KU-255-878

THE MAKING OF
ANDREI SAKHAROV

By the same author

Germans
Munich
Armageddon in Prime Time
Kontinent Four: Contemporary Russian Writers

GEORGE BAILEY

THE MAKING OF

ANDREI
SAKHAROV

ALLEN LANE
THE PENGUIN PRESS

ALLEN LANE THE PENGUIN PRESS

Published by the Penguin Group
27 Wrights Lane, London w8 5tz, England
Viking Penguin Inc., 40 West 23rd Street, New York, New York 10010, USA
Penguin Books Australia Ltd, Ringwood, Victoria, Australia
Penguin Books Canada Ltd, 2801 John Street, Markham, Ontario, Canada l3r 1b4
Penguin Books (NZ) Ltd, 182–190 Wairau Road, Auckland 10, New Zealand

Penguin Books Ltd, Registered Offices: Harmondsworth, Middlesex, England

First published 1989
A translation of this work, entitled *Sacharow: Der Weg zur Perestroika*, appeared in German in 1988, published by F. A. Herbig
Material from Zhores A. Medvedev's *The Rise and Fall of T. D. Lysenko* is reprinted by kind permission of Columbia University Press, © 1969 Columbia University Press

Copyright © George Bailey, 1988

All rights reserved.
Without limiting the rights under copyright
reserved above, no part of this publication may be
reproduced, stored in or introduced into a retrieval system,
or transmitted, in any form or by any means (electronic, mechanical,
photocopying, recording or otherwise), without the prior
written permission of both the copyright owner and
the above publisher of this book

Printed in Great Britain by Richard Clay Ltd, Bungay, Suffolk

Filmset in Monotype Lasercomp Photina

A CIP catalogue record for this book is available from the British Library

ISBN 0–713–99033–3

To the memory
of
ANATOLY MARCHENKO

In the scientific, political and human destiny of Andrei Sakharov we find the motives and accents of a debate that always ac- companies the adventure of man in the conquest of what Plato called 'human wisdom'. Not by chance has he been placed in the company of Copernicus, of Galileo and of Giordano Bruno. Not by chance is the book chosen in accordance with a medieval rite for the laureation of Sakharov *The Dialogue of the Two Greatest Systems* by Galileo: a choice meant to recall the spirit of liberty that animated the growth of the new science and the will which moved the scientist in the exploration of the still hidden mysteries of the universe.

From the laudatio delivered by Fabio Roversi Monaco, rector of the University of Bologna, on the occasion of conferring upon Andrei Sakharov the honorary degree of doctor in astronomy on 9 of February 1989.

CONTENTS

I

'QUID SI NUNC COELUM RUAT?'

In its infancy humanity asked the same questions a child asks. Every child is its own cosmologist; it discovers the world gradually as it grows into adolescence and thence into maturity. And every account of the world begins with Genesis, the Creation, and centres on the order of things. This particular child, the protagonist of this account, was no exception. On the contrary, born the son of a Muscovite physicist and the great-grandson of an Orthodox priest, this child was born and bred to be inquisitive.

But the inquest is inevitable in any case, because the sun, the moon and the stars, moving, mark time – the change from day to night, night to day – sunrise, sunset, moonrise, moonset; the rhythm of seasonal succession, sowing and harvest, the onsurge of winter, its surcease and supplantation by spring:

> The year's decline is ruthless, steady:
> Doomed is summer's elf, –
> Junker Schmidt with pistol ready
> Means to shoot himself.
> Rash fool! Desist! Within, upon or
> From the burial urn,
> Junker Schmidt, my word of honour, –
> Summer *will* return.

Behind the name 'Kozma Prutkov', the signatory author of this verse, crouched the small collective of Count Alexei Tolstoy (no relation) and the brothers Zhemchuzhnikov, Alex and Vladimir Mikhailovich. They wrote satirical verse in Old Russia (mid

I

nineteenth century). This specimen was published in good time for that country, which is to say, thirty-four years later.

It is touching to read the earliest attempts of humanity as a child to explain the apparent order of things. Why does summer return? What holds the world up? What prevents it from falling through space endlessly? According to the Hindu myth the world rests on the back of an elephant which in turn stands on a tortoise which in turn stands on a lotus flower. To ask what is under the lotus flower is taboo.

For the Babylonians, Egyptians and Hebrews the world was not their oyster but an oyster was their world – with water underneath and water overhead, indeed safely enclosed like a babe in the womb. The earth was a hollow mountain, fixed in the middle of the oyster with a solid dome above it. Water seeped through the dome as rain or rose through the floor in fountains and springs. The sun, the moon and the stars entered through doors in the East of the dome and disappeared through doors in the West.

But the question came anyway: would it hold? Would it last? There is the legend of the derivation of the *quidnunc*, the 'what now?' of the querulously curious. It is said that a small group of emissaries from an Eastern satrap visited an ancient Greek court. The visitors had the peculiar habit of looking continually at the sky and asking: *'Quid si nunc coelum ruat?'* (What if the sky falls down now?)

The question 'What if the sky falls down now?' came from an ignorance that seems quaint today. But today the same question arises from the appalling knowledge that such a thing is entirely possible – thanks to a breed of men known as physicists who have invented the infernal machine capable of destroying the world, of blowing up the universe, of undoing Creation. These men, the physicists, might be called the horsemen of the apocalypse. They have brought a finality to the considerations of mortal man – the prospect of instantaneous and universal combustion. Whereas the ancients feared the wrath of the gods, moderns fear the wrath of men, of men who are empowered and accoutred like gods, who can do anything in the way of destruction and are at least as unpredictable as the gods they have succeeded.

This is an account of Andrei Dmitrievich Sakharov, the foremost of the horsemen of the apocalypse. Such an account requires some presentation of the history of science in general and the

2

history of physics in particular. The study of physics begins with the Creation. So does the study of religion. This indicates the necessity of beginning at the beginning, when the confrontation between religion and science began.

But the central idea of this undertaking is to put Andrei Sakharov in context. He is the product of the contending forces of the blanket confrontation that has as many names as it has aspects: east–west, north–south, Soviet–American, Communism–capitalism, humanism (technology)–anti-humanism (conventional religion), environment–heredity, etc. Sakharov, the unconfessed Christian, the secular *salvator* to all those who troop to his apartment in Moscow – now again as before his exile – seeking sentence and solace, is not a throwback but a 'throwforward', the first citizen of the as yet unfounded United States of the World.

Andrei Sakharov's formal confrontation with the Soviet establishment came in 1973, when he was summoned to appear before the deputy prosecutor general of the USSR. This occasion, its prelude and aftermath show striking parallels with the appearance of Galileo Galilei before the tribunal of the Inquisition in Rome in 1633 and with the Oppenheimer case three centuries later, namely with the hearings of J. Robert Oppenheimer before the Atomic Energy Commission's personal security board in Washington, DC in 1954. Galileo went back to the ancient Greeks and picked up the thread of scientific development. His return to the source of pure science led to results that were taboo in his time and place, his cosmological discoveries demanding a universal philosophical revision, even a theological one. In much the same way, following Galileo's lead, Robert Oppenheimer directed and presided over the invention of the atomic bomb, and found himself thinking in apocalyptic terms about foreign policy and military strategy. Sakharov in his turn, having received the same tradition from his father's hand, invented the hydrogen bomb and underwent a trial of another and far more severe kind.

There is thus a direct line leading from Galileo to the nuclear bomb and the pollution of air, soil and water in the industrial nations of the world. In this connection Sakharov, the inventor of 'the Super', the discoverer of the secret of the solar phoenix – that is, the sun's capacity for perpetual combustion – is the chief executor of Galileo's will and testament. But he is also more than this: the deadly work he did as a scientist proved to be the chrysalis out of which emerged the human-rights champion and Nobel laureate for world peace. The relevant reminder here is that human rights includes the conservation of the world's natural treasures as well as that of its cultural endowment.

Both Galileo and Oppenheimer tried to retain their standing with the authorities they served. Not so Sakharov. Sakharov defied point-blank the state and homeland he served – one man against the whole totalitarian empire of the Soviets in the most dramatic confrontation since Galileo. For Sakharov's trial, unlike Oppenheimer's demeaning 'review', was by ordeal. And unlike both Galileo and Oppenheimer, it was Sakharov who prevailed.

The Greeks had a word for the order of things: κόσμος, *kosmos*. Originally the word meant simply 'order'. It later devolved, via 'good order', 'good behaviour', 'government', 'ornament' (beautiful order), into the meaning 'world' or 'universe' (from its perfect order). The Greeks also had a word for young humanity's inborn habit of seeing the hand of God in every aspect of nature and reading spiritual or mystical significance into every fact of life. The word was δεισιδαιμονία, *deisidaimonia*, literally fear of daemons, but fear rather in the sense of the English word 'dread', as in 'holy dread', connoting reverence and awe. This was the word for the atom of faith before it was split into its two components of religion (when used in the good sense) and superstition (when used in the bad sense). The split came when Greek colonists in the Middle East (little Asia) in the eighth century BC came into contact with the bewildering variety of peoples, customs and religions of that area. There and then they discovered so many radically different religions and mythologies, each with a different explanation of the genesis of the world and the order of its phenomena, that the serious inquirers among them found themselves forced to abandon religious and mythological approaches to the problem altogether. This was the beginning, perhaps, of the Great Divorce between religion and reason, which resulted in the emergence of 'Ionian' atheism. The only rational approach to the problem of the *kosmos* that came into the ken of the early Greeks was that of the Babylonians. By dint of watching and registering the movements of stars and planets over a period of years they divided the day and night into twelve sections each and the year into twelve months – in accordance with the twelve moons of the year. The word 'moon' is related to the word 'month'. In Russian the same word serves for both 'moon' and 'month': '*myesats*'. (It was left to the monarch to make up the underlap by decreeing a leap year whenever he felt like it.) The Babylonians used the sexagesimal system of numbers. As good an explanation as any of why the Babylonians used a system based on multiples of the number six is given by Philo of Alexandria (*c.*20 BC). In his *On the Account of the World's Creation Given by Moses*, he explains why God took six days to make the world:

> Six days are mentioned because for the things coming into existence there was need of order. Order involves number, and among numbers by the law of nature the most suitable to productivity is the number 6, for if we start with the number 1 it is the first perfect number, being equal to the product of its factors [i.e., $1 \times 2 \times 3$], as well as made up of the sum of them [i.e., $1 + 2 + 3$], its half being 3, its third part 2, its sixth part 1. We may say that it is in its nature both male and female, and is a result of the distinctive power of either. For among things that are it is the odd that is male, and the even female. Now of odd numbers 3 is the starting point, and of even numbers 2, and the product of these two is 6. For it was requisite that the world, being most perfect of all things that have come into existence, should be constituted in accordance with a perfect number, namely 6; and, inasmuch as it was to have in itself beings that sprang from a coupling together, should receive the impress of a mixed number, namely the first in which odd and even were combined, one that should contain the essential principle both of the male that sows and of the female that receives the seed.

The Egyptians for their part marked off 360 degrees in a circle, apparently on an analogy to the yearly circuit of the sun. They also divided the year into 360 days with each of the twelve months containing thirty days. It was not until the thirteenth century, apparently, with the invention of the mechanical clock, that the minute was marked as a division of the hour. (The Babylonians used the minute as one-sixtieth of a unit – *pars minuta prima* in medieval Latin – in their sexagesimal system of fractions and the second – *partes minutae secundae* – as a re-division of the same.) Another three hundred years passed before the second was marked in the improved timepieces of the late sixteenth century.

Greek curiosity, always boundless, had something like a shopping list of questions. The Greeks borrowed a whole catalogue of Babylonian inventions such as the calendar and the rudiments of geometry and mathematics and went on to adapt them and improve them to their purposes. They were the first to geometrize geography. This they did by superimposing triangles, squares and circles on makeshift maps (often enough in the sand), using them as geographical frames of reference, coordinating points within the figures and plotting courses. This was a very considerable improvement since the descriptions of coastlines at that time gave only the distances between places, indications of seaboard foothills and changes in the configuration of coast, without exactitude of direction. In the same way, the highways constructed by the Persians in the Middle East boasted official distance markers, but the Persians apparently had no maps on which the distances and directions and the patterns they formed were traced. The Greeks tried everything, and often enough their inventions and adoptions were wildly inappropriate. But even when mistaken they were often able to get some use out of their mistakes because the latter provided reference points, however awkward. Greeks were always notorious in this regard. Some fifty years after the appearance of the first map and description of the earth by Heketaios, Herodotus complained about the 'rape of reality by geometric schematisms'. He poked fun at the 'Ionians' who believed that the earth was round – 'as if it had been turned on a potter's wheel' – and that the earth was surrounded by an ocean-sea that enveloped the rest of the globe. At about the same time – in the first half of the fourth century BC – Eudoxos of Knidos (it was probably he) covered the earth with the same grid of latitude and longitude we use today. There was the same problem with time as with space – that of orientation by providing points or frames of reference in order to chronicle events of the past. To do this it was necessary of course to choose some events in the past as fixed points of reference from which to list events forward and backward, the present being obviously unsuitable to this purpose since it is continuously shifting. Thus Christians now use the date of the birth of Christ as their reference point (BC and AD). The ancient Romans used PUC (*post urbem conditam* – after the construction of the city – that is, Rome) to the same purpose. The classics scholar Kurt von Fritz refers to all those who refuse to conform in the use of the almost universal BC and AD 'as pedantically consistent non-Christians who are forced to use such terms as "before our era" and "after our era"'.

But the Greeks had trouble with plotting time past. Heketaios took the list of Spartan kings as his frame of reference and allotted to each king an average reign of forty years. He then accommodated all known events to this list by cross reference. Unfortunately, the legendary founder of the Spartan dynasties was Hercules, not the only but certainly the most blatantly fictitious monarch in the Spartan succession. The Greeks had more trouble than the Hebrews in divorcing historical fact from the sagas that surrounded their beginnings. Their various attempts at a standard chronology were far less happy than their applications of geometric schemata to geography.

But the really revolutionary discovery of the Greeks came in the area of theology–philosophy. Or, rather, it began there. One of the fragments of the works of Xenophanes of Kolophon (570–450 BC) contains this statement: 'If someone says something very true [very much to the point] about the Gods, he does not come by this knowledge through direct observation but only on the basis of its seeming so to him.' This is the first recorded instance of a process in the achievement of knowledge that is not based directly on the perception of the senses but rather on conclusions drawn from sensory perceptions. It was a process involving a good deal of contemplation and reflection. Here, apparently for the first time, there arose the thought that the understanding of the world consists not only of the awareness of phenomena and their interrelationships but that there was something behind the phenomena that could be discovered only by virtue of hard thinking. This was likewise a process that resulted more than two thousand years later in an approach to art that found expression in the half-joking, half-serious statement, 'I paint what I don't see.' What this statement means is that 'all artistic creation is absolutely subjective', as Oscar Wilde put it in his dialogue, *The Critic as Artist*: 'The very landscape that Corot looked at was, as he said himself, but a mood of his own mind.' In other words it was a process which rejected the mere accurate representation of things as they are or acknowledgedly appear to be. As such it was the controversy *in nucem* over whether an educational system is to cultivate the memory (learning by rote) or the imagination. And as such it was to repeat itself according to the temper of each succeeding age down through the centuries and millennia. The periodic recurrence of the controversy stems from the existence of two kinds of truth: factual truth and imaginative truth. By way of corollary came

Xenophanes' inkling that the understanding of things would necessarily have to concern itself with the conditions of human perception imposed by the very nature of the apparatus of the human mind.

At about the same time, Pythagoras developed his doctrine of numbers. Some time before, Greeks had noticed the connection between mathematics and music. They discovered that certain pleasant and harmonious tones could be produced by strings of the same kind whose lengths were in simple numerical relation to each other – that the same tones and tone combinations could be produced by other instruments when the same relationships were established. These and like discoveries concerning frequencies and pitch led Pythagoras to his famous conclusion that 'all things are numbers', or, 'all things are composed of numbers', or, 'numbers are the essence of things'. From music Pythagoras and his pupils went to geometry, as in the discovery that three sticks whose lengths are in the relation of 3, 4, 5, to each other will form a triangle containing a right angle and that, regardless of the magnitude of the sticks, the same triangle would result if the 3, 4, 5 proportion were maintained. Finally, the Pythagoreans made the observation that the orbital movement of the planets was regular and the interrelationship of these movements could to a certain extent be numerically comprehended, a discovery that quickly led to the conceit of 'the music of the spheres'.

But there was a great deal of mysticism involved in the Pythagorean doctrine. The arrogance of the totality of the Pythagorean claim (*mathesis universalis*) included the demand that justice, the institution of marriage, various animals and a good many other things be subjected to the numerical calculation of their essential quality. There were various ways of arriving at a numerical calculation of an essential quality, one of the most memorable being that recommended by the philosopher Eurytos at the beginning of the fourth century BC: the basis number could be determined by discovering how many pebbles were required to produce the recognizable outline of, say, a horse. Despite such vagaries, in laying the groundwork for the development of science in the modern sense the Pythagorean thesis was probably the most important of any Greek finding: it signalled the beginning of the quest to mathematize the world, to measure everything in life as precisely as possible. The curious thing is that here as elsewhere an interaction took place between the mythical–mystical and the strictly or at least predominantly rational approaches to the problem. Astronomy grew out of astrology. Indeed the two were inseparable and virtually indistinguishable until late into the Middle Ages. Even Kepler and Galileo drew up horoscopes for their princes and patrons and other notables at large. They did so without reluctance and with no little interest. For that matter even today, quite apart from its continuing general popularity – what mass-circulation publication would dare drop its daily, weekly or monthly horoscope? – captains of industry and statesmen among others pay good money to have their horoscopes drawn, often refusing to take any important decision until this is done. In the same way alchemy with its myriad crackpot projects and seemingly impossible dreams gave birth to and nourished chemistry. And the mystification of numbers (particularly certain numbers – like three, seven, nine and eleven) gave an enormous impulse to the study of mathematics. Indeed, it was this fanaticism with regard to the magic omnipotence of numbers that led the Pythagoreans to the discovery of incommensurability – the fact that between certain quantities there is no integral or fractional common measure. This discovery came as a great shock, because the Pythagoreans believed that all relationships could be reduced to whole numbers. As unsettling as it was, this discovery nevertheless led in turn to the invention of a criterion to accommodate the fact that the process of mutual subtraction recedes in a given direction into infinity – as in the case of the symbol that indicates the ratio of the circumference to the diameter of a circle, giving the incommensurable quantity 3.14159265. The Pythagoreans were the first to discover pi in the sky, as it were.

One of the eternal quests in Greek scientific history was the attempt to determine the nature of matter – particularly whether there could be such a thing as empty space, an area devoid of anything. If any such thing or no such thing (where the presence of nothing is not just a contradiction in terms) could be posited, then true being must be divisible into a variety and plurality of particles capable of penetrating the void and keeping some distance from one another – somethings interspersed with nothings, as it were. If this were true then there must be some sort of minima, particles that were so small they were indivisible. The concept of ultimate

9

indivisibility gave the atom its name: ἄτομος a-tom (from the Greek verb ἀτέμνω, not to cut, that is, uncuttable). The Greeks also posited that the atom had weight and with it also the 'power of weight', namely gravity. The concept of a physical body was necessary to the sense apprehension of any sort of causal relationship between physical bodies and their parts, 'a double stipulation', as Kurt Lasswitz called it, concerning the possibility of changes in space as well as the possibility of making something the subject of these changes from which they could be asserted as evidence. The sensory reality and interaction of bodies must be firmly attached to the concept of substance, otherwise nature and matter elude perception and it would be impossible to achieve an objectization of the subjective sensory experience. The concept of the atom has proved itself to be indispensable to the securing of the objectivity of sensory experience as the dynamic interaction of substances.

But since the end of the nineteenth century the concept and theory of the atom have undergone and continue to undergo turbulent, headlong developments. Atoms are no longer indivisible – indeed they are growing steadily larger in terms of the number of particles they are discovered or presumed to contain. Many of these particles, moreover, are of an extraordinarily elusive nature. They are described as 'presence' or 'presences'. They can hardly be said to exist in the form of substance: they are, rather, sometimes described as 'waves' or 'continuing fields of force'. While it is hard to see how the atom as a conceptual term of reference could disappear after some two and a half thousand years' yeoman service, yet the velocity of change in the field of physics is so great and so likely to continue that predictions of any kind would be foolhardy.

The Greeks had another word for it, μηχανή, which is the same word as mechanic or mechanics. Originally the word meant 'artifice', or 'trick', or 'contrivance'. In Greek saga Daedalus is the patron of everything mechanical, the father of the machine. It was he who fled his captor-king by fitting himself and his son, Icarus, with wings of wax and feathers. During the flight Icarus, who was curious, flew too close to the sun. The wax on his wings melted and he fell to his death. This is the classical and classic lesson in hybris. Nevertheless it would be impossible to exaggerate the importance of the role of the contriver of mechanism in Greek history.

The Greeks invented construction engineering. And Greek mechanics made tremendous strides under Archimedes (287–212 BC) who discovered the laws of the centre of gravity, of leverage (by attribution his is the statement: 'Give me the right place to stand and I shall move the earth'), of the screw, of the inclined plane, of buoyancy (specific gravity and hydraulics). He also improved the invention of the block and tackle. The Greeks performed prodigies in architecture; they built bridges and bored tunnels, coming from the opposite sides of mountains and meeting with great accuracy in the middle. (It should come as no surprise to the reader that most if not all Greek engineering feats were connected with military campaigns or sprang from communion with military considerations.) But the strange thing was that the natural sciences remained virtually untouched by the whole thrust and sweep of Greek mechanical innovation and development. The reason for this omission is of great significance. The Greeks had a great, inborn reverence for nature which they gave the name φύσις – *physis* – from which we get the words 'physical' and 'physics'. What is more, the Greeks considered anything mechanical not only non-natural but 'anti-nature'. Nature-worship is the leitmotiv in Greek life. Aristotle expresses this pointedly in the preface to his 'Concerning Mathematical Problems', which is attributed to be part of his *Mechanics*:

> One is astonished at what happens in accordance with nature, the causes of which are unknown to us, and at what happens contrary to nature by means of technical intervention to the advantage of humankind. For in many things nature conducts itself in such a way that is to our disadvantage. For nature always works in the same way and in accordance with simple laws. What is useful to us, on the other hand, is wrought by changes in all sorts of ways. When it becomes necessary, then, to do something against nature one is confronted by difficulties and therefore must take recourse to art [τέχνη]. Hence we call that part of art which is of help to us in such difficulties by the name 'mechanics'. For, as the poet Antiphon has described it, so indeed it is: by means of the technical we gain the upper hand whereas otherwise we would be worsted by nature.

The dilemma is clearly stated. And what could have been an extraordinary chapter in the history of applied natural sciences through the invention and development of instruments of precision remained quiescent for as long as a thousand years. For in answer to the question: does one live in accordance with nature or does one conquer nature, does one accept the world as it is or does one change the world by the tricks and devices of artful invention and doing violence to nature? The Greeks, with their inborn awe of what they were given, came down very clearly on the side of going along with the world as it was.

As for astronomy, the Greeks did not accept their own or any of the original mythologies with which they came in contact. The refusal to accept mythological explanations for natural phenomena forced the Greeks to disregard the primary evidence of their senses, that is, the evidence of mere appearances. They reasoned their way out of the dead end imposed by the impression that up and down were directional absolutes and therefore the earth was the centre of the universe. By the middle of the fourth century BC (355) the earth and the other visible planets were recognized to be in orbital as well as other movement and the sun the fixed centre of the heavens. A gigantic first step in the direction of the Copernican system had been made. In the cosmology of Philolaos (which is the first recorded pre-Copernican version) there are a number of 'Mack Sennett' aspects, such as the assertion that all forms of life on the moon were fifteen times larger than those on the earth. This was because the author had determined the 'moonday' to be fifteen times as long as our day (that is, half a month).

It is significant that the Greek reverence of nature – this time in the form of the Pythagorean–Platonic conviction of the harmony and godliness of the cosmos – acted as a brake on the development of a precisely ordered heliocentric system, and particularly as regards the idealistic demand that all planetary orbits be concentric circles (the perfect circle) and that all planets in their orbits travel at the same speed or at speeds commensurable with one another. At the same time it was just this insistence on strict conformity and perfect circles that spurred the Greeks (just as it spurred Copernicus two thousand years later) on the way to the Copernican system in the first place. And yet: Aristarchos of Samos (320–250 BC), the astronomer responsible for the most highly developed heliocentric system models among the Greeks, came within an ace of being charged by the Greeks for irreverence (ἀσέβεια) because he tried to move the 'centre of the universe' from its place by assuming that the heavens stood still while the earth moved in a slanted circle around the sun and turned on its own axis. But as superb as the heliocentric construction of Aristarchos was, it was passed over by the most careful observer among the Greek astronomers, Hipparchos of Nicaea, who chose to develop the geocentric model of Apollonius of Perge. It was the improvement of this model that finally found approval with Ptolemy, who further refined it.

There are no very cogent explanations for this fateful turn of events. Certainly the arithmetic explanations of the orbits involved in the geocentric system were easier and more flexible than those imposed by the heliocentric system. Likewise Ptolemy found it difficult to believe that anything so obviously massive and heavy as the earth could move so fast through space and turn so rapidly on its own axis as the heliocentric system of Aristarchos demanded. Most important, probably, was the consideration that it is easier to carry out constructive mathematical calculations if one can assume the fixed and unchanging position of the observer – as we have seen, whether dealing with calculations in time or space. It is certain that the traditional Greek insistence on conformity of geometric figures and commensurability prevailed far into the Middle Ages and beyond. Even when astronomers were forced to abandon the perfect circle, the notion of omnipresent concentric circular planetary motion persisted. It was Johannes Kepler (1571–1630) who finally figured out that planetary motion as registered through pure and simple observation could be explained by positing elliptical orbits. Apparently shocked by the necessity of giving up the cherished 'perfect and most appropriate idea of the circle', he found solace in the discovery that the new figures were 'perfect' ellipses (*figura perfecta elliptica*). Such is the pertinacity of fixed ideas.

Thus the two main approaches in Greek scientific exploration were epitomized in the heliocentric and geocentric theories of universal order. The one, prematurely abandoned by the Greeks themselves and all but entirely forgotten by those who followed them, was right; the other, the Ptolemaic, enthusiastically embraced and dutifully cherished for two thousand years, was wrong. Worse than ignorance, runs the old saw, is the illusion of knowledge. The Ptolemaic system was a sterile diversion of scientific progress, a labyrinthine roadblock that simply absorbed the best efforts of the finest minds and yielded nothing. Theologically and politically, however, the Ptolemaic–geocentric system was literally made to order. Here is Ptolemy on the subject:

13

Having set ourselves the task to prove that the apparent irregularities of the five planets, the sun and the moon can all be represented by means of uniform circular motions, *because only such motions are appropriate to their divine nature* [author's italics] . . . We are entitled to regard the accomplishment of this task as the ultimate aim of mathematical science based on philosophy.

At base the Ptolemaic approach was unscientific; the impulse that produced it was theological. 'In the year 1500,' wrote Professor Whitehead, 'Europe knew less than Archimedes, who died in the year 212 BC.'

The decisive turn in the direction of modern physics was taken with the introduction of a system of coordinates entirely independent of the objects to which it was designed to apply, through René Descartes (1596–1650), and then by means of the development of analytical geometry, that is, through the arithmetizing of geometry, then through the invention of infinitesimal calculus by Isaac Newton (1643–1727) and Gottfried Wilhelm Leibnitz (1646–1716), which made possible the mathematization of physics. These were the breakthroughs underlying the spectacular advances in physics from Newton's time to the present.

Yet none of these breakthroughs could have been accomplished or even conceived if they had not been preceded by a revolutionary cast of mind, an atmosphere conducive to thought in radically new terms – or, rather, in terms so old that they appeared to be radically new. Erasmus (Gerhard Gerhards), Copernicus (Nikolaus Koppernigk) and Martin Luther were all born within a generation of each other in the second half of the fifteenth century. Erasmus published the first edition of the original Greek New Testament and translated the original text into Latin, thus revealing the corruption of the Roman Vulgate. All three – Erasmus, Copernicus and Luther – went back to the Greek texts, the two theologians to the Bible, the astronomer to Pythagoras and Archimedes. It was here among the old Greeks that Copernicus came across the work of Aristarchos of Samos and his advanced model of the heliocentric system. (In his own manuscript Copernicus crossed out in ink his reference to Aristarchos and substituted a somewhat obscure forerunner, Hicetas of Syracuse. One can only speculate why he did this.)

If Erasmus ushered in the Reformation it was Luther who gave it body and broke the hold of the Catholic Church by replacing faith in authority with the authority of faith as revealed by the written word of the original texts of the Bible and interpreted by every man according to his conscience. And yet it was the work of Copernicus that signalled and set the tone for a revolution closely connected with the Reformation but of far greater portent. In a section of his *Geschichte der Farbenlehre* entitled 'Change from the Old to the New Age', Goethe described the effect of Copernicus' work on the consciousness of the civilized world:

> And yet among all the discoveries and new assurances nothing could have had a greater effect on the human spirit than the teachings of Copernicus. Hardly was it realized that the world was round and confined within itself when it also became necessary to renounce the tremendous prerogative of being the centre of the universe. Perhaps there has never yet been a greater demand made of humankind: what was it that did not go up in smoke and flame by way of this admission – a second paradise, a world of innocence, poetry and piety, the testimony of the senses, the conviction of a poetic-religious faith; no wonder that no one wanted to let all this go, that one resisted such a doctrine in every possible way, a doctrine which entitled and challenged all those who accepted it to a hitherto unknown and even unsuspected freedom of thought and grandeur of sentiment.

At this juncture in time – a point of pause in historical progress but one marking an extraordinary confluence of motive forces, recoveries of lost heritages, inventions and interventions – the stage was set for the entrance of Galileo Galilei.

The fire stolen from the gods by Prometheus and given to man was used to forge instruments – weapons and tools. With the increasing production of instruments has come the passion for mechanistic abstraction. And the great and fascinating, deceptive allure of mechanistic abstraction is the eternal promise of perfection. Despite all the caveats the technologists, technicians and engineers can raise, that promise is always there. And with that promise comes the belief that is false – the *pseudopistis* – that man can do anything. In this sense it was a downright sinister stroke of fortune that René Descartes should have followed and complemented Galileo (either one of them makes Dr Faustus himself look like a dabbler in trivial *occulta*).

So infatuated with the new scientific method of mechanistic abstraction was Descartes that he could exclaim, 'Give me matter and motion and I will construct the world.' He became the personification of the hybris of the new science. Indeed, altogether, Descartes's was a curious performance: he based his claim to the ability to construct the world – the whole of organic life (here was cosmogony for fair!) – on the Galilean principle of the reduction of all life to the quantifiable. But he reserved all that was unquantifiable – the spiritual, the sensual, that is, all the 'secondary qualities' of colour, taste, sound and sensation in general – to the Church and left it unstudied and unapplied. In short, he abandoned it.

In much the same way and with equal aplomb Descartes reserved virtually all political rights to the state, the king, the emperor, the tyrant, the despot: 'the single unifying mind as the source of absolute order'. Descartes was an absolutist. As such he was responsible for the making of much of the mould into which the modern scientist has been cast – that of a reliable, willing and perfectly docile servant of the state. It is not a very far cry. The attempt to make machines very much like men is closely akin to the attempt to make men very much like machines.

All this for the sake of order – which is, so far as the human mind can conceive it, in itself mechanical. According to Philo, this was why it took six days to create the world: '. . . because for the things coming into existence there was need of order. Order involves number . . .'

It was a question, then, of conditioning men to absolute obedience. And it is precisely this question that makes Andrei Sakharov so much more important a figure even than he seems to be. In like fashion the struggle he took up is far larger and more significant than 'just' a confrontation between two 'superpowers', a struggle that can and will be resolved in any of a number of ways short of mutual or alternative destruction. It is a confrontation of man with himself. And since the blue planet – insofar as anyone has been able to discover – is the sole and only bourne of life in the universe, it is a question of the death of life or – if the conformists succeed in conditioning men to absolute obedience – a question of a life of death, of the elimination of the individual as a personality.

II

GALILEO

Ivan Nikolaievich Sakharov, a lawyer by profession, married the heiress Maria Petrovna Domukhovskaya in the middle of the 1880s. The inheritance in question, a small estate called Budyaevo, was in the Smolensk region. Ivan Nikolaievich sold Budyaevo in 1899 and moved to Moscow, where he bought a large house in 1901. Ivan Nikolaievich had need of a large house: Maria Petrovna bore him six children, five boys and one girl – Sergei, Ivan, Dmitri, Nikolai, Yuri and Tanya. Of the six, in their turn, only Dmitri produced sons: Andrei, born in 1921, and Georgi, born in 1926. Dmitri was also the only one of the children to become a scientist. He had established himself as a physicist even before the birth of his first son. And this despite an enforced sojourn of two years in the Caucasus where he and his bride were marooned – cut off by the revolution and the civil war – and he made his living by playing the piano in a silent-movie theatre. His bride was Yekaterina Alexeyevna Sofiano, whose ancestry (as her surname indicates) was fixed in the Greek colony of time immemorial on the north shore of the Black Sea. The bride's father was nevertheless a native Muscovite and it was in Moscow the couple met and married in 1918 (he was twenty-nine, she was twenty-five). Both had been on the faculty of a private school, Dmitri as a teacher of mathematics, his bride as an instructress in gymnastics.

Dmitri Ivanovich quickly recognized the intellectual potential in his older son, Andrei, and devoted himself to the boy's mathematical and scientific education. Since his first son expressed an early interest in his father's chosen discipline, physics, there was a meeting of the minds on the subject of his future profession from the very beginning. Said Andrei Dmitrievich in later years: 'I never wanted to be anything but a physicist.'

The quality of his education was assured from the outset, his father and his father's colleagues tutoring him in the natural sciences (to the exclusion of any formal schooling whatever until he was twelve years of age) and his grandmother, Maria Petrovna, reading to him from the Russian classics. Both these courses of instruction left their mark on the boy and the man. The tutorial sessions laid the disciplinary groundwork for the future physicist and foreshortened his childhood, making an academic recluse out of what should have been a schoolboy. But, by confining him to the home, the tutorial sessions also brought him the warmth and support of a large and harmonious family. The long reading sessions with Maria Petrovna endowed him with a knowledge and relish of literature that added a cultural dimension to his character and imbued him with a lifelong gratitude and admiration for his benefactress.

Dmitri Ivanovich wrote the first popular book on physics in the Russian language. In tutoring his son he was inevitably reminded of the man who wrote the first book ever on physics, setting the course of its development as a modern science. For this outstanding scientist Dmitri Ivanovich inculcated in his son a healthy respect at an early age. There was also the fact that the transformation symbolized in this historical figure, the evolution from priest to scientist as the predominant model of a public figure, took place in three generations in Sakharov's own family: from grandfather Nikolai to grandson Dmitri Ivanovich. Dmitri Ivanovich had good reason to remember Galileo. Thus, for the double purpose of imparting something of Andrei Dmitrievich's intellectual background and the general context of the study of the natural sciences and particularly physics, the present chapter of this account is devoted to the father of modern physics, Galileo Galilei. But there is another, broader reason for the inclusion of this titan. The struggle of Galileo against Church dogma concerning the nature of the cosmos epitomized the great, inevitable and continuing clash between religion and reason or, as modern parlance has it, between science and religion. The Church's insistence on one world with the earth at its centre was based, of course, on the necessity of maintaining doctrinal unity, the unity of the faith. It would be historically wrong to leave the impression that the emergence and flourishing of Christianity was a break or an extended disruptive intermission in the development of science. It was rather the other way around. It was Christianity that saved civilization, preventing the fall of Rome from becoming a universal catastrophe. The Church absorbed, preserved and recreated the cultures of Israel, Greece and Rome, giving the European Middle Ages their distinctive, traditional unity. In the matter of faith the Greeks stood in contradistinction to the Jews. That contradistinction was absolute. The Greeks had many gods, the Jews one. He who serves more than one master serves none. The sum of many gods is less than one. Polytheism is an entirely different experience from monotheism. Hercules, the king of the Spartans, like Christ, the king of the Jews, was half-god and half-man, but he was one among many and therefore less than one. In the Incarnation the eternal Logos, the word, became flesh and finite form was given to the infinite and formless. The assumption by the Godhead of human nature limited − necessarily − but by no means exhausted the divinity. Rather it established the claim of the invisible Church by making it visible. Christ, the first priest of the Church, became the Church. And this process in itself, with its necessary limitations and exposures to contingency, was the beginning of the visible process of secularization. Hercules became a cult that lasted a few centuries in the Old World and sometimes crops up today as a pathetic incongruity as when, for example, a condemned man prays for deliverance, not to Christ, but to the heavyweight champion of the world ('Save me, Joe Louis!') as the current incarnation of Hercules.

In contrast, the Church became the great, inclusive ordering factor of the medieval world. In its exposure to contingency the *corpus Christi*, the *corpus mysticum* of the invisible Church, became a corporation, a constitution, a universal civic institution. This, adds Philip Sherrard in his book, *Greek East and the Latin West*, was a 'degeneration' of the sacramental understanding of the Church into a 'social and corporational organism'. The great contingency in the history of the Church was the conversion of the Emperor Constantine to Christianity, wherewith the Church became the state-Church and the empire became the Church-state. Over the centuries thereafter the function and significance of the Church changed from the observation and reflection on the Mysteries to the administration and control of the human spirit in its temporal activity. Aquinas in his writings frequently replaces liturgical idiom by juristic idiom. In a process that received its stamp of official approval in the corporational doctrine of the Roman Church in 1302, by Pope Boniface VIII in his bull *Unam Sanctam*, the *mystical person* of the sacraments became the 'fictitious person', the *persona representata* or *ficta* of the jurists. The sacramental idea of the *corpus mysticum* had been reinterpreted into a sociological and juristic concept. Sherrard notes that it was frequently debated in the theological circles around Pope Boniface VIII whether a jurist or a theologian could better care for the souls of the Christians. And so the Church veiled itself in the law. In the upshot, by way of cumulative jurisprudential enfleshment, as it were, the *corpus Christi*, Christ's body, became the body politic of the Western world.

Galileo Galilei was born in Pisa on 15 February 1564, in the same year that William Shakespeare was born. He was the son of Vincenzo Galilei, a Florentine whose family had ranked among the first in his native city for more than two hundred years. Galileo embodies a crucial juncture in the history of Europe. Three days after his birth Michelangelo died in Rome; less than a year after Galileo's death in 1642 Isaac Newton was born. Galileo's life thus spanned the end of the Italian Renaissance and the beginning of the age of Enlightenment. But he also marked and worked the introduction of a new age in the history of humankind overall: he was the father of modern science.

However, the age makes the man more than the man makes the age. It was, indeed, as if all occasions did conspire to produce such a man as Galileo. It was a time of wars between the Italian city-states and rapacious neighbours like France, Spain, the Holy Roman Empire of the German nation and the Ottoman Empire. It was not so long after the introduction of gunpowder in Europe from China and less than a hundred years after the first appearance of mobile field artillery in France. The phenomenon of artillery itself provided a strong inducement to the study of spheres in motion – in the form of cannon balls and their trajectories. From this fact alone there sprang up a race of ballistic experts, engineers, artillerists, specialists in mechanics and dynamics. The nonce-term for these professionals, under which they were known far and wide, was *virtuosi*.

Man invents in order to answer a need. The need was there and it was pressing: where there was no war in progress there was always the threat of war. Something very much like a permanent and universal arms race was going on. Whenever anyone invented anything at all his first task was to demonstrate its usefulness in armed conflict. Anything that secured military advantage over the real, prospective or imagined enemy was at a premium. Galileo was such a *virtuoso*. But he was also a virtuoso in the fullest sense of the term; a Renaissance man *par excellence*, he was a philosopher, an accomplished musician and a man of letters. He knew most of Virgil, Ovid, Horace and Seneca and could quote them from memory. The same was true of the poems of Petrarch. He also knew the whole of *Orlando Furioso* by heart: Ariosto was his favourite author. He early developed into a master of the new demotic Italian language, using it to great effect in setting his views and theories before the broad public. Until Galileo broke with tradition in so doing, the use of Latin confined philosophical and technical discussion to the learned élite. Here again, Galileo's having been born a Florentine nobleman was a lucky throw of the dice: the Florentine dialect, thanks to Dante Alighieri, was destined to become the Italian national language.

But Galileo's first love was geometry and his first real teacher, Ostilio Ricci of Fermo, himself one of the *virtuosi*. Ricci held the same title, 'First Mathematician of the Archduke of Tuscany', that Galileo was to receive some thirty years later. Ricci was also professor of the classical geometry of Euclid. It is one of the wonders of this world that the thirteen books of geometry by Euclid are still in use in classrooms throughout the world today – unchanged. Galileo had the same fixation on Euclid that Einstein conceived in this century. Einstein described his book of Euclid as his only consolation and companion throughout the dull years of his conventional schooling. Indeed, Albert Einstein began his journey to the discovery of the theory of relativity by questioning one of Euclid's axioms.

From Euclid Galileo graduated to Archimedes, the arch-technician and prime mover of the old world, as it were. Thus by chance or providence Galileo came as a student to the neglected side of Greek science. He undercut the feckless abstract theorizing of the schoolmen and held to the practical, mechanical line of approach, that of inventing and using instruments of precision in the pursuit

21

of inquiry. This was in stark contrast to the use of the times that was given to devotion to the traditional teachings of Aristotle – as poorly conceived and falsely understood as that tradition was.

The choice of Euclid and Archimedes by the young Galileo was like picking up a main line of development that had lain buried for almost two thousand years. Moreover the *virtuosi* study of ordnance suited eminently with the study of order in the heavens: a knowledge of ballistics provided an excellent basis for the observation of the movement of celestial spheres while, in return, planetary motion proved to be a grandiose demonstration of observed ballistic principles. With such practical experience it seemed easier to believe that the earth circled the sun in the course of a year than to believe that the sun and the planets circled the earth in twenty-four hours. Galileo found himself at the door of Copernicus and his work *De Revolutionibus Orbium Coelestium* (*Of the Revolutions of Celestial Spheres*). Before the end of the century Galileo had become a closet Copernican, enthusiastic but private. Mindful of the censure and the ridicule that had been heaped upon Copernicus posthumously (Copernicus's masterpiece was published only a few days before the author's death in 1543), Galileo was prudent enough to await further proofs, his own among them. He was unimpressed, however – indeed, he was put off – by Kepler's work, *Mysterium Cosmographicum*, which was produced to prove the Copernican theory. Galileo found it too mystical and not based enough on precise measurements and mathematical findings. He continued his experiments, particularly those with a copper sphere rolling down a plane set at various angles of inclination. But he had to wait another ten years. Then the great breakthrough in astronomy came with the invention of the telescope.

Galileo did not invent the telescope, but he co-invented it or reinvented it. The moment he heard of the Dutch invention of a system of lenses capable of magnifying distant objects he divined the principle and set about building his own telescope. When he succeeded in doing so he became famous overnight. The *signoris* of Venice, in whose republic Galileo held the chair of professor of mathematics, entrusted him with the invention (rather than buy an offered import sight unseen and at an exorbitant price), rewarded him with preferment and doubled his salary to the amount of 1,000 gulden per annum. This was not the result of unprompted gratitude. Galileo had done a magnificent job of salesmanship. Here is a quote from his letter accompanying the invention:

> Invaluable advantages are assured through the bringing up close of objects through this instrument both by land and by sea . . . On the seas we will be able to discover the ships and sails of the enemy two hours before he can become aware of ours; by determining the number and kind of the enemy's ships we can assess his strength in order to decide to pursue him, engage him or flee from him; in the same way the enemy's camps and entrenchments within his fortified areas as well as in the open field can be observed from distant vantage points and also the enemy's movements and preparations in the open field can be made out and assessed to our advantage.

A man had come forward with two lenses in a length of pipe. Although Galileo was at best only a co-inventor of the telescope (no patent was ever issued for the invention: there were too many claims and counter-claims from Dutch lens-grinders) he was the first to look at the firmament through a telescope and record his findings. There is a lapse of some three months between the time of his invention and his first letter describing his examinations of the heavens (7 January 1610). This certainly does not mean that it took Galileo almost three months to aim at the stars or have a look at the moon with his new instrument. It is far more likely that scanning the night sky through a telescope for the first time proved to be more difficult than we can now appreciate, for the early models of the telescope were crude. The original telescopes magnified by a ratio of two to one. Galileo's first effort produced a telescope magnifying by a ratio of ten to one. He improved subsequent models in short order, achieving ratios of twenty to one and finally thirty to one. For decades Galileo produced the best telescopes in the world. Himself a master craftsman, he employed a master craftsman in the person of the lens-grinder Alessandro Piersanti at the head of a group in the Venice Arsenal which Galileo used as a workshop. His glass he drew from the famous Venetian works at Murano, then as now unrivalled in the production of fine glass. Galileo's residence in Venice thus proved to be another happy coincidence. He could not have been in a better place as far as the quality of the material needed was concerned. Moreover the Republic of Venice was the most liberal, forward-looking and independent government in the whole of Italy if not in

23

the world. Galileo was swamped with requests for telescopes. He confined himself to fulfilling the wishes of kings and ruling princes.

On 13 March 1610 550 copies of Galileo's first book (it ran thirty pages) appeared under the title *Siderius Nuncius* (*Messenger* – or *Message – from the Stars*). In it Galileo described his discovery of the four satellites of Jupiter and stated the fact that the moon gives no light of its own, but merely reflects the light of the sun. With his book Galileo included instructions on the care and use of the telescope, stipulating that lenses with a magnifying ratio of twenty to one were necessary to the practice of observing celestial bodies. As short and as matter-of-fact as *Siderius Nuncius* was, the booklet gave philosophers and theologians plenty to think about. Concerning the Milky Way Galileo drily and routinely delivered a statement of stupendous significance: 'At whichever of her segments one directs the telescope, his gaze is met with a tremendous multitude of stars of which many are rather large and very conspicuous; the number of the small stars however is simply incalculable.' Since the time of Hipparchos of Nicaea (190–120 BC), the astronomer who catalogued a thousand stars, humanity had made do with that round number. Here was the invitation to the heresy of Giordano Bruno, who believed that there were innumerable worlds outside this one, and who was burned at the stake ten years before in Rome for his public persistence in his belief (Cardinal Bellarmine had sat up all night with Bruno on the eve of the latter's execution, trying to persuade him to recant). But Galileo did not draw any inferences from his findings. In his conclusion, however, he did make a statement of purpose: 'I shall, namely, prove that she [the earth] moves and that she exceeds the moon in brilliance, and is not a swill made up of the dirt and dregs of the universe, and I shall also support this with hundreds of reasons drawn from nature.' But it was another twenty years before the book, heralded under the title 'The System of the World' in Galileo's conclusion, finally appeared.

The appearance of *Siderius Nuncius* marked the beginning of a struggle between the immemorial orthodoxy (actually it was about four hundred years old) and the new (which, as we have seen, was actually much older than the old orthodoxy but just as long forgotten). But this was not by any means merely a struggle within the confines of a scientific field. This was a direct confrontation along a front that stretched into infinity and as such exemplary of the age-old struggle inherent in the paradox within the nature of man. The world of the Middle Ages had been whole and hale, all of a piece throughout. That world had already been shaken by the Reformation and was in the midst of being shaken again by the Counter-Reformation. In the Middle Ages churchmen had become the successors of the philosophers of antiquity, the Catholic Church had taken over from the Academy and the Lyceum which had disappeared. The Church set, asserted and established the whole scale of values for humanity and with it the climate of culture and the course of learning. Now a new civilization was emerging. What was at stake was an entire *Weltanschauung*, a universal theological and philosophical system. Hitherto man had been at the centre of God's creation. Man's home, the world, had been the centre of the universe. But what was at stake was not only planetary order but every kind of order – most importantly social order, an order under the control of a consistent philosophical motivation. This was what the Catholic Church was all about. Galileo clearly foresaw the breakdown of this basic order when he was informed that Professor of Philosophy Cosimo Boscaglia at a social occasion of the Tuscan court in Pisa had said that the movement of the earth was something incredible in itself and could not take place for the especial reason that holy scripture expressly and unambiguously contradicts this version of natural phenomena. It was here the battle was joined. In a letter to the Benedictine monk Benedetto Castelli, Galileo set forth the dangers and the impropriety of bringing the Bible into scientific discussions.

If the original holy authors had had the purpose of instructing the people concerning constellations and the movements of heavenly bodies, they would not have treated these subjects so scantily that it is nothing in comparison with the infinitely many and sublime and wonderful conclusions which science opens up to us.

But earlier in the letter he made a more important point:

How much greater disorder would result if one should add things according to the demands of people who – quite apart from the fact that we do not know whether they speak out of divine inspiration – nevertheless make it perfectly clear that they totally lack the knowledge necessary, I will not say to refute but rather even to understand the procedures which the most subtle sciences employ in the confirmation of their conclusions.

Chroniclers and scholars point out that Galileo was singularly ill-starred in his conduct of public and private controversy – particularly with the Jesuits. This is true enough: Galileo possessed great powers of impromptu expression, he was probably the foremost literary stylist in the whole of Italy, he had a quick, incisive mind and a prodigious memory, and he disposed over a vast amount of experience, both practical and theoretical. He was, moreover, eminently gregarious, he delighted in banquets and in spirited discussion and, particularly, in putting down pretentious discussants. But what drove his opponents to fury and made implacable enemies of them was something else: Galileo was a very prolific inventor. He seemed to shake inventions out of his sleeve like a magician. And they were important, indeed revolutionary inventions, not just trivial curiosities. He was continually delighting and amazing the public at large and the rising entrepreneurial class especially. And he did so, of course, in Italian, not in Latin. This meant that his books could not be understood outside Italy, as Latin would have been; but it also meant that they would be understood inside Italy, as Latin would not have been. (As Melchior Inchofer, one of the three Counsellors of the Inquisition at Galileo's trial, was to put it in his examination of the text of the *Dialogue*: '. . . he goes on to arm the Copernican opinion with new arguments that no ultramontane ever suggested, and he does so in Italian, surely not the language best suited for the needs of ultramontane or other scholarship but the one most indicated to bring over to his side the ignorant vulgar among whom errors most easily take hold.' Inchofer either forgot or remembered pointedly that most of the apostles were illiterate.) Before the telescope Galileo invented a thermoscope, a forerunner of the thermometer. Some three years after the telescope he invented a micrometer for his laboratory work that was a very considerable improvement over everything until then available. Not long thereafter he invented a floating forerunner to the ship's chronometer in order to replace the very dangerous procedure known as dead reckoning for the ascertainment of longitude at sea. Then in 1624 he surprised the world with his *ochialino* – the microscope as the logical complement to the telescope. As with the telescope Galileo's copyright to the microscope is controversial. But here again he was at least a co-inventor and the instruments he produced in his workshop were the best to be had. The letter accompanying his present of the microscope to Prince Cesi is typical of the onrush of Galileo's enthusiasm for the unknown:

> I have observed with boundless admiration a great many animals among which the flea was the most horrible and the mosquito and the moth on the other hand were very pretty. I have observed with great satisfaction how flies and other small animals are able to walk on the surface of mirrors, incidentally also with their heads downward. But your excellency will have the opportunity to observe thousands upon thousands of details, the most notable of which I ask you to make known to me.

Even though Galileo made do with very little sleep – he spent several hours every night watching the stars – his time was limited. He chose to follow the great and the distant rather than to inspect the small and the near – the macrocosm rather than the microcosm. But it was just this never-ending series of inventions and the technical and theoretical use he put them to (in 1594 he published the *Golden Rule of Mechanics*, concerning the preservation of mechanical energy) that shocked, dismayed and infuriated his opponents-cum-enemies, in particular and the ecclesiastical and the academic establishment at large. The discoveries gained by new methods of observation kept coming. He could argue from unprecedented, unsuspected, steadily unfolding evidence from new sources of information. It was maddening. But of course the very newness of Galileo's approaches had its disadvantages. The bulk of the Italian establishment resisted Galileo's findings by simply ignoring them. A great many scholars and other dignitaries refused point-blank to look into Galileo's telescope. Often enough those who did look professed to see nothing of the sort clearly discerned by Galileo and his friends. But the broad public did not ignore them: it could not.

However the real trouble ran deeper than this. The underlying cause of the failure to resolve the dispute over the planetary systems of Ptolemy, Tycho Brahe and Copernicus was the fact that the theory of cognition of the schoolmen was radically different from the theory of cognition of the new science, so different indeed that the schoolmen refused to admit any of the tenets of the new theory. (The schoolmen were not interested in the truth about nature but in the nature of truth – or, as it was put by William Jennings Bryan in the Scopes Trial three hundred years later, they

27

were 'not interested in the age of rocks but in the "Rock of Ages"'.) Cardinal Bellarmine warned in a letter to the Carmelite monk Foscarini that only in the presence of 'conclusive proof' to the contrary could one question the passage in the Bible which states that the sun revolves around the earth and then only by saying that we do not understand the passage but certainly not by asserting that the contrary had been proved. Bellarmine went on to say that he doubted very much that 'conclusive proof' could ever be brought. He knew what he was talking about. For whereas Galileo promised to bring a 'thousand proofs' he could not bring the one 'conclusive proof' that would have resolved the dispute. For example: Galileo could demonstrate that the planet Venus appeared to have horns in certain phases. There were monks willing to look through his telescope who were fair-minded enough to admit what they saw. But it is one thing to say: 'If the planetary system is Copernican then Venus will show phases,' and quite another thing to say: 'If Venus shows phases then the planetary system is Copernican.' What Galileo was faced with if he tried to argue with the schoolmen on their terms was the virtually insuperable problem of producing negative proof. This was put to him by Cardinal Barberini in a duly chronicled conversation in Rome in 1615. 'Do you believe,' asked the Cardinal,

> that God could have ordered and moved the planets or the stars in another way than in the sense of the Copernican theory or that He could have arranged matters so that everything which is manifested in heaven or that is claimed with regard to the movements, sequence, position, distance and order of the stars could be explained in a satisfactory way? If you say no then you must prove that the production of these appearances in any other way than the one you have conceived is self-contradictory. Because God in his infinite power can do anything that is not self-contradictory . . .

At this Galileo is said to have fallen silent, as well he might have, for there is no practical answer to this line of reasoning. If Galileo had put horns and a tail for good measure on every planet in the firmament he still would not have proved that God in his infinite power could not have produced these appearances in some other way that is not self-contradictory. But there was more to this than the obvious logical strait-jacket. To declare that the Copernican conception of the universe is the only possible and true one would be to deny the omnipotence of God and bring down upon oneself the charge of heresy. A hair-shirt went with the strait-jacket. Barberini's argument was by no means new. At the University of Paris in 1277 theologians with the help of the local bishop and the subsequent approval of the pope declared 219 philosophical theses heretical. By this means the natural sciences were chained to the ecclesiastical establishment along with philosophy. Actually, this was the Church's answer to the new-found freedom consequent upon the re-discovery of Aristotle and the claims of scholarship to the right to independent research and ratiocination. Within two hundred years the fresh wind that rose with the introduction of Aristotle blew cold enough to freeze the master's works into glacial dogma. Reliance by the medieval academic establishment on the letter of the Aristotelian text had been gradually corrupted and become superstition. This made the confrontation and conflict between the old faith and the new science inevitable because it split the ranks of the scholars: superstition in scholarship will not remain uncontested for very long.

Within a year after Galileo had written his letter to Castelli, copies of the same were in circulation, some of them deliberately distorted. Two of these falsifications have come down to us. Whereas Galileo wrote that there were scriptural passages which 'taken in the strict literal meaning, look as if they differed from the truth', one of the copies reads '. . . which are false in the literal meaning'. Likewise, Galileo's original statement that scripture sometimes 'overshadows' its own meaning was changed to read 'perverts' its own meaning. Within the year a Dominican monk had denounced Galileo as a heretic in a sermon in Florence, was reprimanded by his superiors at Galileo's insistence, but went on undaunted to register a formal complaint against Galileo with the Inquisition. The inquisitors rejected the complaint and no case was made. Galileo's letter to Castelli and his expanded follow-up letter to the Grand Duchess Christina of Tuscany were laid *ad acta* in the Inquisition, but not forgotten.

The cat in the form of a kitten was out of the bag: the intent of the two letters was clear; it was a challenge in keeping with Galileo's promise (namely, to prove that the earth moved) made five years before in his first book, *Siderius Nuncius*, that would sooner or later have to be answered. At this point, March 1616, Foscarini, a Carmelite monk from Naples, published a book in defence of Galileo and Copernicus. Preaching in Rome, Foscarini challenged all comers to public discussion about his book and sent a copy to Cardinal Bellarmine which elicited the response already cited. By this time a good deal of skirmishing was going on behind the scenes. Galileo was assiduously using his many and illustrious connections to further his case in the Vatican, in the universities and in society at large. In fact he pushed his case too hard. The pope, Paul V, in consultation with Bellarmine decided a stand would have to be made; he therefore decreed to summon the theologians of the Holy Office to give a formal opinion on the Copernican theory. The decree of the theological experts (Qualifiers) of the Holy Office found the first proposition (namely, that 'the sun is the centre of the world and wholly immovable of local motion') to be formally heretical. The second proposition (that 'the earth is not the centre of the world nor immovable . . .') they found to be equally objectionable but did not pronounce heretical. This decree, in turn, was adjudged to be too severe by some of the cardinals; it was not published for a full seventeen years after it was made. Instead the General Congregation of the Index issued a decree in which the word 'heresy' was missing. The Holy Congregation decreed that Copernicus's work, like that of Diego de Zuniga on Job, 'be suspended until they be corrected'. The book by Father Foscarini, however, was 'altogether prohibited and condemned'. It was, in short, placed on the Index with no prospect of reprieve.

There was thus a certain amount of hedging on the part of the Vatican. Copernicus's book remained on the Index just four years. The corrections made in 1620 consisted of the omission or alteration of nine sentences in which the heliocentric system was represented as certain. Galileo was nowhere mentioned in the decree. There ensued the general appearance that nothing had really changed; there were no reins on discussion of scientific matters as long as they remained theoretical in nature and did not specifically encroach upon the theoretical domain. Galileo thought that he had won the round on points even though he had been called in for an interview with the pope – it lasted three-quarters of an hour – and was surely admonished to observe the proprieties as they had just been set forth. Two days later Galileo was summoned to appear before Cardinal Bellarmine who admonished him – at the direction of the pope – to abandon his opinion that the sun was the immovable centre of the universe and that the earth moves.

This admonitory procedure contained the clause 'in the case of his refusal to obey, that the Commissary is to enjoin on him, before a notary and witnesses, a command to abstain altogether from teaching or defending this opinion and doctrine and even from discussing it . . .'

To scotch rumours that he had been humiliated and punished, Galileo petitioned Bellarmine for a certificate that nothing of the sort had taken place. Bellarmine obliged: '. . . Galileo,' he wrote,

> has not abjured, either in our hand, or the hand of any other person here in Rome, any opinion or doctrine held by him; neither has any salutary penance been imposed on him; but that only the declaration made by the Holy Father and published by the Sacred Congregation of the Index has been notified to him, wherein it is set forth that the doctrine attributed to Copernicus . . . is contrary to the Holy Scriptures and therefore cannot be defended or held.

This certificate must be regarded as proof that no absolute injunction was served on Galileo, leaving him free to discuss the Copernican doctrine at his discretion. It is supported by a minute of the Holy Congregation dated 3 March. Seventeen years later, at the trial, it was contradicted by a minute from the Vatican files which is widely regarded as a forgery and a crude one withal. But the result of this skirmishing was a kind of stand-off, an uneasy truce. Galileo published nothing for the next seven years.

The occasion for Galileo's publishing his famous *Il Sagiatore – The Assayer* – coincided with an auspicious event. The suspicious and sulking Paul V was replaced as pope by Galileo's friend and admirer Maffeo Barberini, who ascended the throne as Urban VIII in 1623. Barberini was a worldling (he conspired with Gustavus Adolphus, the Protestant leader and generalissimus, against the Holy Roman Empire), a man of letters (he translated passages from the Bible into hexameters) and a celebrated wit (on learning of the death of Richelieu he is said to have remarked: 'If there is a God, Cardinal Richelieu will have much to answer for; if not, he has done very well'). Galileo had every reason to expect a turn for the better in his affairs in general and in his scientific pursuits in particular with this ascension. In 1620 Barberini had written an ode in honour of Galileo. The title of the ode was 'Adulatio Perniciosa' or 'Pernicious Adulation' – an ominous title if ever there was one. And indeed, Barberini and Galileo were said to constitute a mutual adulation society. But there was another side to Barberini that was less encouraging: he had a colossal ego. He was the first pope to allow a monument to be erected to him in his lifetime (a fact that prompted Arthur Koestler to remark that Barberini's vanity was monumental). He was also famous for the remark that he 'knew better than all the cardinals put together'. His gutting the bronze ceilings of the Pantheon for the casting of cannon in the course of fortifying the Castle of St Angelo supplied the stuff for the epigram: 'What the barbarians could not do, Barberini did.' Considering that Galileo was himself hardly a shrinking violet (he had insisted on occasion that 'he alone had discovered everything new in the sky') the mutual adulation society might also have been qualified as 'pernicious'. In any case Galileo made the most of the coincidence of publication and ascension by dedicating *The Assayer* to Urban VIII. Not only that but the book contained in addition to the dedication an encomium in which Urban VIII was hailed as a Maecenas and protector of the arts and sciences. The pope was duly impressed; he had *The Assayer* read to him at meals and let it be known that he was delighted with it. *The Assayer*, whose subject matter is the nature and origin of three comets that appeared in the autumn of 1618, is a polemical pamphlet directed at the Jesuit Father Horatio Grassi, who had published his views concerning the comets in 1619, and a dispute via third persons and pseudonyms so characteristic of the age developed. Although it contains some gems such as the distinction between primary qualities (position, number, shape and motion) and secondary qualities (colours, odours and tastes) in nature, *The Assayer* is chiefly remarkable as the first known instance of the perfection of Galileo's prose style in the new demotic Italian language. As such it is a masterpiece and all the more effective as a diatribe for being so. Once again Galileo had made an implacable enemy of a Jesuit. There is, nevertheless, a real question as to whether this continual polemical skirmishing made any appreciable difference in the nature and finality of the verdict and sentence at Galileo's trial. While trying to research the subject of comets in the course of the controversy with Father Grassi, Galileo tried to take recourse to the recently published work on comets by Johannes Kepler, *Epitome Astronomiae Copernicanae*, only to discover that the work had been banned (although it had nothing to do with the Copernican theory *per se*) in the wake of the decree of 1616. This simple act of denying information, to a scientist or an artist, is worse than insults: he cannot function in such an atmosphere. The lines of battle had long since been drawn; the opposing forces had aligned themselves on either side and were spoiling to try conclusions. Galileo had many and powerful friends who not only urged him on but also brought pressure to bear on him. He had promised well over a decade before in his first book, in all solemnity, to 'prove that she [the earth] moves ... and ... support this with hundreds of reasons drawn from nature'. He was now over sixty years of age and it was time this matter was decided. Galileo sent up a trial balloon in the form of a refutation of a refutation of Copernicus published eight years before by a lawyer from Ravenna who had since become Secretary of the Propaganda Office of the Faith in Rome, Francesco Ignoli. He did so under the pretext, as he explained, of showing the Protestants that the Church had outlawed the Copernican theory not as a result of its ignorance thereof but out of reverence for the authority and superiority of Holy Scripture. Galileo's work was circulated in the form of samizdat. The pope had a copy of the work read to him (the reading took an estimated two hours) and was yet again charmed by the eloquence of his fellow Florentine.

The contents of the long-promised book had for some time been clear to Galileo; he had discussed them with friends and opponents any number of times over the years. He had touched on the subject and more than that in his books often enough and much of his correspondence had been taken up with it. There was also no question of what the main theme would be – the example adduced by way of the required 'conclusive proof' that the earth moved. It was to be Galileo's theory of the ebb and flow of the tides which he held to be the most convincing demonstration citing purely mechanistic factors (in contrast to Kepler who posited that the moon had some mysterious influence on the regular rise and fall of the waters of the seas). Another attractive aspect of this subject matter was that Aristotle had no explanation whatever for the phenomenon of the tides. Indeed, Galileo had communicated his intention of giving his prospective work the title 'A Study of the Ebb and Flow of the Tides'. The pope himself dissuaded Galileo from doing so.

Galileo was in poor health for the last twenty years of his life: he suffered from flu and fevers, he was rheumatic and his eyes were bad, over-sensitive to light and subject to frequent infections. The work that was to change the course of the world was six full years in the writing. It emerged as a dialogue between three people, Salviati (Galileo), the Copernican, Sagredo, the Ptolemaean and Simplicio, the Aristotelian. It took its title from its nature: *Dialogue on the Two Greatest Systems of the World, the Ptolemaic and the Copernican.* The *Dialogue* lasted four days, each day's discussion constituting a book. It is a curious piece of work – a masterpiece of propagandistic writing, a simplification, a popularization of a scientific treatment. As a scientific work proper the *Dialogue* leaves a good deal to be desired. Galileo was wrong in his theory of the tides. The gravitational pulls of the sun and the moon have more to do with tidal movement than do the rotation and orbital movement of the earth and, in any case, Galileo's theory accounted for only one ebb and flow during the diurnal round, whereas in fact there are two. Even so, Galileo's theory points the way to the true explanation. The movement of the earth around its own axis and in orbit around the sun does indeed have something to do with the tides – via the gravitational pulls of the sun and the moon. Isaac Newton, born in the year Galileo died, discovered the true explanation sixty years later. But it was his enthusiastic reading of Galileo's *Dialogue* in his youth that set him off – and in the right direction.

The particular form and style of the work were carefully chosen. The dialogue had become especially popular after the rediscovery of Plato and the stilted, extravagant language of the courtier was still very much in vogue. Also, Galileo took the precaution of bringing in and deferring to Urban VIII's favourite argument at the end of the work. Simplicio admits that Salviati's theory (the Copernican) seems the more persuasive but can nevertheless not be accepted as convincing proof:

> Always fixed in my mind's eye rather is the unshakeable bastion of doctrine which a highly placed personage once gave to me. The question is: can God by virtue of His unlimited power and wisdom impart by other means to the element of water the alternating movement which we observe than by moving the seabed? I know that your answer to this question will be that He possesses the power and the wisdom to do this in many ways that surpass our understanding. Acknowledging this I come straight away to the conclusion that it would be an impermissible audacity to attempt to limit and constrict divine power and wisdom within the narrow confines of one man's whimsy.

This was the argument Barberini produced in 1615 and it was said to have reduced Galileo to silence. This time, however, Salviati (Galileo) has the last word. In fourteen years Galileo had found an answer. It was this:

An admirable, indeed angelic doctrine! And fully in accord with it is that other divine statute which certainly permits us to seek to examine the structure of the universe, and yet forever forbids us to perceive and comprehend fully the work of His hands – perhaps with the intention of thus assuring that this activity of the human spirit does not wither and die. Let us therefore use this God-given and God-willed capacity of the human spirit to the end of recognizing His greatness, fulfilling ourselves all the more with wonder the less we discover ourselves capable of penetrating the limitless profundities of His unending wisdom.

Modern critics are apt to find this language – particularly the term 'angelic' – ironic to the point of scurrility. In so doing they misjudge the temper and conventions of the age. Four censors could find no fault with this language – although the whole procedure of the granting of the imprimatur, the permission to publish, developed into a kind of comedy of errors. And this not least because of two tragedies, the Thirty Years War (which took up an inordinate amount of an ambitious pope's time) and the outbreak of the plague in Florence in 1630 (coming from the north). When Galileo arrived in Rome with a copy of the manuscript, Urban VIII did not have time to read it or have it read to him. Under the pressure of his assumed field captaincy in the ongoing war Urban VIII had only enough time to receive Galileo once. The latter, who often boasted that his tongue was mightier than his pen, did not have the opportunity to bring his Florentine eloquence to bear. Before the year was very old, moreover, much of Italy was under quarantine because of the plague. This made travel largely impossible and split the machinery of the granting of the imprimatur between Rome and Florence with two censors operative in each city.

The result of this constellation of circumstances was a great deal of confusion. This was further compounded by the fact that none of the censors was remotely qualified for the task of passing judgement on the text. The chief censor, the Maestro del Sacro Palazzo, a Dominican monk known as Pater Monstrum because of his tremendous girth, believed that the planets were set and kept in motion by angels. He was well disposed to Galileo, having given his most enthusiastic permission to *The Assayer* when it appeared six years earlier. There ensued a back-and-forth between the two cities. Changes, but very few of them, were made in the manuscripts and there were no cuts. Apparently each of the four censors relied on the other three to exercise the necessary acumen. The book appeared in February 1632, two years after it had been submitted to the authorities for approval. On the obverse side of the title page appeared the four official stamps of the approving censors.

The first responses to the *Dialogue* were altogether ecstatic. Tomasso Campanella praised the work as a 'philosophical comedy'. 'We need not envy Plato,' he wrote. 'Salviati is a superb Socrates, who acts as a midwife for the thoughts of others rather than giving birth to his own, and Sagredo is a genuine free spirit who, without having been mutilated by the schools, adjudges everything with the greatest wisdom . . . These truths from old problems, from new worlds, new stars and new systems are the dawn of a new era.' And so it went for six months. Galileo, in the midst of a tenacious eye-infection (he had to have the notices read to him), sunned himself in praise that seemed to come from every side.

Then, in mid-August, the blow fell: the printer and publisher Landini received instructions from the Vatican to stop all sales of the book. What happened in Rome in the six months between February and August is a blank. But from the reports of the Tuscan ambassador at the Holy See, Niccolini, to the effect that the pope 'was so incensed that he treated this affair as a personal one' and including Urban's 'bitter remark' that Galileo had deceived him, it is clear that there had been a concentrated campaign in progress at the Vatican to turn Urban against Galileo. Galileo's enemies made the most of an unprecedented opportunity. It was a comparatively easy matter to play on the vanity of Urban and convince him that the representation of his and the Church's standpoint in the *Dialogue* by the simpleton Simplicio was an indelible affront to both his person and his position. The representation of a point of view by a character in a fictitious dialogue could be turned to disadvantage as well as to advantage. As the saying goes, 'Affronts are as they are taken.' The masquerade in literature, like its modern example the *roman-à-clef*, is convenient but also dangerous.

By the same token Galileo was convinced that, given a fair chance to defend himself and his works, he could, relying on his native eloquence, succeed in setting matters aright. Despite the harshness of the initial proceedings, the summons and the threats of punishments upon failure to comply, his plea of illness and incapacity was honoured and Galileo was granted a four-month delay (after doctors sent by the Vatican had examined him). He arrived in Rome in February of 1633, staying as usual in the Tuscan embassy. But three months passed before he was called for his first interrogation at the Holy Office.

When Galileo finally arrived in Rome he was likewise faced with a series of unpleasant discoveries. The first of these was the basic procedural rule of the Inquisition to keep the accused in ignorance of the charges made against him. Instead, the accused was asked if he knew or could guess why he had been summoned. For those who have had occasion to experience or to inquire into the standard procedure of Communist governments in court interrogations of those summoned, this will strike a familiar note. In his treatment of this aspect of Galileo's trial in his book *The Sleepwalkers*, the late Arthur Koestler, who had made a thorough-going study of Soviet official interrogation procedures and techniques in researching his novel *Darkness at Noon*, supplies a footnote at this point:

This has also become the standard procedure in trials by the Soviet State Police. The 'inquisitorial character of OGPU [later NKVD, MVD and KGB] methods' is more than a figure of political jargon. The absolute secrecy enjoined on the accused regarding the proceedings and even the fact that he is under investigation; the absence of lawyers for the defence, and the assumption that he is guilty unless proved innocent; the methods of psychological pressure, the alternation between threats and paternal reassurance, and above all, the metaphysical axiom of the 'union of wills' between Church and penitent are only the more salient features which the OGPU copied after thorough study of the Inquisition's methods and procedure.

In like manner, Josef K. in Kafka's *The Trial* is never able to discover the nature of the charge brought against him.

But there was another, even more devastating discovery awaiting Galileo at his first interrogation. This was that inquisitorial procedure allowed no discussion: the accused was restricted to answering questions put to him by his interrogators. Thus Galileo was deprived of his favourite and most effective weapon: his eloquence.

Then came the news that with the beginning of the trial he automatically became the prisoner of the Inquisition and would thus be taken into custody and kept there throughout the proceedings. Through the intervention of his host, the Tuscan ambassador Niccolini, with the pope, Galileo was allowed to stay in a specially provided room with a servant who brought his meals and acted as a personal valet in the Palazzo del Sant' Uffizio. He was thus spared the discomfort and indignity of being confined in a dungeon of the Inquisition. There is no doubt that these and other evidences of preferential treatment confused the old man Galileo had become as to the true nature and significance of the proceedings against him.

The special commission formed to investigate the case of Galileo on the occasion of the publication of his book had made three findings. The first was that Galileo had contravened the papal decree in deviating from the hypothetical treatment of the Copernican theory; the second was that he had erroneously ascribed the phenomena of the tides to the Copernican theory; the third was that he had practised deceit in the article of the command laid upon him by the Holy Office in 1616, namely 'to relinquish altogether the said opinion . . . nor henceforth to hold, teach or defend it in any way whatsoever, verbally or in writing'. This third finding was based upon the minute produced as evidence of the serving of an absolute injunction on Galileo in 1616 in connection with the decree outlawing the Copernican theory. But Galileo had petitioned and received a certificate from Cardinal Bellarmine to the effect that no such injunction had been served. And that settled the matter. The two documents are mutually exclusive. One of them has to be a forgery. Bellarmine's certificate cannot be questioned: it was signed, sealed and delivered. But it is utterly fascinating that seventeen years later a highly irregular (a copy with no original on record), painfully obvious jobbing of a document should be produced on just this very point. This curiosity is significant as a symbol of the controversial nature of the trial. It is clear that the 'minute' was fashioned – perhaps, indeed, as early as 1616 – to reinforce the decree against the Copernican theory by silencing its foremost and most effective advocate. But not only him. In the light of the lifting of the decree against the Copernican theory after the few corrections already mentioned had been made, the situation was still ambiguous. It is certain only that the Church was not entirely in charge of itself in the whole matter. There were those who believed that an accommodation of some kind to the new science and its new discoveries had to be made. It was clear to most of the cardinals as it was to the pope himself that the Church was fighting a rearguard action, the object of the exercise being to prevent a breakthrough (the breakthrough already made by Martin Luther was bad enough). In the Thirty Years War the Church was on its way to losing all but one of the budding industrial nations of the north. In this light the trial of Galileo can be seen as the ceremonial symbolizing of the great tragedy of mankind, the final act of the fall from grace, the last exodus from Eden, the divorce of humankind from nature. For with Galileo the scientific–technical revolution was visibly peeking over the rising shoulder of the industrial revolution.

Then, too, the means at the disposal of the Vatican to accomplish the defence of the faith were none too impressive. The Index itself was hardly an awesome threat any more: two of the three theologians who sat on the committee of experts adjudging the Copernican theory in 1616 were later to have works of theirs placed on the Index – moreover, one of these was a cardinal, Oregius. Bellarmine himself for that matter, he who was considered to be the best-versed theologian in the college of cardinals, had one of his works placed on the Index. As Georgio de Santillana in his book *The Crime of Galileo* put it: '. . . the feeling seems to have been current in Rome that the Index was a kind of administrative misadventure that occurred sooner or later to anyone writing on serious subjects and that it was a matter of waiting until the official line changed again.'

And as for the Inquisition, what of it? The special ecclesiastical courts for the juridical persecution of heresy were instituted by the Emperor Frederick II (Hohenstaufen) in 1232. Gregory IX, mindful of the age-old hegemonic strife with the German emperors ('who is going to do the thinking around here?'), lost no time in claiming this office for the Church. He appointed papal inquisitors selected from the members of mendicant orders, especially Dominicans and Franciscans, whose theological learning and asceticism seemed to render them qualified for the work. The Inquisition, then, was the first organized secret state police, 'entitled to do exactly anything' (di Santillana) which is always the formula for disaster. It was an emergency tribunal creating and changing its own administrative law at will. It was also the 'thought police' of Western Christianity, the guardian of 'revealed truth' as a whole (this meant not only Scripture and dogma but also the whole 'deposit of Faith', that is, the entire heritage of Christianity through tradition). Under the decision *publice cremandum fore*, books were burned in the public square by the executioner, whereas the decision *prohibendum fore* meant merely that a book was prohibited. The powers of the Inquisition were therefore wholly discretionary, a principle that was horribly abused by the Spanish Inquisition. But the larger point is that there was never a German Inquisition. 'Had it existed in Germany in good working order,' wrote the medieval scholar H. C. Lea,

> Luther's career would have been short. An Inquisitor like Bernardo Gui would have speedily silenced him . . . In Germany there was no national Church; there was subjection to Rome, which was growing unendurable for financial reasons, but there was nothing to take the place of the Inquisition, and a latitude of speech had become customary which was tolerated so long as the revenues of St Peter were not interfered with.

But this does not explain why there was no Inquisition on the home ground of the institution's *spiritus rector*. The explanation is simple: '*Rübe ab!*' ('Off with the head!') Within a year after his appointment, the first and last Grand Inquisitor of Germany, Konrad von Marburg, was dead by an assassin's hand. The same fate befell any inquisitor who became too inquisitive. The Probst of Berlin was killed when he tried to exert his authority overmuch, as some thought. By way of punishment, and since the culprits could not be found, the pope excommunicated the whole of Berlin. In other words, there was no Inquisition in Germany for the same reason there is no trade-union movement in Sicily: a Sicilian trade-union leader is a dead trade-union leader.

'If Galileo had only known how to retain the favour of the Jesuits,' said Father Grienberger, the leading Jesuit astronomer at the time, 'he would have stood in renown before the world, he would have been spared all his misfortune and he could have written what he pleased about everything, even about the motion of the earth.' Just so. But this statement can be turned around to much greater effect. If the Jesuit astronomers had not gone over-board in their hatred of Galileo and their fear of the new science, they could have rendered incalculable service to the Church and to the whole of humankind withal. They could have – in coopera-tion with Galileo – accommodated the new science by degrees into the body of Church doctrine. This after all was the chief function of the Jesuits. Theirs was the hold on education, theirs the whole of the 'humanistic' programme on which they had brought up the ruling classes. As it was, all the positions proposed and promoted by Galileo, theological as well as scientific, were subsequently accepted by the Church, the subsequence having extended over a period of two hundred years with great damage to the Church and the humanities in the main and untold and untell-able collateral damage at large.

The cause of the tragedy of Galileo which is the tragedy of humankind was the failure of the Jesuits to perform their educative function in terms of high policy: they were there to prevent the pope from making a fool of himself. The Jesuits failed because they panicked. They panicked because they had the precedent of Martin Luther before their eyes. Like Galileo Luther had been a master of the vernacular who had gone to the people and spoken to them in their own language. Moreover he had invented a means of com-munication utilizing the printing press for the first time on a mass basis in the form of the pamphlet – six to eight pages for a price anybody could afford.

But there was never any question of silencing Luther. The German lands were fiercely guarded by the seven Electors, each supreme on his own territory. But even the petty princes of fringe regions managed to exact sweeping concessions from Rome in return for revenue: in the German tradition a kind of ecclesiastical Danegeld. There was the saying: 'The Duke of Cleves is pope in his own territories.' There was another saying that came out of the German lands and prevailed: 'Cuius regio, eius religio' (the ruling prince determines the religion of the land). This arrangement was part and parcel of the result of the Investiture Contest which ended in compromise. The compromise meant that somewhere down the centuries Luther would be waiting. But as for the Inquisition, Galileo would have been out of its clutches and safe from its toils in the neighbouring Republic of Venice: this assurance was the other side of the warning from Galileo's friends when he quit

Venice to return to his Tuscan home. As it was, the Inquisition did great service to the papacy and greater disservice. The worst thing it did – notwithstanding the hideous aberrations in Spain – was to stand model for Communist and then Nazi security services in this century.

Thus Galileo, in spite of his age and infirmity and the dimensions of the scandal, must have entered upon this 'administrative mis-adventure' with a certain bravado. In his first sessions with the interrogators of the Inquisition he flatly denied that he had presented the Copernican theory in his book in such a way as to favour it over the Ptolemaic theory. This assertion was made in a summary answer to a series of questions as to whether he had received an absolute injunction against discussing the Copernican theory. Galileo of course denied having received such an injunction and produced a copy of Bellarmine's certificate to support his denial. Nothing daunted, the Inquisitor put the same question some five or six times, with some variations on the theme. He asked if perhaps others had been present when Galileo had been admonished. Galileo denied this but finally conceded that it had been a long time ago, that his memory might be faulty and that it was just possible that others might have been present. The Inquisitor then turned, tacitly assuming that Galileo's statement was tantamount to an admission that he had indeed received an absolute injunction, to the question of Galileo's application for the imprimatur. Had he informed the censor that he, Galileo, had been commanded to cease and desist from favourable discussion of the Copernican theory? Galileo replied that he had not considered it necessary to do so, 'for I have neither maintained nor defended in that book the opinion that the earth moves and that the sun is stationary, but have rather demonstrated the opposite of the Copernican opinion, and shown that the arguments of Copernicus are weak and not conclusive'. On this note the hearing ended.

Three experts, who had been appointed by the Inquisition to examine the contents of the book, had no trouble producing abundant evidence by way of quotations from the book that Galileo had discussed the Copernican view as an hypothesis, defended and promoted it, spicing the account by describing those who did not hold the Copernican view as 'idiots', 'mental pygmies' and 'hardly deserving to be called human beings'. Koestler calls Galileo's 'pretence' in the teeth of this evidence culled from his own book 'suicidal folly'. Shortly before this, however, Koestler is far more persuasive in pointing out the many defects of Galileo's (that is, Salviati's) argument for the Copernican theory. He emphasizes the weakness of the theory of the tide which is paraded as the main and would-be conclusive proof of the rightness of the Copernican theory. Koestler professes astonishment that a scientist of Galileo's stature and accomplishments would dare present so slovenly constructed a model as proof of anything. The only explanation for this eccentricity to Koestler's mind is the 'quasi-pathological contempt which Galileo felt for his contemporaries'. And then there is the second finding of the special commission, namely, that he had erroneously ascribed the phenomena of the tides to the Copernican theory. Scientifically, at any rate, according to these assertions Galileo was fully justified in denying that he had presented or represented the Copernican theory in such a way as to favour it over the Ptolemaic or any other theory. In terms of polemics, of course, there can be no question but that he gave the palm to the Copernican theory. It is possible to draw the inference that in spite of a well-planned and carefully constructed literary edifice Galileo's very considerable polemical talents were given enough rein to run away with the work. It is more likely that the author was attempting to construct a number of escape routes leading out of the edifice so that anyone inclined to avail himself of one of them could easily do so. This would also explain why it took the Vatican six months to come to the conclusion that the work was deceitful (because it had passed four censors) and affrontive (because it could be taken that way: 'affronts are as they are taken'), and they took another three months to prepare the case. It would also explain why Galileo thought that he would be able to talk his way out of any dilemma the work might pose.

The Inquisition broke out of the impasse resulting from Galileo's stubborn insistence on his innocence by taking recourse to a shift that has become all too familiar in the twentieth century. It was, as Georgio di Santillana put it, as if Ivanov came to Rubashov. This was an allusion to the hero and his interrogator in Koestler's novel *Darkness at Noon*. The Commissary of the Inquisition, Firenzuola, wrote a letter to the pope's brother, Cardinal Francesco Barberini, one of the judges at the trial. In his letter Firenzuola suggested that since

Galileo has in his examination denied what is plainly evident from the book written by him, since in consequence of this denial there would result the necessity for greater rigour of procedure and less regard to the other considerations belonging to this business ... I suggested a course, namely, that the Holy Congregation should grant me permission to treat extra-judicially with Galileo, in order to render him sensible of his error and bring him, if he recognizes it, to a confession of the same.

Permission was granted. In a surprise visit to Galileo, Firenzuola quickly attained his object, bringing Galileo 'to a full sense of his error, so that he clearly recognized that ... he had gone too far in his book'. This Galileo did with much feeling, 'like one who experienced great consolation in the recognition of his error'. Galileo agreed to confess but asked for time to consider the formulation of his confession. Time was granted. Firenzuola closes his letter:

> ... I trust that His Holiness and your Eminence will be satisfied that in this way the affair is being brought to such a point that it may soon be settled without difficulty. The court will maintain its reputation; it will be possible to deal leniently with the culprit; and, whatever the decision arrived at, he will recognize the favour shown him, with all the other consequences of satisfaction herein desired.

Two days after the interview described Galileo appeared for his second hearing and the awaited statement. Here he explained that he had reread his book (having been at liberty to send his servant out to look for a copy) which he had not seen for so long that it appeared to him like a new book by a strange author. He added:

> I freely confess that in several places it seemed to me set forth in such a form that a reader ignorant of my real purpose might have had reason to suppose that the arguments brought on the false side, and which it was my intention to confute, were so expressed as to be calculated rather to compel conviction by their cogency than to be easy of solution.

Galileo listed two arguments in particular:

> ... the one taken from the solar spots, the other from the ebb and flow of the tide – which, in truth, come to the ear of the reader with far greater show of force and power than ought to have been imparted to them by one who regarded them as inconclusive, and who intended to refute them, as indeed I truly and sincerely held and do hold them to be inconclusive and admitting of refutation.

His mistake had been 'one of vainglorious ambition and of pure ignorance and inadvertence'. Galileo then offered a supplementary statement, returning to the hearing after he had been dismissed. The interlocutors in his work already published, he said, had agreed to meet again after a time to discuss problems of Nature. This would afford him the opportunity of adding other 'days' or chapters. 'I promise,' Galileo concluded, 'to resume the arguments already brought in favour of the said opinion, which is false and has been condemned, and to confute them in such most effectual manner as by the blessing of God may be supplied to me.'

Ten days later at a purely formal hearing Galileo submitted his written defence in which he denied deceitful intentions and stated that he had been unaware of a 'specific and absolute injunction in 1616'. He then repeated his statement already made with the offer to make good all harm done by writing a sequel to the condemned book. Finally, he added a personal appeal:

> Lastly, it remains for me to beg you to take into consideration my pitiable state of bodily indisposition, to which, at the age of seventy years, I have been reduced by ten months of constant mental anxiety and the fatigue of a long and toilsome journey at the most inclement season – together with the loss of the greater part of the years to which, from my previous state of health, I had the prospect ... And I would equally commend to their [the most Eminent Lords] consideration my honour and reputation, against the calumnies of ill-wishers, whose persistence in detracting from my good name may be inferred from the necessity which constrained me to procure from the Lord Cardinal Bellarmine the attestation which accompanies this.

Sentence was passed against Galileo six weeks later on 16 June. Koestler cites the decision as it was entered into the acts:

> ... Sanctissimus decreed that said Galileo is to be interrogated as to his intention [in writing the *Dialogue*] under the threat of torture; and if he kept firm he is to be called upon to abjure before plenary assembly of the Congregation of the Holy Office, and is to be condemned to imprisonment at the pleasure of the Holy Congregation, and ordered not to treat further, in whatever manner, either in words or in writing, of the mobility of the Earth and the stability of the Sun; otherwise he will incur the penalties of relapse.

Three days later Galileo was called for his third and last

examination. He was questioned under oath about his real conviction with regard to the two cosmological systems. Galileo answered that he had considered that either opinion might be true in nature until the decree of 1616. '. . . After the said decision,' he went on, 'assured of the wisdom of the authorities, I ceased to have any doubt; and I held, as I still hold, as most true and indisputable the opinion of Ptolemy, that is to say, the stability of the earth.' He was then confronted with the manner in which he treated the subject in the *Dialogue* and informed that by the very fact that he had written the book he was presumed to have favoured the Copernican opinion. To this he answered that his only aim in writing the book was to set forth the argument for both sides. He then repeated: 'I do not now hold the condemned opinion, and have not held it since the decision of the authorities.' The question was put to Galileo a third time: on the basis of the contents of his book, the *Dialogue*, he was presumed to support the Copernican view – or, at least, to have done so when he wrote it – therefore 'unless he made up his mind to confess the truth, recourse would be had against him to the appropriate remedies of the law'. Galileo replied: 'I do not hold, and have not held, this opinion of Copernicus since the command was intimated to me that I must abandon it; for the rest I am here in your hands – do with me what you please.'

Thus Galileo remained *vehementer suspectus* (he died under imposed penitence and was refused burial in hallowed ground as forever *vehementer suspectus*). His sentence reads:

> We say, pronounce, sentence and declare that you, the said Galileo, by reason of the matters adduced in trial, and by you confessed as above, have rendered yourself in the judgement of this Holy Office vehemently suspected of heresy, namely, of having believed and held the doctrine – which is false and contrary to the sacred and divine Scriptures – that the Sun is the centre of the world and does not move from East to West and that the Earth moves and is not the centre of the world; and that an opinion may be held and defended as probable after it has been declared and defined to be contrary to the Holy Scripture; and that consequently you have incurred all the censures and penalties imposed and promulgated in the sacred canons and other constitutions, general and particular, against such delinquents.

The division here is complete; it is the stand-off confrontation of two theories and systems of cognition, the theological and the scientific: the nature of knowledge as against the knowledge of nature. Galileo can truthfully and tranquilly say that since the decree of 1616 he had no longer held the condemned Copernican opinion. This was a matter of form. 'Affirmatively' he must not hold certain opinions. Just so. And as to Galileo's real opinion on the matter? Well, then – who was to convince Galileo on his own terms, which is to say on scientific grounds, that he should hold the one opinion and not the other? It was a question not only of holding an opinion but of holding the line – the battle line. Galileo had outlined the dilemma in a letter already cited:

> How much greater disorder would result if one should add things according to the demands of people who – quite apart from the fact that we do not know whether they speak out of divine inspiration – nevertheless make it perfectly clear that they totally lack the knowledge necessary, I will not say to refute but rather even to understand the procedures which the most subtle sciences employ in the confirmation of their conclusions.

He had also stated his position clearly in a letter to the lawyer Francesco Ignoli:

> In matters concerning Nature the authority of man counts for nothing. You, indeed, as a student of law, seem to put great stock therein, but Nature, my dear sir, scorns the directives and decrees of princes, emperors and monarchs and would not change its course one iota at their behest. Aristotle was a human being, saw with the eyes, heard with the ears and thought with the brain, of a human being. I am a human being, I see with the eyes and a great deal more than he did for that matter; with regard to thinking, I believe that he thought about more things than I have; but whether he thought more and better than I about the things which have been the objects of contemplation for the both of us – this will be shown by the reasons we adduce and not by those in authority above us.

Thus each of the two disciplines had its own proper area of validity and neither had any business in the bailiwick of the other. The difficulty was that in trying to draw the demarcation line between the two provinces one was inevitably perceived as trespassing by the other side. In theology the atmosphere was as rarefied as in the higher reaches of the natural sciences. Galileo was certainly ill-advised to venture into theological considerations –

47

particularly when citing St Augustine as an unimpeachable Church authority. Even so, his works – whether banned, burned, prohibited or 'permanently' placed on the Index (it took the Vatican almost two hundred years to take the name of Galileo off the Index) – withstood all attempts at suppression. 'Manuscripts,' in the famous phrase of Mikhail Bulgakov, 'do not burn.' It was this factor, not a fact, that accounts for the myth that Galileo, at his final hearing and through clenched teeth, muttered the words: *'Eppur si muove'* ('And yet it moves'). It was not he who spoke; it was his works.

And so Galileo remained a highly privileged prisoner for the rest of his life. He changed residence several times, in embassies, palaces and villas. His final sojourn on this earth was spent in his home, the villa at Arcetri. He never spent a day or a single minute in prison. He was allowed to work and to write, and indeed it was during this period – in 1638 – that he produced his most important work, *The Discorsi . . . Investigations and Mathematical Demonstrations Concerning Two New Sciences, Mechanics and the Laws of Gravity*, a book that was soon hailed and is still regarded as the 'first modern textbook of physics'. He spent the last seven years of his life in darkness, being totally blind. For such a man blindness was a tragedy on a scale with the deafness of Beethoven. He gave fitting expression to his plight in a letter to his friend Diodati:

> Alas, your friend and servant Galileo has been for the last month hopelessly blind; so that this heaven, this earth, this universe, which I, by marvellous discoveries and clear demonstrations, have enlarged a hundred thousand times beyond the belief of the wise men of bygone ages, henceforward for me is shrunk into such small space as is filled by my own bodily sensations.

The confrontation of the two theories of cognition, the theological concern with the nature of knowledge and the scientific concern with the knowledge of nature, is not just a formal reversal of concepts. Lewis Mumford in his book *The Pentagon of Power* points out a deeper significance of the trial of Galileo Galilei:

> But actually Galileo committed a crime far graver than any of the dignitaries of the Church accused him of; for his real crime was that of trading the totality of human experience, not merely the accumulated dogmas and doctrines of the Church, for that minute portion which can be observed within a limited time span and interpreted

in terms of mass and motion, while denying importance to the unmediated realities of human experience, from which science itself is only a refined ideological derivative. When Galileo divided experienced reality into two spheres, a subjective sphere, which he chose to exclude from science, and an objective sphere, freed theoretically from man's visible presence, but known through rigorous mathematical analysis, he was dismissing as unsubstantial and unreal the cultural accretions of meaning that had made mathematics – itself a purely subjective distillation – possible.

While this comment smacks of the quip about the scientific approach as a way of learning more and more about less and less, the key phrase 'the cultural accretions of meaning' and the charge of its dismissal as unsubstantial and unreal are the undersong of a chorus of complaints, alarms and caveats by modern critics and observers. In *The Use of Poetry and the Use of Criticism*, T. S. Eliot elaborates on this theme: '. . . when morals cease to be a matter of tradition and orthodoxy – that is, of the habits of the community formulated, corrected and elevated by the continuous thought and direction of the church – when one man is to elaborate his own, then *personality* becomes a thing of alarming importance.' (Gerhard Szczesny cites 'the craving for personality among the masses of antiquity just as they were being set free by the dissolution of the older social forms'.) In the same essay Eliot then adds: 'The number of people in possession of any criteria for distinguishing between good and evil is very small.' Harry Levin, in one of the conclusions arrived at in his remarkable book, *The Gates of Horn*, brings a pertinent insight to the concerns of the Vatican then as now: 'What matters, then, are not the articles of belief but principled patterns of behaviour: not the controversies of theology nor enhancements in the manner of Chateaubriand, but a unique means of countering the forces of self-interest.'

Between Galileo and the authorities it came to a showdown, as Georgio di Santillana says, about 'who is going to do the thinking around here'. (Galileo was made to promise, under oath and *sub poenis*, that 'should I know any heretic or person suspected of heresy, I will denounce him to this Holy Office'.) It is extraordinary how often this pattern emerges: 'Kepler complained in a fervent petition to the Church Council in Württemburg; the Council answered in a long, patient and paternally chiding letter that Kepler should stick to mathematics and leave theology to the theologians.'

But who was to decide what constituted heresy? Galileo wanted to be part of the establishment, which was still theological, to guide it, advise it like the loyal consultant he was. But the entire controversy involving Galileo should be examined on the basis of his discovery or premonition that in one way or another everything is measurable. 'One must measure,' he is purported to have said, 'everything that is measurable and make measurable whatever is not.' Once again: Galileo himself may never have uttered these words but his works and his teaching made the statement for him. In any case he wrote to the same effect and far more eloquently: *'La natura e scritta in lingua matematica'* ('Nature is written in the language of mathematics').

This is the basic legacy, the 'Open Sesame' to the cult of human omnipotence. Prometheus was chained to a rock where an eagle came every day and beak-tore his liver as punishment for his having stolen fire from heaven and given it to humankind. Prometheus the fire-giver and Lucifer the 'light-bearer'. For the Church there was something Promethean and also Luciferian in the exploits and perception of Galileo. For with Galileo the wheel had come full circle in a process that started with the separation of Olympian religion and Ionian philosophy. The rise of Ionian atheism was the compensatory reaction to the decline of the state religion of the Greeks which had hardened into a carapace of ritual and routine with the consequent loss of that cosmic consciousness which had generated religion in the first place. With Galileo final causes became mere superstition, with Galileo the awesome spell cast over humankind by Nature had been broken, and the indomitable reverence of the Greeks for Nature replaced by the thirst to plumb the depths of Nature's mystery regardless of the consequences. (What we are witnessing here is the birth of the idea of 'Faustian man'.) But transcendental justice and moral values had been inseparable from the instinctive reverence for Nature and the natural order as divinely ordained. Nothing in life – plant, insect, metal or angel – was outside the divine order. 'This little stone,' said Richard Basehart in the film *La Strada*, 'if this has no purpose then everything is senseless – even the stars.' Nothing was outside the hierarchy of values. Everything had its reward, its punishment and its meaning. With what was humankind to replace the loss of this 'God-given' system of values? By what right and under whose authority were the social forces in dynamic societies to be kept under the control of a consistent philosophical motivation? It had taken how long to build the edifice now being demolished? No one knew. A thousand years? Two thousand years? One hundred thousand? Who could tell? How old were these 'cultural accretions of meaning'? Lewis Mumford goes a great deal further than this. In his book, *The Myth of the Machine*, he states that man is the result of a billion years of evolution. His pedigree, then – his cultural, physical, biological provenance – is simply unfathomable.

The explosion of the first atomic bomb in Alamogordo in 1945 and what happened since then has generated a new interest in the history of the natural sciences. While interpretations of the significance of the development of nuclear physics and other aspects of the mechanistic obsession of humanity vary widely and even radically, there is general agreement among qualified observers that the path of development of the natural sciences and particularly physics is mistaken, that the root cause of the mistake was the divorce of humanity from nature which began with the rise of the natural sciences and has been accompanied throughout by the progressive secularization of Christianity. In tracing this process emphasis unerringly falls on the quantification of matter as the key development and on Galileo as its author and original culprit. Thus the crime of Galileo has assumed dimensions undreamed of until the mid-twentieth century. Within the scope of these studies emphasis has also been placed on the exchange of roles effected on different levels – the displacement of Christianity as the unquestioned authority and its gradual replacement by science – most recently in the form of advanced or high technology, the passing of the old priesthood (of theologians) to make way for the new priesthood (of scientists) and the leitmotiv in both cases but more especially in the new authority and the new priesthood of an umbilical connection from the very first between mechanics and then physics with warfare, specifically with the business of fortification – tunnels, moats, trenches, earthworks, walls and towers – and arms production. The military uses of technology and its products have always enjoyed first priority. The Greeks had a saying (Heraclitus), made popular by the Germans in modern times: 'War is the father of all things.'

III

❧

THE GREAT ROLE REVERSAL:
MAN BITES GOD

Perhaps the strongest urge in the psychic make-up of the human animal is the craving for personality. The emphasis on the significance of the individual in Christianity at the beginning of the Christian era was the most attractive element of the new religion to the masses. The replacement of 'attrition' and 'contrition' for the absolution of sins beginning in the eleventh century by means of the institution of the confession had the effect of privatizing sin, of separating the two kinds of regret springing from fear and love, respectively, of probing the individual's psychological state to determine which kind of regret was dominant. The institution of private confession, which gradually replaced public penance, made the deity partner to the individual's ability to express sincere sorrow in confessing sins. This was a tremendous breakthrough in the development of Christianity and one that in no small part anticipates Luther.

Toward the end of the eighteenth century the Enlightenment and the rationalist conception of religion loosened the strictures of traditional religious dogma. Luther had liberated the conscience of man from both great traditional institutional monopolies – the ecclesiastical and the synagogal. When Luther declared that 'the place in which we must learn to live together with God as man and wife is the conscience', he made the conscience – and the consciousness – of man the centre of the universe. He also brought about a direct relationship, an intimacy and a confrontation, between God and the individual being that declares an equality in the relationship between the human and the divine. With his reversion to Holy Writ, to the Word, as the sole authority in all matters of faith, Luther took the implement of exegesis (by means of which the Church could interpret and reinterpret Holy Writ to suit its hierarchic purposes) out of the hands of the hierarchy and placed it in the hands of the individual. In short, he replaced the belief in authority with the authority of belief. It was a feat that almost belittles the term 'Promethean'; Moses received the tables, but Luther turned them. He thus drew the problems of conscience into the province of reason. This was a complete turnabout from the traditional Thomist ecclesiastical use of subordinating reason to faith. It was a revolution without parallel in history, and the influence of Luther's feat on the course of history can hardly be exaggerated. This is mainly because Lutheranism marked the beginning of the development of philosophic and scientific thinking in Europe and of its redevelopment (after a respite of some two thousand years) in the world at large.

But the Lutheran revolution was just as important in that it opened a main line of access to the development of the human personality. It is clear that both these beginnings, the philosophic and the scientific, are interconnected and mutually auxiliary. 'When God gave him [Adam] reason, he gave him freedom to choose, for reason is but choosing,' wrote John Milton in the *Areopagitica*. The thirst to develop one's own style can be characterized as an attempt to determine the offshore limits of the personality, an undertaking to discover the *kosmos* (both ornament and order) in the microcosm of the individual. 'I sometimes think,' said Edmund Kean, 'that the display of extreme emotion is merely bad acting.' But acting, good or bad, presupposes choice. The fields of choice that underlie the development (conscious or unconscious) of personality limit the scope and therefore the quality of the acting. Where there are few if any fields of choice there is either bad acting or sterility. There can be no doubt that the personal aspect of Christianity as a creed, in the person of the deity and in the person of every one of his conscious creatures, both broadened and intensified the individual search for personality. In like fashion, progress in the discovery and development of personality refined and also broadened Christian religious thought to an extent where the life of Christ came to be considered as in itself the beginning of the process of secularization. And in any case the bulk of theology is far too impressive – especially in its myriad cultural ramifications – to be brushed aside on a take-it-or-leave-it basis. This was

53

Galileo's standpoint in his conviction that his creed could sovereignly accommodate any systemic discovery – whatever its basis – and that he had the right and his Church had the right to make every effort to do just that. In this he was the direct follower of Luther, whose exclusion predetermined the rejection of Galileo's works for some two hundred years. But, the theme of Lutheranism remaining constant, it is impossible to overlook the central figure in modern history responsible for the state of affairs and the affairs of state, for the system of government and the entire quality of life, into which Andrei Dmitrievich Sakharov was born late in the first quarter of the twentieth century.

Karl Heinrich Marx was the product of two revolutions whose enlightening influence struck his father's family in the reverse order of their historical succession. The French Revolution – in the person of Napoleon – freed German Jews from their ghettos; the Reformation – in the form of conversion to the Prussian state religion of Lutheranism – offered a second, definitive escape when the ghettos reclosed around them. Herschel Levi became Heinrich Marx and a successful Prussian lawyer. His eldest son was born Karl Marx. Reformation and revolution gave the Jews of Europe a taste of freedom they found difficult to forget or hold lightly. Marx enrolled as a law student at the University of Bonn in his native Rhineland in 1835. He changed to Berlin the next year and in that hotbed of Hegelianism (it was only five years after Hegel's death) became a Hegelian. He ultimately took his degree of doctor of philosophy at the University of Jena in 1841. The title of his doctoral dissertation was 'On the Differences between the Natural Philosophy of Democritus and Epicurus'. He was thus well grounded academically, a philosopher trained in universities that numbered among the best in the world. The rudiments of much of the system Marx was later to develop are evident in the dissertation. It was entirely Hegelian in its assumption of the World Spirit as a vantage point for a critical attack on the irrationality of the empirical world. Here he parted company with the Young Hegelians in the article of the identification of self-awareness with the historical process. If there were to be any real prospect of such identification, wrote Marx, then it would have to come from the immanent forces of history itself and not from some rational construct superimposed from without. The purpose then must be to find the conditions that can make history rational and in keeping

54

with the consciousness of its participants while eliminating that false consciousness that contemplates the world but is not yet the world's self-consciousness. The embryo of Marxism is there. 'Epicurus tried to free mankind from dependence on nature by, in effect, transforming the immediate aspect of consciousness, its being-for-itself, into a form of nature. But in fact we can only become independent of nature by making it the property of reason, and this in turn requires us to recognize the rationality of nature in itself' (Kolakowski). It is not surprising that Marx went back to the ancient Greeks to find the stone on which to build his church. The Young Hegelians were Greek scholars because Hegel himself was a superb Greek scholar.

Marx had laid the foundations and complete floor-plan of his system by the time he was thirty-five years old (1848) and living in exile in Paris (off and on and not for long; in 1849 he moved definitively to London). Marx was a theoretician. His long suit was not observation; he spent the greater part of his working life at his writing desk and in the reading room of the British Museum. This latter statement has a double significance. Marx was quintessentially German (precisely because of his Jewish background) and anywhere out of Germany he was a fish out of water. He had no understanding of English life or of the English. He didn't like them and had no contact with them worth mentioning. He was thus the victim of a twofold isolation, national as well as political. But in actuality all this was of no great moment; he was by nature withdrawn and his source material was overwhelmingly academic in any case. It made very little difference to him where he lived so long as his books and periodicals were available. One of the reasons for this combination of contentment and concentration was that Marx, like Bismarck, was blessed with a very happy and harmonious family life. The reason for the wealth of source material that awaited him was his coming at a time that was conjunctive of the forces freed by Reformation and French Revolution, philosophically, theologically and sociologically. He was in a position to gather in and bind together the variety of theory and empirical information that had accumulated. To this task he brought a wholly extraordinary devotion: 'The nineteenth century,' writes his biographer Isaiah Berlin, 'contains many remarkable social critics and revolutionaries no less original, no less violent, no less dogmatic than Marx, but not one so rigorously single-minded, so

55

absorbed in making every word and every act of his life a means towards a single, immediate, practical end, to which nothing was too sacred to sacrifice.' The result of this whole-hearted and single-minded devotion was late in coming but equally extraordinary. It was, to quote Isaiah Berlin again, 'the most formidable, sustained and elaborate indictment ever delivered against an entire social order, against its rulers, its supporters, its ideologists, its willing slaves, against all those whose lives are bound up with its survival'. Moreover the indictment came, as Berlin adds, at a moment when bourgeois society had reached a pinnacle of its material prosperity, when Gladstone in a budget speech congratulated his countrymen on the 'intoxicating augmentation of their wealth and power'. It remains to examine this achievement.

Marx did not merely collect and bind the strands of theory and data that a fruitful conjunction of events had placed at his disposal. He wrought a revolutionary theory by standing his master, Hegel, on his head in a philosophical *tour de force*. (Quite naturally Marx claimed that he was standing Hegel on his feet – here Marx was actually speaking to Hegel's remark that 'philosophers walk on their heads'.) To generalize for a moment: if the idea of the German idealist philosophers seems far-fetched, that is, that man somehow created nature by or through his perception of it; then looking back through history at the progress of the pilgrim – especially if one takes the scientific theory seriously, that is, his emerging from the primordial slime and developing by evolution over hundreds of millions of years to become what he is today – then man did indeed create the world because he has established himself as the sole recording perceiver, the unique supplier of the history and with it a context for the world which is not only an awareness but also an awareness of the awareness of the world and hence the world itself. For the world without this awareness would be nothing but matter. And that, of course, is the contention of the idealist philosophers. As Descartes said: 'Give me matter and I shall make the world.' Speaking as a representative of knowing man, a *homo sapiens*, Descartes did just that. But he did it as the product and heir of a billion years of evolution. Man is a creature of an incredibly vast and intricate complex of dependencies. He is an inseparable link to the past of his kind.

Having perceived the world, it is a question of what one makes of one's perceptions. This fact, of course, highlights the importance of history in the broadest sense. History makes man and man makes history; these are considerations that heighten the question of any man's immediate and intermediate antecedents. In the case of Marx, the collector and assimilator of theory and data, the in-gatherer who brought all the dominant strains of thought of the time to bear on a single, burning focal point, this question is of crucial importance. Who were the thinkers who stood behind Marx, whose intellectual estates he plundered in the synthesis of his doctrine? The first of these, in stature and chronology, was Kant.

Without Luther, Immanuel Kant (1724–1804) would not have come upon his major theses. The *Critique of Pure Reason* is an advertisement of the basic result of Luther's revolution. But Kant was also, and perhaps more consciously, influenced by Galileo. Beginning his career as a mathematician deeply interested in physics, Kant's first major work bore the title *A General History of Nature and Theory of the Heavens.* In it he developed the idea of a number of rotating galaxies in the firmament. Kant opted for reason, but in so doing he defined the natural limits of reason in terms of setting forth the categories of perception. In these, time and space figure as the warp and woof of the human apparatus of apperception, the presence of two different objects in the same place constituting time and the presence of two different objects at the same time constituting space. Proceeding from this restriction in the natural endowment of the human being to take in and appreciate sense perceptions, Kant concluded that human knowledge of absolute reality, *das Ding an sich* (the thing in itself), is categorically impossible. Kant's *Critique of Pure Reason* is an exposition of what reason can and cannot do in the light of the categorical limits of perception imposed by nature, of which man is a part. But the *Critique* is also a study of the act of cognition. To begin with, Kant distinguishes between matter and form: 'In a phenomenon I call that which corresponds to the sensation its *matter*; but that which causes the manifold matter of the phenomenon to be perceived as arranged in a certain order, I call its *form.*' Matter is given to us a posteriori (as the result of a cause), but form is imposed on the matter by the mind itself, hence form is already in the mind – a priori – 'and must therefore be capable of being considered as separate from all sensations'. This distinction corresponds to Kant's distinction between perception and judgement,

57

perception being the simple sensual registration of objects as they are given whereas judgement is the intellectual activity the mind exercises upon them. In the first case the mind is merely the passive recipient of an impression; in the second the mind legislates over nature insofar as it imposes law and order. 'Time,' writes Kant, 'is nothing but the form of our own internal intuition.' Space is the complement of time.

This is the duality established by Kant: man at once as the passive victim of contingent phenomena and the legislator who imposes order on nature, at once the slave and lord of nature. In Kant this essential dichotomy between the passive and active in man goes through a whole series of correspondences – the division of the world into what is perceived and what is thought, between the contingent and the intellectually necessary, between happiness and duty, between free will and law, between the phenomenal world of causality and the world of the *Dinge an sich* (things in themselves), the absolute ideal, freedom and independence of mind. But there must be a way to overcome the essential dichotomy, a way to reconcile subject and object, free will and law, to achieve a synthesis of happiness and virtue. In the empirical world these things are opposite poles and limit themselves mutually: one man's right to swing his fist ends where the nose of his neighbour begins. The solution clearly required a Promethean effort. And indeed, Kant made a Promethean effort in the *Critique of Pure Reason*: the result was stupendous, but it was not enough. His conclusion was that the Absolute was unreachable, unattainable by the human mind. It was a beacon lighting the way of progress of knowledge, which is endless. The prospect before man, then, was that of an unending progress towards self-deification in the sense of achieving perfection. Perfection, once achieved, would negate the power of contingency over freedom. The problem, posed by Galileo's discovery and invention of modern scientific methodology, was clear. The mind schematizes nature (by imposing form on matter) for the purpose of quantifying it, measuring it and making calculations on the basis of measurement. This involved a split between consciousness and the external world. Descartes had given a sinister twist to Galileo's methodology by declaring manipulation of nature to be the scientific goal, paraphrasing Archimedes' 'Give me a place to stand and I shall move the world' with 'Give me matter and I shall make the world' – the ultimate arrogance and the ultimate arrogation. Actually, of course, this was merely making explicit what was implicit in Galileo's methodology. But Descartes was primarily a philosopher and Galileo was not, with the result that the problem has remained set in Cartesian terms and philosophy has largely accommodated itself to the Cartesian framework ever since: how to bridge the gap between consciousness and the external world, between nature and freedom, between desire and duty, between passive existence dependent on contingency and active existence which eliminates contingency (which is to say the elimination of the possibility of unfortunate accidents, that is, evil). What Kant did was demonstrate the kind, condition and limitation of the tools at man's disposal for the achievement of the 'Cartesian' task. It was a *tour de force*, this demonstration, but it was not encouraging to the faithful. And Kant had made every effort to be just that.

But the exposé of the duality of man and nature was not a revelation. Mortal man discovered this great and consternating truth. The man was Galileo. Galileo was the scientific executor of Martin Luther's will and testament. Luther's heirs were Kant and Hegel. It was Georg Wilhelm Friedrich Hegel who charted the progress of consciousness toward the Absolute. What Hegel wrote in the whole corpus of his works was, in the words of Leszek Kolakowski, nothing less than the autobiography of the mind. *The Phenomenology of the Spirit* (or *Mind* – in German, *Geist*) is the most important of Hegel's works in that it details the development of the mind through the continuing bombardment of the 'slings and arrows of outrageous fortune' in history, toward perfection or absoluteness. Specifically, Hegel describes the development of consciousness through self-awareness and the ramifications and consequences of self-awareness. His book is a handbook on how the mind works. The mind itself is the only reality. It is the subject which discerns the object in the outside world. An object is something alien to the subject, different from it, inimical to it. The object is the natural enemy of the subject. This comes to light in the word 'objection'. Etymologically the word 'object' is from the Latin *ob-jectus*, the past participle of the verb *ob-jicere* (*ob* + *jacere*, to throw) and means 'something thrown against or in front of the observer'. The enmity is etymological. The subject befriends the object, as it were, by way of the mind's awareness of its knowledge of the object. What was an object has become knowledge of an object, being has become being-in-itself-for-consciousness. By so doing, the mind negates the negation constituted by the object and so removes it by assimilation. The mind overcomes the conflict between Reason and reality not by denying or destroying the object but by absorbing it. And the mind enriches itself in the process. This is the Hegelian dialectic of thesis (subject), antithesis (object) and synthesis (fusion and enrichment). Of course, the resultant synthesis takes place at a higher level of understanding than that of the original conflict between thesis and antithesis. Thus the dialectic is the locomotive of progress. Thus, too, the development of the mind (consciousness), the only reality, is synonymous with the history of the world in that the mind develops through a progress of ordeals by combat with contingency. This makes for the rationalistic determinism of the historical process. It is a development through successive negations. Instead of Kant's progress toward infinity, the idea of unlimited self-perfection, Hegel posits authentic infinity 'as the consummated return into self, the relation of itself to itself, its being – but not indeterminate, abstract being, for it is posited as negating the negation; the image of true infinity, bent back into itself, becomes the circle, the line which has reached itself, which is closed and wholly present, without beginning and end'. The meaning of true infinity in Hegel is the self – through the progressive development of self-awareness – finally discovering itself – through the achievement of complete self-awareness. This is both a return and an advance to an Absolute that is freedom – hence the perfect circle as the symbolic metaphor; in freeing itself from contingency the spirit frees itself absolutely. History becomes intelligible as a whole if one regards it as the gradual development of the consciousness of freedom to the achievement of the final salvation which is the return of the self, enriched to the point of perfection, to itself. Only the actual historical process is creative of values. 'Action,' wrote Hegel, 'is namely nothing more than the pure translation out of unformed being (potential) into the being of form (actual) . . . the individual can therefore not know what he is until he has brought himself to reality through action . . . Talent is likewise nothing other than the original individuality regarded as inner means or the transition of purpose to reality.' The value of the individual consists only in the 'element of divinity' within him, and it actualizes itself *as a value of the Absolute*. Moreover, the rationalistic determinism of the historical process has nothing whatever to do with the pursuit of happiness: 'The history of the world is not a scene of happiness. Periods of happiness are blank pages in it, for they are periods of harmony – periods when the antithesis is in abeyance.' No: the lot of humanity is struggle and antagonism, suffering and oppression in order to meet its destiny, which is also that of the world spirit: 'Man is an object of existence in himself only in virtue of the Divine that is in him – that which was designated at the outset as Reason and which, in view of its activity and power of self-determination, was called Freedom.'

Hegel posits a tribunal of Reason to distinguish between what is truly real and what appears to be real but is only the empty husk of a bygone reality. The tribunal of Reason is the state. The systematic coercion of individuals is the hallmark of an immature society; progress leads to a situation in which the subjective and the general will coincide spontaneously as a result of acts of understanding of the world. But for as long as there is no complete and voluntary accord between the subjective will and universal Reason, who is to decide what the universal will requires? Since there is no other institution which could assume this role, and since the state by definition is the incarnation of Reason, in cases of conflict it must play the role of the medieval Church, that is, the sole authorized interpreter of the divine message. The perfection of the state as an institution would result or coincide with the disappearance of the need for compulsion.

But there was a middle ground between the philosophers and theologians. This was occupied by the socialists or proto-socialists, most of whom were French, although the impulse for the socialist movement, which was the onset of the Industrial Revolution, took place in England. In 1767 James Hargreaves invented the spinning-jenny, the weaving machine that revolutionized the textile industry. In 1790 James Watt invented the steam engine; just twelve years later the first steel rolling mill driven by steam engines was in operation. In 1814 George Stephenson built the first locomotive. Hardly six years later he built the first railway, running between the English towns of Stockton and Darlington, and just two years later he founded the first locomotive construction company, complete with factory. The Germans followed this feat by building the first railway on the continent – between Nuremberg and Fürth – in 1835.

With this development began the urbanization of mankind; it

was specifically the mass exodus from the country to the cities that presented 'the thinking reed' with an entirely new set of problems generally concerning the art of living and working together in the mass at close quarters. The beginning of the Industrial Revolution coincided with the end of feudal allegiance buttressed by the flying arches of the medieval Church. Necessity is the mother of invention: the result of the end of the one and the beginning of the other was the birth of socialism.

An unprecedented social upheaval during the gestation of socialism was to influence its course in subsequent ages considerably if not decisively. This of course was the French Revolution. In its wake there took place what has been hailed as 'the first active manifestation of socialism'. The reference here is to the conspiracy of Gracchus Babeuf. Babeuf and his followers, called 'Babouvists', founded their philosophy on Rousseau and the utopianists of the Enlightenment. The Babouvists considered themselves the successors of Robespierre and, after the latter's execution in 1794, they organized a conspiracy to overthrow the revolutionary government. Considering that the masses were not yet capable of exercising power, the Babouvists volunteered, as it were, to exercise it for them. Politically they were radical egalitarians and the first to hit upon the idea of private property as the source of inequality and to formulate economic arguments against private property as the foundation of society. The conspiracy was exposed and Babeuf was executed in 1796. But the projected role of the Babouvists in the wake of the French Revolution bears a strong resemblance to the actual role of the Bolsheviks in the wake of the Russian Revolution.

The first of the social or 'socialist' philosophers were amateurs and for good reason: the study they undertook was new, no such academic discipline existed (there are those who would argue that no such academic discipline exists even now). But as they began, tentatively or rashly, they moved toward a new appreciation of the Church or, at least, of the Church's function in society. But it was another discipline that served as a model for their efforts. Claude Henri, Comte de Saint-Simon called for a political science as positive and reliable as the physical sciences. Another Newton was needed, he said, to unify the body of knowledge accumulated since his day. This was the great task that faced scholars – to lead their nations toward happiness (Saint-Simon had fought in the

American War of Independence). From 1814 to 1818 Saint-Simon worked out plans for the political and social reorganization of Europe, including parliamentary government on the British model and even a supranational European assembly for the preservation of peace, the practice of cooperation between states, but on the basis of liberalism rather than theocracy. In his work, *Industrie* (1817) Saint-Simon concluded that the function of the state was to concern itself with productivity while applying the methods of industrial management to social questions. He further concluded, along the lines of historical materialism, that political change was the result of the evolution of the means of production, that poverty was caused by free competition and the anarchy of production and exchange that result. The Great Divide, for Saint-Simon, was between those who produced and those who merely battened off the productive process. In his future society industry would be managed by the producers of wealth while production was to be planned to fulfil social needs. Private property would be changed in character and function, subordinating its use to the general good and not to the owner's whim, inheritance would be abolished: only those who had earned the right to possess property by ability and application would be allowed the privilege. In his last major work Saint-Simon worked his way around to Christianity. This was *Le Nouveau Christianisme* (1825). Here Saint-Simon asserted that political science needs must be based on religious principles. Industrial society must be made to fulfil the central tenet of Christianity, which was love – 'To love thy neighbour as thyself'. Self-interest could not serve as a basis of social organization, religious feeling was a permanent feature of human existence.

The school of Saint-Simon's disciples that followed emphasized the religious strain of his writings. Also, the state was to be kept more or less as it was but with modified functions. The new Christianity was to be suffused with the spirit of science and technical progress. For the rest, Saint-Simonism proved itself capable of development in opposite directions, like all doctrines. If most of his followers were basically traditionalists he also had disciples like Louis Blanc and through him Ferdinand Lassalle, the founder of the German Social Democratic Party. It was also Blanc who modified Saint-Simon's doctrine with the formulation 'From each according to his ability, to each according to his needs.'

There was, obviously, a strong Romantic strain in Saint-

Simonism. This was predominantly but by no means exclusively French. But in France the dawn of the Industrial Revolution was accompanied by strong Romantic overtones. Engineers and businessmen were seen as knights errant of the new world of applied science. The same thing happened in Germany, first and foremost in the writing of the poet Novalis. But the amount of Romanticism involved in socialism was always only a matter of degree. The theory of socialism naturally divides into a pragmatic (reformist) and a utopian (revolutionary) wing. But they were the wings of the same 'bluebird of happiness'. And even the hard-headed and hard-hatted (he was a factory worker who became a factory owner) Robert Owen (1771–1858) was convinced that socialism was a heaven-sent discovery and unique. One extreme begets the other. In the England of Owen's time six-year-old children worked fourteen to sixteen hours a day in the spinning mills. It was only in 1819 that the Factory Act, the passage of which was largely Owen's doing, limited the working time of children in the textile industry. In his own factories Owen reduced working hours to ten and a half and he refused to employ children under the age of ten years. He arranged for free primary education and comparatively hygienic working conditions. As a public figure Owen attacked the Church for keeping the masses in poverty and ignorance. In his view the most harmful and erroneous of the Church's doctrines was that of holding the individual responsible for his character and actions. He organized trades unions and cooperatives and planned a new type of society. His attacks on religion and private property generated violent reaction, under the pressure of which he went to America in 1824. There he tried to set up communist societies and found the New World in space even less hospitable than the New World in time had been. He returned to England just five years later and devoted himself to organizing the British proletariat through the promotion of trades unions and cooperatives. Perhaps his most interesting idea resulted in his advocacy of a 'labour currency' that was meant to fix the price of products at their real value, reckoned by the average labour time in their manufacture. He also organized a 'labour exchange' to eliminate the middleman. Owen's attempt to introduce a new concept of currency failed because it was tantamount to an attempt to eliminate the market. But any serious thought of eliminating the market is based on more profound assumption. Owen adopted the view of the eighteenth-century utilitarians that man is not responsible for his character and conduct, which are exclusively the product of his upbringing and circumstances – his environment. The theory that a man cannot change himself is curiously leglocked to the theory that someone else can change him. For Owen, man's knowledge and convictions are the result of education. 'The idea that man can be moulded at will,' writes Kolakowski, 'and that there can be a social harmony which does not do away with private interests but reconciles them through education is part of the stock-in-trade of the Enlightenment.' From this stock Owen drew practical conclusions intended to revolutionize the social system through educational and labour reform. Reform is slow going. Owen finally concluded that the workers would have to look to themselves for any improvement in their lot.

Charles Fourier (1772–1837), quite possibly the most utopian of the utopians on record, was born the son of a rich merchant in Besançon. After an apprenticeship as a commercial agent he founded a firm of his own only to be ruined by the upheaval of the revolution and the speculation that ran riot in its wake. Soured forever on the idea of free enterprise, Fourier concluded that human nature, its needs and passions, was ineradicable, but led to unhappiness only because society was badly organized. Fourier was sent off on his speculative odyssey by comparing the price of apples on a trip from Rouen to Paris. He noted a wide difference in price even though the climate and conditions of produce were the same. This finding led him to pronounce all middlemen anathema. The system that Fourier devised in order to remove the antagonisms of mankind and induce general harmony was a unit he called the 'phalanstery'. This was a settlement or a building containing a total of 2,000 people who in turn constituted a 'phalanx'. The design was calculated both to satisfy and redirect all human passions to constructive ends. Fourier distinguished twelve passions in human nature: four were passions of sentiment (love, friendship, ambition and family feeling), one passion was assigned to each of the five senses and the remaining three he called 'distributive' – the longing for change, the love of intrigue and the urge to unite in competing groups. Fourier calculated that the combinations of these passions totalled 810 different types of character. Work within the phalanx was to be reorganized so that everyone had an occupation suitable to his character. No one would be forced to

65

remain at the same kind of work. This kind of freedom was possible because everyone would be trained in at least forty different aptitudes, thus allowing an individual to change his occupation several times a day if he so desired. The dirty work would be done by children, who loved to play in the dirt anyway. The phalansteries would be hotels rather than barracks. Fourier fore-ordained the emancipation of women, there was to be complete equality, family life would be abolished and children cared for communally at public expense. Moreover, sex was to be free, without any restrictions. Fourier considered asceticism to be harmful and unnatural. For him the liberation of man meant the liberation of his passions. Monogamy could be practised if that was what people wanted, but love was to be free and brothels would become respected institutions. (Features such as these brought the charge that Fourier's utopia was Rabelaisian rather than socialist.) Inheritance, private property and economic inequality while not abolished would somehow lose their antagonistic character. Minimum subsistence for all would be provided – even for those who did not work. But in Fourier's view there would be no idlers in his society; everyone would want to take part in the pleasure of working under the new circumstances, that is, production by cooperatives whose income would be determined by the usefulness of their output. Individuals would work in various groups, drawing different wages in each group according to performance. Everyone would be entitled to share in the capital of the cooperative, but safeguards would prevent exploitation. Political institutions would become superfluous, public affairs would be decided democratically and government would be stripped to the administration of economics. There would, however, be a system of titles, dignities and representative functions to excite emulation. Fourier reckoned precisely how many phalanxes would be required to cover the world and constitute the world state of 'omnarchy' (rule by all). Theretofore, wrote Fourier, the faulty organization of society had also corrupted the animal and vegetable kingdoms. His system, when introduced, would transform these in the course of the assertion of man's dominion over all nature. The salt water of the Seven Seas would be converted into orangeade, deserts would bloom, glaciers melt, spring would be eternal, wild beasts would become tame and as friendly as dogs. Man would have 'anti-lions' and 'anti-whales' at his beck and call. There would be only one language for all mankind, etc., etc. Here Fourier's utopia is less Rabelaisian than paradisiacal – humanity before the Fall.

Fourier's 'system' is a prime example of the dangers involved in trying to explain or harmonize human affairs in accordance with universal laws discovered and established by scientific investigation.

> The pursuit of knowledge was to him a form of worship, and the laws of nature were divine decrees. Newton's law of gravity applied to souls as well; all human passions were instances of 'attraction', all were natural, therefore divine and deserving of satisfaction. The universe was a kind of phalanster composed of heavenly bodies in a hierarchical order: the planet copulated, the stars had souls, and so on. Fourier . . . believed that the human soul and the universe were constructed according to an identical schema.
>
> (*Kolakowski*)

Despite the extravagances of his system, many of the ideas contained in Fourier's writings became part and parcel of socialist theory. He had no illusions about changing human nature but sought rather to remedy the human situation within the framework of a new social order. The establishment of workers' consumer cooperatives was a direct result of his system as was the sometime establishment of producer cooperatives with workers as shareholders. Both stood as models for similar organizations common enough today.

Pierre Joseph Proudhon (1809–65), like Charles Fourier, was born in Besançon. He was the son of a brewery worker. He had some schooling, but not much; he completed his apprenticeship as a printer. His first pamphlet, written in 1840, entitled *Qu'est-ce que la propriété?*, received a mixed reception made up of equal parts of admiration and fury. Thereafter Proudhon was always associated with the slogan 'Property is theft', although the phrase had actually been introduced before the revolution by Brissot. Proudhon, however, did coin the expression 'scientific socialism'. But the slogan 'Property is theft' begs more questions than it answers. By reviving the slogan of Brissot Proudhon opened Pandora's box.

He did not recommend the abolition of property, but he was too impetuous a writer ever to overcome the sloganizing of his own disjointed message. He called for the 'generalizing' of property and left it as vague as that. And yet he gave expression to a verily prophetic vision of Communism. He called the Communists power-hungry fanatics whose aim it was to establish an omnipotent state on the basis of public property. In their system the individual would not be allowed to own property. Instead the 'whole law-lessness of its use' would be transferred to the state. The state would own everything, the country's resources, its wealth over all 'and the bodies of its citizens as well'. Everything, the lives, talents and aspirations of human beings would become state property and thus the source of all social evil, namely the monopoly principle, would be driven to an extreme. All Communism had to offer, he concluded, was the police state.

Proudhon knew what he didn't like. On the positive side he favoured what he called 'industrial democracy', the workers' con-trol of the means of production. Society was to consist of a federa-tion of producers, agricultural as well as industrial. This was the only way to solve 'the furious conundrum of the machine' which, in its successive perfections as a means of production, was a boon to mankind but also a curse in that it created unemployment. There was also the problem of the division of labour, the fact that industrial production fragmented the work process into various menial functions and thus reduced the individual to a mere part of himself. The whole man in his capacity as artisan and master-workman was out of it forever. There is an almost overpowering nostalgia evident here. Proudhon could never reconcile himself to the fact of property in hands that had not earned it. Anything over the proper amount a person needed represented a theft from other workers. And this went particularly for unearned income such as interest on capital, rent and dividends.

There are names in the history of socialism that are important if only because they serve to denominate the two main trends in the movement. Louis-Auguste Blanqui (1805–81) transmitted the heri-tage of Babouvism to the revolutionary generation of 1848, thus linking the Jacobin left and the nineteenth-century radicals and introducing the concept of revolutionary conspiracy into the wor-kers' movement. Blanqui was also the author of the idea of a 'dictatorship of the proletariat', not to be exercised by the proletar-iat itself but rather by a highly organized élite of professional revolutionaries working in the name of the proletariat. Louis Blanc (1811–82) was a moderate socialist theoretician who proposed an extensive programme of reforms and public works when a member of the provisional government in 1848. He was a deputy of the moderate republican left from 1876 until his death. In 1879 he inspired the law granting amnesty to the Communards. Blanc was a practical reformer who did not want to provoke a violent upheaval but to prevent one. Blanqui's ideas were adopted by Tkachev and Lenin; Blanc's by Ferdinand Lassalle and the modern social democrats.

In the immediate aftermath of Hegel's death in 1831, Hegelianism became something very like the official doctrine of the Prussian state. Apologists for the Prussian state drew on the twenty volumes of the collected works as an unprecedented wealth of theory. Authorities filled university chairs, particularly in Berlin, with Hegelians. Within a few years, however, the same authorities discovered that there was trouble in paradise. The Young Hegelians, as they were called, soon demonstrated that they were inclined to adopt and develop the more radical ideas to be found in Hegel's works. The celebrated aphorism, 'What is actual is rational', which seemingly sanctioned any factual situation, turned out to be only half of the aphorism, which went on to proclaim, 'and what is rational is actual', indicating that the empirical fact only deserved to be called 'actual' if it conformed to the demands of historical reason. But most alarming for the authorities was the fact that the Young Hegelians displayed a penchant for attacking established religion. For the Young Hegelians the dominant theme in Hegel's works was the principle of permanent negation as the ineluctable law of spiritual development.

Young Hegelianism was the philosophical creed of the republican, bourgeois-democratic opposition in the Prussian state. It criticized the Prussian feudal order and looked to France for inspiration. (Hegel called Napoleon 'the World-Spirit on horseback'.) Prussia's western provinces, the Rhineland and Westphalia, had been under French hegemony for some two decades and hence benefited from the Code Napoléon which abolished the feudal estates and established equality before the law. When these provinces were annexed to Prussia in 1815 they became a hotbed of opposition to the Prussian monarchy. From this radicalized area came the poet Heinrich Heine and other literary lights such as Ludwig (actually Loeb Baruch) Börne who led a group known as Junges Deutschland (Young Germany). In time these were replaced by the Hegelian radicals (most of them in Berlin) who included a club of philosophers and theologians given to interpreting Christianity in a Hegelian spirit. Prominent among these was David Friedrich Strauss, whose book, *The Life of Jesus*, was a bestseller. *The Life of Jesus* wielded enormous influence for decades after its appearance in 1835 (Friedrich Engels forswore his belief in Christianity after reading it) and was translated into most European languages. It was translated into English by George Eliot under her real name of Marianne Evans, although her name did not appear in the original English edition. Eliot, who was deeply offended by the book – especially in its treatment of the crucifixion (she used the notorious third edition in German – in the other editions Strauss had some-what modulated his attack on his subject) – found the book heavy going; the German original appeared in three volumes and ran some nine hundred pages. Eliot received the princely honorarium of £20 for her efforts. Undoubtedly the fact that George Eliot was the daughter of a clergyman added to her discomfiture. Strauss's masterpiece was the well-nigh inevitable result of the development of Hegelian Reason. What could be more reasonable than turning this finely honed surgical instrument on the founder of the Christian religion, the cornerstone of the entire edifice of civilization? Strauss dismissed the Gospels: they were not a system of philosophical symbols but merely Jewish myths. He went on to question the existence of a historical Jesus, as Voltaire had done many years before. What nettled Strauss particularly here was the conceptual architecture of his Hegelian background against the myth of a single incarnation of the Absolute in an historical person. He remained convinced of the complete immanent presence of God in history, but rejected the idea of a personal God.

Despite her discomfiture with Strauss's famous book, George Eliot was soon to accept the task of translating a far more important book by a far more important writer – *The Essence of Christianity* by Ludwig Feuerbach. (To impart some idea of the dimensions of this feat, Eliot's active knowledge of the German language was not good enough to permit a meaningful conversation.) Feuerbach had already written *A History of Modern Philosophy from Bacon to Spinoza* and studies of Bayle and Leibnitz. As a writer he called for the philosophical rehabilitation of nature and he criticized Hegel for giving nature short shrift in his concentration on the spirit. In *The Essence of Christianity* Feuerbach argued that 'the secret of theology is anthropology', in other words, man's knowledge of

God was really only the mythicizing of man's knowledge of himself. The Greek myths among others stood as proof of this. This is really nothing more than a logical extension of Luther's reversal of theology and philosophy (indeed, Feuerbach often referred to himself as 'Luther II'). The Greek practice of depicting gods as descending to earth in the form of men or swans or whatever was merely the reverse of what it claimed to be. It was man's knowledge of man (or beast or tree) posing as a supernatural event in a double masquerade: under the masquerade of god as man there was the masquerade of man as god. Hence, concluded Feuerbach, the real truth of religion is the denial of God and the affirmation of man – in short, atheism. Basically this is the familiar notion of the mutual dependence of subject and object: the subject constitutes itself in self-knowledge by separating itself from the object, the object is constituted in the projection of self-knowledge by the subject. Hence God is the imaginative projection of man's species-essence, his powers and attributes being assigned to the deity. But this, in turn, introduced alienation: the transference of the best qualities of man by man to an imaginary deity results in the tyrannizing of man by a fiction of his own creation. The more religion enriches an imaginary divine being, so runs the argument, the more it impoverishes man. There was, in this regard, the symbol of ritual blood sacrifice in the primitive stages of Judaism and Christianity and in other primitive religions to emphasize the humiliation of man before God. But even now, in modern Christianity, humanity must be humiliated, deprived and degraded in order that the Deity may shine forth in greater majesty – *ad maioram dei gloriam.* 'Man asserts in God what he denies in himself.' To assert himself *ad hominem* man must realize that religion is *ab(h)ominable*, as the word was spelt in English until the seventeenth century and so appears invariably in Shakespeare. (The true derivation is from *ab + omen*, meaning to deprecate as an ill omen, which serves the purpose almost as well.) Thus, writes Feuerbach, in order to save the true values of religion, which are those of humanity, man must overthrow religion. In the polarization of God and man, moving away from God is perforce moving toward man and vice versa. Having accomplished the turning from God toward man, men will be able to create genuinely humanistic societies, and here Spinoza's principle of *homo homini dei* (man is God to man) is brought in. 'If the essence of man is the supreme essence for man, then the first and supreme law of action must be man's love for man.' (Incidentally, George Eliot also translated Spinoza.)

As time went on Feuerbach became more and more anthropocentric in his views: man was the only value, all others being ablative, merely deductible from this central, living, finite, concrete entity. In his *Lectures on the Essence of Religion*, published in 1851, he stated that religious feelings stem from man's inability to interpret his own situation in nature properly. It was man's feeling of dependence on nature that triggered religious imaginations (an idea he could have found as a schoolboy in almost any Greek text). In the end, Feuerbach rejected the whole of Hegelianism because of its idealism, which he regarded as merely a continuation of religious fiction. By this time Feuerbach had come to see religion as the root of all social evil. The historical stage was being set for the entry of the great materialist himself. *The Essence of Christianity* was an immensely influential book. It was a heavy-artillery attack that left the philosophical landscape permanently changed. Above all the book radicalized the anti-religious wing of the Young Hegelians. One of these was a young academic-cum-journalist from the German town of Trier on the Mosel River, which becomes the Moselle when it enters France just six miles away. This was Karl Marx.

In at least one of his films the Hollywood actor Burt Reynolds plays the part of a philosopher-detective (he reads Karl Jaspers). While investigating a lead in a Greenwich Village bookstore he abruptly suggests an assignation to an exceedingly well-proportioned salesgirl. When she affects surprise and indignation the philosopher-detective reasons with her: 'You did not,' he says quietly, 'receive that body of yours overnight.' The bookish salesgirl (she also reads Karl Jaspers) concedes that she did not, that – indeed – she is the sole recording perceiver of the microcosm she represents. The interlude between the philosopher-detective and the bookish salesgirl proceeds accordingly.

Karl Marx rejected 'the assumption of pure self-awareness' as the starting point in a dialectic because it posited a subject able to apprehend itself in isolation – independent, that is, of its environment in nature and society. In Marx's reckoning, nature was not a reality already known nor was man its product. It was impossible to contemplate nature in isolation from man's active contact with it. Thus from the multi-billion-year passage of man the pilgrim, the creature of an incredibly vast and intricate complex of dependencies, Marx chose 'the true starting point' anew, shifting it from consciousness, where Hegel placed it, to man's 'physical commerce with nature' as he elsewhere calls it. This is the transfer of the authorship of the creation from God ('merely an outer – eschatological – projection of man') to man himself but only through the instrumentality of labour. Thus labour, in the abstract and concretely, becomes the holy of holies in the Marxian theogony–cosmogony, and man becomes a kind of lesser God. This transfer is a progression (or regression) from the transfer from God to consciousness effected by Luther.

Marx brings the whole of human activity under the common denomination 'labour' – Galileo peeping through his telescope, Alexander leaving Pela to conquer the world . . . it was all 'labour'. Labour for Marx is the means by which man creates himself and the world around him. It is the ultimate sanctification. But only *after* the process of abstraction does the consciousness (self-consciousness) exist. In other words, in the beginning was the work; it was work that quite literally transformed mankind from mud to man: 'Labour is the realization of the essence of man.' From this it becomes perfectly clear why the proletariat must be the chosen people or, rather, the chosen class. The very fact that it is the working class brings its sanctification. But not only that: Marx develops a whole soteriology – a sequence involving the Fall from grace and the promise of salvation. It was the curse of the machine that drove man from his pre-mechanized Eden. The improvement of tools forced the division of labour which is the first source of the alienation process. The alienation process is the cause of the creation of private property. This comes about because the division of labour leads inevitably to commerce which is 'the transformation of objects produced by man into vehicles of abstract exchange-value'. When matters have gone this far and things have become commodities, the basic premise of alienation is already given. At this point we have the true beggaring of the human individual by the machine. For it is by virtue of the machine that wealth is accumulated. 'Private property' is used as a synonym for accumulated wealth that has been abstracted from the common weal. This ultimate beggary Marx calls 'depersonalization' – 'the subjection of individuals to the work of their own hands and brains'. The only salvation is to regain control over the inanimate forces which have gained mastery over their very creators. The saviour in this passion play is the proletariat – the working class that produces the wealth in the first place by virtue of its 'labour power'. This the proletariat has been destined to do by the very nature and course of the struggle. And here is where the concept of historical materialism comes in. 'The history of society is the history of struggles of opposed classes one of which must emerge triumphant, although in a much altered form: progress is constituted by the succession of victories of one class over the other, and that man alone is rational who identifies himself with the progressive class in his society' (Berlin, *Karl Marx*, Introduction). This is the Marxian dialectic that polarizes society between haves and have-nots and makes revolution inevitable. The capitalists will seek to increase production and keep down costs (by holding the workers at subsistence wages) out of sheer greed, in the interest of the further accumulation of capital. But here the magic of the machine enters again. Technological progress is vital to capitalism because it cannot thrive without constantly revolutionizing the means of production – which is to say that capitalism is the necessary historical condition of technological progress. Marx sees the social movement not as a process but as *the* process of natural history. Here he establishes the most intimate bond possible between socialism and natural science. 'Human consciousness is merely the expression in thought of a social relationship to nature, and must be considered as a product of the collective effort of the species.' In Marx everything is reduced to the practical – of course, this is materialism, which constitutes the scientific approach as practised in the natural sciences and adapted to philosophy, sociology and politics. Thus Marx is simplifying in the name of science. But not only in the name of science – also in the name of man: 'For man,' writes Marx, 'the root is man himself.' 'We deny,' he wrote in *The German Ideology*, 'the validity of metaphysical and epistemological problems engendered by the false hope of attaining to some absolute reality beyond the practical horizon of human beings.' In short, Marx turns the method of abstraction, used so effectively by Hegel, against Hegel by disqualifying abstraction altogether. It is not a matter of providing new answers to questions of metaphysics and epistemology, but of denying their validity. Alienation cannot be cured by thinking about it; one must remove its causes, a consideration that leads naturally to the most famous of quotations from Marx: 'The philosophers have only interpreted the world in various ways; the point, however, is to change it.' The problem was to contrive a form of social organization that would reconcile the selfish interests of each with the needs of all. This Marx never did. He was far more interested in organizing the revolution than in trying to blueprint the society that was to follow it. By 1844, in the Paris journal *Vorwärts*, Marx had already formulated the idea that socialism was not to be the mere replacement of one type of political structure by another. It was to be the abolition of politics altogether. He thus provided the prime example of the messianic or apocalyptic nature of socialism – of breaking all the eggs to make an omelette and thus ruling out the possibility of any succeeding administration putting Humpty-Dumpty together again. In this sense a Communist party is not a political party; it is a religious party preaching a chiliastic absolute by way of a social message. Hence its thrust is actually anti-political. Here there is a foreshadowing of the German National Socialist (Nazi) Party which, like the Soviet Communist Party, insisted on a one-party state. In a one-party state the one party is not political but religious in that it proceeds from a millennial assumption toward an eschatological goal whether that goal be Communism or *'das tausendjährige Reich'*. Marx was more than clever enough to realize that if he dwelt in his writings on the nature of the ultimate goal he would reveal it as utopian. But even as it was, the presupposition that there can be a 'perfect identity between collective and individual interests . . . that private egoistic motives can be eliminated in favour of a sense of absolute community with the whole' raises questions. How does one know that the 'absolute community' has been achieved without ever so closely checking? 'Trust is good, but control is better.' Here Marx was waiting for Lenin. And so the collective itself was to become a control mechanism, an association of regularly reporting stool-pigeons. But that is not all. The Marxian ideal of a perfect identity between collective and individual interests is an oxymoron. Marx is trying to have it both ways. If the private 'egoistic' interests are eliminated in a sense of absolute community, then the individual as an individual is eliminated just as surely as the individual is eliminated in any philosophical Absolute. Kolakowski paraphrases Marx: 'Successful ideas must be the expression of some mass interest (the "idea" has always been a fiasco when divorced from "interest") but whenever "interest" takes the form

75

of an idea it goes beyond its real content and must present itself delusively as a general interest and not a particular one.' In this regard it is extraordinary to what extent the public assignment of a private motive to an enterprise can demean that enterprise, or the private assignment of a public motive can enhance an enterprise. A political motive can ennoble even the foulest deed, including murder and massacre – *vide* international terrorism (the thug as hero) – whereas a private motive, once publicly assigned, can degrade the noblest cause to the point of the worst ignominy (literally 'ignominy' means the loss of name – i for *in*, meaning 'not' + *gnomen* for *nomen*, meaning 'name' = 'no-name'). The essence of private property is an individual's possession of his name, because his name is the sign of his identity. In assigning private motives publicly the particular is posed against the general because identity involves 'self' (*idem*) and, when counterposed against the public, the individual identity always appears 'selfish'. In this context the private individual becomes a 'privateer' and privacy the equivalent of 'privateering', and friendship, which is a private matter, the equivalent of conspiracy. What Marx did was to outlaw privacy. He banned and ostracized the private individual from society. But there can be no freedom without privacy. Without privacy 'freedom of association' is meaningless. Communism is the sanctification of the general at the expense of the particular, the individual, the private: to be successful the idea 'must present itself delusively as the general interest and not a particular one'. In short, the final consequence of the whole effort is the polarization of the common weal and freedom. Thus Marx created a secular religion with all the necessary elements, including a new system of values: Communism, which would solve all mankind's problems and usher in the lost elysium, replaced salvation and paradise. The proletariat replaced the ecclesia in general while the collective replaced the Church in particular in all its pastoral functions. The Communist Party replaced the clergy. Marx, as the prophet of socialism, wrote the movement's Bible, the indisputably authoritative work sanctifying labour, canonizing revolution and anathematizing the bourgeoisie which is a blanket-term accommodating private individuals engaged in private enterprise using private capital – three principal evils rolled into one. But most important, Marxism contained the tergiversation indispensable to its credibility as a religion: it formally and ceremoniously forswore all religion and proclaimed itself a science – the ultimate science of man. And so the proletariat had its creed, its holy book and its sword.

Unfortunately, Marx was not a scientist. He was a messianic ideologue with all the fanaticism peculiar to such spirits and more. The secularized salvation he preached was taken straight from the book of Sir Thomas More, *De optime statu rei publicae deque nova insula Utopia*, in which work the author presented the world with the concept of utopia – literally 'no place' (from Greek *οὐ* = not and *τόπος* = place), figuratively 'too good to be true'. More's island was a depiction of the perfect political, social and legal system modelled after Plato's Republic. Unfortunately, the panacea More hit upon to secure his earthly paradise was the abolition of money. Here is the finale of Utopia:

> But these most wicked and vicious men, when they have by their insatiable covetousness divided among themselves all those things which would have sufficed all men, yet how far be they from the wealth and felicity of the utopian commonwealth. Out of which, in that all the desire of money with the use thereof is utterly secluded and banished, how great a heap of cares is cut away. How great an occasion of wickedness and mischief is plucked up by the roots. For who knoweth not that fraud, theft, rapine, brawling, quarrelling, squabbling, strife, chiding, contention, murder, treason, which by daily punishments are rather revenged than refrained, do die when money dieth. And also that fear, grief, care, labours, and watchings do perish even the very same moment that money perisheth. Yea, poverty itself which only seemed to lack money, if money were gone, it also would decrease and vanish away.

Marx's theory of alienation rests squarely on the premise of the intrinsic evil of money. 'Since money, as the existing and self-operating concept of value, exchanges and "mischanges" all things [*verwechselt, vertauscht*],' wrote Marx, 'so is it the general exchanging and "mischanging" [misconceiving] of all things, that is, the world turned upside down, the exchanging and mischanging [misconceiving] of all natural and human qualities.' Marx, like More, held money to be the coeval and interactive cause of the division of labour. In his rejection of the conventional economists ('vulgar economists' he called them) he rejected the idea of money (it was for him the 'incarnation of capital') as an indispensable technical instrument for the regulation of economic relationships. He completely overlooked the fact that money, with the concepts of profit, loss, credit, cost accounting and estimates, etc., is the *sine qua non* of industrial commerce. The use of money is the only way to *quantify* (as the basic scientific method) commercial transaction. Money is a standard of measure. Instead of analysing the concept (but of course quite a number of conventional economists had already done that) Marx, like the fanatic ideologue he was, demonized it. With Marx demonization was a habit of mind. In this instance the habit was to have untellable consequences as revolutionary socialism made its way through some nine decades of the twentieth century.

IV

❦

COMES THE REVOLUTION

In the year 1831 Alexis de Tocqueville arrived in America. He was twenty-five years old. Four years later the first two volumes of his work, *De la Démocratie en Amerique*, were published. At the end of the second volume there appeared the following now much-quoted passage:

> There are today two great peoples on this earth who, having started from different points, seem to be advancing toward the same goal: these are the Russians and the Anglo-Americans.
>
> Both have grown in obscurity; and while the attention of mankind was directed elsewhere, they placed themselves suddenly in the first rank of nations, and the world took cognizance of their birth and size at the same time.
>
> All other people seem to have attained more or less the limits which nature has set for them and have nothing to do but maintain themselves in their present state, but these [two] are growing . . .*
>
> The American struggles against the obstacles that nature opposes to him; the Russian struggles with human adversaries. The one combats the wilderness and barbarism, the other combats civilization equipped with all its weapons: hence the conquests of the American are achieved with the ploughshare, those of the Russian with the soldier's sword.
>
> To achieve his goal the first puts his faith in personal interest and lets main force and individual reason play their parts without trying to direct him.

* Here there is a footnote to the effect that 'Russia, among all the nations of the ancient world, is the one whose population is growing the most rapidly – all things being equal.'

The second concentrates, after a fashion, the entire puissance of society in a man.

The principal means of action of the former is freedom; of the latter, servitude.

Their points of departure are different, yet each seems called by some secret design of providence one day to hold in his hands the destinies of half the world.

This account and prophecy highlights the two salient factors in the development of the Russian empire: the tradition of servitude and the fact of a four-century-long carrying wave of Great Russian fertility, the highest birth-rate in the ancient world. There was, of course, a great deal more – and a great deal less – than just these two factors at work in what remains to this day the largest contiguous land empire on the face of the earth. The Christianization of Rus', which celebrated its first millennium in 1988, was and remains an event and a condition of profound and scarcely measurable importance. The Christianization of Russia did not create the now familiar traditional servitude of the Russians but it reinforced that servitude, sanctioned and sanctified it institutionally. It was a fateful and most unfortunate coincidence in one sense, in the sense of developing civic responsibility – *Zivilcourage*, as the Germans bluntly call it. But it suited the sons of Rurik and their companions-in-arms after the Norman conquest of Novgorod and Kiev to accept the Christian faith according to the Eastern rites when they came, saw and were conquered by Byzantium. In many ways the Byzantine faith, which broke with Rome over the indivisibility (as against the duality – *filioque: and* the son) of the Godhead, was the ideal creed for the fighting man as well as for his leader. The mystagogical, spiritual inward-turning of the Greek Orthodox faith prefigured the withdrawn spirituality of the Russian Orthodox tradition. But it also brought with it the $\mu\epsilon\gamma\acute{a}\lambda\eta$ $\emph{\iota}\delta\acute{\epsilon}a$, 'the big idea' – the vision of empire, of world dominion. After the fall of Constantinople Moscow came to be regarded as the New Rome, the seat of a newer, purer ecumenicity. In this regard there is a striking parallel between the transfer of the Holy Roman Empire to the German nation (after the fall of Rome) and the transfer of the Byzantine Empire to the Russian nation. 'The big idea' of the Roman Empire as the universal and eternal ordering factor haunted the Germans until very recent times. (Hitler himself was a distorted version of the Holy Roman Emperor of the German

Nation and much of his appeal to the German people was based on their instinctive reverence and appreciation of the greatest religious–political tradition the world has ever seen.) In much the same way, but with perhaps an even deeper, certainly more mystical instinctive reverence and appreciation, for a great many Russians, Russia is not merely a state. It is a world, a spiritual empire – the true way (after the original Christian device which was 'the way'). The Orthodox patriarch became the successor of the displaced Christian emperor, and the Russian nation inherited the *mission civilisatrice* of the Eastern Roman Empire to reshape the world. But this Orthodox version had a special feature: the world was to be reshaped in accordance with the exclusively spiritual values proclaimed and catechized by the Eastern Church – especially against the materialism and secularism of the West, against the dynamic involvement in worldly affairs characteristic of Roman Catholicism and, later, to an even greater extent, of Protestantism. (It is Max Weber's thesis, long since broadly accepted, that it was Protestantism that played the decisive part in creating and establishing the values and attitudes, in short, the psychology of an industrial society.) Now this, the very spiritual withdrawnness or other-worldliness of Russian Orthodoxy, seems to have been part of 'some secret design of providence' to prepare the way for another spiritual discipline that was to come many centuries later, emerging to blend with a displaced puritanism forever at arms against the superficiality and tawdriness of the bourgeoisie. The strong tendency of Orthodoxy in Russia was to leave the field of worldly affairs to the field commanders. De Tocqueville sensed this; his sense of it is clear in a remarkable passage in *Démocratie en Amerique* which, again, contains a double prophecy:

> But I think that if one does not succeed in introducing little by little democratic institutions and to establish them among us finally, and that if one renounces the effort to give to all citizens the ideas and sentiments which at first prepare them for liberty and later permit them to use it, there will not be independence for anyone, not for the bourgeois, not for the noble, not for the poor, not for the rich, but an equality of tyranny for all; and I foresee that if one does not succeed in establishing among us a peaceful empire of the greatest number, we shall arrive sooner or later at the fact of the unlimited power of one man.

In Russian history that one man of unlimited power was various men at various times. 'The rulers of Russia,' said Ivan the Terrible, 'have not been accountable to anyone, but have been free to reward or to chastise their subjects.' Peter the Great, for a prime example, was a revolutionary from above. Comparisons are facile and they have often been made between Peter the Great and Lenin and now recently between both leaders and Mikhail Gorbachev. It is extraordinary how these patterns repeat themselves: Western education in the upper ranks of Russian society in the eighteenth and nineteenth centuries 'was alien to the Russian masses' (Berdyaev) – the teachings of Voltaire on the one hand and mystical Freemasonry on the other – while the people continued to live by the old religious beliefs and regarded the gentry as an alien race (which they in part, at least, were: Russian aristocrats loved to claim descent from Ruric and still do); they were the 'hidalgos' – 'the sons of somebody' and those somebodies were the Viking conquerors of Russia. They spoke French as a native language and were not always able to speak Russian well if at all. In Pushkin's *Eugene Onegin* the entire stanza describing the heroine at her morning toilet is in French. The author explains that there are no Russian words for the articles he is required to describe in the scene. Now the *nomenklatura* and pre-eminently the KGB enjoy much the same privileges as did the gentry in the eighteenth and nineteenth centuries. While Western influence strengthened the privileged classes it worked to debilitate the masses in Russia. This left the visceral feeling in the Russian masses that Western influence was *per se* against the people and for an élite that was alien to the people and its true interests. Thus this struggle between East and West in Russia did not begin with the Slavophiles and the Westerners. It began at the beginning when the Viking masters of the Russian people embraced Eastern Christianity – Byzantium and not Rome per geographical force. The same river that carried them to Kiev carried them on to the Black Sea and Byzantium. Russia is Eastern Christianity. The doctrine of Moscow as the Third Rome was expounded by the Monk Filofei. In his letter to the Tsar Ivan III he wrote:

Of all kingdoms of the world, it is in thy royal domain that the holy Apostolic Church shines more brightly than the sun. And let thy majesty take note, O religious and gracious tsar, that all the kingdoms of the Orthodox Christian faith are merged into thy kingdom. Thou alone, in all that is under heaven, art a Christian tsar. And take note, O religious and gracious tsar, that all Christian kingdoms are merged into thine alone, that two Romes have fallen, but the third stands, and there will be no fourth. Thy Christian kingdom shall not fall to the lot of another.

Much has been written about the inconsistency of the Russian spirit and the inorganic confusion of Russian history. Any sort of organic unity was impossible because the place was simply too big. There were no boundaries, there was no form. And, as in America, the whole place was very thinly inhabited and then mostly by various kinds of nomads. There was one thing: expanse – *prostranstvo*. It was hard to hold anything. Some of the nomads were not so nomadic – like the Tartar Khans who subjugated the Russians and kept them that way for some three centuries. There was a good deal of very bloody back-and-forth, rebellions that rose up spontaneously and almost took the day. Or if they did not they kept the place in an uproar, as Pugachev did, for years on end. The Russian overran the expanse in the end but he had great difficulty holding it and still more difficulty trying to cope with it once he held it.

Then, too, from the very first there was the problem of the soil. In much of Russia proper the soil was not especially fertile, fit for grazing rather than for planting, a fact that had much to do with a nomadic way of life. It is tempting to see the general infertility of the soil as at least a partial cause of the strange divorce of the Russian from reality, the Russian penchant for living by ideas alone. This was never more apparent than in the case of the intelligentsia's perennial infatuation with social ideas with no opportunity – because of political conditions – of putting these ideas to practice or otherwise discovering for themselves whether there was any basis in reality for them. As a result the Russian was much given to political and social – or, rather, socialist – day-dreaming. They had no Renaissance, no Reformation, no Age of Reason. 'We have lived, as it were, outside of history,' wrote Chaad-ayev in 1829, 'and have remained untouched by the universal education of the human race ... Isolated from the world, we have given or taught nothing to the world.' Of course, reality – Russian reality – was the spur to fantasize. A religious cast of mind blended nicely with the belief, fed anew every day, that there must be some way to get out of the mess the Russians quite clearly saw themselves embedded in. Faith rests on paradox. The great bulk of the Russian people was held firmly in the grip of serfdom. They had never done anything. They lay prostrate, prone. The very fact that they had never done anything fed the belief that they would one day rise up. They were prone, but prone to do what? It was an extraordinary situation. More often than not the indomitable tendency to seize upon every new idea as the ultimate panacea, every scientific theory from the West honestly proffered as nothing more than a hypothesis was taken by the Russian intelligentsia as dogma, as a kind of religious revelation. Russia was imbued with the eternal expectation of miracles, a sort of anticipatory receptivity, eagerly waiting for the key, the insertion of which into the wards of the prevailing hopeless situation would change everything and usher in the ideal future. In Russia the 'rock of ages', the rock on which the Christian Church was built was indeed the foundation of the Russian state, the Russian people, the Russian identity.

The creed fulfilled the need and the need was great. With the introduction of ideas disruptive of the specific faith, ideas from the French Enlightenment and the German Romantic and idealist philosophers, they were seized upon with the same religious fervour because the need remained unchanged and the need was great. There was, there is and there will be this great thirst for the answer to this problem, this paradox: the Russian people was and is miserable and yet is the master of a vast empire – the greatest on the face of the earth, unprecedented in the whole of recorded history. Hence there must be an answer. The power is obviously there: 'Look around you; what do you see?' More often than not this tendency to seize upon new ideas with a dogmatic, totalitarian frenzy has seemed like a clutching at straws. To the consternation of Marx the first Marxists were Russians. The appeal of Marxism was automatic because it contained the two elements most attractive to the Russian intellectual: socialism and science – two panaceae in one.

The transfer of religious conviction from the Godhead as revealed in the institution of the Church was not peculiar to Russia. The same phenomenon took place at approximately the same time in Western Christianity. Most notably, the same convictions were embraced and developed by religious activists like John Henry

Newman and Søren Kierkegaard and perhaps most notably and programmatically by Félicité Robert de Lamennais (1782–1854) in France. In 1834 Lamennais published his most famous work, *Paroles d'un croyant* (*Words of a Believer*), the central theme of which was that Christ lived in and for the masses, an idea that re-emerged more than a century later in the worker-priest movement in France. Lamennais conceived of the masses and appealed to them as 'the new non-institutional embodiment of Christianity'. For him the institution of the Church was no longer representative in either direction: it did not represent the people and it had ceased to be an effective instrument of the deity in dealing with earthly affairs. Rather, Lamennais saw the mysticism of the masses, the inertness combined with latent omnipotence as the new repository of the divinity: 'God had by-passed the institution of the Church.' Christ in history had passed through many different manifestations, each in keeping with the essential nature of the succeeding age. It was a question of working out relations between the Godhead and society in keeping with developing conditions. For Lamennais the new incarnation of divine reality, the locus of the contemporary Christ, was popular liberty. This in turn was a matter of legislating improvements or influencing the legislation of improvements in urban–industrial commercial society in accordance with new or at least relevant interpretations of holy writ. When socialist priests organized a banquet in 1849 for workers to celebrate the advent of the Second Republic, the celebrants toasted Jesus Christ as the father of socialism.

Some members of the Church saw the process of secularization as the alienation of the Godhead and tantamount to the arrogation of the divine functions of creation and redemption, of the divinity itself, by mankind. This arrogation established the autonomy of the human being. The ancient Greeks began by making their gods like themselves; modern men, beginning with Galileo, began to make themselves like their God, which is to say they began to assume control, or the possibility of control, of the functions of nature – this is why physics played so great a role in this arrogation. The investiture contest takes on a different light when seen from this point of vantage. The German emperors strove to secure to themselves the divine right of kings at the expense of the Vicar of Christ. But the first to establish a secular imperium was Napoleon, and his taking the crown from the cardinal and crowning himself was more than an empty gesture.

The American Revolution inspired the French Revolution and both served to create the notion and the model of 'the new man'. The 'new man' was free. Indeed, he was more than free: he was sovereign. Democracy could be described as a breaking down of sovereignty into an infinite number of constituent parts. Each new citizen of the world's 'first new nation' was a part of that fragmented sovereignty. It took no great leap of imagination for Johann Gottlieb Fichte to see in the French Revolution the model for his new system of thought, 'the first system of freedom' as he called it, and to establish man 'in his first principle as an autonomous being'. The breakdown of sovereignty in statehood that came with democracy runs parallel to the fragmentation of the Godhead that came with secularization. The liberation of mankind was a liberation on two levels, religious and political, and as such it was and remains ambiguous. This was a double-track process for the laying of the charge that led to an explosion of pluralities with the premium placed upon interpretation. In short, there is no norm. This, in turn, means that there is and will be a continuing struggle to create and establish a norm. Without the sheet-anchors of established religion and a stable political system there can be and have been and are hideous excrescences in place of a norm.

Napoleon destroyed the Holy Roman Empire of the German nation and set himself up as an emperor in the first secular imperium instead. And he invaded Russia. Hitler followed Napoleon in a caricature restoration of the Holy Roman Empire of the German nation. And he invaded Russia. In the case of Hitler the breakdown of Christianity (specifically, the deterioration of Christian polity) and the fragmentation of the Godhead worked for the perpetration of atrocities on a totally unprecedented scale. As William A. Clebsch in his book, *Christianity in European History*, put it: 'Hitler took on to himself the power and action of God in judging the nations' (including his own).

In the Russian Empire the process of secularization, the humanization of the sacred, took a radical turn. In their increasing disillusionment with Christianity because of its failure to improve the lot of the peasant, the Russians instinctively turned to a primitive form of socialism. The suffering, which the Russians saw all around them, fairly forced the adoption of socialism. This was as basic as 'misery loves company'. But the problem of the justification of suffering, the problem of evil itself as the Russians saw it, gave the Russian concept of socialism a strong atheistic element. Yet the Russian renunciation of religion was a religious renunciation. As Nikolai Berdyaev points out, 'All the subsequent atheism of the Russian revolutionary socialist and anarchist tendencies was Russian religiousness turned inside out, Russian apocalyptic.'

Vissarion Belinsky (1811–48) was the forerunner and prototype of the Russian revolutionary intelligentsia which was to play so signal a role in the development of Russian Communism. Belinsky was 'a man of the people' in the sense that he was a *paznochinets*, that is, he belonged to no class or guild and was not a nobleman. He was typical of the Russian at large in that he was sectarian, intensely devoted to ideas (particularly those concerning improvement of the social order), intolerant and not very well educated. He knew no foreign languages. And yet he possessed a remarkable susceptibility to cultural influences and nuances. He was an outstanding literary critic. He was, in all probability, the model for his friend Dostoyevsky's character Ivan in *The Brothers Karamazov*. He was certainly the inspiration for the figure and message of the Grand Inquisitor in that novel. It is in Belinsky that the original source and headwaters of the Russian Communist movement are first and most clearly visible. He was uncompromising in his rejection of everything that did not contribute directly to the betterment of the human lot – and that meant an unmistakable and irreversible improvement in the social order. Belinsky in his person and in his persona sums it up: the Russians became atheists and socialists because they could not bear the evil they saw everywhere around them. They rejected God because he failed them – he had created an incomplete world full of suffering with no prospect of surcease. The Russians thus sought to take matters – the fate of mankind withal – into their own hands. This fact alone goes far to explain the demonic, totalitarian character of Russian socialism–Communism. Here was an arrogation that was cosmic, definitive and fatal in its dimensions and presuppositions, the most desperate adventurism imaginable, the ecstatic acceptance of the insupportable burden and infinite fatefulness of the Godhead. This was the Luciferian presumption itself. Small wonder that the Soviet leadership spoke with such strange, mechanical finality: the self-appointed lords of the universe were pronouncing *ex cathedra*. Small wonder the awkward, lumbering, infantile pomp so infallibly characteristic of Soviet ceremony. There are several stages in the transfer of the Godhead from the sacred to the secular: hieros to ethos, ethos to pathos, pathos to bathos. From the sublime to the ridiculous. Perhaps the Hungarian humorist Ferencz Karinthy captures the spirit of the situation best in a tableau about a bored businessman who amuses himself by looking through high-powered binoculars from his office high in a skyscraper into neighbouring office rooms. On one occasion he spies a middle-aged executive chasing a comely secretary around his desk. As it happens the observer knows the building in which this drama is taking place and can even make out the name of the occupant from the plaque on his desk. He consults the telephone directory and gives the culprit, who is still trying to force his attentions on the secretary, a ring. When the culprit answers the telephone the observer announces himself as God Almighty and tells him to stop molesting the young woman in his employ. The culprit, thunderstruck and unable to account for the observer's exact knowledge of what has been going on, falls on his knees in a paroxysm of fear and wonder and begs forgiveness. The observer roundly berates the culprit who swears he will do anything to make amends and promises never to sin again. Hereupon the observer informs the culprit that he can indeed make amends by lending him 100 pengö. The answer, of course, is a burst of profanity and the abrupt termination of the call. Karinthy then draws his moral: if you want to play God don't try to borrow money, a precept Soviet leaders might have done well to honour in their dealings with Western nations which they were also trying to bully and browbeat, flaunting eschatological pretensions and military power the while.

It was in this broad riverbed of Russian socio-political geography that perhaps the strangest of Russian intellectual phenomena was generated and developed: nihilism. Nihilism in Russia was in fact the very turning inside out of Russian religiousness. Nihilism in Russia was the codification of Orthodox asceticism turned against religion itself and toward the social welfare of the common people – it conceived and tried to implement a contradiction in terms: socialism as a secular religion. It is curious in the extreme how Orthodox asceticism should have been turned against the Church to such paralysing effect. For this was a development that compromised the Church definitively in the struggle over Russian polity by diverting the intelligentsia from the Orthodox faith to an

Orthodox un-faith. It was a double corruption – an inverted orthodoxy sanctifying politics and politicizing sanctity. As a result of this creed of negation for a cause there appeared in Russia a new type of man, the archetype of the Bolshevik, the vanguard of the working class which had otherwise nothing to do with the working class, the cadre of professional revolutionaries whose duty and destiny it would be to lead mankind up out of the swamp to Communism, into the new dawn. This was 'the iron man in the leather coat' like Commissar Davidov in Mikhail Sholokhov's novel *Virgin Soil Upturned*. There is an unforgettable description of the new man in Nadezhda Mandelstam's *Hope Against Hope*: he is young, lean, unsmiling and unbending; he does not mix with others, he is laconic, he does not drink – there is a single-mindedness about him that is chilling. A new age had begun in Russia, the union of Soviets in the Soviet Union: it might appropriately have been called 'the importance of being sternest' – an inflexible and unmerciful devotion to the cause, a *Kadaver-Gehorsam*, a deadbody obedience that would have made the most docile German civil servant wince with embarrassment.

When religion is detached from the sacred, from the reverence for the unseen, from the mystery of life there arises – witness the Russian experience – the need to justify everything in life anew and in terms perforce unfamiliar and difficult to fix. The pervading suspicion that marks the Russian character is never so dismaying as when it applies to traditional fundamental values. Russian Orthodox asceticism suspected the justifiability of culture itself. This suspicion was based on the instinctive perception common to all religions that cultural creativity is sinful. There is a basic religious sense that all human creativity, but particularly cultural creativity, is *per se* an arrogation of divinity, hence culturally operative words like 'enthusiasm' and 'inspiration' have at their roots the designation of divine ordinance, as if to ticket the activity as God-given and mark the function as on loan from the Almighty, as it were, so as to prevent any misapprehension or misappropriation. But the nihilists went even further. They broke with all established life including the state, law and traditional values, indeed even with the family. This, as Berdyaev confirms, was because they considered these things had been made use of to justify the enslavement of man (the problem of justification again).

The constriction of this ethos led the nihilists to settle on materialism as the only permissible philosophy. This was inevitable: anything more abstract or, indeed, anything at all abstract was suspect. By the same tenets the nihilists were led to place a premium on the natural sciences as the only fitting means to surmount prejudices and expose the canons of established religions as mere superstitions. Thus materialism became dogma, as hard and fast as that of any theology. Materialism for the Russians was a theology without a *theos*, without a God – but with an idol; the idol was science. Dialectical materialism promises, as a matter of 'scientific certainty' and 'historical necessity', the establishment of an earthly paradise for peasants and workers.

There was another aspect of nihilism that was carried over magnified into Communism. This was the hatred, the blank detestation of the bourgeoisie. The rejection of anything even remotely smacking of the bourgeoisie was eagerly adopted by nihilism; it was not original with nihilism. Actually the Russian hatred of the bourgeois is part and parcel of the turning inside out of Russian Orthodoxy. Moreover it plays into the much larger polarization of East and West, of Eastern spirituality against Western civilization. Basically, surely, the rejection of the West by the Russians was motivated by their resentment of their own sense of dependence on the West. Traditionally this dependence was marked by the very controversy – intense and enduring – between the Westerners and the Slavophiles, the former convinced that salvation for Russia could come only from the West, the latter certain with a religious profundity of conviction that only Russia could save the world. Surely in this love-hate relationship with the West the Russians were persuaded in the main by Alexander Herzen, whose role in the shaping of the Russian nation would be difficult to imagine or evaluate in the history of any other people. For his part Herzen was the archetype of the Russian *émigré*. He lived for decades outside Russia, in Switzerland, in Paris and in London. He founded the famous Kolokol (Bell) publishing company and magazine in London which undertook to publish all Russian authors whose works could not be published for whatever reason in Russia itself. He was thus one of the first and most effective Russian champions for the rights of man with freedom of speech first and foremost. Herzen's experience in the West was formative for the Russian experience with the West as a whole. Herzen, the revolutionary, who lived for the Revolution of 1848 and was crushed by its failure, was appalled by the pettiness he found everywhere in the West. The ideal of the knight had degenerated into the ideal of the small shopkeeper (Napoleon had dismissed the English as a 'nation of shopkeepers'). Herzen was the first to recognize the possibility of a bourgeois socialism. But in this the Russians, as a whole, did not follow him. Out of the general disgust and disillusionment with the West came the iron resolve of the Russian intelligentsia never to undergo the experience of bourgeois capitalism. The rejection was a priori. The Russians had no direct experience of the prime motive force in the economics of the nineteenth and twentieth centuries as a sample from which to judge. With the lack of the experience of capitalism, moreover, the Russians lacked experience of most if not all of the political phenomena accompanying capitalism, such as liberalism. It was this combination of absences, particularly of the mollifying influence of liberalism, that made the Russian Communist approach to the problem of ordering human existence relatively narrow and entirely one-sided. Russian Communists, as a result, when the workability of the system they had established with so much sacrifice and difficulty became obviously unworkable and dangerously inappropriate, had no tradition of experience to fall back on as an alternative. The high priests of the Party (for the Party was still at least semi-sacred) had pronounced capitalism anathema and the anathema remained. The hatred of the bourgeoisie and the hatred of capitalism went hand in hand. These were religious hatreds that blocked the ordinary exits open to industrial nations when they find themselves in economic crisis. Hence these various lacks were from the beginning guarantees that the crisis, when it came, would not be just an economic crisis but a general crisis involving all aspects and basic principles of Russian-Soviet life. The system was and remains totalitarian and hence affects the totality – nothing less.

In the meantime, however, the capitalist system in its Western, conventionally democratic guise was not the shining contrast to the better it had once stridently and still somewhat plaintively claimed to be. The boisterous frivolity of the American model was enough to disconcert and disgust the Russians whose seriousness in most matters has always bordered on manic-depression. Thus, willy-nilly, the crisis – even without the specific problem of nuclear (and massive conventional) disarmament – concerns the whole of humanity and not just the Soviet Union and its satellites. It is, moreover, not just the lack of leadership (the enduring American public quest for 'credibility' in leaders comes to mind) but the lack of conscious models of leadership that matters here. Hitler's use of the Parteitag hoopla like the batteries of searchlights used to form 'cathedrals of light' in the sky and all that massive, neoclassical architecture – the whole of totalitarian elephantiasis was necessary to dwarf the individual and put him into his psychological corner. Something had to be done, after all, to restore the sense of awe that was lost with the downgrading and discrediting of the Church in the West as well as in the East – not merely in Communism and its offshoots as in Fascism but in the conventional democracies as well. Is not the problem of 'disciplining democracy', of setting values and asserting them, clear proof that without this achievement no harmonious or even meaningful co-habitation of the planet is possible? Surely the thirst for an unacceptable authority, for a national if not universal father figure, is responsible for the extraordinary popularity of the present pope. John Paul II, considering his unbending insistence of the traditional tenets of the Roman Catholic Church, would hardly be popular in Catholic countries let alone in the Protestant and industrialized West were it not for the manifest need to believe in somebody or something. The rise and fall of the 'televangelists' in the United States would hardly be the scandal it unquestionably is without this need.

The horrors and bestialities of the Third Reich in its twelve long years' existence can be compared in the reach of human history only with those inflicted or conduced by the other more powerful and more lasting of modern attempts to replace Christianity: Communism. The materialistic façade of Communism has inveigled any number of observers into mistaking its nature and intent. In his *A Short View of Russia* the economist John Maynard Keynes scores a clean miss. 'Leninism,' he writes,

> is absolutely and decisively non-supernatural; its emotional and aesthetic messages concern the conduct of the individual and society with regard to the love of money ... I do not mean that Russian Communism changes human nature or even tries to; that it makes Jews less fond of money or Russians less wasteful than they were before. I only mean to say that it erects a new Ideal. I mean that it makes the attempt to establish a society in which the profit motive as a driving force will have a different relative significance and in which social values will be differently hefted and behaviour which

had been regarded as normal and respected will cease to be the one or the other.

This is indeed a short view. Communism most manifestly and explicitly preaches and promises deliverance, a life lived in fulfilment and truth, the abolition of injustice, an end to 'the exploitation of man by man'; this was, or was clearly calculated to be, the transfer of Christianity's hereafter to the scientific materialistic here and now. Communism replaces Christianity's salvation with revolution, the revolution that transforms all things and ultimately but most importantly of all, man himself. 'Man will become immeasurably stronger, wiser, and subtler,' wrote Trotsky at the conclusion of his *Literature and Revolution*, 'his body will become more harmonized, his movements more rhythmic, his voice more musical . . . The average human type will rise to the heights of an Aristotle, a Goethe or a Marx. And above this ridge new peaks will rise.' And what does this deliverance in Communism hinge upon? As Keynes easily perceives, it hinges upon the individual's ability to renounce the love of money, to fall out of love with money. Nothing is so essentially characteristic of Communism as its dogmatic detestation of money as both the instrument and symbol of wealth, property, the whole concept of possession. The first thing a Communist regime does when it comes to power is to dispossess the population of all except its most trivial holdings. If it were at all possible Communists would do without money altogether. In short, Communists – following Marx – regard money as the primary source of deception in general. Communists, as a matter of intriguing fact, have always – then as now – preferred barter, primitive bilateral trading, to the use of money or any other instrumentality.

The invention and use of money as a unit of calculation and hence as a means of measuring quantity as distinct from quality was anathema to the Russian soul from the very beginning. Russian Orthodox asceticism always regarded the very idea of business – activity for a profit, occupation and preoccupation, thinking about material gain – like any saint or monk of the Church as a sin. Who can forget the scene in Dostoyevsky's novel, *The Idiot*, in which Rogozhin throws tens of thousands of roubles into the blazing hearth because Nastasia Philipovna has spurned him – while the startled guests fight down the impulse to salvage as

93

much as possible from the flames? *'Negotium,'* runs the passage in the *Decretum Gratiani, 'negat otium neque quaerit veram quietam, quae est deus.'* (Business negates leisure and does not seek true quietude, which is God.) Money is the measure of quantity in default of quality and hence no measure of true value at all. Worse still, money is the stuff of usury and speculation (the Christian ban on usury is based on the rabbinical bans against usury for the Jews and the railings against money-lending for interest in the Old Testament). It was, in short, the stuff that thoughts about money – 'thinking in terms of money' – are made of. And it is this, the thinking in terms of money, that is the most distasteful aspect of the bourgeoisie to the Communist at large – not just to the Russian Communist or to the Russian Communist ascetic. For the same reason in Friedrich Wolf's play, *Thomas Münzer*, the sixteenth-century Anabaptist and peasant leader can present the invention of double-entry bookkeeping as one of the great crimes in history. The deed was done by Fra Luca Pacioli in 1494 and was hailed by Goethe as 'one of the most beautiful inventions of the human spirit'. Werner Sombart, author of the classic *Modern Capitalism*, was more explicit in his praise:

> Double-entry bookkeeping was born of the same spirit that informed Galileo and Newton. With the same means as these it orders the phenomena in an ingenious system and one can characterize it as the first *kosmos* to be built on the principle of mechanical thinking. Double-entry bookkeeping opens up for us the *kosmos* of the world of economics after the same fashion as that later used by the great physicists with the *kosmos* of the firmament ... Double-entry book-keeping rests on the logically applied premise of conceptualizing all phenomena as quantities.

The whole of modern finance was built on this rock.

It is not difficult to see why Communist dogma is opposed to the whole concept and practice of high finance. The very existence of the institution negates the central tenet of Communist faith: the forswearing of the very concept of private property. There was, of course, a major lapse officially condoned and even initiated by Lenin himself – the NEP period in the early twenties – after Lenin had seen and recognized that the Soviet experiment was about to end in famine. He lost no time in throwing the game open to the acquisitive instincts of his fellow Soviet citizens. The New Economic

Programme lasted five years in which the team of writers, Ilf and Petrov, celebrated the first Soviet millionaires in a comic novel entitled *The Golden Calf.* Ilf and Petrov knew what they were writing about. In its all too short a lease, the NEP period proved that the Russian people, if left to their own devices, could produce what was needed and a good deal more. But the comedy was followed by a tragedy. With all its sectarian severity the secular religion was reimposed and the collectivization of agriculture carried out by main force. As a result millions of people, mainly peasants in the Ukraine, died of starvation. The superinduced famine in the Ukraine remains the outstanding Bolshevik atrocity.

But ideology alone cannot explain the inflexibility of the Communist position *vis-à-vis* profit-making and profit-taking. There must be, as Spengler suggests, a religious mystique somewhere in the foundation of this edifice of credenda. 'Regard the lilies of the field, how they grow: they do not toil neither do they spin.' To the religious nature this gentle injunction has lost none of its original appeal. And yet it has spelled disaster in the Russian Communist production drive. It is at dialectical cross-purposes with any sort of effective work ethic in the modern world. For what is striking in the never-ending debate over 'unearned income' in the Soviet Union is the semantic difficulties the Soviets encounter in trying to come to terms with the concepts and categories they themselves have created and sought to assert.

The institution of private confession is just as firmly established in Russian Orthodoxy as it is in Roman Catholicism, and practised there on even stricter terms. Its influence, then, on the individual's struggle to discover and develop personality is comparable to what has taken place in Western Christianity. At least that. For what writer has done more to take the measure of the off-shore limits of the personality than Fyodor Dostoyevsky? The abrupt secularization of Russian society (and European society with it, but with different effect) is the leitmotiv of the corpus of Dostoyevsky's work. And yet, for all the scope and depth of Dostoyevsky's work (or precisely because of it), his achievement remains the portrayal of the negative hero, the man without God, without faith and hope and with very little charity. It is an utterly fascinating but withal a very dismal picture. Few if any writers have managed to equal Dostoyevsky in showing what man without God is up against. Consequently, the historical effect of Dostoyevsky's work was to heighten the consciousness of urgency in the quest for salvation by whatever means. In this sense Dostoyevsky not only joins the mainstream (which was a torrent) of Russian intellectuals; he leads it. Thus, the nineteenth-century intelligentsia moulded the totalitarian mentality of the Soviets. As Berdyaev sums it up, 'The whole history of the Russian intelligentsia was a preparation for Communism.'

In 1883 Karl Marx warned the Russians, whom he did not like, against their habit of 'interpreting passages from Marx's writings and letters in the most contradictory ways, just as if they were texts from the classics or the New Testament'. (Marx once refused to appear on the same platform as Herzen, as he put it in a letter to Engels, 'since I am not of the opinion that "old Europe" can be rejuvenated by Russian blood'.) And yet Marx found his St Paul in a young Russian student of admixed German and Chuvash ancestry – Vladimir Ilyich Ulyanov, also known as Lenin. Lenin was the archetype of the 'true believer'. He had found his religion. 'There is no other man,' wrote Lenin's sometime colleague Axelrode, 'who is absorbed by the revolution twenty-four hours a day, who has no other thoughts but the thought of the revolution, and who, even when he sleeps, dreams of nothing but the revolution.' Leon Trotsky recalled in his book, *My Life, an Attempt at an Autobiography*, how impressed he was to note, on meeting Lenin for the first time (they were in London), that Lenin referred to everything in life as either 'ours' or 'theirs' – 'theirs' meaning any and every thing belonging to capitalists. Since Trotsky's introduction to Lenin took place in the autumn of 1902, when Russian Communists owned little more than what they carried in their suitcases – if indeed so much as that – Trotsky's noting this attribute in passing gives some idea of the degree of Lenin's besetment by the revolutionary idea. Lenin's belief in economic determinism as the prime motive force in history was simply overpowering. From it he drew his absolute conviction of the rightness of every conclusion he arrived at and every position he saw fit to adopt regardless of circumstances and the apparent odds against him at any given time. And yet his doctrinaire certitude had no effect on his ability to sense and assess the main chance in any situation. He was a superb tactician. According to the pamphlet issued by the Novosti Press Agency Publishing House in 1986, 'the mere enumeration of Lenin's contributions to Marx's theory would take up more than a few pages ... Both Marxism and Leninism make up a single integral theory of social development. That is why we call it Marxism–Leninism ...' It is safe to say that without Lenin the Bolshevist revolution in 1917 would not have occurred. His single-handed, single-minded bravura performance in engineering the Bolshevik revolution is attested by all witnesses. His theoretical contributions to Marxism, however, are questionable, but not in the Soviet Union. There Lenin's writings, like those of Marx before him, became Scripture. One of his *tours de force* was his arbitrary inclusion of the peasantry in the proletariat, whereas Marx had considered the peasantry petty-bourgeois and reactionary. Lenin forbade any reference to differences between the peasantry and the industrial workers. By 1964, however, the Soviets had conveniently forgotten this particular Lenin innovation when they officially explained that Communism in China had failed (this was after the Sino-Soviet break) because the Chinese movement had been built exclusively on an agrarian uprising. Communism, the Soviets maintained then, could not be constructed without an industrial proletariat.

But Lenin's greatest and most fateful 'contribution' to Marxist theory was made in the most crucial area of all revolutionary thought: how to seize and hold power. Whereas Marx and Engels had declared that 'the emancipation of the working class is the work of the working class itself', Lenin quickly perceived that this view was wholly incompatible with any effective revolutionary formula. He therefore conceived of the idea of a 'socialist vanguard', a cadre, a hard-core of professional revolutionaries trained and indoctrinated to lead and inspire the working class. In a very real sense, then, Lenin created a corps of revolutionaries in his own image. Here Lenin's tactical genius is clearly evident. He fashioned a weapon that was also an instrument of precision for the job – for 'job' it was – of revolution. Moreover and most importantly, the cadre of professionals was his, Lenin's, instrument, totally under his control. It is obvious that he could not have done what he did in bringing the October Revolution about if he had not had this instrument at his exclusive disposal. It was the *sine qua non* to his success.

But the job of revolution is not pretty. It does not consist in the main of long, earnest late-night discussions in accordance with the precepts laid down in the *Agitator's Notebook*. The title, in the original Russian version of General Petro Grigorenko's *Memoirs*, is *In the Underground You Meet only Rats*, a soldier's way of apostrophizing the fact that the underground is inseparable from the underworld. By the same token the immediate goals of the underground are often of necessity the same as those of the underworld. The presence of Josef Vissarionovich Djugashvili, known as Stalin, and more especially that of Lavrenti Beria among the Bolsheviks was in no small part due to the fact that both were professional Georgian bandits who specialized in bank robbery. The underground, like the underworld, is always in need of money: Stalin and his Georgian specialists were the ones who supplied the Party with much of the cash it so desperately needed. In providing the wherewithal for the Party to dispense they made themselves indispensable to the Party – 'from each according to his ability, to each according to his needs'. Oswald Spengler pointed out that the criminal element in society was also an essential element of the proletariat. Such was the stuff and such were the circumstances that Lenin had to deal with. Moreover, in the process of honing the instrument of the professional revolutionary cadre to the cutting edge required, Lenin was forced to simplify and 'sloganize' theory and hence radicalize an already radical group of men and women. Lenin brought the necessary drive to answer this challenge in the form of his unquenchable passion for control. This passion for control is evident throughout Lenin's thought and actions. It is always there, the well-spring of the rigidity that informs the system he created: centralized economic planning, universal censorship, administrative coercion and the calculated use of terror. In short, all the attributes of the police state *par excellence. Les extrêmes se touchent*: the police state is by definition a criminal institution.

This was a devastating turn of events because it provided a precedent for the new era by bringing over reinforced and reinvigorated all the root evils of the old era. Of course, this is the fundamental dilemma of the revolutionary situation in general. It was this consideration – the fighting of evil with evil, 'driving out the devil with Beelzebub' – that prevented the German resistance in 1944 from resorting to measures drastic enough to remove Hitler. Colonel Clauss Schenk, Graf von Stauffenberg could not see the sense in ending one bloodbath with another bloodbath – which is to say that von Stauffenberg rejected Lenin's choice, that of starting a new era with a bloodbath.

It is the role of Lenin as mass-murderer that gives many a would-be admirer pause. Lenin murdered thousands by direct order, tens of thousands by general order and millions by decree. A Polish Catholic priest who, in a strange interlude, befriended Lenin after the revolution has written that the head of the new Soviet state was deeply troubled by the fact that he had been forced by circumstances to order the execution of so many people. But this was not a confession: Lenin was unrepentant; he could not see how he could have done otherwise and still won through. Historically there is an explanation adduced to excuse the extreme severity of his action. It is this:

> The tsarist government had conscripted over eight million men altogether – far more men that it could ever equip or handle at the front – it had torn them up by the roots from their own villages, and great multitudes of these conscripts were now practically brigands living upon the countryside. Moscow in October and November 1917 swarmed with such men. They banded themselves together, they went into houses and looted and raped, no one interfering. Law and administration had vanished. Robbed and murdered men lay in the streets for days together.
>
> This we have to remember was the state of affairs when the Bolsheviks came into power; it was not brought about by their usurpation. For a time in their attempts to restore order anyone found bearing arms was shot. Thousands of men were seized and shot, and it is doubtful if Moscow could have been restored to even a semblance of order without some such violence. The débâcle of tsarist Russia was so complete that the very framework and habit of public order had gone. 'They had to shoot,' President Masaryk once told the writer H. G. Wells. And then he added, 'They went on shooting – unreasonably, cruelly.'

In this account the basic facts of the situation are stated accurately enough apart from the general conclusion that, 'the very framework and habit of public order had gone'. However, the explanation for the actions taken is less satisfactory and even intrinsically self-contradictory: '. . . It is *doubtful* if Moscow could have been restored to *even a semblance* of order without *some such* violence.' Nothing less than the bloodbath was attempted, and the result remained the same – a legacy of merciless and unreasoning suppression. And the main cause of marauding by Russian soldiers was the number of decrees issued by the Soviets themselves. The

99

legacy also remains a millstone around the neck of Lenin as an historical figure. It was the boast of the 'Hollywood Nine', the group of writers and directors who were blackballed and subpoenaed to appear before the Congressional Committee on Un-American Activities, as agents of the Soviet government, that their contribution to the cause consisted not in what they had done (which was precious little if anything) but in what they had prevented. At the top of the list of the evils they had prevented was the making of a Hollywood film based on the life of Lenin – *The Lenin Story*.

The criminalization of the Russian state-Party and Party-state was a *donnée*. As a proverb of somewhat later vintage has it: 'Those who identify with the Soviet system are conventional criminals and those who keep their distance from it are "political criminals",' and are so characterized by the state they refuse to serve. But the worst of the Lenin legacy was what has now come to be called 'democratic centralism' but during Lenin's last years was called by the young Trotsky 'egocentralism'. Indeed Trotsky, like Maxim Gorky, saw the inevitable outcome of the establishment of Lenin's cadre of professionals as the vanguard of the working class: 'The organization of the Party takes the place of the Party itself; the Central Committee takes the place of the organization; and finally the dictator takes the place of the Central Committee.' Which is exactly what happened in the case of Stalin, who had the precedent of Lenin to guide him. And de Tocqueville's prophecy was fulfilled: '. . . If one does not succeed in establishing among us a peaceful empire of the greatest number, we shall arrive sooner or later at the fact of the unlimited power of one man.'

What was so devastating was the fact that the Soviet system as conceived and partially developed by Lenin was not new but only the same old Russian absolutism dressed up in the trappings of revolution. This fact made the further totalitarian development of Soviet Communism under Stalin a foregone conclusion. The Soviets, in merely continuing the tsarist tradition of misrule, had a great deal of Russian history to draw from – the father figure of the tsar above all, and all the patriarchal pettifoggery that emanated from it. Under Nicholas I all works on logic and philosophy were prohibited. A historian was not allowed to write that Roman emperors had been assassinated: Roman emperors could only 'perish'. Censors struck out such phrases as 'the forces of nature' and 'the majesty of nature', as possible reflections on the almighty tsar. In the same spirit Lenin, in his book *Materialism and Empirio-Criticism*, attacked as 'reactionary idealists' all those who attempted to bring dialectical materialism into line with the revolutionary new concepts in physics. 'You cannot eliminate even one basic assumption,' Lenin wrote, 'one substantial part of this philosophy of Marxism, without abandoning objective truth, without falling into the arms of bourgeois-reactionary falsehood.' This in the face of the fundamental standpoint of physicists that it is essential to question *all* basic assumptions in order to advance objective truth in the study of nature. In applying this fundamental scientific approach physicists have been obliged to forgo the use of the Marxian dialectic in their pursuit of truth.

But such dogmatism was well within the tradition of the Russian intelligentsia. And even those figures in Russian history and literature who stood outside that tradition, such as Pushkin, provided plenty of fuel for the fire of this sectarian fanaticism. In his poem *Freedom* Pushkin foretells and exhorts the liquidation of the tsar and all his family:

> Thou autocrat of evil deed,
>> On thee and thine my execration!
> With fierce delight I yield thy seed
>> To death, and thee to thy damnation!

The result of the October Revolution was not a new beginning; it was a recommencement of the old urges but reinforced with a new faith – a faith in unfaith, a virulently inverted orthodoxy, a new bullet-in-the-back-of-the-head ruthlessness, a new set of rules and a new set of values loudly proclaimed but untried and unreflected. It was the introduction of a new rhetoric. There was a strong foretaste of this in Bogdanov's description of Lenin's style as 'quotational shock treatment'. The Soviet Union came by its addiction to sloganeering directly from Lenin via the ritualistic repetition of slogans, a kind of political enchantment induced by the religious chanting of slogans drawn from the quotations of Lenin. But the most effective manifestation of the new rhetoric was as an expression of the new ruthlessness, the new rules and the new would-be values. One of the first acts of the Bolsheviks in government was to change the word 'strike' to 'sabotage'. And the workers found themselves faced overnight with the fact that their new employers were forever enshrouded in the anonymity of the government of the state. The poet Mayakovsky later tried to bridge the gap that opened up between employer and employee by addressing the state as 'comrade government'. To be sure, 'comrade government' is a pathetic apostrophe: it was used by Mayakovsky for the last time as a form of address in his suicide note. (One of the motive forces in Mayakovsky's suicide was the sudden prohibition of his travel abroad.) But the re-christening of the industrial strike as 'sabotage', a capital crime summarily adjudicated, clarified the situation between labour and management drastically. The abolition of private property made the state sole owner of everything, with the ability to turn the full panoply of state power directly and immediately on the workers at will. Ivan the Terrible's statement reverberated down the corridors of time with the volume increased: 'The rulers of Russia have not been accountable to anyone, but have been free to reward and chastise their subjects.' The gap between subjects and masters had grown alarmingly; it had become an abyss.

And yet, despite all the obvious difficulties and disjointures – despite even the stark horror – of the time, the immediate aftermath of the revolution was a time of hope. There was the exhilarating atmosphere of great expectations. Moreover, the Bolsheviks had made extravagant promises ('Promise them anything if it will help us come to power!' was the sense of Lenin's repeated adjurations) all along the line, beginning with the promise of immediate and general betterment of the food situation as soon as Russia withdrew from the Alliance and the war against Germany. The greatest of these promises was that concerning land reform in which every peasant was promised that he would receive a sufficiently large plot of land for his own. On 15 November 1917 the All-Russian Central Executive Committee of the Soviets (controlled by the Bolsheviks) issued a decree, a 'Declaration of Rights of the Peoples of Russia', that promised ethnic equality and the right to self-determination, including 'total separation and the constitution of an independent state' (the right to secession). This decree hastened the dissolution of the Russian Empire. It served the Reds well in the civil war which loomed in the very act of the October Revolution, foiling the attempts of White commanders to rally nationalities to the colours of 'Russia'. When General Denikin came up from the south in his campaign to liberate Moscow, he failed to enlist the crucial help of the independence-minded Ukrainians because he appealed to them in the name of Russia. This was the greatest and most sustained promise made by the Bolsheviks: indeed the right to secession is still on the books, having weathered all subsequent revisions, it remains in the present Soviet constitution. The Russian saying, 'We have a constitution but it is never implemented,' is subject to at least one exception. The exception came at the beginning of Bolshevik rule when Finland, which had belonged to Russia since 1808, was allowed to secede and constitute itself as an independent sovereign state in 1917. This was an act that made a considerable impression at the time: it did much to lend credence to Soviet promises.

In a *Pravda* editorial dated 18 November Lenin exhorted Russian workers to 'install a very strict control over production' and to 'arrest and bring before the people's revolutionary justice anyone who dares to harm the cause of the people'. But it was not until 5 December that a Bolshevik edict did away with the old judicial system, courts, investigating magistrates, prosecuting attorneys, juries, bar associations, *et al.* New judges were to be elected by the Soviets and by popular vote. The edict also established 'revolutionary tribunals' which were charged with the prosecution of 'counter-revolution, sabotage, speculation, and criminality'. To complete the sweep, *all* legal codes were abolished. Since it was some time before new legal codes could be established (1 November 1918), the authorities in their prosecution of the active opposition were obliged to fall back on such sweeping generalities. Indeed, perhaps the most momentous initiative in the history of post-revolutionary Russia and one that stood model for any number of modern police states was taken without a legislative mandate. This was the establishment of the All-Russian Extraordinary Commission against Counter-Revolution, Speculation and Sabotage (Vserossiiskaya Chrezvychainaya Komissiya). The acronym of this title in Russian is *Vecheka* and the organization soon became known and notorious by an abbreviated version: *Cheka.* This was the revolution's central agency for the formation and control of regional secret police organizations. Here was 'an emergency tribunal creating and changing its own administrative law at will', after the fashion of the Holy Inquisition. The Cheka's first director, Felix Djerzhinsky, summed up the situation, as the Bolsheviks saw it, exactly: 'We don't at present need justice,' he declared; 'we are engaged in a life-and-death struggle.' This was the first declaration of the permanent political emergency that was to be re-proclaimed periodically for the next forty years – until it was re-coined as an ideological emergency in the era of détente. A state of acute revolutionary urgency was simulated and made the statutory foundation of Soviet society.

On 25 December the revolutionary committee of the city of Samara (today's Kuibyshev) arrested nineteen 'capitalists' and freed them on payment of what came to be known as 'forced loans', a practice that became widespread throughout the following year, in keeping with the Bolshevik slogan coined in December 1917, *'Grab nagrablennoye!'* ('Rob the robbers' – literally, 'Plunder what has been plundered!') On 27 December all private banks were nationalized to become branches of the Soviet Central Bank. Private treasure was confiscated. Safe-deposit-box owners were required to report their holdings to the new authorities. One of the bookkeepers appointed by the revolutionaries to the exacting task of sorting out and evaluating the Kremlin jewellery with an eye to its sale on the international market was Tatiana Matveyevna Bonner, née Rubinstein in Nikolayev, a village in Siberia founded by the tsar during the Crimean War for the express purpose of housing political exiles. Tatiana Bonner was a widow. Her husband, Grigori Aramovich Bonner, also a native of Nikolayev, had committed suicide in 1906, a year after the abortive Communist revolution. Tatiana, like her husband, was the grandchild of one of the forced founders of Nikolayev. In founding remote, official-exile villages for revolutionaries the tsar had unwittingly, and witlessly, groomed revolutionary tradition as a family institution. If a political prisoner was not a revolutionary before arriving in Nikolayev or its like, he very soon became one. And if not he himself, then his children.

There was also what chroniclers refer to as the 'incipient' civil war in Russia. In fact, the civil war in Russia was part and parcel of the revolution itself. It was the revolution fighting itself out. The revolution had not succeeded until the civil war was over. There was no one on the side of the Whites, a number of able field commanders notwithstanding, with anythiɲg like the genius of Lenin or Trotsky. The subsequent fitful and insubstantial intervention of the Allies on the side of the Whites did more harm than good. Out of the sheer and inborn resentment of the Russians (as distinct from the Ukrainians and other affected nationalities) against foreign interference, the presence of British, French and American troops on Russian territory actually helped consolidate the gains of the revolution. Strangely, too, and yet logically in the extreme situation obtaining, the very ferocity of the revolution worked as a kind of guarantee in the intoxication of the moment and long after, that the old absolutism had been destroyed forever, that there could be no turning back after such an apocalypse, and that the future – whatever else it might be – would be different and if it were different it would have to be better.

In many respects the year 1918 was the turning-point in the process of the October Revolution. It was the year in which a number of major issues were not so much solved as resolved – for better or for worse. On the other hand a number of initiatives were taken which, however temporary they were meant to be, proved to be lasting. On 1 February the old Julian calendar was officially abolished and replaced by the revised Gregorian calendar. The Gregorian calendar had been in use in most of Western Europe since 1582. A day later a government edict announced the separation of Church and state. Freedom of worship was proclaimed in all official solemnity while at the same time all religious teaching, whether public or private, was prohibited. As a matter of course all churches and religious associations were denied the right to own property and their effects of whatever nature were confiscated. In mid-February the Germans launched a major offensive that overran the Russian front line in many sectors but particularly in the south, in the direction of the Caucasus, and in the north, endangering Petrograd. With the Russian forces in complete disarray, Lenin and the Soviet People's Committee (Sovnarkom) agreed to sign a peace treaty with Germany. This was the Treaty of Brest-Litovsk which marked the victory of Imperial Germany on its Eastern front. With this victory Germany acquired Poland, Lithuania and part of Byelorussia. Likewise the Soviets were obliged to recognize the independence of the Ukraine, of Finland, Latvia and Estonia, while Kars and Batum were ceded to Turkey. The victory of the Germans in the East in World War I was a many-sided disaster. The event in itself had calamitous consequences and it set a baleful example for both the Germans and the Russians. It planted in the German mind the idea that Russia could be militarily defeated, and that with comparative ease. The German campaigns on the Eastern front, as almost contra-distinct from their campaigns on the Western front, were crowned with a series of spectacular military victories. And the Germans remained intoxicated with them: they made beautiful memories. The Russians, on the other hand, who had always been impressed by the disciplined power, the sheer efficiency of the Germans, were now more impressed than ever. Lenin, who was starstruck by the prodigies performed by the German wartime economy, took it as a model for the Soviet economy where it served virtually unchanged for the next seventy years, to the general detriment of the Soviet commonweal and the ultimate bankruptcy of the Soviet state. In immediate terms the German victory wrought an anarchic and anomalous situation with a peace the Western Allies, who were still at war with one of the parties to it and still allied with the other, could not respect. Hence two days after the Treaty of Brest-Litovsk was signed, the French and the British landed troops at Murmansk to protect Allied bases in northern Russia. This was the beginning of the 'foreign intervention' during the civil war in the Soviet Union.

The presence of Allied troops on Soviet soil encouraged the Whites in the seesaw of battles that raged back and forth over the Russian and Siberian landscapes (the Japanese landed in Vladivostok on 5 April and made it clear that they were not just visiting). With various large cities such as Kazan and Omsk in the hands of anti-Bolshevik forces and various other key positions more or less directly threatened by the Whites, the Soviet government decided to move quickly where it could and establish *faits accomplis.* For this reason and acting on orders from Moscow a Cheka detachment reinforced by Latvian guards proceeded to Yekaterinburg, where the tsar and his family were being held. The detachment entered the detention area, a villa, and shot to death the tsar, the tsarina, the tsarevich and all four tsarevnas in a group. They also shot to death the tsar's doctor and the imperial family servants, hacked the bodies to pieces and threw them down a mine shaft nearby. They then emptied sacks of lime over the remains. These extreme measures were taken to forestall the liberation of the tsar and his family by the advancing White forces which entered Yekaterinburg just eight days after the massacre occurred. There were any number of witnesses and there can be no doubt that the tsar, his wife and all his children perished as a result of this operation. The extinction of the tsar's family in its entirety and beyond any possible doubt was the purpose of the exercise. The so-called 'Anastasia affair' was finally laid to rest on 7 March 1967 when a Hamburg court of appeals rejected Anna Anderson's claim to be the daughter of the last tsar of all the Russias. The motives of confidence men (and women) aside, there is a simple explanation for the inevitable genesis of the myth of Anastasia's miraculous survival. The name Anastasia comes from the Greek *anastasis*, which means resurrection. Only those members of the various branches of the imperial family who managed to make their way abroad escaped the toils of the Cheka.

The Yekaterinburg massacre took place in mid-July. Earlier in the year, on 16 March, a government decree transferred the capital from Petrograd to Moscow. Lenin and Trotsky moved into the Kremlin while Felix Djerzhinsky and his Cheka commandeered a nearby insurance company building in the central Lubyanka area, since when the headquarters of the secret police under its successive titles has been known as the Lubyanka. Before the German advance was stopped by the Treaty of Brest-Litovsk the Soviet government restored the death sentence, pleading imminent danger to the 'socialist motherland'. Djerzhinsky and his Cheka, working through the 'extraordinary commissions' they had established in various cities and under orders from Lenin, formed flying courts or *troikas*, as they were called (they were made up of three Cheka agents) to sit in summary judgement – executions were carried out on the spot – of 'looters, hoodlums, counter-revolutionary agitators and German spies'. The next day, 22 February, two new categories were added to the list: 'saboteurs and other parasites'. The use of the word 'other' in this subsequent addition is revealing. It was not so much the devaluation through inflation of the term 'saboteur' (just another parasite) as the equation of parasites at large with saboteurs. This was class warfare with a vengeance. There is evidence that the National Socialist regime in Germany studied and adopted the Cheka's flying courts. During the last months of the German occupation of France in 1944, the Vichy government passed a law creating courts-martial, tribunals composed of three non-magistrate judges whose names were not divulged and who sat in secret inside the prisons where the death sentences that were inevitably pronounced were carried out then and there – in the courtyard of the prison. These arrangements were as bare as their Cheka models, there being neither prosecutor nor defence counsel provided. The flying courts in France were made up of militiamen who in almost all cases escaped detection and any sort of retribution after the war. They were created on the insistence of the Germans as a means of repressing the activities of the Resistance. Neither the Germans nor their French minions, however, adopted the Soviet method of executing by firing a bullet into the back of the condemned's head. The Soviets favoured this method because the bullet, exiting the head through the face, destroyed the features and prevented recognition.

On 3 April a Sovnarkom edict ordered all newspapers to devote their front pages to government decrees and the resolutions of local soviets. This edict, which is still in force, contributed much to making the Soviet press what it soon became – almost unrelievedly dull. On the same day the Moscow Cheka issued a circular urging the population to denounce 'enemies of the people'. This was the first in a series of appeals encouraging individual and hence anonymous or pseudonymous denunciation. On 22 April Trotsky, who had meanwhile become people's commissar for war, devised a new and crucial policy for the Red Army. In addition to the restoration of strict discipline and the recognition of military competence, the new policy foresaw the systematic enrolment of former tsarist officers as 'military technicians'. It also foresaw the introduction of political commissars for the express purpose of monitoring the tsarist officers. The tsarist officers, some of whom remained in or later rose to general rank, have long since disappeared; the political commissars now known as *politruki* (political leaders) were soon given a much wider mandate: monitoring and instructing the armed forces at large – including the merchant marine – and down to platoon level. This was therefore the beginning of the institutional infiltration of the Soviet armed forces by the K GB.

In one of the most curious incidents in the civil war, the Czechoslovak Division formed by Tamás Masaryk after the February 1917 revolution from prisoners and deserters from the Austro-Hungarian army clashed with Red Army forces all along their lines of march from the Urals to Siberia (on their way to the Pacific where they meant to embark for service in France). The Czechs and Slovaks, who were far better disciplined than anyone the Russians could put up against them locally, soon occupied a number of towns in Siberia, the Urals and in the region of the middle Volga. In the wake of this strange campaign a number of anti-Bolshevik governments were set up in various cities, such as Samara, while in others – Omsk, for example – local Soviets were overthrown before the Czechoslovak legion reached the scene. This was altogether a freak development, a twentieth-century anabasis whose only goal in Russia – like that of the original 'armed promenade' of approximately the same number of men in Persia two thousand years earlier – was to reach the sea. By the same token, the 'conquests' of the anti-Bolshevik forces along the Czechoslovak line of march could not in the nature of things be of long date. Under Trotsky's new common-sense military policy the Russian Fifth Army defeated a clutch of detachments from the Czechoslovak Division and retook Kazan. It was the turning-point in the civil war. This was in mid-September. By the end of November Trotsky had tightened the screws on Red Army discipline still further. Commanders were ordered to shoot all deserters and burn the house of anyone hiding a deserter. Indeed, Trotsky systematized countermeasures against desertion. 'Barrage detachments' were organized behind the lines for the express purpose of rounding up or intercepting deserters. Such operations depended on the massive participation of Cheka troops for whom this kind of 'back-up' activity became standard procedure. In World War II Stalin informed Ambassador Averell Harriman that in the Soviet system it took a great deal more courage to try to defect than to fight the enemy. Stalin's 'secret army', the NKVD (now the MVD and the KGB), with perhaps as many as a million men under arms, executed, deported or otherwise disposed of several millions of Soviet citizens – instead of opposing the invading Germans in World War II.

Likewise in 1918 food rationing was introduced – in four categories and on a declining scale – for workers, Red Army men, the liberal professions and last and least for 'non-working' elements of the population. On 5 September, on the heels of a decree published by the People's Commissariat of Justice encouraging 'Red terror' tactics, the Cheka was granted discretionary powers including the power to pronounce and carry out the death sentence. At the end of October the Communist Union of Soviet Youth – Komsomol for short – was formed. (Earlier in the year, on 8 March, the Party decided to dispense with 'social democratic' as a title and adopted the word 'Communist' instead. It was thenceforth known as the Communist Party of the Soviet Union.)

Meanwhile the Soviets, under Lenin's unflagging leadership, nationalized everything. They abolished all taxes, water and electricity charges, room and house rents, public transportation tickets – everything was free! Quite naturally, within a very short time this policy produced a colossal state budgetary deficit and with it runaway inflation. This development in turn prompted Lenin to do away with money altogether, apparently acting on the assumption – in addition to Marx's behest – that if there were no such thing as money there could be no such thing as a deficit.

When World War I ended with the armistice signed at Compiègne on 11 November, the Soviet government lost no time in denouncing the Treaty of Brest-Litovsk as 'intolerable'. At the same time the Soviets did their best to encourage and abet the revolution in Germany and Austro-Hungary, who now followed imperial Russia into the turmoil of defeat. In Berlin, Hamburg, Munich, Leipzig and Dresden, 'soviets' were formed out of the same stuff as the original soviets in Russia – marauding soldiers and sailors, intellectual rebels, romantics and dreamers – a good many recognized poets among them. But the situation in general was nothing like the same as the Russian model. It is true that Bela Kun proclaimed a 'soviet republic' in Hungary and managed to hold out in Budapest for a few months (21 March to 1 August 1919) before being swept away by Hungarian troops under their regular leaders. 'The Soviet Republic of Bavaria', headquartered in (and confined to) Munich, made up of irregular troops and political fantasts, was of even shorter duration. The 'German revolution' and its neighbouring facsimiles were not the work but the play of political mice while the cats were away. When the cats returned in relatively good order at the head of their troops, the game was over.

By the end of the year 1918 the Soviet government, having already made several peace overtures to the Western Allies, sent a note to President Wilson in Washington. In it Wilson was asked to use his good offices to put an end to foreign intervention in Russia. There was an 'or else' attached to the request. It was this: if the intervention could not be stopped it could very well lead to the 'total extermination of the Russian bourgeoisie by the desperate masses'. This, too, the holding of an entire class – the bourgeoisie – hostage against the kind of Allied behaviour desired by the Soviet government was to serve as a model for Soviet dealings with the

West. Yet the note was drafted in language conciliatory enough to pass the musters of Woodrow Wilson and Lloyd George. However, both Premier Georges Clemenceau and President Raymond Poincaré refused to enter into any negotiations whatever with the Bolsheviks. And there the matter rested.

By the end of the year 1920, however, the Soviets themselves had solved the problem of foreign intervention. The last British and French troops were withdrawn after the defeat of General Denikin in the Caucasus. (Denikin was replaced by his second-in-command, Baron Wrangel.) Shortly before that a more serious threat to Soviet power had been overcome when Admiral Kolchak, who had made substantial inroads into Red territory out of Siberia, was defeated and executed. Nevertheless the Soviets were still far from consolidating their position. Indeed, quite the contrary, the almost superhuman efforts involved on the part of the Reds in their prosecution of the war, coupled with their extravagant demands on the people, enforced with well-nigh maniacal severity, created a situation throughout the vastness of the country that was clearly intolerable. Peasants were no longer interested in sowing their fields – what for? They were obliged to deliver up everything they produced (not even excluding what they needed for their own survival) and received nothing in return. The harder the peasant worked the more severely was he penalized with 'taxes in kind'. This, of course, was the formula for disaster. At times Russian peasants bound tax collectors between two planks – like a human sandwich – and sawed them into pieces. At times they separated a new 'master' from his testicles and then sent the latter to the Ministry of Agriculture labelled 'eggs' (Russian slang for testicles) and thus part of the 'tax in kind'. There was a complete breakdown of the economy accompanied by widespread famine. Nothing worked and tens of thousands were dying from hunger. There were spontaneous revolts throughout the countryside. The situation was on the point of getting completely out of hand. Galloping inflation accelerated the process. The Soviets tried to reintroduce money to establish order in the economy. On the black market the tsarist gold rouble was worth 200,000 Soviet paper roubles in 1922 when the authorities reintroduced the institution of the state bank. Krestinsky, the commissioner for finance, estimated the money volume at ten trillion paper roubles. By that time every newly printed rouble note was issued in a denomination ten thousand times greater than its forerunner. It was only when the gold rouble was reintroduced that it became possible to establish tolerable financial conditions.

The crisis culminated in the revolt of the marine garrison at the port of Kronstadt at the Neva estuary. This was a great shock to the revolutionaries; the garrison at Kronstadt had been the pride of the revolution, its sailors having played a key role in the early phase of the October coup. The Kronstadt uprising was put down in blood with the singular ferocity characteristic of the Bolsheviks. But even the most fanatic of the professional revolutionaries realized that something more would have to be done, something basic, general and organizational. It was clear, in short, that a new policy was needed. Lenin, who had a sense of reality that sometimes suited oddly with his ideological vision, realized that a return – or, at least, a partial return – to capitalism was under the circumstances inevitable. But he encountered resistance so strong on the part of the entrenched functionaries (who clearly discerned their own downfall in the return of a capitalist economy) that he was forced to compromise. The compromise took the form of a decree to the effect that thenceforth all parties and groups except the Bolshevik Party were outlawed. This was the horrendous price of the 'unanimous' resolution in favour of the New Economic Policy (NEP) at the Tenth Party Congress in 1921. What was even worse than this proclamation of a one-party state was the supplemental prohibition of factions or interest groups. This spelled the doom of intra-party democracy: it was the formula for 'cadaver obedience' (as the commissar for education and enlightenment remarked when a British journalist complained that the Soviet Union did not have habeas corpus: 'No, but we have habeas cadaver!'). The baby was thrown out with the bathwater. But not only that: the Tenth Party Congress with its habeas cadaver provided a ramp for the accession to power of Josef Vissarionovich Djugashvili, called Stalin.

Lenin was perfectly frank: 'On the economic front,' he said, 'in the attempt to achieve the transition to Communism in the spring of 1921, we suffered a defeat that was more serious than any defeat Kolchak, Denikin or Piłsudski inflicted upon us.'

The Soviets introduced the New Economic Policy because they had to – there was no choice: they were presented with a bill for their success in accomplishing the impossible. They owed their success, the whole of it, to one man: Lenin. It was Lenin alone who made the revolution. And it was he alone who accepted the bill and realized that it had to be paid immediately. But introducing the NEP proved to be the most difficult prodigy Lenin ever performed. For with the restoration of a form of capitalism, the throwing open of the economy by and large to the market, Lenin confirmed the arguments of the opposition within the Party – the 'rightists' (Mensheviks, Social Democrats and cadets, remnants and reminiscents) – and therewith confounded, frightened and infuriated the Party faithful who were Lenin's closest and most loyal followers. (He was able to achieve the statutory 'unanimity' in the passage of the resolution only after repeated threats to eject nay-sayers from the Party.) The bill presented by the Party faithful for their extreme obedience came immediately thereafter in the form of the decree establishing the one-party state, a step no less fateful in its consequences than the passage of the Enabling Act in National Socialist Germany twelve years later. But the worst of the yoking of the two decrees, NEP and the exclusion of legal opposition, was that a paradoxical situation was thereby created: it was the yoking of a fire and water combination – the prospering of whichever one of the two meant the blight of the other. As it turned out, the NEP was a very considerable success and indeed (for many) a spectacular success. Within a year there were wares on sale in the shops, the farmers produced fruit and vegetables and sold them on the open market for ready money, and within three years Russia's budding industry achieved a gross national product equal to that of the pre-war high. Moreover, the NEP brought with it a flourishing of the arts and sciences.

But the better the worse. The very fact that Russian (and worse still, minority) businessmen were thriving to some extent, that speculators were becoming well-to-do, that private farmers enjoyed something like a monopoly of the production of food, was repulsive in the extreme (they were even exhorted publicly by Nikolai Bukharin, a leading member of the Politburo, 'to enrich themselves'). The hardliners, the professional revolutionary cadres (Stalin: 'The cadres decide everything') asked themselves: 'Is this what we fought for and sacrificed ourselves for?'

V
❦
'TWO HOUSES BOTH ALIKE
IN DIGNITY...'

The year 1921, the year of Andrei Sakharov's birth, marked the end of the revolution in the sense that by that time armed hostilities on any sort of mass scale were a thing of the past. It was thus a pivotal year, a point of pause for assessment and the taking of bearings. The trouble was that the mark at the end of the revolution was a question mark. The revolution was a success, but the price of success proved to be hideously exorbitant. The country – its history, its tradition, its values, its culture and, above all, its economy – lay in ruins. The comparison which, then as now, suggested itself insistently was that between the French and the October Revolutions. The French Revolution was the only model the Soviets had. All their revolutionary leaders had studied it more or less thoroughly and were even in the habit of using the vocabulary of the French Revolution to describe events current in their own. Some of the similarities were indeed striking. Tsar Nicholas II was an acceptable double for Louis XVI, his German wife Alexandra Feodorovna equally acceptable as a facsimile of the Austrian Marie Antoinette. The 'Great Incorruptible', the fanatic and cruel Robespierre, bore a strong but by no means complete resemblance to Lenin (of whom Gorky once said that 'he wanted nothing for himself personally'), the eloquent Danton, organizer of the armed uprising, suits with the figure of Trotsky, while Marat compares closely with the merciless and hysterical Djerzhinsky. But even the political parties involved in the two revolutions were similar. The Girondists were on an historical par with the Georgian separatists in the Russian Revolution, Mirabeau's reformists were like enough to the cadets, while the Jacobins were the obvious models for the

Bolsheviks. The question, then, was whether the October Revolution would follow the course of the French Revolution. In the terms of the former, the October Revolution had arrived at the stage known as Thermidor – after the eleventh month (19 July to 17 August) in the French revolutionary calendar which saw the overthrow of Robespierre and the end of the Terror. Would the October Revolution have its Thermidor? Was the NEP the Russian Thermidor? If so, it would last quite some time and perhaps install itself as a permanent arrangement.

But the dissimilarities between the two revolutions were far more important than the various spectacular likenesses. In the first place the real comparison is between the French Revolution and the February revolution in Russia, not the October Revolution. The French Revolution was cut to the national cloth as the February revolution in Russia was meant to be. It had limited objectives most of which – if not all – were capable of realization in the ordinary scheme of things. The October Revolution, on the other hand, regarded itself as the beginning of, the model for, world revolution. It was apocalyptic in nature, a fact that imparted an extraordinary *élan* to it but deprived it virtually by definition of any possibility of achieving its supernatural, utopian ends. The ends of the October Revolution were out of the orbit of reality – exorbitant. As the German poet Hölderlin sang, 'In his desire to make the state his heaven, man made of it the sheerest hell.' The October Revolution could not possibly have succeeded had it not been for its politico-philosophical lineage. This is perhaps best highlighted by two quotes, the one from Friedrich Engels, the other from Nikolai Berdyaev. Wrote Engels in mid-nineteenth century: 'Communism is the natural fruit of German philosophical culture.' Wrote Berdyaev some seventy years later: 'The whole history of the Russian intelligentsia was a preparation for Communism.' If so, it was very largely the work of two men, Marx in the first case and Lenin in the second. Here another comparison of quotes is indicated, both of them already familiar to the reader: 'The nineteenth century contains many remarkable social critics and revolutionaries no less original, no less violent, no less dogmatic than Marx, but not one so rigorously single-minded, so absorbed in making every word and every act of his life a means towards a single, immediate, practical end, to which nothing was too sacred to sacrifice.' Of Lenin his colleague Axelrode wrote,

'There is no other man who is absorbed by the revolution twenty-four hours a day, who has no other thought but the thought of the revolution, and who, even when he sleeps, dreams of nothing but the revolution.' In the lineal descent from God to Communism there are many illustrious names, giants of the mind and spirit: Luther, Galileo, Descartes, Rousseau, Newton, Locke, Kant, Hegel, Feuerbach, Marx and Lenin. But it would not have come to Communism without the last two names. Marx and Lenin not only preserved the continuity of the line; they also reinforced it, broadened it, shored it up, underpinned it and finally – in the case of Lenin – imposed it. Marx created a philosophical platform large enough to accommodate an alternative. Despite all the rigid schematics of the dialectic and the 'fierce optimism' that informed all his works, Marx never committed himself on anything that had to do with how Communism was to be achieved. There occurred, consequently, a split between those who favoured the path of parliamentary reform and those who were convinced that only the bloodiest of revolutions would suffice to overthrow capitalism and establish the proletariat in its place. Thus the socialist parties in both Russia and Germany split into two factions, the Bolsheviks and Mensheviks in the former and the Socialists and Communists in the latter. But it was Lenin who forced the original split, in the London Party Congress in 1903, and who turned Marxism definitively on to the path of world revolution ('Proletarians of all countries unite!') and the 'dictatorship of the proletariat'. Lenin combined within himself the Russian revolutionary tradition and the most radical form of Marxism. He set the course of the Communist Party of the Soviet Union. The course was uncompromising in principle but flexible in tactics and strategy, hence Lenin's characterization of the NEP as a 'temporary retreat'. Far more so than Marx, Lenin was a prodigiously prolific writer: his collected works number fifty-five volumes. Anyone who knows Lenin's works well can find a suitable quote for almost anything. But the main point to be made is that both Marx and Lenin were something on the order of supermen. Both were possessed of well-nigh superhuman energy, enormous intellectual power, unflagging devotion to the cause and – in the case of Lenin, anyway – a highly developed fighter's instinct for the main chance. The second point to be made is that because of these superhuman qualities both men – and especially Lenin – were able to overcome the natural

boundaries and obstacles in the way of their pursuit. The result –
again, particularly in the case of Lenin – was that their victories
and achievements and, in the end, their legacies were unnatural.
The demands implicit and explicit in the latter were simply too
great for the mass of humanity to satisfy. The departure from all
the established norms of social behaviour (with a large entailment
on human behaviour as such) amounted to a leap into the dark
because the utopia although proclaimed had never been surveyed
and charted or even properly identified. In this sense the demands
made by the legacies of Marx and Lenin were intrinsically unnatural. In sum, the demands of Marx and Lenin converged in the
central demand for the junking of religion and all that it stood for.
As Marx put it, 'the critique of religion is the prerequisite of all
critique.' And again, he describes Feuerbach's greatest deed as 'the
proof that philosophy is nothing other than religion clothed in
thought and set forth in rational terms; and therefore likewise to
be condemned as another form and existential means of the alienation of the human being'.

In working out a blueprint for action impossible to follow in its
utopian exactions, in playing over the heads of their fellow men in
the drawing of the entire floor-plan of their basic assumptions,
Marx and Lenin paved the way to disaster of a very particular
kind. It is historically spectacular that Marx, whose main and
indeed exclusive concern was man, who could write, as already
quoted, that 'for man, the root is man himself', and further that
'We deny the validity of metaphysical and epistemological problems
engendered by the false hopes of attaining to some absolute reality
beyond the practical horizon of human beings,' could do exactly
that. It is historically scurrilous that Marx could declare war on
the alienation of the human being and then proceed, under the
aegis of anti-alienation, to alienate humankind in a way and on a
scale that beggars description and pygmies all precedent. It is
flabbergasting that he could engender a span of expectations and
desires brighter than any 'arch-in-heaven' (as the French call the
rainbow) that was far 'beyond the practical horizon of human
beings'. And as for Lenin: it was Russia's and the world's tragedy
that the implementary genius of Lenin should have followed so
closely on the heels of the innovative genius of Marx, that backward and isolated Russia, a political monstrosity from any point of
view, should have replaced Germany as the classic scene of socialist

revolution. By 1917 Maxim Gorky, the archetypal proletarian author, had seen through Lenin: 'Vladimir Lenin,' he wrote,

> is conducting a socialist form of government in Russia in accordance with the prescription of Nechayev: full steam ahead smack through the swamp! The people have already paid for this experiment with tens of thousands of lives and will be forced to pay with still more. This tragedy does not disquiet the slaves of dogma of Lenin and his comrades. For him life, with all its complications and entanglements, is something foreign. He does not know the masses of people, he has never lived among the people. But he knows perfectly well from books how to cause an uproar among the masses of the people, how to incite the instincts of the people. The working class for him constitutes the same element that ore does for a metallurgist. He works like a chemist in the laboratory. Only, a chemist works with dead materials and produces splendid results for living people. Lenin does just the opposite.
>
> The working class must understand that it is being made the subject of a horrible experiment which will destroy the best that is in the working class and for long years will postpone the normal development of the Russian revolution.

Gorky's description of Lenin as the chemist in the laboratory working with the masses as though they were chemicals is precisely to the point. The *raison d'être* of Communism is the scientific approach. It was the intoxicating prestige of science – particularly the natural sciences – that sanctioned the 'horrible experiment' and covered the multitude of sins the experiment demanded. It was science that licensed mankind as God. It takes a brilliant mind to make a really colossal mistake: let us admire the ingenuity with which Marx and Lenin deceived themselves. And the ingenuity and perseverance with which they deceived others. 'The idea in question,' wrote Nadezhda Mandelstam in *Hope Against Hope*,

> was that there is an irrefutable scientific truth by means of which, once they are possessed of it, people can foresee the future, change the course of history at will and make it rational. This religion – or science, as it was modestly called by its adepts – invests man with a God-like authority and has its own creed and ethic, as we have seen. In the twenties a good many people drew a parallel with the victory of Christianity, and thought this new religion would also last a thousand years ... All were agreed on the superiority of the new creed which promised heaven on earth instead of other worldly

rewards. But the most important thing for them was the end to all doubt and the possibility of absolute faith in the new, scientifically obtained truth.

Basically the 'fierce miscreed' of Marxism–Leninism did two things: it made demands on mankind that were impossible to fulfil and it codified broad penalties for failure of fulfilment. This was laying the foundation for an entire structure of euphoric, programmatic deceit, of pious fraud on a scale no Christian society could have imagined. What the idolatry of science came to specifically was the imposing of comprehensive quantitative norms on society as a whole. The imposition of the quantitative norm is, of course, a direct descendant of the quantification of matter, which was 'the crime of Galileo'. The result was general disaster, both blatant (forcing the adoption of the NEP) and insidious (going unnoticed and even unsuspected for decades). But the worst aspect of the imposition of impossible demands was that it led directly to the criminalization not only of politics but of society as a whole – in much the same way, although on a far grander scale, that the passage of the Eighteenth Amendment prohibiting the manufacture, sale and transportation of intoxicating liquor in 1919 led to the criminalization of American society (effective enforcement became impossible because of popular disregard of the law). John Stuart Mill considered the fact that in the mid nineteenth century 'nearly half the United States have been interdicted by law from making any use whatever of fermented drinks, except for medical purposes', a prime example of the 'gross usurpations upon the liberty of private life'. His indignation was ethical, which is to say that it was based on his sense of what sort of laws can and cannot be enforced in human society.

The criminalization of Soviet society was the work of Vladimir Ulyanov, known as Lenin. Lenin anticipated the decree proclaiming the one-party state in 1921 by ten years when he formed the professional revolutionary cadres as a sort of political Praetorian guard, bound by oath to ruthless obedience in accordance with Nechayev's *Catechism of a Revolutionary*. The result was a highly disciplined organization made up of ideologically indoctrinated professional criminals. The use of both terms – 'professional' and 'criminal' – is advised. The one thing distinguishing the professional revolutionary from the common criminal is the difference in

119

motives: the revolutionary murders, maims or robs for a political or religious cause, never for himself. His act is selfless, often involving self-sacrifice. However, although the law sometimes recognizes extenuating aspects in motivation – as in crimes of passion – it sees no extenuating aspect whatever in crimes committed for a higher cause, even if the cause is common to the government in power. To the contrary, a crime committed for a cause is likely to come under the heading of 'premeditated' and warrant a more severe penalty. Thus the sanction of selflessness in the commission of a crime is altogether suspect. Marx almost managed to make a case for selflessness in the service of the general good. Basing his argument on the general tenets of socialism he outlawed privacy (by connecting it with property in 'private property') and forced a polarization of the commonweal on the one hand and freedom on the other (because there can be no freedom without privacy) to the disadvantage of the latter since the *raison d'être* of Communism is the general good – at least, that is the proclaimed purpose of the system. The polarization of the commonweal and freedom is implicit; it underlies the basic Marxist position. For a Marxist the very idea of freedom as it is understood in the West is a bourgeois concept and as such categorically rejected. Morality is an instrument in the class struggle, nothing more. The worth of an individual is restricted solely to his function as a component in the collective. According to Marx, Communism is a society in which the 'bourgeois freedoms', including human-rights guarantees, are meaningless because each and every citizen identifies fully and freely with the community. (It is to be noted that in Marx's concept of the worth of the individual's being restricted solely to his function as a component in the collective, the imposition of the quantitative norm is clearly visible.)

The above expositional foray may provide some inkling of the lengths (and depths) to which Marx went to shore up the rationale of his system, standing Hegel on his head and reversing the basic tenets of Christianity. It was indeed Lenin who criminalized the Soviet state. But the theoretical spadework, the underlying conceptualizations necessary to the process of criminalizing the state and society, was done by Marx. The sum total of their efforts worked the predestination of the Soviet system. It was not the organizational and conspiratorial superiority of Stalin over all his rivals in the struggle to succeed Lenin. In any sort of political situation except the one that actually obtained in the Soviet Union, Stalin would have been no match for at least five of his rivals. His only strength on the face of the situation was his obvious weakness, his lack of the necessary qualities of leadership – none of his victim–rivals was ever able to imagine Stalin as Lenin's successor. But Lenin had prepared the way for Stalin – even without knowing it: Lenin had criminalized the state and therewith presented Stalin with an insuperable advantage. For Stalin was the only professional criminal in the Soviet leadership. As a bank-robber he had been schooled in terror and intrigue – all the machinations necessary to hold bandit gangs together (for these were the people he dealt with and commanded for years on end) in operational discipline. He worked with a boldness and a sure knowledge of human weakness and corruptibility that were utterly foreign to his bookish rivals. Stalin was in his element; his rivals were – and remained – at sea: to a greater or a lesser extent they had misconceived the entire enterprise.

There were, of course, strictures imposed upon the official criminality of the state. These were due to circumstances over which the Soviets had no control. In the two years, 1921–2, at least five million people died of starvation in the Soviet Union – one million of them in Kirghizia. An All-Russian Aid Committee for the Starving was created in July of 1921 with no particular attention paid to the political purity of its composition, its membership including a large number of non-Bolsheviks and liberal intellectuals. (The Norwegian explorer, Fridtjof Nansen, a League of Nations high commissioner, headed the European Aid Committee for the Starving in Russia.) Maxim Gorky wrote open letters appealing 'to all honest people in the world' to come to the aid of the starving in Russia. He then turned to Herbert Hoover, president of the American Relief Administration, which was active throughout war-torn Western Europe, with the request for food supplies *en masse*. Less than a month later Maxim Litvinov, commissar for foreign affairs, signed an agreement with the American Relief Administration for both the transport and distribution of powdered milk, chocolate, flour, sugar and tea among other foodstuffs throughout the huge territory under Soviet sway. It is estimated that in the following year American Relief supplies kept fifteen million people alive. The number of those saved from starvation could have been considerably larger particularly in the Ukraine where the Bolsheviks, fearing insurrection and the fomenting of Ukrainian nationalism, insisted on controlling all aspects of the distribution process. Two months later, in October, the Soviet government signed an agreement with Armand Hammer's Allied Drug and Chemical Corporation for the exchange of art objects (the Soviets had no idea of the worth of the paintings lost to the national treasure in this fashion), caviar and furs in return for the supply of one million poods of wheat (about 18,000 tons!). At the time Hammer, who was the son of one of the founders of the American Communist Party, was twenty-seven years old. Just six days after this agreement was signed, the Soviet government granted Hammer a twenty-year concession for the mining of asbestos in the Urals.

Meanwhile the general governmental tumult continued unabated. Hardly more than a month after its formation the All-Russian Aid Committee for the Starving was forcibly dissolved and most of its members arrested. Once again Lenin proved himself to be especially bloody-minded in the pursuit of his set goals; he was determined, particularly, to get rid of the constitutional democrats (cadets) who were widely represented on the committee. Only Nansen's intervention and the protests of the representatives of the American Relief Administration managed to save the lives of many of the members of this pathetic organization. On 1 September another blow fell. The execution by firing squad of sixty-one members of the so-called 'Combat Organization', an allegedly counter-revolutionary group of intellectuals (the arrests had been made on 5 June), was announced by the Petrograd Cheka. Among the victims was the poet Nikolai Gumilyev, formerly a tsarist officer and the husband of Anna Akhmatova, in her own right one of Russia's most famous poets of the twentieth century. The execution of Gumilyev was and remains a scandal. No such thing as a 'Combat Organization' ever existed. But even Party members were not safe. In a *Pravda* article dated 21 September, Lenin exhorted his colleagues to 'purge the Party of scoundrels, bureaucratized and dishonest Communists, softies and Mensheviks who have repainted their faces but who remain Mensheviks deep down within themselves'. Lenin's appeal brought about the first major purge of the Party after the revolution. In one year 140,000 members – or about one-fifth of the Communist Party's total membership – were drummed out.

There was, however, one refuge, one walk of life, one pursuit that, from the very beginning and for ten blessed years thereafter, was largely exonerated from the vicious whims and preposterous vagaries of the security organs of the new state. During this decade, because of the enormous prestige with which they were held – a prestige bordering on sanctification – the sciences provided an inviolable asylum from almost any kind of persecution-cum-prosecution. But it is wise to emphasize the 'almost'. There were, of course, exceptions: Professor Nikolai Koltsov, the famous cytologist and biologist, was arrested and sentenced to death in 1918 by reason of his having been a cadet. He was saved by Maxim Gorky who interceded directly with Lenin. It is also true that the Soviet Union lost a great many of its foremost scientists through flight and emigration. These included Igor Sikorsky (he designed the first multi-motor airplane in 1913), who left Russia illegally in 1919 and emigrated to the United States where he made a spectacular career in aviation technology as the designer of the helicopter. There was also Georgi (later George) Kistiakovsky, a young chemist who left Petrograd and emigrated to America where, as a leading specialist in explosives, he played a key role in the construction of the atomic bomb at Los Alamos. Nor were the *émigrés* and refugees by any means confined to the sciences. Their name was legion, a legion of the élite: Bunin, Balanchine, Chagall, Chaliapin, Prokofiev, Rachmaninov, Stravinsky, Kandinsky, Nabokov, Pavlova, Karpovich. The intellectual blood-letting through flight legal or illegal – the 'brain drain' resultant from the October Revolution – was comparable to that of the French Revolution.

But quite apart from their being the presumptive founding disciplines of the socialist–Communist system itself, its rationale and *raison d'être*, the sciences – and above all, the natural sciences – were at a categorical remove from anything political (there was always the almost sacred traditional neutrality of the sciences: always and only on the side of man in the most general sense possible), so that no one could associate them actually or historically with any political party or movement. Peter the Great founded the Academy of Sciences on the model of European academies, introducing the ideas of Copernicus, Galileo, Kepler and Newton. The Soviets simply took it over. Even so, a very high percentage of the members of the Academy of Sciences were aristocrats by birth and all of them were aristocrats by calling. Moreover the average income of a member of the Academy was twenty to thirty times higher than that of an industrial worker, a fact that levered them into the upper class. As a result very few academicians sympathized with the radical social forces at work in pre-Revolutionary Russia. No, the sciences in the Soviet Union in the year of reckoning 1921 were in themselves sanctuary – and, indeed, the only sanctuary in the system. Anyone working in the sciences, regardless of his origins, class or family connections, was likely to be excused, excepted and exempted instinctively and automatically. There is the story, for example, of Professor Gamov, a distinguished physicist, who tried to cross the border illegally in 1930 – long after the decade of grace for scientists and after the Soviets had intensified border control many times over in order to stanch the flow of peasant farmers after the beginning of forced collectivization. Gamov first tried to cross the mountains into Afghanistan. When he was caught by Soviet soldiers he explained that he was a mountain-climber – it was his favourite sport. His excuse was accepted. On the next occasion he tried to cross the Black Sea in a small boat *en route* to Turkey. When he was hauled up by the Soviet Coast Guard he explained that another favourite sport of his was sailing. This, too, was accepted. Not long thereafter the government, its suspicions – *mirabile dictu* – still unaroused, allowed Gamov to attend an international conference abroad. He never returned, but went on to the United States where he made a name for himself as a biologist some twenty years later. Anyone working in the sciences who came from a family of scientists – where scientific study was a family tradition, as it were – belonged just as surely, just as automatically to the only aristocracy the Communist doctrine implicitly foresaw. In the very worst of possible cases, one in which, say, all occasions including noble birth conspired against the subject, the pursuit of a scientific profession – as will become amply clear in this account – entailed a special status. That at very least.

Into this special status-cum-sanctuary in the chaotic Communist world of the Soviet Union was born on 21 May 1921 Andrei Dmitrievich Sakharov. His father, Dmitri Ivanovich Sakharov, as already noted, was a physics professor who wrote a number of books on physics, one of which was used as a standard text in the Russian secondary-school system. In an autobiographical note Andrei Sakharov adds that the favourite composers of the former movie-house pianist were Chopin, Grieg, Beethoven and Scriabin. 'My childhood,' writes Andrei, 'was spent in a large communal apartment most of whose rooms were occupied by our relatives, with only a few outsiders mixed in. Our home preserved the traditional atmosphere of a numerous and close-knit family – respect for hard work and ability, mutual aid, love for literature and science.' This was the house that Ivan Nikolaievich Sakharov had bought in 1901. Came the revolution several families were moved into the house, but Ivan Nikolaievich was allowed to stay with his family, occupying several rooms. The grandmother and *grande dame*, Maria Petrovna, had her own room. The piano of Dmitri Ivanovich was in the parental bedroom. There were three rooms occupied by the Sakharovs all heated by the same flue. Thus Andrei Sakharov grew up in the same house with his parents, his grandparents, four uncles and one aunt. Small wonder he writes that family influences were especially strong in his case. As noted, Andrei Sakharov was tutored at home until he was almost twelve years old: he was then sent to school where he was admitted to the (Russian) fifth grade. His parents thought that he should have been admitted to the sixth grade. After six months they took him out of school and had him tutored at home again for the second half of the year. Thereafter, while still in his twelfth year, he was admitted to the seventh grade. Because of this, he writes, he 'then had difficulty relating to [his] own age group'. All this, of course, is by way of saying that Andrei Sakharov led a sheltered life. In fact he enjoyed the advantages of a double shelter: his father, Dmitri Ivanovich, provided the shelter afforded by the scientific profession; his family, close-knit as it was, provided a shelter-within-the-shelter by tutoring him at home and thus shielding him from virtually the whole of the Soviet primary-school system.

And yet the Sakharov family did not remain unscathed. There was Uncle Vanya. Ivan Ivanovich had been a classmate but not a friend of Bukharin's in the pre-revolutionary Moscow school system. An engineer by first profession, Uncle Vanya had decided to study for the bar as 'a better way of helping society'. He was arrested in 1923 when a client of his managed to escape the Soviet Union by crossing the border illegally. The Soviet state held Uncle Vanya responsible, accusing him of being an accessory before or after the fact. There were two trains of speculation in the Sakharov family. One was that Uncle Vanya knew nothing of the whole business and was merely a victim. The other was that Uncle Vanya knew about it but deliberately kept quiet so as not to hurt the chances of his client. Nobody believed that Uncle Vanya had been an accessory *before* the fact. Uncle Vanya was sent away 'for several years'. When he returned he was 'a second-class citizen', but he resumed his law practice. He was arrested a second time in 1933 and sent to a region of the upper Volga where he became the director of a hydro-electric station. In 1941 Uncle Vanya travelled to Moscow illegally to attend the funeral of his mother, Maria Petrovna, who had died at the age of seventy-nine. Uncle Vanya died two years later.

Uncle Kolya (Nikolai Ivanovich) divorced and married again. Aunt Tanya had two daughters, Katya and Valya. Katya, who is seventy-seven at this writing and lives in Moscow, and Andrei Sakharov see each other from time to time. Sakharov's most vivid memories of his childhood concern his beloved grandmother, Maria Petrovna. She was the life and soul of the family, she held everything together – her husband, Ivan Nikolaievich, being a more peripheral figure ('as is usually the case, apparently'). The family (but not Sakharov's immediate family) kept beautiful dogs. There was Dzhalma ('an Indian name after some hero or heroine in Indian history or folklore') who was killed in the street by an automobile: 'for the family that was a tragedy.'

The 'difficulty' Sakharov mentions in relation to his own age group can and should be read as his remaining aloof from his classmates throughout most of his schooling. He graduated at the top of his class in 1938 at the age of seventeen. In 1942 he graduated from Moscow State University where he was said to have presented 'the most brilliant thesis ever offered in physics' at the university. To be sure, the classes of the physics department of the university were evacuated from Moscow to Ashkabad in the Turkmen Republic near the Iranian border in 1941 at the outbreak of World War II and Sakharov did not escape many of the hardships connected with the Soviet retreat before the invading German armies. The summer of 1942 was difficult for everyone in the Soviet Union and Sakharov was no exception. But he was exempted from military service (and rightly so) and that made all the difference. Sakharov was sent for a few weeks that summer to work in Kovrov (east of Moscow on the mainline to Gorky) and then he was employed 'on a logging operation in a remote settlement near Melekess' (in the western Urals). There he gained his 'first vivid impression of the life of the workers and peasants'. In September he was sent to an arms factory on the Volga where he worked as an engineer until 1945. He recounts that he 'developed several inventions to improve quality-control procedures at that factory', and that in his university years he did not manage to do any original scientific work. He adds that in 1944, while still working at the factory, he wrote several articles on theoretical physics and sent them to Moscow for review. None of these articles was ever published, but they gave him, as he puts it, 'the confidence in my powers which is essential for a scientist'. In 1945 he entered the Lebedev Physical Institute as a graduate student. His adviser happened to be Igor Tamm, the outstanding theoretical physicist who was later to become a member of the Academy of Sciences and a Nobel laureate. In 1948 Tamm included Sakharov in his research group which succeeded in developing a thermonuclear weapon. With this the course of Sakharov's career as a nuclear physicist was set.

Thus, except for the summer of 1942 when for several weeks he 'roughed it' in the western Urals, Sakharov was more or less comfortably ensconced in the socio-political cocoon provided by the academic–scientific disciplines within the Soviet system. But contrast provides the truest perspective. By way of contrast, that same Tatiana Matveyevna Bonner, the bookkeeper appointed by the revolutionaries in 1917 to catalogue and evaluate the Kremlin jewellery, bore a daughter at the turn of the century. This was Ruth Grigorievna Bonner who, like her mother and grandmother, was born in the official-exile village of Nikolayev in Siberia. Ruth Grigorievna moved with her mother to Petrograd where she met and married Gevork Alikhanov, an Armenian and member of the Communist Party (Bolshevik) since 1917. The year was 1921. Two years later a daughter was born of the union, Elena Georgievna, and after another two-year interval a son, Igor Georgievich. Meanwhile Ruth Grigorievna had become a member of the Communist Party of the Soviet Union (1924). Ten years later Ruth Grigorievna entered Moscow University as a student of construction engineering; her husband Gevork had meanwhile advanced to the position of head of the personnel department of the Comintern. 'On the morning of 27 May 1937,' she told this writer fifty years later, 'my husband left for work wearing a light summer suit for the first time that year. I remember the occasion vividly because we had quite a row over the suit: I wanted him to

127

wear something warmer. "Nonsense," he said, "it's spring!" I never saw or heard from him again. About a year later I heard that he had been shot in March 1938 – so he spent about ten months in that light suit!' A few days after the arrest of her husband and the day after she had received her diploma as a construction engineer, Ruth Gregorievna was arrested as 'ChSIR' (member of the family of a traitor), an arrest category that is the exact counterpart of the Nazi German *Sippenhaft* (kin arrest). Ruth Gregorievna was asked fifty years after the event whether she had been able to practise her newly won profession of construction engineer while in prison. She answered in the affirmative. 'What did you construct while in prison?' she was asked. 'Prisons,' she answered. After her arrest her two children, Elena and Igor, went to live with their grandmother, Tatiana Matveyevna, and their uncle, Ruth Grigorievna's brother, in Leningrad. In October of 1937 the uncle was arrested for the crime of family relationship with a traitor and imprisoned while his wife was sent into exile. This left Tatiana Matveyevna alone in charge of three grand-children (the third being her son's two-year-old daughter). Her grandchildren survived the Second World War. Tatiana Matvey-evna did not: she died of starvation during the siege of Leningrad. Ruth Grigorievna spent seventeen years in prison camps and exile. She was released in 1954 (a year after the death of Stalin), rehabili-tated and granted a special pension. Her husband, Gevork, was likewise rehabilitated, perforce posthumously. The odyssey of Ruth Grigorievna Bonner and her family – antecedents and descendants (among them especially Elena Bonner) – not only provides a con-trast to the general shelteredness of the scientific community in the Soviet Union; it also constitutes a natural – an organic – complement to that phenomenon.

But the fate of Ruth Grigorievna and her family in the Soviet Union is typical of that of Jews in general who became involved with the Communist Party of the Soviet Union either as members or merely as people – in either or both capacities the Jews played a key role. As Ruth Grigorievna used to say: 'I know nothing about Judaism. I speak not one word of Hebrew or Yiddish. The only language I know is Russian; the only culture I know is Russian. And yet I am Jewish.' In capsule form, this was the problem. The Jews failed to meet Stalin's specifications for ranking as a people because they had no territory. Also, like as not – and like Ruth

Grigorievna – Jews were as Russian as Russian could be. In 1928 the Soviet government made 'the somewhat grotesque attempt to create a national Jewish home' in Birobidzhan, on the waste borders of China. It may be imagined with what success: in the 1959 census the Jewish population of Birobidzhan numbered 14,000 and made up 9 per cent of the total population of the 'national Jewish home' and less than one half of one per cent of the Jewish population of the Soviet Union.

Because they were rejected by conservatives and, in any case, associated conservatism with their own age-old oppression by the establishment of whatever country they happened to be in, Jews inclined overwhelmingly – and especially in Russia – to the political opposition. In pre-revolutionary Russia Jewish youth provided the cadres of revolutionary parties and organizations in large part. This was especially true of the Bund, which was in a class by itself. The Jewish Social Democratic Union (Bund), although specifically Jewish, was the oldest, most active and for a long while the most effective element of the Russian social democratic movement. 'When the first Zionist congress met in Basel in 1897 and in the same year the first all-Russian congress of the Bund took place,' runs the report, 'giving expression to both national and social radicalism, the enthusiasm aroused among the Jews of Russia was vast and overwhelming.' From the very first, then, the contest between Zionism and Communism was given. Theodor Herzl, the founder of Zionism, with his idea of the agrarian production collectives or *kibbutzim*, was a socialist of the first water. The Bund became wholly devoted to Zionism, ultimately providing the leaders and cadres for the founding and building of the State of Israel.

The Bolshevik Party was no exception to the other revolutionary parties: about one half of the Central Committee's members were Jews. All key positions and posts of power within the Central Committee were occupied by Jews. There was Trotsky, the commander and in no small part creator of the Red Army and the political leader second only to Lenin. There was Sverdlov, who headed the regime and was Lenin's right-hand man; Zinoviev, leader of the Comintern and Party boss of Petrograd; Kamenev, Lenin's first deputy in the Council of People's Commissars, manager of the Soviet economy and head of the Moscow Party organization. In the Politburo of 1921 all members excepting only Lenin and Stalin were Jews.

The reason for this extraordinary state of affairs was not only that, to quote a Soviet official, 'formerly we did not have our own intelligentsia, so we had to rely on Jews . . .' but also the comparative lack of Russians in the opposition. As Ruth Grigorievna put it: 'When I grew up in Nikolayev at the beginning of the century I met all sorts of exiled political radicals – Jews, Armenians, Ukrainians, Tartars, Georgians, Circassians – any minority you could shake a stick at – but very, very few Russians.'

Came the revolution all this began to change. Those Russians who had been right to be afraid and afraid to be right suddenly or gradually saw their chance and joined the Party. Inevitably this movement changed the membership proportions of the Party: the massive Jewish membership of a small party became a minority in the larger party and conspicuously concentrated at the top of the power structure. At the Fourteenth Party Congress in December of 1925 Stalin removed the Jewish Party leaders from the centres of power. Trotsky, Zinoviev and Kamenev remained in the Central Committee, but only until the next congress, in 1927, when all three were expelled from the Party. After that it was very seldom indeed that a Jew was elected to the Central Committee. The only exception to this rule was an ominous one: Stalin allowed and – it must be assumed – deliberately cultivated the prevalence of Jews in the police – the Cheka, the OGPU and the NKVD – until the mid-thirties. (Yagoda, whom Stalin 'entrusted' with the organization of the Great Purge, himself became a victim of it when Stalin had him shot in 1938.) The prevalence of Jews in the secret police led to a particularly vicious identification of Jews with rabid Communism on the one hand and of anti-Communism with anti-Semitism on the other. One of the little known chapters of this grim history is the slaughter of Jewish NKVD officers and agents stationed abroad during the Molotov–Ribbentrop Pact period.

Immediately after World War II the Soviet government and its counsels gave little if any thought to the Jewish problem internationally. It should have. For the Soviet vote in the United Nations Organization in favour of the establishment of a Jewish homeland in a partitioned Palestine (or anywhere else outside the Soviet Union) was very much against Soviet interests as these are perceivable or given to be understood by the Soviet Union itself. Instead, the generalissimus and wisest of leaders, now in his declining years and the prey to mounting paranoia, launched a propaganda campaign against 'cosmopolitanism' and 'internationalism' culminating in the so-called 'doctors' plot' in which nine doctors, seven of them Jewish, were arrested on charges of poisoning high-ranking Party officials or causing their deaths by deliberate malpractice.

The 'doctors' plot' provocation was designed by the NKVD to function as a trigger for the mass deportation at short notice of Jews from all the main cities of the USSR. This operation was of course patterned after the mass deportation of the Chechens, Ingush, Kalmyks, Crimean Tartars, Volga Germans and other national minorities to remote regions. As the historian Roy Medvedev reported in his essay of May 1970, 'The Middle East Conflict and the Jewish Question in the USSR', 'In certain areas of Kazakhstan barracks were hurriedly erected for Jews. The text of an Appeal to the Jewish People was prepared for signature by certain prominent representatives of science and culture of Jewish nationality . . .' Grigorii Skvirsky, a former member of the Soviet Writers Union now living in London, recounted the episode of the 'open letter' in some detail:

> 'Establishment Jews' gathered at the *Pravda* combine to put their signatures to an article approving the deportation of all Jews, down to and including children at the breast, purportedly to save them from the wrath of the people . . .
> Lev Kasil, who signed this document after poet E. Dolmatovsky, historian Mints, and others ('How can one get out of doing it?' he muttered), related how Ilya Ehrenburg got up and staggered uncertainly to the door . . . He was the only one who did not append his signature. They looked at him in horror, as at a man falling out of the window of a skyscraper . . .

Ehrenburg wrote a letter to Stalin explaining why the Soviets, in the Jewish question, could not have it both ways. Here are the pertinent passages of the letter:

> I fear that a collective statement by a number of Soviet cultural figures united only by their ethnic origin may strengthen nationalistic tendencies. The text of the letter contains the term 'Jewish people', and this may embolden nationalists and people who have not yet grasped that there is no Jewish nation . . . When the question has been raised on various commissions and at press conferences why there are no Jewish-language schools or newspapers in the

Soviet Union, I have invariably replied that after the war no centres of the former 'pale of settlement' were left, and the new generations of Soviet citizens of Jewish origin do not wish to isolate themselves from the people among which they live. The publication of a letter signed by scholars, writers and composers who speak of a community of Soviet Jews may whip up the loathsome anti-Soviet propaganda that the Zionists, Bundists and other enemies of our fatherland are now conducting . . . I am convinced that it is necessary to fight energetically against any attempts to resurrect Jewish nationalism, which inevitably leads to treason . . .

The death of the dictator forestalled the implementation of this product of delirium and spared the Soviet Union a public-relations nightmare that just might have changed the course of history. The very idea of the mass deportation of Soviet Jews from their urban residence to a barracks life in Kazakhstan – and this on the heels of the Holocaust – belongs to the Cloud-cuckoo-land of political grotesquerie: it overtaxes credulity. And yet even without this Wagnerian encore, the signal dupes in the revolutionary process in the Russian empire were the Jews. They aided and paid for the prospered treason of the Russian Revolution – man for man, woman for woman – as no other people aided and paid. The Jewish revolutionaries, in their great majority, were Mensheviks, the original social democrats who envisioned the new Russia as a loose federation of autonomous nation states. They ran afoul – not by choice but by fate – of both the Bolsheviks (whose centralism ruled out any sort of effective autonomy) and the Ukrainians (whose separatism opposed any sort of autonomy within the traditional borders of the Ukraine – and most Jews lived in the Ukraine). Hence the Jewish problem in the Soviet Union remained not only unsolved but unaddressed.

In the Russian (Plekhanov) reading of Marx's tenet, all historical changes are due to the development of tools. It is hardly surprising that this view should have been popularized in 'the homeland of socialism' since the theory and foundation of socialism itself was the result of the application of scientific method to the regulation of human society. 'Karl Marx, Friedrich Engels and Vladimir Ilyich Lenin were, above all great thinkers and scientists,' wrote Zhores Medvedev in his book, *The Rise and Fall of T. D. Lysenko*:

They were creating Communism as a science concerned with the forms of development of human society. They were establishing the

132

doctrine of Communism as a social and economic system, acceptable to all mankind, guaranteeing the equal, just, rapid and friendly development of all nations on earth. The scientific method of Marx, Engels and Lenin was the method of proofs, the method of analysis of facts and of arriving at truth. It is precisely because of this that Marxism has always attracted the minds of progressive scientists.

It is a statement that suits oddly with the saga of Ruth Grigorievna Bonner and her family – but is therefore all the more effective in the provision of contrast between the real and the imaginary. But then Medvedev is describing the situation, from firsthand knowledge, in the scientific community up to but not including the year 1935.

An unprecedented number of discussions took place in 1935–7 in all fields of science, the arts and literature. As a rule, because of the historical conditions, they all were harsh. Differences of opinion, approach, method and evaluation of facts are completely natural occurrences in science. Truth is born from argument. But in the environment of the massive repressions of the thirties, the spy hunts and centralized inflaming of passions, and under the conditions of a feverish search after the 'enemies of the people' in all spheres of human activity, any scientific discussion tended to become a struggle with political undertones. Nearly every discussion ended tragically for the side represented by the more noble, intellectual, honest and calm men, who based their arguments on scientific facts ... In that period, making political accusations was the easiest and most tempting method of vanquishing opponents who could not be subdued by the force of scientific argumentation. There were some who took that road, which often led not only to a rout but also to actual physical elimination of scientific opponents.

The struggle described by Medvedev broke out in 1929 first, specifically, in biology and then in genetics. The outbreak, of course, was not unconnected with the final phase of Stalin's consolidation of his power and the beginning of the intensive drive for the collectivization of agriculture which led directly into the great famine in the Ukraine and north Caucasus. Quite the contrary; it was the great famine that led to the Great Purge.

VI

❧

LYSENKO:
'THAT WAS THE MOST TERRIBLE YEAR'

Much, if not everything, that happened in the series of purges in the thirties in the Soviet Union was conceived in the shadow of the famine of 1932–3. The event itself was the result of a reaction to the New Economic Policy in the twenties. The Bolsheviks, in their fear of a return to capitalism, looked with increasing apprehension at the liberated and enfranchised peasants. In 1927, 98.3 per cent of the sown area in the Soviet Union was owned by individual peasants. As a result of the NEP and its seven-year flirtation with a market economy the percentage of kulaks (*kulak* means 'fist' in Russian and is used here in the sense of being 'tight-fisted') had risen from 2.8 in 1922 to 6.1 in 1925. The label kulak, as applied by the Bolsheviks, was extremely elastic, including as it did the variation 'semi-kulak'. Originally anyone with two horses, two cows, enough land to provide a square meal throughout the year with something left over to sell qualified for the designation. In the event the Bolsheviks used the term to target anyone they wanted to dispossess.

Another problem contributing to the classical motivation to collectivize was the fact that while the peasants were 'flourishing', the saleable surplus for the town markets was diminishing. Bread rationing was introduced in the provinces in 1928 and in Moscow and Leningrad in 1929. Hereupon Stalin suddenly reversed Lenin's policy of non-violent persuasion of the peasantry and launched a crash programme for the total collectivization of agriculture. The consequence was incredible turmoil bordering on civil war in the countryside. In three months, January to March 1930, 10 million peasant holdings were collectivized. Over half of all peasant holdings were collectivized in five months. The peasants defended their property with shotguns, daggers, axes and knives. And they slaughtered their livestock rather than leave it to the collective farms. Finally, they refused to stay in the kolkhozes. The collectivization drive was a fiasco and recognized as such.

But nothing happened. The reason why nothing happened is to be found in the nature of the Party. It had been observed as early as the Kronstadt revolt that whenever the Party came under fire for whatever reason there was a tendency on the part of Party members to stop bickering among themselves and close ranks in the solidarity of a perimeter defence. This is what happened most signally after the failure of Stalin's all-out collectivization drive, which even Stalin admitted was a mistake, while blaming over-zealous subordinates. Then, instead of taking advantage of the great groundswell of disgust and defiance in the countryside and in general that followed, the 'Rightists' in the Politburo – Bukharin, Rykov and Tomsky – made it known that they would never dream of siding with the peasants against 'the Party'. This attitude appertains generically to the code of thieves' honour – the anathema of 'ratting' on the gang and particularly the gang-leader, regardless of what the issue may be. It also lays bare the mechanism that made Stalinism inevitable, namely the siege mentality of the Party. This was what Lenin meant in 1923 when he said, 'We are living in a sea of illegality.' Either the Party laid siege to the population or the population laid siege to the Party. It is the core-meaning of the Marxist–Leninist slogan, 'who [does what to] whom?' Since Stalin had taken over the leadership of the Party and directed its main actions, this meant the equation of Stalin with the Party and hence siding with Stalin in the name of the Party in any and all failures of policy. Policy successes, on the other hand, accrued of themselves to the advantage of Stalin.

The result of all this was that Stalin did not regain but was regiven the initiative. It was restored to him by his opponents acting in true solidarity. He went on to reorganize and intensify the total collectivization drive, and compounded the disaster. Thus the siege mentality of the Party contributed directly to the fabrication of the only man-made famine in world history, the famine of 1932–3 in which anywhere from 5 to 6 million people died, at least 3 million of them Ukrainians ('the men first, then the children and finally the women'). This, then, is what was behind 'the environment of the massive repressions ... the spy hunts and centralized inflaming of passions ... a feverish search after the "enemies of the people" in all spheres of human activity in which "any scientific discussion tended to become a struggle with political undertones", with nearly every discussion ending tragically for those who based their arguments on scientific facts.' In this passage Medvedev is describing what came to be known as the Great Purge.

The struggle in biology and then in genetics in the Soviet Union was thus by no means merely the age-old controversy between heredity and environment, or between 'nature and nurture' as the modern alliteration would have it. In the Russia of Lenin and Stalin the controversy inevitably received the twist of the 'biological versus the social'. The revolutionary founders of the Soviet Union believed that they could build a 'new Soviet man' by creating a new social environment. This, after all, was what Marx was all about and it was what kept them going: that it was possible to re-make man in the image of an ideological absolute by changing his environment. Under pressure of the politicization of everything, this tenet forced the entry of ideology into the sciences. 'Some, however, especially among the younger scientists,' writes Med-vedev, 'broadened the front to include "bourgeois tendencies" in science, extending it to many areas of natural sciences. They attempted to apply the class approach even to problems that could only be worked out experimentally, under either a socialist or a capitalist environment.' The dispute in the science of genetics involved 'the problem of inheritance and acquired characteristics and the reality of the gene as a hereditary substance'. But even marking the impatience of a political leadership made up of revolu-tionaries imbued with a totalitarian ideology, the creation of the 'new Soviet man' was obviously a long-term project susceptible to a wide variety of theoretical animadversions. There were also more practical and far more pressing projects. In 1935–6 genetics was no longer merely academic. The science was also called upon to serve as the theoretical basis of plant and animal selection, seed growing and plant breeding. The emphasis on plant and animal breeding came as a result of the drought and crop failures of 1921 and the famine that followed. This predicament also led to a radical change in the method of crop distribution. Considering the depleted state of its finances and its lack of various other resources, such as qualified agronomists, the Soviet Union made a massive effort to improve and expand its agricultural productivity, sending teams of scouts to enlist foreign experts, and new hybrid specimens and information. (Tsarist Russia, although predominantly an agricultural country, had probably the most backward farming practices in the civilized world.) But the driving force of the Soviet state was an explosive mixture of great needs, great expectations and great convictions, the latter stemming from the central certainty that they were in possession of a creed-cum-science which, if correctly applied, could solve any and all problems. All this made for a situation which was virtually destined to produce one or more like Trofim Denisovich Lysenko.

Lysenko was a botanist who was catapulted to fame with his discovery of 'vernalization', which is described as 'an agronomic practice whereby winter crops are obtained from summer planting' (Medvedev). Working in what is now Kirovobad in Georgia, Lysenko discovered that winter forms of cereal sown in the spring instead of the autumn will produce spikes after first exposing the seed to cold. This was widely hailed in the Soviet media as the transformation of winter into spring cereals. In 1929, some three years later, Lysenko's father had sown seeds of the winter variety (which wintered under the snow) in the spring and had obtained a yield of twenty-four centners per hectare. The sensational aspects of this achievement, for which Lysenko the younger in effect took credit, were heightened against the background of the massive losses of winter crops in the Ukraine because of frost in the years 1927–8. Vernalization was seized upon as a possible saviour from further disasters of this sort. A special department of vernalization was created in the Odessa Institute of Genetics and Breeding by decision of the commissariats of agriculture of both the Ukraine and the USSR and Trofim Lysenko installed therein. It was the beginning of a wholly extraordinary career.

In the period 1931–4 Lysenko advanced a theory of 'the phasic development of plants' which was hailed in the thirties as 'an outstanding achievement of Soviet science'. But meanwhile it developed that vernalization was not the panacea it had been taken to be. It was soon shifted to use with spring forms since the yields of the winter varieties first used were found to be decreasing. The shift involved soaking the seeds of wheat and other crops for several days, turning them over constantly, under controlled humidity and temperature conditions – a complicated and time-consuming procedure. Seeds sown in this moist, swollen condition were supposed to have a vegetative phase that was shorter by several days. If the second half of the summer was too dry this treatment forestalled or at least foreshortened the exposure of the crop to drought (which allayed the parallel shift from the fear of frost to the fear of drought). It was soon discovered, however, that Lysenko's real talent lay in the detection and application of political analogies. Here, as an example, is a passage from Lysenko's speech at the Second All-Union Congress of Shock Collective Farmers in 1935. The speech was delivered with Stalin and all members of the government in attendance:

> In fact, comrades, while vernalization created by Soviet reality could in a relatively short period of some four to five years become a whole branch of science, could fight off all the attacks of the class enemy (and there were more than a few), there is still much to do. Comrades, kulak-wreckers occur not only in your collective farm life. You know them very well. But they are no less dangerous, no less sworn enemies also in science. No little blood was spilled in the defence of vernalization in the various debates with some so-called scientists, in the struggle for its establishment; not a few blows had to be borne in practice. Tell me, comrades, was there not a class struggle on the vernalization front? In the collective farms there were kulaks and their abettors who kept whispering (and they were not the only ones, every class enemy did) into the peasants' ears: 'Don't soak the seeds. It will ruin them.' This is the way it was, such were the whispers, such were the kulak and saboteur deceptions, when, instead of helping collective farmers, they did their destructive business, both in the scientific world and out of it; a class enemy is always an enemy whether he is a scientist or not.

At the end of the speech Stalin exclaimed: 'Bravo, Comrade Lysenko, bravo!' Stalin understood, namely, that the gathering storm within the Soviet scientific community over genetics was a great deal more than a controversy over planting and breeding theories and practices or even a resolution of the heredity or environment issue. What was at stake here was the assertion or the disavowal of Marxism as a creed. What was at stake here was the assertion of Marxism as the central science of all sciences. 'You cannot eliminate even one basic assumption, one substantial part of this philosophy of Marxism,' wrote Lenin in his book, *Materialism and Empiric Criticism*, which became the Soviet Bible, 'without abandoning objective truth, without falling into the arms of bourgeois-reactionary falsehood.' Lenin had swallowed Marx whole and there was nothing for it. (There was a parallel development at the first congress of the Soviet Writers Union in 1934 when the theory of socialist realism was propounded and included in its statutes: 'Socialist realism, which constitutes the basic method of Soviet artistic literature and literary criticism, demands from the artist a truthful historico-concrete representation of reality in its revolutionary development.') Science, however, in general and in particular, is international, objective and neutral by its very nature. It was clear to Stalin as it had been to Lenin that Marxism would either dominate science or science would dominate Marxism – and ultimately destroy it. This was particularly so since Russian science was comparatively weak – a number of outstanding theorists not-withstanding – as compared with the rest of the civilized world. (The first sixteen members of the Russian Academy of Sciences were imported from Western Europe by Peter the Great, its first students were eight young men from Vienna.) Since Marxism claimed to be wholly scientific the Soviet Union was quite simply constrained to adopt an aggressively arrogant and arrogating posture in regard to the rest of the world on any and all scientific matters. Science was the Achilles heel of the Soviet Union because the Marxian claim to scientific legitimacy was fraudulent. The spirit of orthodox Communism is thoroughly unscientific. In the teeth of Vladimir Lenin's above-quoted *noli me tangere* attitude to the basic assumptions of Marxism, the first principle of the scientific approach is the vigilant criticism and constant questioning of *all* basic assumptions. There is nothing sacred in science except this principal method. Lenin's outlawing of the civilized industrialized world as 'bourgeois-reactionary' was in reality the outlawing of the Soviet Union itself. This was the essential element in his criminalization of the Soviet state. The gradual realization of this fact in the comity of nations brought down upon the Soviet Union such epithets as 'rogue elephant' and more recently 'evil empire'. But this constraint of Soviet policy – domestic as well as foreign – worked a self-imposed quarantine of the Soviet Union among the nations chiefly in communications but also in all other transactions as well – excepting only espionage. The case of Trofim Denisovich Lysenko was made to order for the Soviet purpose of claiming a monopoly position on all sciences on the grounds of a new departure in plant breeding unencumbered by bourgeois prejudice and, above all, productive of sensationally successful yields. If Lysenko's claims had been scientifically valid and borne out in the event, the Soviets would have been in a key position from which to continue their psychological war of conquest of men's minds. As it was the Soviets were in much the same position as the schoolmen in Galileo's time: they were not interested in the truth about nature but in the nature of truth – of which they firmly believed themselves to be in possession. In the spring of 1937 a fifteen-year-old schoolboy named Andrei Sakharov read an article in *Izvestia* that was a blistering attack on 'Morganism and Weismannism',* shook his head and shuddered. 'That,' he said fifty years later, 'was the most terrible year.'

But the Communist Church was young and its claims were fully as extensive as those of the Catholic Church and its enemies even more numerous; the main struggle lay ahead. Lysenko twitted the classical geneticists with the fact that no one had ever seen a gene regardless of the strength of the microscope he might be using, an attitude not unlike those Churchmen who refused to look into Galileo's telescope or could not make out the rings of Saturn when they did. In much the same fashion as in Galileo's time the argument shifted from theoretical discussion to *ad hominem* attacks and accusations of disloyalty. This was, of course, the time of the Great Terror, of the Kremlin show trials in which Stalin rid himself of the entirety of the old Bolshevik leadership, culminating in the executions of Kamenev, Zinoviev and Bukharin, in addition to tens of thousands of Party officials and army officers (among them Marshal Tukhachevsky) on the pretence of treason, styling his victims 'wreckers' and 'enemies of the people'. It was the orgiastic triumph in the long process of a master-criminal's settling accounts. This long process of annihilation served as a reservoir for the Party faithful in the sciences or on the fringe of the sciences from

* A major obstacle in the way of Lysenko and 'Soviet science' was the person of Gregor Johann Mendel (1822–84). It was he who discovered the 'Mendelian', or hereditary, laws which categorically deny that acquired characteristics can be inherited in man. Two of his most significant disciples were the American Nobel laureate Thomas Hunt Morgan (1866–1945) and the German August Weismann (1843–1914). On Lysenko's side there stood Ivan Vladimirovich Michurin (1855–1935) who wrote a book called *Concerning the Inapplicability of Mendelian Laws in Bastardization*.

which they could draw for their political attacks on the scientists proper. Thus all 'classical scientists', that is, those who refused to bend scientific principles to suit the interests of the Party, were labelled 'Trotskyite agents of international Fascism', 'knights of the gene', 'minions of Bukharin' and accused of using science as a front for espionage, etc. The scientist turncoat who was willing to prostitute his profession to the Communist cause was worth his weight in diamonds. Thus the safest man in the Soviet Union was undoubtedly Lysenko. His enemies were too noble to resort to underhand methods to encompass his downfall while his friends, although ideological thugs, were too dependent on him and what he represented even to dream of removing him for whatever reason. The most endangered of the species by the same token was Nikolai Ivanovich Vavilov, Lysenko's chief opponent by virtue of his standing as a noted scientist and his capacity as president of the Lenin All-Union Academy of Agricultural Sciences (LAAAS) and the All-Union Institute of Plant Breeding (AIPB). Vavilov, moreover, was a man of character and highly regarded internationally. Given his integrity it was precisely his prominence that spelled his doom: he was the perfect 'fall-guy' for the system. It took just half a dozen years of concentrated slander to bring Vavilov to ground. He was taken on 6 August 1940 while on a plant gathering expedition in the western Ukraine. His interrogation began on 12 August 1940 in the 'internal prison', as it is called, of the NKVD (today's KGB) in Moscow. First Lieutenant Khvat (a relevant name: it means 'grab' or 'catch') began the interrogation with the words: 'You are under arrest as an active participant in an anti-Soviet wrecking organization and as a spy employed by foreign intelligence services . . .

'Do you admit your guilt?'

According to the Soviet report Lieutenant Khvat cannot have been satisfied with Vavilov's answer because he went on to interrogate the wretched innocent who stood before him an even 400 times in the eleven months before his trial, which lasted less than ten minutes. (In these interrogations Vavilov was forced to stand for as long as ten hours at a time.) It took Khvat twelve days to break Vavilov ('. . . the investigating judge was an inquisitor of the Beria school . . .'). On 24 August Vavilov signed his confession. But Khvat achieved much more: he forced Vavilov to compose a completely fantastic twelve-page declaration entitled 'Sabotage activity in the Institute for Plant Research, which was directed by me from 1929 until my arrest on 6 August 1940'. What Khvat could not do was force Vavilov to confess to espionage for a foreign power. But what Vavilov had confessed to, his declaration with the resounding title, was more than enough to suit the purpose of his tormentors. Here the author of the report has an interesting comment: 'Not only torture, humiliation and sleepless nights forced Vavilov to write such a thing, but rather his firm conviction that his fate had been decided in advance, that it made no sense whatever to stand on his rights and deny the slanders, that it was senseless to offer resistance.' This supposition, if this is all it is, is not far-fetched. Vavilov had lived through the Walpurgisnacht of the Great Terror in which the Party and military leadership had been cut down like so many weeds. After the spectacle of the show trials no one in the Soviet Union close to the events could believe that, once arrested, there was in any case brought before the courts the slightest chance that justice would somehow assert itself.

Even so, these matters were far better managed by the Soviets when the science in question was clearly relevant to military needs. Sergei Pavlovich Korolyev, physicist and aeronautical construction engineer, like his colleague and rival Wernher von Braun, had the fortune in misfortune to come under military sponsorship at an early stage of his career. Korolyev had the particular misfortune, as it turned out (having formed GIRD – Group for the Study of Rocket Propulsion), to catch the eye of Marshal Tukhachevsky, 'the best brain in the Red Army', who was executed as a traitor in May 1937 in the course of the Great Terror. (Wernher von Braun, with his group, came under the wing of the German General Staff at the same time, the year 1931.) In addition to Korolyev among the dozens of aeronautical engineers arrested and imprisoned in the wake of the Tukhachevsky execution was Korolyev's friend, Alexander Tupolyev, one of the foremost aeronautical designers in the country.

In 1939 Stalin had the foresight to transfer Tupolyev to a factory prison in the centre of Moscow for the purpose of constructing military aircraft. Tupolyev demanded the assistance of Korolyev who was thus saved from a death-camp in Siberia. Korolyev, like Tupolyev, remained a prisoner until 1945 when he was sent on a special mission to the German V–2 factory at Peenemünde. There he picked up several of the V-2 propulsion engines developed by the Wernher von Braun group and returned to an aeronautical construction complex at Kapustin Yar on the southern Volga. From these he developed the first in the Soviet series of propulsion engines RD-107. Korolyev was given the rank of colonel of artillery (shades of Galileo and the *virtuosi*) as a reward for this achievement. But he was still kept under surveillance, even though no longer a prisoner. Indeed, he did not lose his 'tail' until Stalin died. Then he was offered Party membership, which he was quick to apply for as a means of enjoying greater independence.

In 1956 Korolyev persuaded Khrushchev that he could steal a march on the Americans by being the first to send an artificial satellite into orbit in celebration of the Universal Geophysical Year, 1957. This was the conception of the Sputnik sensation, which was followed by the first man in space, Yuri Gagarin. The sensation of the Soviet space lead was complete – complete but of brief date: in less than ten years the Americans had put men – and a jeep, a 'moonmobile' – on the moon, a feat the Soviets have been unable to duplicate or otherwise trump to this day, at the close of the second decade after the event. Korolyev was a genius of improvisation, working with the aeronautical equivalents of shoestring and sealing-wax. He had nothing like the wealth of facilities and materials available to the Americans. The American moon-shot was a triumph of Korolyev's inveterate rival Wernher von Braun and his team. The von Braun group was brought over to the United States more or less intact, given American citizenship and virtual *carte blanche* in a crash programme to win the race to the moon. Korolyev did not live to see Armstrong put his foot on the moon: he died in January 1966 of a heart attack in his sixtieth year, well aware that the Soviet Union had already lost the space race.

As for Vavilov, on 9 July 1941, the military collegium of the Supreme Court, consisting of three persons (the traditional *troika* favoured by Communists and Fascists), after sitting for only a few minutes (the statutory period in both Communism and Fascism) found him guilty under Article 58 of the Soviet Criminal Code on a number of counts: belonging to a rightist conspiracy; spying for England (Vavilov was elected president of the International Congress of Genetics in Edinburgh in 1939; he was denied permission to travel); leadership of the Labour Peasant Party; sabotage in agriculture; links with White *émigrés*, etc. Vavilov denied all charges. He was sentenced to death. His sentence was later commuted to ten years' imprisonment where he died in late 1942 of malnutrition and exposure (Vavilov's imprisonment coincided with the German invasion of the Soviet Union with the result that he had to be moved, apparently several times, during the winter of 1941–2).

With the fall of Vavilov, Lysenkoism emerged triumphant in all sciences in the Soviet Union with an agricultural application, a remarkable parallel to Lysenko's controversy with the geneticists having taken place in agronomy with the grassland system advocated by the academician V. R. Vilyams. This was a system of planting in the rotation a 30 to 40 per cent mixture of legumes and cereal grasses for the induction and maintenance of soil texture, which Vilyams considered to be all-important. For this method of planting in fine-textured, lumpy soil (according to Vilyams the only fertile kind) he claimed that yields could be increased tenfold. These claims were based on no data whatever – no experiments were performed (Vilyams refused to allow experimental comparisons of his system with any other method of crop rotation) – the only basis being the 'abstract consideration of the water-holding capacities of different kinds of soils'. How, asks Medvedev, was Vilyams able to hypnotize the planning organs into accepting on faith 'his fantastic promises of 100 to 160 centners per hectare yields of wheat merely from the decomposition of roots of perennial cereals'? Medvedev concludes that behind Vilyams's apparent use of dialectics lay demagoguery, 'a calculating talent for slandering, discrediting and defaming his scientific opponents. Vilyams and his school were people who knew how to exploit the tragic atmosphere of the reigning personality cult for their own ends.' Employing the methods described, they were directly responsible (as was, of course, his friend Lysenko to an even larger extent) for the incarceration and death – either by execution or suicide – of dozens if not indeed hundreds of scientists. For this Vilyams and Lysenko were officially praised, not blamed. By accusing the pupils of the eminent botanist D. N. Pryanishnikov, who held the chair of plant breeding at the Moscow Agricultural Institute, Vilyams encompassed the arrest of twelve scientists in the All-Union Institute of Fertilizers including its director Zaporozhets (the institute was the brain-child of Pryanishnikov). This feat was hailed in the central press of the Soviet Union: 'For a long time,' wrote one Lyashchenko, a follower of Vilyams,

a group of the enemies of the people operated in the institute ... These, if you will forgive the expression, 'agricultural chemists' undertook to work out the methodology of map-making. Yearning for the kulak economy where from time immemorial they had conducted experiments on fertilizers, these latter-day 'agricultural chemists' used all possible means to turn soil maps into a break against raising yields ... The enemies of the people operating in the institute were unmasked and rendered harmless ... But sabotage in this area is not yet weeded out. The commissariat, the LAAAS and the Fertilizer Institute do nothing to crush the nests of enemies.

At times the contrasting sobriety of the classical scientists under attack provided a kind of comic relief. Thus, at a plenary discussion of soil maps by the section of agricultural chemistry and soil science of the LAAAS, it was noted that

the conduct of the chairman of the session, Pryanishnikov, was surprising. Every time a comrade went beyond the framework of purely technical matters and touched on the wrecking activities of the enemies of the people ... the chairman would interrupt him.

The plenary session condemned the speech and the behaviour of Pryanishnikov at the meeting as being unworthy of a Soviet scientist.

Later, in an article entitled 'Mercilessly to Uproot the Enemies and their Riff-raff from Scientific Establishments', Pryanishnikov was commemorated again:

The last plenary session ... provides an example of the attitude of some academicians towards the problem of liquidating the consequences of sabotage. The scientific community remembers that the chairman, Pryanishnikov, openly declared: 'It is not the business of the Academy to occupy itself with the consequences of sabotage; that is the prerogative of other organs.' And the Academy presidium never even discussed this revolting fact.

The upshot of the discussions on soil maps was the acceptance of Vilyams's proposals. These foresaw the continuation of soil maps but without the designation of the chemical content of the soil. Instead the maps, following Vilyams's bent, were to provide morphological descriptions and characterizations of soil texture.

Indeed, with the help of such vigilantes as Vilyams the Lysenkoists carried the day and dominated Soviet agriculture, replacing most of the conventional scientists in key positions in relevant institutes, academies and ministries by the end of the thirties. But their domination, fortunately for the Soviet Union, was never complete. Hence despite Vilyams's unflagging crusade against chemical fertilizers, Pryanishnikov and his colleagues were able to insist on the construction of fertilizer factories, readily convertible to the production of explosives. It would be difficult to exaggerate the importance of the existence of such factories when the Germans invaded without warning on 21 June 1941.

VII

'OPPIE': THE RISE...

Galileo – his persona, his achievements, his faults and failures, his fame, his trial and his fate – symbolizes as no other contemporary figure the caesura, the watershed, between the old and the new histories and the Old and the New Worlds. Not by coincidence did Cristoforo Colombo and Amerigo Vespucci set forth from the same traditional environment, the same country and in the same general era to discover the New World and give it their names. The same urge that drove mankind to leave the old era behind them and enter a new one ... the same knowledge that the whole course of civilization had somehow gone wrong ... that same urge drove men across uncharted seas to seek a New World, a fitting place for mankind to make a new start. There is also a clear coincidence, a perfect superimposition of the one – historical – concept on the other – territorial–geographical. The coincidence was deliberate: the beginning of the New World was the beginning of a new history, perhaps even the beginning of a new era with no history. Two New Worlds, one in time and one in space. That there should have been an interaction between these two concepts – the desire for the one spurring the desire and acquisition of the other – and that the men and women from the old time and the old place with all their old ways still about them and all their old sins on their heads should be the ones to undertake this acquisition effecting yet another interaction, one between the old and the new – all this is obvious enough. But the plenitude of new impulse that should inevitably come from so vast and splendid a new place – in sum an entire hemisphere – who could have foreseen this – so overwhelming a promise? In this regard the sheer sparsity of inhabitants in both North and South America played an immense role in the colonization and, later, in the decolonization and political liberation of the New World, particularly of North America. What Galileo really did was give the two New Worlds to each other – in a colossal explosion of unforeseen, unsuspected and undreamed-of possibilities, potentialities, urges, impulses, drives, obsessions, passions and convictions – all of them connected with the dream that was one with the reality of the one planet in the firmament which Galileo had never seen in his telescope, the *terra incognita* of his own earth, the Western hemisphere.

In this regard, too, the horrible simplifications introduced by the Galilean methodology were made to order for the conquistadors, the explorers, the frontiersmen and the pioneers. Simplification means a *reductio ad usum* but it brings with it a concentration on a select few to the exclusion of everything else. Because of this the new science received in its turn a tremendous impulsion from the New World.

In the history of humankind there have been three great all-embracing tides of romantic influences. Christianity (as the foremost of the world religions), science (particularly the natural sciences, more particularly physics, most particularly the technological revolution), America – the 'other world', 'real world' and 'new world' respectively. The romanticism involved in all three movements – and we are dealing with a convergence of all three when we treat modern history since Galileo – increased the simplification explicit and inherent in Galileo's methodology. It became, in the romantic view, a magic formula. There was also a radical simplification manifested in the dealings of the new men of the Old World with the old inhabitants of the New World, a savagery on the part of the cultured Europeans which is perhaps best summed up in Pizarro's statement to the Inca king: 'We Europeans are here because we suffer from a terrible disease for which there is only one cure: gold!' Add to this the fact that the New World was virtually untouched, let alone civilized. The conquistadors had some reason to believe that they were dealing with savages, at least enough to justify their own brutality regarding the natives in the eyes of the civilized world for several centuries. The roughness and readiness of the American pioneer, hunter, trapper, cowboy, lumberjack *et al.* promoted simplification applied and imposed as a way of life. A running roughshod over the niceties, the subtleties, the nuances, the *caveats* and qualifications and, above all, the proprieties of any situation has always been one of the chief American behavioural delights. It was the informing spirit of American vaudeville and remains the guiding principle of American comedy.

But the savagery of the conquerors and the natives was as nothing as compared with the savagery of the American climate in most places – extreme heat and humidity in summer and extreme cold in the winter. This was nature in the raw as few Europeans had even imagined it. Nature in America did not ask or require inventiveness; it demanded inventiveness. The only answer to the challenge of the New World was the machine. For the pioneer, life is a permanent revolution. Demands had to be met on a daily basis. By the middle of the nineteenth century the United States of America began to make themselves felt as a prime force in the Industrial Revolution.

On terms of polity the United States exercised an equally strong attraction to the tired and disillusioned humanity of Europe. In *An Inquiry into the Rights of the British Colonies* (1766), a Stamp Act pamphlet, Richard Bland affirmed that Americans had exercised their natural right of quitting the country (Great Britain): 'Becoming private adventurers, they established themselves, without any expense to the nation, in this uncultivated and almost uninhabited country.' Expatriation, Bland pointed out, is an implicit rejection of the contract with the sovereign: 'When men exercise this right, and withdraw themselves from their country, they recover their natural freedom and independence. The jurisdiction and sovereignty of the state they have quitted ceases.' This argument was picked up by Thomas Jefferson in his instruction to the 1774 delegation when he observed that Americans 'possessed a right, which nature has given to all men, of departing from the country in which chance, not choice, has placed them, of going in quest of new habitations, and of there establishing new societies, under such laws and regulations as to them shall seem most likely to promote public happiness'.

This is an expression of what became, knowingly or unknowingly, the *raison d'être*, the ideological charter of all emigrants-cum-immigrants everywhere for as long as the rule by law under the principle of equal representation should last.

Of course these principles and considerations derived directly from the dangers the colonists had known, the risk they had willingly taken and the ordeals they had survived. There is this essential connection between the roughness and readiness that characterized the New World and the political, moral and cultural philosophical systems that gradually emerged from it. There is a certain – and altogether prerequisite – recklessness involved in the very act, the implemented decision, of becoming an emigrant-immigrant. Emigration – even so-called 'inner-emigration' – is *ipso facto* a protest. Immigration, on the other hand, is a challenge, a double challenge – to the immigrant himself and to his former country. Thus, as with the historical New World which is in large part the new science, so with the geographical–geopolitical New World that is America there is the eternal promise of perfection – Utopia, but a geographically fixed Utopia: 'We know where it is, if only we can get there.' 'El Dorado', 'gold in the streets', 'where money grows on trees', 'the land of opportunity' where 'every man gets an even break' – the clichés are endless, homegrown no less than foreign-made: the 'Fair Deal', the 'New Deal', the 'Land of Promise' . . . And in spite of everything, the heartbreak of dashed illusions, the raw cruelty of the New World, the hardness of life in America: from the very beginning of mass immigration to America a full 10 per cent of the immigrants sooner or later give up and go back to where they came from – to this day. But in spite of everything and because of everything the promise is always there: the dream that is America, the New World, persists. The attraction of America persists undiminished as does immigration to 'the land of the free and the home of the brave'. The odd thing, the piquant thing, is that because all – or almost all – the claims about America are at best only half true there is the eternal expectation that the other half will come true: the fact that the dream remains un-realized is the very reason the promise of its realization remains upright and fully operative. Of course there is poverty in America (although it is, to be sure, a special kind of poverty); of course there is prejudice – class prejudice and race prejudice – in America. But here again, it is of a very special kind – and reduced. To be rich or poor does not represent a status but a condition. To be sure: America, the New World, is at best a half-truth; but a half-truth in a country that is a continent of unfathomable wealth is pretty good. And then, too, there is no doubt about it: many of the barriers are down. For the formulation of the new order ('*novus ordo seclorum'*) was not just rhetoric – 'We hold these truths to be self-evident . . .' wrote Thomas Jefferson in the Declaration of Independence – it was also manifested and guaranteed in the separation of powers. (German newspapers reported the scandal concerning the Pentagon Papers with headlines proclaiming the 'Supreme Court's Decision against the Government', ignoring the fact that the judiciary is part of the government.) In America, in the New World, you cannot tell who or what a man is by the way he speaks or the way he dresses – neither by his manners nor his manner. Carl Zuckmayer, the eminent German playwright, re-counted his meeting with a man in the Oyster Bar of Grand Central Station whom he took to be a bookkeeper – perhaps a certified public accountant. When the German made bold enough to ask the stranger what he did for a living, the latter obliged forthwith: he was a harpoonist.

The dream of the New World that is half-realized in America and still promised was born in the American Revolution and gave the French Revolution its proudest battle-cry: *'La carrière ouverte aux talents'* (perhaps best translated as, 'What sort of career you make depends entirely and only on your talent'), in place of the Old World's insistence on 'the lifetime fixation of function'. But the geographical–geopolitical New World America offered something still better: this was something also distinctively and genuinely new. As the fame of the 'land of opportunity' spread like wildfire throughout the Old World, America became the reservoir and place of residence of a sort of international élite of the reckless – whether reckless by nature, persuasion or coercion – the collection point where takes place the fraternization of strangers driven to a common destination by their apprehension of peril or worse than peril: boredom and hopelessness: west towards home. Thus the 'heritages' that make up the American nation cannot in any sense be regarded as national minorities. They are rather the opposite. They are in a sense delegate populations from their countries of origin, integrated into a supra-national ethic that happened to be harboured geographically on the continent of North America. This was the original sense of the New World – a homeland for human-ity at large, as couched in the inscription on the base of the Statue of Liberty in New York harbour, facing the open sea.

The American nation is not ethnic in any conventional sense. So many ethnicities as there are in America make for no ethnicity.

Sociologists have noted that it is the lack of ethnic grounding of Americans that is responsible for their quest of status. But the American nation is ethical in every conceivable sense. The all-important point of reference for America is that the *ethos* has replaced the *ethnos*. The informing spirit of the American nation is the ethic. This is why morality and idealism are the insistent strains in the American tradition. For the ethic is the stuff – and it is the only stuff – that binds the nation together: it is not only the basis of national identification, it is in fact the national identity itself. (The American obsession with the literal truth, the national fixation on lying and dissembling as the supreme form of evil stems from the same root. 'Father, I cannot tell a lie: I did it with my little hatchet,' says the child in the myth of George Washington and the cherry tree. European psychiatrists report that Americans alone among their patients drum the word 'hypocrite' to describe people they dislike or hold responsible for wrongdoing.)

It is this new identity based on the ethic rather than on race, religion or ethnicity that constitutes the uniqueness of America. 'Anybody can be an American,' said the German actor Curt Dubois not long ago. '*I* was an American.' Ah, yes. But America is the only nation on earth which lends itself willingly, openly, premeditatedly and triumphantly to this claim. 'The German government,' said a former Soviet naval officer and defector in his late fifties just recently, 'wants me to take German citizenship: after all, I have lived here in Germany more than twenty years now. And yet, I cannot be a German. But I could be an American – I could be an American with every fibre of my being!' The New World that is America offers a new identity – a new personal identity as well as a new national identity: a man can shed his identity (with his old name, if he wishes) and become a new man in the New World.

Shortly after World War II a traveller crossing the English Channel met an American businessman on the Golden Arrow, the crack train running between London and Paris. The traveller noticed that the American spoke with a heavy foreign accent, nothing at all unusual in itself but the traveller thought he recognized the accent and asked accordingly. Said the businessman, 'I immigrated to America from Germany.' Thereupon the traveller began speaking German with the businessman and to his astonishment detected a foreign accent in the businessman's German – and asked accordingly. 'I was,' grinned the businessman, 'a Russian soldier in the First World War and was captured by the Germans in East Prussia. After the war I became a German citizen and had a business in Berlin. In 1938 I saw what was coming and immigrated to America.' An old man can crown his life by becoming an American, as a sort of fulfilment of his striving all along the line. But one of those who emigrated from Germany to America in the last quarter of the nineteenth century was a very young man – a seventeen-year-old boy whose name was Julius Oppenheimer.

J. Robert Oppenheimer, the elder son of Julius Oppenheimer the immigrant from Germany, was a child prodigy who continued to be a prodigy long after he had left his childhood behind. Robert was the adored and pampered child of a prosperous father (the immigrant had become a very successful importer of suit linings and he housed his family in a nine-room apartment on Riverside Drive in Manhattan) and a gentle, cultivated mother. Both parents were members of the New York Society for Ethical Culture ('dedicated to the ever increasing knowledge and practice and love of the right'). They sent Robert and his brother, Frank, through the society's school. Robert grew up multi-lingually: German was a given in his family background and he studied classical languages at school. At the age of nine he is reported to have challenged an older girl-cousin: 'Ask me a question in Latin and I will answer you in Greek.' Studying physics he completed Harvard's undergraduate course in three years and graduated *summa cum laude*. As might be expected, he spent most of his time in the library.

In order to take his doctorate in physics (which he achieved at the age of twenty-three) young Oppenheimer was obliged to go to Europe: until the Second World War Europe was still the home of the advanced sciences. Oppenheimer went first to Cambridge (where he met the great men of physics: Bohr, Dirac, Rutherford, Born) and then to Göttingen in Germany to receive his doctorate. He also studied at the University of Leyden, where he was taken to task for his sloppiness in thought and expression and sent to Zurich to learn discipline. He was homesick, he was a loner and subject to deep depressions. At the age of twenty-five he returned to the United States to accept a dual appointment to lecture autumn and winter at the University of California at Berkeley and in the spring at the California Institute of Technology in Pasadena. Within five years he was a full professor of theoretical physics at Berkeley.

At the age of thirty-two Oppenheimer at first blush was the archetypical recluse of the higher sciences. He was a bachelor who lived in a small apartment with neither telephone nor radio. He had never read newspapers nor even magazines. He was, as these data indicate, totally uninterested in ephemera, in 'current events' of any kind. But except for serving as a sure indication of the apolitical side of Oppenheimer's character, these data are misleading. Culturally a polyhistor went with the polyglot; Oppenheimer was interested in everything with the single or half-again exception of politics and sociology. He was vastly read in various literatures and his grasp of general history was extraordinary. But it was particularly in the sciences that the breadth of his knowledge was most impressive. It was said that there was no major problem in any of the sciences that he did not know about and understand. He was also gradually developing into an extraordinarily effective, perceptive and charismatic teacher. He attracted and held a following among students of physics and diverted many a promising young scientist from the school of his choice – usually one of the then more famous universities – to Berkeley. By the late thirties there existed a regular cult of 'Oppenheimer men' in the intercollegiate student body. His signal exhortation to his students during class still echoes in the institutional memory of the place: 'Quantify it.'

Oppenheimer paid for his breadth of knowledge and understanding with his failure to achieve any profound insight of the kind that leads to a major discovery or other breakthrough in the sciences. Unlike many of his close colleagues and friends he never received a Nobel Prize nor was he ever even nominated for the honour. It was as if he were predestined to be what he became – a scientific administrator of genius, a consultant and adviser of finely attuned judicial capacities.

The idyllic-ascetic aspect of Oppenheimer's life came to an abrupt end in 1936 with the outbreak of the Spanish Civil War. In a sense the outbreak occurred in the nature of a delayed-action device, a time-bomb. Oppenheimer, as the son of a German-Jewish immigrant, had relatives in Germany who had been in harm's way ever since the accession to power of Adolf Hitler. Oppenheimer apparently slept through the proclamation of the Nuremberg Laws against the Jews in Germany in 1935. But in 1936 the international left was alerted and alarmed when Hitler and Mussolini declared their support for Francisco Franco. On the other side – in complete isolation as it developed – the Soviet Union declared its support for the Spanish loyalists. With the entry of the Soviet Union as an active sponsor on the scene of the conflict a well-organized international machinery in the form of the Comintern went into action, assuring a great deal of publicity for the struggle on a continuing basis. Oppenheimer, the academic, was drawn into the toils of the local and regional Communist organizations naturally and as a matter of course. Although he had no basic sympathy for the Party and never even considered joining it (his brother Frank did join), Oppenheimer more than once stated – half-jokingly but accurately – that he had 'probably belonged to every Communist-front organization on the West Coast'.

The year 1936 was a watershed for Oppenheimer because it bore in upon him two dominant phenomena of his times: the Great Depression at home and the rise of Fascism abroad. Both issues led him into association with leftist elements on campus and off. Himself fairly affluent (he had a salary of $15,000 a year – a princely emolument at the time – plus stock dividends), Oppenheimer was generous to a fault with friends and colleagues in need: the period marked the nadir of capitalism in America; the Communist Party of the United States reaped an all-time high of 80,000 votes in the 1936 presidential election. (Theretofore the minuscule party, three-quarters of whose members were women, received little more than a thousand votes in presidential elections.)

The rise of Fascism in Europe in the twenties and thirties (in interaction with the rise of Communism) precipitated the Second World War. In the prelude to that conflict a fairly large number from Europe's scientific and professional élites made their way to the traditional refuge and safe-haven of the Old World's emigrants, America. Among the refugee scientists newly arrived in America were those who had knowledge of the phenomenon of nuclear fission and forebodings with regard to its potential uses. Lise Meitner, a German-Jewish assistant to the eminent German physicist Otto Hahn for thirty years, had fled Nazi Germany and found temporary refuge in Sweden (she later moved to Great Britain). Hahn had written to her in Sweden in 1939 describing a recent experiment in which he had bombarded uranium with neutrons and got barium, a totally different element. Could he have split the atom? he asked. Lise decided that he had done just that and told her visiting nephew from the United States, Dr Otto Frisch, late of Vienna. News of this nature travels fast in scientific circles. Another emigrant-physicist, Dr Leo Szilard, a Hungarian Jew, initiated and supervised an experiment in the Pupin laboratories at Columbia University later in 1939 and demonstrated that the fission of uranium produced fast neutrons. The neutron, discovered by Sir James Chadwick in 1932, has a binding energy of from one to two million electron volts. The splitting of the atom convinced Szilard that the vast energy binding particles in the entity of the nucleus could be released, causing an explosion of colossal power. It would be releasing – in part – the latent force of the cosmos. At least that. Another question was whether, once this path was taken, it might come to releasing more than just a part of the latent force of the cosmos. The dramatic scientific advances of 1939, it has been said, and the outbreak of the Second World War constitute one of the most striking and sinister coincidences in history. The question of coincidence can be set aside, perhaps, in the confirmation of yet another, if most spectacular, example of the link between dramatic advances in the natural sciences and military requirements in time of war or approaching war. 'Great powers cannot be exerted,' wrote Samuel Johnson, 'but when great exigencies make them necessary.'

What bothered Leo Szilard was not so much the prospect of inadvertently blowing up the world and possibly disrupting the order of the solar system as the simple fact that the atom had been split by a German scientist working in Germany. This posed the distinct prospect of the Germans coming up first with such a super-bomb and using it to conquer the world in the conflict already in progress. Szilard started a one-man campaign, enlisting the help of his fellow-immigrants Albert Einstein and Edward Teller among others at an early stage, to convince the top echelons of the American government of the necessity of mounting a crash-pro-gramme for the production of a nuclear bomb. When he succeeded two years later, the task of selecting, recruiting, organizing, guiding and leading, comforting and inspiring a group of scientists, many if not most of whom were European immigrants, ultimately devolved upon J. Robert Oppenheimer. In studying the crisis that led to the outbreak of the war and the various movements that helped bring it about and then fostered it, there is difficulty in avoiding the conclusion that 'Oppie' was somehow predestined by his experience, his character and his family background as a first-generation American to lead this motley of *prima donnas*, naifs, eccentrics and dreamers – probably the greatest collection of technical and theoretical scientific talent ever assembled – to the successful completion of the most ambitious and fateful scientific task ever proposed. For the first time in history humanity did something that definitively changed the nature of war – and peace. After the production of the atomic bomb and its use against the Japanese at Hiroshima and Nagasaki, life on the blue planet Earth would never be the same.

From the moment the atom bomb was first successfully tested at Alamogordo, New Mexico in 1945 the men in charge of the programme and their superiors, the President of the United States, the secretary of war and the secretary of state particularly found themselves confronted with an historically unprecedented situation. The question that posed itself with the birth of the bomb was this: can we answer for the possession of this, the ultimate weapon – a weapon that is more than a weapon since it represents the ready means of creating a manmade apocalypse, the destruction of the world and all of humankind – can we answer for the possession of this by one nation? Is it not, rather, clear that this weapon must be put in the service of all humankind and secured so that it cannot be used for any partisan purpose whatever? For this reason there was immediate controversy among the scientists as to whether the bomb should be used at all, whether it did not behove the United States to inform the Soviet Union of the discovery immediately and offer joint control with the Soviet Union and our allies at the very outset.

The problem that posed itself with the birth of the bomb was that no one was prepared for it: the scientists working on the bomb were taken by surprise – no one had expected anything so big, so powerful, so insidious as this. Watching the first explosion, the student of Sanskrit Oppenheimer recalled the lines of the Hindu epic, the *Bhagavad Gita*:

> If the radiance of a thousand suns
> Were to burst at once into the sky,
> That would be like the splendour of the Mighty One . . .
> I am become Death,
> The shatterer of worlds!

157

Worse still, the scientists had woefully underestimated the potential for radioactive fallout. No one, in fact, had known what he was doing; they had stumbled into a New World no one had bargained for, a complete and potentially terrible *terra incognita*. But of most concern was the simple fact that the world was not ready for the nuclear age. On a policy level the secretary of war, Henry L. Stimson, was only slightly better prepared. When Harry Truman succeeded Franklin Delano Roosevelt as president, Stimson informed him that within four months the United States would 'in all probability have completed the most terrible weapon ever known in human history, one bomb which could destroy a whole city'. Considering the new technology with respect to 'the world in its present state of moral advancement' Stimson concluded that 'modern civilization might be completely destroyed'. By April 1945 it had long been clear that the war was nearing its end, Germany was finished and Japan merely had to be convinced that she had already lost the war. Hence when Stimson warned Truman that the United States could not expect to keep the atomic bomb as a monopoly for very long, the only country 'which could enter into production within the next few years is Russia'. International control of the weapon would be extremely difficult: no such machinery existed. Because of this, 'the question of sharing it with other nations and, if shared, upon what terms, becomes a primary question of our foreign relations'.

The greatest misfortune concerning the birth of the bomb, which Stimson did not touch on because it was so obvious, was that the dominating factor in the equation was the military one. The country was still at war: to be sure Germany was finished and Japan effectively beaten, but the convincing of Japan might well cost, in the estimate of George Marshall, the American chief of staff, from half a million to a million American casualties. Thus while the when, if and how had not even been discussed at this time the target of the bomb – if there was to be one – was a foregone conclusion: Japan. In fact, of course, the prospect of half a million to a million American casualties if the war were to be fought out on a conventional basis in effect also foreclosed the decision of whether to use the bomb at all. There remained the question of whether, when and how to inform the Soviet ally. Informing the Soviet ally was the clear route to at least some sort of internationalization of the bomb and the great majority of the scientists working on the bomb favoured doing so. Once again the indefatigable Leo Szilard started a one-man campaign to convince the American leadership of the necessity of informing the Russians and sharing with them so as to avoid the worst of all possible eventualities, namely, a nuclear-arms race between the United States and the Soviet Union. For this reason Szilard was against using the bomb against anybody or even indulging in some sort of 'demonstration' of what the bomb could do – it would only alarm, anger and spur the Russians to emulation. While Szilard's efforts failed (despite his gaining access to the highest government circles), he succeeded in bringing to a head an issue that had developed steadily throughout the war – the increasing alienation between the scientists and the policy-makers.

It was at this point that it became perfectly clear that the policy-makers had failed to produce a policy as far as the bomb and everything about it were concerned. In part this was simply bad luck: the demise, in the last months of the war, of the most charismatic president in American history. If Roosevelt had done any thinking about the bomb he had kept it strictly to himself. The new president, Truman, had not even known of the existence of a bomb project until briefed by Secretary of War Stimson. For the most part, however, the lack of a policy was due to the state of emergency in connection with the ongoing war and the consequent predominance of the military. It was with the military, therefore, that the scientists saw themselves in principal contention and disagreement. There was also the fact that the communication gap between the two sides had widened with the introduction of nuclear physics into the field of armaments. Technical and operational problems of the bomb had become so intricate and complex that the policy-makers, military as well as civilian, lost all comprehension and hence oversight of what was going on. The policy-makers had become, in the words of Galileo in his letter to the Benedictine monk Castelli, '. . . people who . . . totally lack the knowledge necessary . . . even to understand the procedures which the most subtle sciences employ in the confirmation of their conclusions'. In Galileo's time it was the clergy and the laity who were hopelessly ignorant of the new science, now it was the military – the very contractors could no longer understand the operative principles of the weapons they had contracted for. General George Marshall, chief of staff of the United States Army, had sent back the literature on the bomb because he found it impenetrable. This was a turning-point. In full view of the failure of the policy-makers to make policy – any kind of policy, let alone cogent and logically consistent policy – for lack of comprehension of the principles and issues involved, the scientists found themselves, *nolens volens*, in a position of unprecedented power and responsibility, responsibility not to their contractors and hierarchical superiors but to humanity at large. Indeed, the scientists found themselves all the more responsible in view of the fact that they were now the only ones who could fathom and interpret the nature and dimensions of their original responsibility.

Decision-making has been a salient weakness of American government in the twentieth century. The indomitable fatuity of the decision-making apparatus of the American government in 1945 is well known through the colossal gaffe of neglecting to secure a geographical access to the Allied position in Berlin in negotiations with the Soviets. This cardinal consideration was lost sight of due to the chronic infighting of the military services, each of them too eager, in the words of the assistant secretary of war, John J. McCloy, to employ its own forces to conclude the war. In 1983 McCloy told the writer, Peter Wyden, that the decision-makers interpreted political decisions as a sign of weakness. 'Groves [the general in charge of the atomic-bomb project] and Truman were exactly the right guys to open this [nuclear] Pandora's box,' he said. 'They didn't step back to get the whole picture, they didn't look ahead.'

When Szilard's campaign to ban the bomb came under severe criticism by General Groves, Szilard's immediate superior at the Chicago Metlab, Arthur Compton, responded in a cogent memorandum:

> I believe the reason for their action is that their responsibility to the nation is prior to and broader than their responsibility to the army . . . They have had little assurance that serious consideration of [the atom's] broader implications is being given by those in a position to guide national policy. The scientists will be held responsible, both by the public and their own consciences . . .

Compton went on in his memorandum to criticize the secretary of state for his failure to explain the atomic dilemma to the founding conference of the United Nations which was the prospective institution of international control: 'His appreciation was so limited as possibly to serve as a hazard to the country's welfare.' Compton blamed General Groves for not having briefed the State Department properly. (In November 1944 Secretary of State Cordell Hull was succeeded by Edward Stettinius as 'acting secretary of state'. Prior to this appointment Stettinius had been under-secretary for about one month. He had had no previous diplomatic experience. Just seven months after his appointment Stettinius was replaced by James F. Byrnes, a close friend and adviser of Harry Truman.)

There was a tragi-comic episode occasioned by Oppenheimer's use of the word 'demonstration' in one of a loose but persistent series of discussions among the scientists concerning the morality of using the bomb at all. At a unique meeting of some fifty of the scientists at Los Alamos, presumably to scotch what might have turned into a mutiny against the completion of the project, Oppenheimer came up with a scenario: since a United Nations Organization was going to be formed within a few months, what was needed was a demonstration of the bomb before that happened. The world public would be so overawed by the power of the bomb that the statesmen convening for the funding of the United Nations Organization would ban the bomb then and there. This idea satisfied the would-be mutineers who thereupon dispersed never to reconvene. The UNO was founded several months before the bomb was ready, but by this time the momentum of the programme was such that nothing mattered except the set goal: build the bomb. Yet the idea of a demonstration persisted. When Bacher, the liaison officer from the obstreperous Chicago Metlab group – Compton, Szilard *et al.* – presented the view of his colleagues that the bomb was not needed to win the war, he was countered by Oppenheimer's question – 'How do we know?' Similarly, the discussion of the possibility of demonstrating the bomb harmlessly for the Japanese resulted only in an agreed formulation of what – by default – was the consensus of the scientists: 'Once you know how to make the bomb it's not your business to figure out how not to use it.' Note the negative: '. . . how *not* to use it'. The negative got everybody off the hook and implanted the tacit assumption that the non-use of the bomb was a foregone conclusion. In short, the scientists were back on the track of automaton irresponsibility. Once again the question of 'who is going to do the thinking around here?' had been decided as in the case of Galileo.

It took the clear-thinking, incisive physicist, Isidor Rabi, friend, colleague and six years Oppenheimer's senior, to reduce the 'demonstration theory' to its illogical components. The only meaningful demonstration would have to be the real thing. Anything less than the real thing would fail to convince the Japanese that the war was lost. Only the destruction of a town would serve as 'incontrovertible' evidence. Bainbridge, the Harvard physicist in charge of the 'Trinity test' (its code name) at Alamogordo, suggested that buildings be erected at various points and distances from Ground Zero of the blast area. This was vetoed by the Army on security grounds: construction would require the presence of construction workers. Rabi is quoted by Wyden as saying in 1975 that 'You would have to have built a model town to make a realistic demonstration'. He might have added: '. . . and put real people in it'. Any realistic demonstration under the circumstances would have been *ipso facto* a surrealistic demonstration – the first science-fiction 'happening'. Anything short of that would have been denounced as a 'Potemkin village' set up for the purpose and hence a set-up for the purpose. On top of all this there was the question of time. The decision-makers would not have felt that they could spare the time for such an undertaking. Time meant casualties.

Thus, instead of trying to figure out how *not* to use the bomb, the Army command was trying to figure out how best to use the bomb for maximum military and public-relations effect. For this reason the favourite target of General Groves was the holy Japanese city of Kyoto, which was also an architectural gem and a cultural site of inestimable value. The annihilation of Kyoto complete with the massacre of most of its citizens and the radioactivization of the surviving rest would indeed have been a public-relations masterstroke. There is something almost comic in the boy-scout eagerness of such a suggestion. The secretary of war himself struck Kyoto from the list. He and Mrs Stimson had spent part of their honeymoon in Kyoto and cherished the memory of the place as surpassingly beautiful. At the end of May 1945 the question of forewarning the Japanese was discussed in formal sessions and at the intervening lunch by Stimson, Byrnes, Compton, Lawrence, Oppenheimer and company and laid to rest. Byrnes performed the obsequies when he said: 'If the Japanese were told that the bomb would be used on a given locality, they might bring our boys who were prisoners of war to that area.' (The unfortunate fact is that in war there are only two sides: to favour one side automatically disfavours the other side; to disfavour one's own side, for whatever reason, is political suicide.) Interestingly enough, it was the soldier, George Marshall, who argued for forewarning the Japanese of a military bomb drop. In a statement to the secretary of war as recorded by the assistant secretary of war, McCloy,

> General Marshall said he thought these weapons might first be used against straight military objectives such as a large naval installation and then if no complete result was derived from the effect of that, he thought we ought to designate a number of large manufacturing areas from which people would be warned to leave – telling the Japanese that we intended to destroy such centres. There would be no individual designations so that the Japs would not know exactly where we were to hit – a number should be named and the hit should follow shortly after.

Marshall 'emphasized the moral value of giving the Japanese advance notice' (Wyden). 'Every effort,' said Marshall, 'should be made to keep our record of warning clear ... We must offset by such warning methods the opprobrium which might follow from an ill-considered employment of such force.' But the meeting at the end of May, in which Marshall participated, ended with the decision to drop the bomb without warning on a place where it would produce 'a profound psychological impression on as many of the inhabitants as possible'. Compton did not inform his colleagues and charges at the Metlab in Chicago of this decision (he had been sworn to secrecy), but the news he did give them was negative enough to prompt the drafting of the Franck Report by Leo Szilard and James ('Pa') Franck. This report warned against a surprise attack against Japan and made the point that such an attack would foreclose the concept of international control:

> This kind of introduction of atomic weapons to the world may easily destroy all our chances of success. Russia ... and even neutral countries may be deeply shocked. It may be very difficult to persuade the world that a nation which was capable of secretly preparing and suddenly releasing a weapon as indiscriminate as the [Nazi] rocket bomb and a million times more destructive, is to be trusted in its proclaimed desire of having such weapons abolished by international agreement.

This line of reasoning now has the clearly traceable cogency of an historical development. Maurice Couve de Murville, who was France's foreign minister at the time, in defence of the French development of the atomic bomb, made the now famous statement: *'Le propre de la bombe atomique est que c'est national'* (The essence of the atomic bomb is that it is national).

At the time, the spring and early summer of 1945, the two points of view formed the horns of a dilemma. As Peter Wyden in *Day One* couched it: 'The scientists hoped to shock the entire world into disarmament. Stimson and his men wanted primarily to shock Tokyo into surrender.' But there was not, in fact, a consensus among the scientists. Oppenheimer had become a political realist; he dismissed any alternative to military use as academic. The Franck Report never made its way to the Interim Committee formed on 25 April to advise on the 'various questions' about the handling of the bomb. The committee was dissolved less than three months later. Oppenheimer – it was pre-eminently he among the chief scientists of the United States – looked to it that the Franck Report like the various petitions and polls taken of the scientists concerned never reached any meaningful destination. The magnitude of the exigency, namely the Second World War, that necessitated the exertion of an effort so powerful as to succeed in creating an atomic bomb – that same exigency in its undiminished magnitude would carry the project through to its foreintended conclusion, namely the military use of the bomb in wartime. Oppenheimer saw that, recognized it as a sort of categorical imperative, a *force majeur* that was simply not to be gainsaid. Everything else was embroidery, *la guerre de la dentelle*, and Szilard's one-man campaigns set against the alternative that their purpose implied – a war that might last another full year and more with the cost of perhaps another million American casualties and totally unforeseeable contingencies – look shamefaced and ridiculous. These were the considerations that justified his professional duplicity in dealing with his colleagues, convincing them when they needed convincing or tricking them when they had to be tricked. In so doing he spared them serious embarrassment and antagonized some of them – particularly Edward Teller – to the blood. But more important than any of this, more important even than antagonizing Edward Teller definitively, was the fact that in doing as he did Oppenheimer antagonized himself. The result was a double exchange of roles: Oppenheimer made a hawk of the dove Teller, and a dove of the hawk Oppenheimer.

Another of the great and powerful exertions of effort necessitated by the great exigency of the war was Oppenheimer's bravura performance as director of the Los Alamos laboratory. If any one man was chiefly responsible for the invention and implementation of the atomic bomb it was J. Robert Oppenheimer. Above all, Oppenheimer was responsible for creating and maintaining the enthusiasm, the 'Gung-ho!' atmosphere that characterized Los Alamos throughout. In a very real sense Oppenheimer was the personification of the American dream, the son of an immigrant, who rose to wealth (the site of Los Alamos is near a ranch Oppenheimer bought in the thirties) and world fame. In his single-mindedness to complete his assigned project 'Oppie' had the myth of America going for him. Had it not been for this it is seriously questionable whether the leading scientist in the project could have been fobbed off with lame pedestrian explanations of what was being done about the moral problems posed by the sudden coming-into-existence of the bomb. There is Teller's account of Oppenheimer's final explanation of why the last minute petition not to drop the bomb should not be circulated at Los Alamos: 'He conveyed to me in glowing terms the deep concern, thoroughness and wisdom with which these questions were being handled in Washington. Our fate was in the hands of the best, the most conscientious, men of our nation. And they had information which we did not possess.' The 'best, the most conscientious, men of our nation' are the new (super)men of the new supernation, a nation that is not a nation but 'the last, best hope of humanity'. That hope combined with the faith and naïveté of the scientists to accept the military demand that the bomb be dropped on Japan.

And then it happened. On 6 August 1945 Oppenheimer mounted the podium in the auditorium at Los Alamos and, clasping his hands over his head like a victorious prizefighter, informed his colleagues that the first atomic bomb had been detonated over Hiroshima. It was several days before the figures of the destruction became available. But when they came it was like the shockwave of the explosion itself: 78,000 killed, 13,000 missing, 37,000 wounded, three-fifths of the entire city totally destroyed. At one blow. The scientists were horrified. And this, as they all divined, was by no means the end of the bad news. There was more, much more to come. Just three days after the strike that wiped out Hiroshima there followed the strike against Nagasaki with the atomic bomb named 'Fat Man'. Final estimates of the casualties put as many as 70,000 killed. Forty-four per cent of the town was destroyed. The Japanese surrendered five days later. Sixteen days later the Association of Los Alamos Scientists, with the acronym ALAS, was formed with the object of striving to influence postwar nuclear policy. The prime goal of the association was to avoid military control over the atom. In this they were quickly disappointed: the bill passed by the government a few weeks later did not bar military men from serving either as the administrator of the new Federal atomic agency or as members of the nine-man overseeing committee. There were also penalties written into the bill against the discussion of scientific matters the government might deem 'secret'. In a House committee meeting Oppenheimer admitted that the authority granted by the bill was too sweeping, but he urged passage as quickly as possible in the interests of international control. Once again the scientists felt let down by Oppenheimer.

VIII

'OPPIE': ... AND FALL

Oppenheimer left Los Alamos in November 1945 and returned to Berkeley to his old position. But within a few months he was called to Washington to help in the preparation of a plan for the international control of atomic energy. This was the plan that was later submitted to the United Nations Organization as the Baruch Plan. It bore the stamp of Oppenheimer's thinking on international control and included the offer of relinquishing America's monopoly of the atom bomb. Oppenheimer spent two months in Washington working on the plan. There can be no doubt, however, that he had thought long and hard on the subject of international control and placed his hopes in the prospect of its realization. By the end of the year Oppenheimer was appointed a member of the newly formed Atomic Energy Commission upon which devolved control of the American atomic programme after leaving the custody of the American Army. He was elected chairman of the commission's general advisory committee at the first meeting of that body. In the esteem of his peers and the American Establishment if not in the eyes of the general public, J. Robert Oppenheimer had become America's premier scientist. He was the obvious as well as the logical choice for the country's foremost position requiring a scientific background. But he had also become generally popular and much sought after. He was frequently invited to lecture and was showered with offers of book contracts. In the summer of 1947 he was offered and accepted the post of director of the Institute for Advanced Study at Princeton University. Indeed Oppenheimer's influence in government policy councils was described as 'ubiquitous', so many were the federal advisory committees of which he was a member and as often as not chaired. The record shows that Oppenheimer was chairman of no less than seven such groups in post-war years. The record also shows that 'Oppie's' influence was, in fact, enormous. Rarely did the findings of any group of which he was a member differ from his. This 'miraculous performance' was due not only to the scope and depth of Oppenheimer's knowledge but also to his consummate skill at summarizing discussions in which he took part. Even after a three-day session of the GAC Oppenheimer could summarize their deliberations lucidly and comprehensively, giving each contribution its proper weight. It rarely happened that a member would append a rejoinder: 'That isn't exactly what I meant.' Considering the stature of the members and the exactingness of the material under discussion, such a record speaks for itself.

The preparation, presentation and reception of the Baruch Plan at the United Nations Organization was the formative experience of American–Soviet post-war relations. The intransigence and even truculence of the Soviet delegation made it clear that the Soviets had been stung by the surprise atomic bombing of Japan. (Stalin was informed orally by Truman at the Potsdam conference a few days before the drop on Hiroshima – and then in only the most general terms.) For one thing the spectacular exhibition by the West of consummate technological expertise as the effective agent ending the war robbed the Soviet Union of its 'effect' in mounting its long delayed attack on Japan and consequently denied the Soviets any real voice in the disposition of the peace treaty and occupation of Japan. (This was a very considerable cause of contention in itself.) For another it simply devastated all Soviet pretensions to emerging from the Second World War as the greatest military power on earth. For the Americans, with Oppenheimer as their chief specialist representative, the Russian attitude came as a shock because the Baruch Plan was as fair as they could possibly have made it. It was a general plan, not a detailed one. The Russians had turned down the general principles of the plan. In effect. They had not vetoed the plan; they had merely abstained and thus rejected the plan by not agreeing to it. The question then became whether the United States should agree to continue the negotiations in the United Nations. By the summer of 1948 the Baruch Plan, while still bearing its original name, had become the United Nations plan for the internationalization of atomic energy. It is interesting to note how quickly Oppenheimer came to the conclusion that the Americans in dealing with the Russians must be especially careful not to give anything up. In his eyes the Acheson–Lilienthal Plan which had been incorporated into the Baruch Plan already gave away too much – that there must be international ownership and management of atomic plants, for example – so that what they had represented the maximum position with regard to concessions that could be made. To give anything more in the interest of achieving agreement would be to court disaster. After four months of vexatious and fruitless negotiations with the Soviets, Oppenheimer perceived that the Soviets were systematically constrained to reject any plan for the internationalization of any power component – let alone nuclear power. This was because their system, which was totalitarian, was essentially antagonistic to sharing power with anybody. To agree to the Baruch Plan would be to agree to the removal of the Iron Curtain and the whole panoply of Soviet controls, domestic and foreign. They could not and would not do this. And yet if the Iron Curtain were not removed any form of international control would be exceedingly dangerous to the United States. Oppenheimer felt that it would be dangerous to continue the negotiations because the Americans would be constantly tempted to make some compromise which 'without our fully realizing it' would put us into the position of having accepted an agreement for the control of nuclear energy, possibly even with prohibition of bombs, but without binding the Russians to remove the Iron Curtain. Oppenheimer went to considerable lengths to persuade the American leadership not to continue the negotiations. Another reason for his strong stand on this issue was his conviction that the Soviets were using the negotiations for propaganda purposes only. Thus, given the Soviet ideological steadfastness, we would be helping them publicize an agreement we could not afford to make. It would be heads they win, tails we lose. The end result would be either an agreement that would be worse for us than no agreement, or no agreement with the Americans bearing the onus for the failure to come to agreement. Here it was that Oppenheimer made out the lineaments of the great American obsession with negotiations. For people used to the blessings of peace, for whom peace was the natural, normal state of affairs the Americans were ill-prepared, ill-constituted and ill-starred for what was coming: a situation that was neither peace nor war and yet both, a kind of international political limbo in which phases of 'détente' alternated with phases of 'cold war', in either of which there was always a strong admixture of the other. In this situation the indomitable American optimism demanded negotiations in the overweening confidence that an agreement could be reached – and with not all that much difficulty for that matter because for the Americans a bad agreement, by very definition, was better than no agreement at all. For Oppenheimer this experience, bitter as it was, was a foretaste of the cult of the summit, a result of the mass of fatuity promoted by the sensationalist media of the free world. The cult of the summit put a tremendous advantage into the hands of the Soviets in their confrontation with the West. But a seismic shift in American political topography had been under way meanwhile.

In the first third of this century the United States was still very much a young country. Moreover, despite its immigrant origins, it remained strangely isolated from the rest of the world. Of course, the very fact that America was so different from the rest of the world contributed to its continental isolation. Nothing that happened as a result of the new nation's first international involvement on a grand scale – the First World War – alarmed the Americans so much as the emergence of Communism in Europe in general and in the founding of the Union of Soviet Socialist Republics in particular. The anti-Communist 'witch-hunt' that culminated in the highly controversial trial and execution of Sacco and Vanzetti (prolonged as it was by a seven-year interim between trial and execution) was one result of this alarm. Another result was the steadfast refusal of the United States to recognize and establish diplomatic relations with the Soviet Union. But then something happened that rather abruptly reversed both the trend and the policy.

Henry L. Stimson, as secretary of state under Herbert Hoover, saw the American conservative's dream smashed to bits on the offshore rocks of the Great Depression, Black Friday, 1929. He witnessed and worked through much of the Great Depression that closed the Creditanstalt of Vienna and pulled down the financial roof of Europe along with that of the United States. In the United States the Crash and the Depression that followed brought Franklin D. Roosevelt and the New Deal to power. In Germany the Depression paved the way for Adolf Hitler and the New Order. (For the Germans, who made up the most conservative nation in Europe, Hitler's greatest attraction was his promise to 'save the nation from Communism'. This of course included doing away with unemployment.) The same cause produced simultaneous but exactly opposite effects: America moved to the left, Germany moved to the right. But the accession to power of the Nazis confirmed Roosevelt in his desire to establish diplomatic relations with the Soviet Union.

Meanwhile, the anti-Semitism of the Nazis, an article of faith of the movement codified in the Nuremberg Laws of 1935 and demonstrated so disgustingly in the Kristallnacht of 1937, dismayed and outraged Jews throughout the world, especially those among the intellectuals and academicians of the New Deal.

But this antagonism was perhaps basically a contemporary projection of the controversy, partially hidden but none the less bitter, within the body politic of the United States itself. This struggle revolved around the theory and practice of economics. When Roosevelt campaigned for the presidency in 1932, in full appreciation of the violent public reaction against the *laissez-faire* capitalism that had brought on the Depression, he took the field against the 'economic royalty' of America. But the brunt of the New Deal attack on the economics of the American conservative establishment was its anti-monopoly sentiment. The main thrust of the three Roosevelt administrations was the creation of precedents and the building of a record for a body of doctrine against 'monopoly, conspiracy and restraint of trade'. This continuing campaign reached its high point when the president gave his message to the Seventy-fifth Congress, 'Transmitting Recommendations Relative to the Strengthening and Enforcement of Anti-Trust Laws'. A main thesis of this speech was that almost all major production in American industry was carried out by corporations, that there was concentration even among corporations.

The most avid New Dealers were those who had given their hearts and souls to the new economics, and the new economics was grounded on trust-busting, its variations and equivalents. The quest of a corrective for the economy involved the diagnosis of the cause of its collapse. This, the New Deal determined, was big business run riot, avarice divorced from social conscience and outside government control, monopolies resultant from the systematic suppression of competition and the unbridled urge to expand, both vertically and horizontally, by means of the conspiratorial formation of interlocking directorates – in short, the cartel. This was the great, well-nigh all-embracing secret evil. In the eyes of the New Deal the great corporations represented a kind of economic Mafia.

It was this aspect of affairs that made the determining contribution to the great syndrome of the New Deal, the passionate rejection of the poison, which was isolated and identified as socially irresponsible big business; the insistence on the antidote, which was government intervention, investigation, regulation and control of the economic life of the nation – that is, big government. It was this activity, the investigation of international cartels involving American firms (as in the case of the United States *v.* Standard Oil), that led the vanguard of the New Deal to the door of the veritable homeland of heavy industrial concentration, the cradle of the international cartel, a nation so imbued with and impounded by private business interests that it poised like an octopus with a tentacular grip on the economy of Europe and beyond. This was Germany – at that time Nazi Germany, the Third Reich. Thus Nazi Germany, for New Dealers, became the prime example and main proof of the quintessential modern evil – big business expanded and concentrated through private (that is to say, secret and uncontrolled) combinations. This was the worst of all evils because it was firmly believed to be the chief cause of war.

This, then, was the conceptual cornerstone of the New Deal. As such, it also served as the rationale of the alliance with the Soviet Union, providing coordinates for the point of view from which perhaps the bloodiest tyrant in history became 'Uncle Joe'. The worst that can be said about it is that it was, as a matter of demonstrable fact, an extreme position. The most dangerous thing about an extreme position is that it is likely to beget an abrupt and violent reaction in the direction of the opposite extreme. Undoubtedly the most fateful 'rush past the position at which it should have stopped' was Roosevelt's proclamation of unconditional surrender at Casablanca in 1942. The propagation of the doctrine of unconditional surrender robbed the German underground resistance of virtually every prospect of success, since it made clear that the only chance of national survival lay in the final victory of Germany. The doctrine of unconditional surrender affixed the penalty of the 'general and formal submission of the national will' as the only price for peace at the virtual beginning of the American prosecution of the war – long before the outcome could be assured or even seriously surmised. It removed the buffer state between the converging Allies, forcing them to deal with each other directly over the fate of an inert Germany and, therefore, sealed the division of Germany and of Europe.

Moreover, the obsession on the part of Roosevelt and most of the members of his staff with the idea of the total destruction of the German state tended to preclude serious, coordinated study of how Germany was to be administered after the cessation of hostilities, except insofar as punitive and preventive measures were concerned. How else is the sustained squabbling among the very junior officers who staffed the working security committee, on the question of jurisdiction over occupation policy, to be explained (including, of course, the matter of access on land to the Allied sectors in Berlin)?

The trust-busters' conviction that heavy industrial concentration in private hands was the underlying cause of war was the motivational source of the most astonishing piece of American foreign policy in the entire era – the Morgenthau Plan. The Morgenthau Plan proposed the complete demilitarization of Germany, the total destruction of the German armament industry and the removal or destruction of other key industries basic to military strength. It also encompassed the cession of East Prussia (or that part of it not destined for the USSR) and the southern portion of Silesia to Poland, the cession to France of the Saar and the adjacent territories bounded by the Rhine and the Mosel Rivers (that is, the whole of the Rhineland), the Kiel Canal and all German territory north of the Kiel Canal. The remaining part of Germany was to be divided into two 'autonomous, independent states', one comprising Bavaria, Württemberg and Baden, the other comprising Prussia, Saxony and Thuringia. In the Ruhr area 'all industrial plants and equipment not destroyed by military action shall be completely dismantled and transported to Allied nations as restitution. All equipment shall be removed from the mines and the mines closed.' Finally, in order to feed the people of Germany and ensure their perpetually peaceful disposition, the entire country was to be 'pastoralized' into a predominantly agricultural area. There is no need to comment on this position: the Morgenthau Plan spoke for itself. When Morgenthau was in Great Britain in 1944 he asked the supreme commander if it would be possible to put the Ruhr coal mines under water the moment the territory came under Allied control. Eisenhower replied that such an act would be 'senseless and criminal'. Within a few weeks after the war it became axiomatic in American Military Government that the most effective way to sabotage the Morgenthau Plan was to lend it unqualified support. For the fact was that no sooner were the members of American Military Government installed in office than they found themselves fighting for the soul of Germany against the Communists, who had a considerable headstart, who were mostly homegrown and who had the full and energetic support of the Soviet Union. It was not long before memorandums were circulating among top officials of the American government damning the Morgenthau Plan as suicidal and asserting that America's real interest lay in rebuilding Germany as quickly as possible 'as a bulwark against Communism'. When the Communist and capitalist systems met at the Elbe in Germany they did so only because they had together succeeded in destroying the one thing that had forced their association in the first place. Hence the meeting automatically became a confrontation: for each there was only one enemy left – the other.

The confrontation in Germany by its very nature exposed the American liberal-left to the charge of sympathy with the Communists. The congressional elections in November 1946 returned a Republican majority to both houses for the first time in fourteen years. In 1947 the House Un-American Activities Committee opened its public hearings on Communism in America. (A year earlier, in the Atomic Energy Act of 1946, the nuclear programme was transferred from military to civilian hands with the requirement that prospective employees of the new Atomic Energy Commission be subjected to a pre-employment investigation by the FBI to appraise employees' 'character, associations and loyalty'.) In 1948 there began, with the sworn denunciation of Alger Hiss as a member of the Communist Party by Whittaker Chambers, a process of investigation and prosecution in the House and Senate that lasted seven years and unearthed the greatest espionage complex in American history. The findings of these investigations were compiled and summarized in a series of government papers published by the Senate's committee on the judiciary, under the title 'Interlocking Subversion in Government Departments', an interesting counterpart, both as a term and as a phenomenon, of the conspiracy of interlocking directorates in big business.

Most unfortunately, this process of investigation and prosecution acquired a partisan aspect from the very beginning: the Democrats were on the liberal, anti-trust, big-government side while the Republicans remained conservative and, above all, anti-Communist. Even though Harry Truman, a staunch anti-Communist, disliked the Morgenthau Plan and gladly accepted its author's resignation as secretary of the treasury, he decided that the fortunes of his administration could not bear the onus of the unprecedented scandal that was bound to come with a major congressional investigation into Communism in America. Hence the investigation was formally launched only in the presidential election year of 1948.

In March 1947 the Atomic Energy Commission, after receipt of a letter and documents from the FBI on the Communist associations of its senior adviser, formally and for the first time opened an investigation of J. Robert Oppenheimer. There was no choice. The sheer bulk of the derogatory material on 'Oppie' was dismaying. As Deputy General Counsel Joseph Volpe put it: '. . . if anyone were to print all the stuff in this file and say it is about the top civilian adviser to the Atomic Energy Commission, there would be terrible trouble. His background is awful.' That was the one side of it. The other was his achievements, as undeniable as they were spectacular. His prestige was Othellian: 'I have done the state some service and they know it.' And so Joseph Volpe concluded his statement to atomic commissioner Lewis L. Strauss accordingly: 'But your responsibility is to determine whether this man is a security risk *now*, and except for the Chevalier incident I don't see anything in this file to establish that he might be.' The Chevalier incident moves through the Oppenheimer story like some implacable red worm. Haakon Chevalier was a professor of French literature at Berkeley. A native American, born of a French father and a Norwegian mother, raised in Europe, he carried both an American and a French passport. When he met Oppenheimer in 1937 he had already published a book on Anatole France and had translated a number of André Malraux's works, including *Man's Fate*. He also attempted a novel or two. He was witty, cultivated and urbane, but no great light. A contemporary described him as 'a good translator but a bad novelist'. Above all, Chevalier was a political nincompoop, a denizen of the polite leftist dream-world, a

'cocktail partisan'. In early 1943, after Oppenheimer's appointment as director of the super-secret nuclear-weapons laboratory at
Los Alamos, Chevalier informed Oppenheimer while he was the
latter's dinner guest that a certain Eltenton, a British engineer
working for Shell in the bay area, was in a position to transmit
secret technical information to the Soviets. Oppenheimer straight
away rebuked Chevalier with the statement that any such activity
would be treasonable and the matter was dropped. No more was
said. But Oppenheimer did not report this 'conversation' (which
took place in his kitchen while he was mixing drinks) to his own
security officers for another eight months. In the end Oppenheimer
decided to report the matter as stated by Chevalier because it
weighed with him that the man Eltenton might indeed be a serious
threat to the Los Alamos project. But in doing so he doggedly
withheld Chevalier's name while attempting to obfuscate the actual
incident with a fabrication of three similar incidents which he
described as having taken place within the Los Alamos compound
and involving scientists employed on the project. He thus inadvertently concocted a fiction far worse than the truth. Instead of
throwing investigating authorities off the scent or mollifying their
professional curiosity, Oppenheimer's trumped-up version only
drew them more persistently on. Oppenheimer withheld the
identity of his informant for another four months and then, in
December, on a direct order from his superior General Groves,
divulged it. Of course by this time the truth – that Oppenheimer
himself had been approached by a personal friend who had nothing
whatever to do with the Los Alamos project, that in order to
protect his friend (whom he considered innocent of purpose or
guile) he had deliberately concocted a story of three approaches by
as many fellow scientists employed on the top-secret nuclear project – against the background of the renounced fiction appeared
the stranger and more troublesome of the two. At the time of the
divulgence, in 1943, General Groves took the view, as he later
testified, that this was really nothing more than an example of a
sort of arrested schoolboy loyalty to a friend. Moreover they were,
all of them, still at the very beginning of the project. At that time
and in that place, America, nobody knew anything very much
about security, its dimensions, its significance and its exactions.
The very concept was new and still indistinct. But as time passed
and the Loyalty Program of the government went into full swing,

as the Democratic majorities in both the Senate and the House of Representatives were replaced by Republican majorities and, finally, when the Democrat Harry Truman made way for the Republican Dwight D. Eisenhower in the White House, security considerations became far more comprehensive and stringent. In radically different circumstances – it was the McCarthy era – hindsight worked a reverse transformation of perspective: the Chevalier incident loomed larger and more threatening on the horizon of the past as time went on. It was simply indigestible; it stuck in everybody's craw. Oppenheimer himself could scarcely stomach it: by 1953 the man he had become found the man he had been ten years before almost entirely incomprehensible. But in 1947 this process had only just begun and the memory of his unique achievement in producing the first atom bomb was still fresh and overpowering. 'Oppie' was cleared by the Atomic Energy Commission with no questions asked.

On 23 September 1949 President Harry Truman announced that the Soviets had exploded an atomic bomb. The news came as a profound shock, particularly to the American specialists concerned, none of whom had expected the Soviet achievement until some time in the early 1950s. The import of the news was clear, above all to the American military: the nuclear-arms race had begun. Specifically this meant a new and hard look at the American programme to produce a hydrogen bomb, 'the Super', as it was referred to. With concentration on the Super, nuclear research entered a new era, if only because the hydrogen bomb – involving the far more complex process of thermonuclear fusion, in contrast to the nuclear fission operative in the atomic bomb – was clearly calculated to be many times (perhaps a hundred, perhaps a thousand) more powerful than the atomic bomb. The Super was patently 'the ultimate weapon' capable (as a matter of mathematically predictable consequence) of destroying the world. The fact that mankind had caught enough of the secret power of the universe to destroy all life as he knew it forced the eschatological question, the 'to be or not to be' for the whole species and its environment. There was no longer any question for the scientists of ducking the moral issue. A great many of them, including Oppenheimer, felt strongly that the hydrogen bomb should never be built and said so. The businessman member of the General Advisory Committee (GAC) in 1954, Hartley Rowe, put it cogently:

'... the use of such a massively destructive weapon could not be realistically confined to strictly military targets.' ('You would be using it against civilization, and not against the military. I don't like to see women and children killed wholesale because the male element of the human race is so stupid that they can't get out of war and keep out of war.') At its first meeting on the subject of whether the United States ought to take the initiative at that time (1949) in an all-out programme, the GAC voted 8 to 0 against taking such an initiative (Oppenheimer withholding his views until the other seven members present – Glenn Seaborg was absent – had expressed theirs). 'I am glad you feel this way,' Oppenheimer is quoted as saying by one of those present, 'for if it had not come out this way, I would have had to resign as chairman.' In the report the GAC submitted to the Atomic Energy Commission the committee stated its conclusion that the Super could be built with an 'imaginative and concerted attack on the problem', but added: 'We all hope that by one means or another, the development of these weapons can be avoided. We are all reluctant to see the United States take the initiative in precipitating this development.' In a separate report, two of the committee members, Enrico Fermi and I. I. Rabi, condemned the H-bomb on moral grounds:

> The fact that no limits exist to the destructiveness of this weapon makes its very existence and the knowledge of its construction a danger to humanity as a whole. It is necessarily an evil thing considered in any light. For these reasons we believe it important for the President of the United States to tell the American public and the world that we think it is wrong on fundamental ethical principles to initiate the development of such a weapon.

After the adjournment of the GAC Oppenheimer conferred twice with Secretary of State Dean Acheson, arguing that the United States could 'provide by example some limitations on the totality of war' by voluntarily forswearing the development of the H-bomb. Acheson was bewildered: 'How can you really persuade a hostile adversary to disarm "by example"?' And yet George F. Kennan, Acheson's principal policy adviser, in a 128-page analysis of the problem of reacting to the Soviet atomic explosion, argued that the Soviets preferred to rely on non-military means of expansion such as subversion, economic pressure, political action – whence he hazarded the guess that the Soviets would not proceed with a thermonuclear weapon if the United States did not. This assumption, that the Soviets would not proceed with the development of an H-bomb if the Americans did not, was fairly widespread – at least among scientists. It can be attributed to general ignorance of the nature and composition of Soviet Communism. But coming from Kennan, who was uniquely rich in experience of Soviets and their ways, this opinion is dumbfounding in its naïveté. But even for those who know better – far better – the wish is father to the thought. In the end, however, all such tentatives of humanity were quashed by the matter-of-fact statement of Major-General James Burns, a special adviser to the secretary of defense, Louis Johnson. Said General Burns quietly: 'It's a fundamental law of defense that you always have to use the most powerful weapons you can produce.'

On 25 June, 1950 North Korean ground forces crossed the 38th parallel and invaded South Korea.

With the sudden outbreak of the Korean War the United States found itself 'not well equipped to deal with problems of limited aggression', as John Kenneth Galbraith, McGeorge Bundy and Arthur Schlesinger, Jr. among others put it in a letter to the *New York Times* in late April 1950. They warned of a US strategy anchored in a 'misplaced faith in atomic weapons and strategic bombing' that 'seems to impair the moral and political strength' of the United States. All this added up, they thought, to a condition which 'may invite the extension of techniques of guerrilla warfare ... in marginal areas, in the confidence that such local activity would incur only local risks'. Prophetic words uttered two months before the outbreak of war and twenty years before the appearance of the urban guerrilla and the homegrown terrorist. The letter's criticism of strategic bombing was far more ominous than it could have seemed at the time. It was not the first such criticism. Testifying before the House armed services committee on 11 October 1949, as spokesman for the Navy's opposition to the Air Force's long-range B–36 bomber, Rear-Admiral Ralph A. Ofstie conjoined moral and military considerations: 'We consider that strategic air warfare, as practised in the past and as proposed for the future, is militarily unsound and of limited effect, is morally wrong, and is decidedly harmful to the stability of a post-war world.'

Thus opposing alignments over the issue of the Super were gradually forming. The Korean War posed the problem of designing

179

and developing tactical atomic weapons, of refining the atomic arsenal already in existence at the cost of neglecting the all-out drive to produce the hydrogen bomb. It was the school of the little bomb against the school of the big bomb. Oppenheimer and the majority of the participating scientists stood squarely on the side of the little bomb. But there were scientists of note – particularly Edward Teller – who were passionately on the side of the production of the big bomb with all possible speed and regardless of expense. This was the central issue of the time and, as Klaus Fuchs was arrested and convicted of turning over atomic secrets straight from Los Alamos to the Soviets and the Rosenbergs were arrested, convicted and executed for their part in the same case of espionage, the issue became all the more passionately contested. Within a week after President Harry Truman's announcement of the go-ahead on the hydrogen bomb (31 January 1950) twelve of the nation's most prominent scientists, including Hans Bethe, made a statement decrying the president's decision: 'We believe that no nation has the right to use such a bomb, no matter how righteous its cause. This bomb is no longer a weapon of war but a means of extermination of whole populations ... We urge that the United States ... make a solemn declaration that we shall never use this bomb first.' The next week Albert Einstein made a statement: 'If [the H-bomb] is successful, radioactive poisoning of the atmosphere and hence annihilation of any life on earth has been brought within the range of technical possibilities ... In the end there beckons more and more clearly general annihilation.'

Oppenheimer's general opposition to the hydrogen bomb formed a pattern of behaviour in committee visible and disturbing to those with access to both his security file and the committee reports. Even Oppenheimer's advocacy of nuclear-weapons diversification became a part of this pattern, because diversification clearly implied a proportionate diminution in the effort to build the big bomb. Even a study of continental air defence co-sponsored by Oppenheimer – among several other scientists – became part of the same pattern in the eyes of the Strategic Air Command (defence being the opposite of offence). To compound the effect, Oppenheimer had the same caustic wit and impatience with ignorance that Galileo had all too often displayed. At a congressional hearing Oppenheimer publicly humiliated Admiral Lewis L. Strauss, a commissioner of the AEC, by exposing the latter's ignorance of the nature of isotopes, one of the prerequisites for producing atomic power. (The issue before the congressional committee was whether the United States should share isotopes with the British government by way of cooperation in matters of nuclear development. Strauss, alone among the five Atomic Energy Commissioners, opposed the sharing on security grounds. Oppenheimer characterized Strauss's concern as 'morbid'. Strauss never forgave Oppenheimer, whose very friends thought he had gone too far. When he stepped down from testifying he asked a friend, 'How did I do?' The friend answered, 'Too well, Robert, all too well.')

Thus by 1953 all occasions seemed to conspire against 'Oppie'. His students kept turning up before various investigating committees, either admitting they had once been members of the Communist Party or taking refuge in the Fifth Amendment. In June 1951 the California Committee on Un-American Activities came to a novel variation of the common conclusion that there is no such thing as negative proof. The reports of Steve Nelson to the Communist Party complaining of the Oppenheimers' 'uncooperative and unsympathetic [attitude] toward Communism', the committee said, were merely a cover-up to throw US agents off the trail. Hence the reports of Nelson were actually indications of the strong ties of the Oppenheimers to the Party. New and much younger people coming to the staff of the Atomic Energy Commission were far more shocked by the contents of Oppenheimer's security file than the older members who could remember what the 'old days' some ten years in the past were really like. America is a country in which the velocity of history is especially great, in which each succeeding decade wipes its immediate predecessor out, a phenomenon that has moved some observers to remark that America has no history but only an eternal present. In America a decade is an era and unique. Compare the Roaring Twenties with the Great Depression of the thirties; or either of the two with the American Century that was crammed into the forties. But even against this background it must be admitted that Oppenheimer had the great misfortune to have been involved in the mightiest transition of all time, a 'generation gap' that is perhaps the great divide of human history, an abyss that opened up in the decade of the forties with the discovery, production and use of nuclear weapons. Not Armageddon but Alamogordo. Before Alamogordo it was philosophically possible and even usual to state that 'nothing ever really changes'. After Alamogordo it was no longer possible: something had changed. Something had changed in the profoundest possible sense. Man had acquired the knowledge and the means of destroying himself and his world. He could negate the Creation. This was the nature of the abyss that separated Oppenheimer from his past. There was no bridging it. He was a different man in a different world.

Theologically, one supposes, Alamogordo could be and should be regarded as the second Fall from grace, the second and definitive loss of innocence. The implications of this change – whatever one chose to call it or however one chose to regard it – were and are simply awesome. Forces were suddenly released, impulses and ideas in the minds of men, that went unrecognized or were misconstrued first and foremost by the very people who harboured them. For the rational among mankind it amounted to something like the confrontation with reality, with an unsuspected reality, and the clear and compelling need to come to terms with it. It seems ironic that the imperative to think in eschatological terms should have come just as the process of secularization, in the industrial world at any rate, had come into full swing and already, to all appearances, triumphantly established itself.

The main consequence of the implications of this change was the unconscious assumption by mankind of Godhood. The assumption was recognized and hence disguised as the assumption of responsibility for the preservation of creation: 'Please don't blow up the world; we are doing the best we can.' This is a premise which explains the sudden emergence of ecology as a science and the primary social concern in the civilized world. Suddenly the burden of custodianship was there for all to see and it could not be denied. But with the assumption of Godhood there came something else. Suddenly all the premises of life on the earth and in the universe were thrown open to question. It was not only a loss of values; it was a questioning as to the usefulness, true significance – the legitimacy – of everything, values foremost. It was a new look at everything. The whole of humanity was caught flat-footed, some sections of it far more so than others. Those nations like China and India that had been drenched in mysticism and otherworldliness to the neglect of technology found themselves at an almost hopeless disadvantage, but were nevertheless not so stupid as to try to opt out of the technological revolution. Other nations, like those in most of Africa and much of South America, were and were to remain so backward as to be virtually without any hope of ever 'making the connection' or 'catching up' with the modern industrial world in its breakaway development of high technology – in short, of entering the computer age. Directly or indirectly the atom bomb and its ushering in of the nuclear age have been responsible for the continuing precipitous technological development that has characterized the post-war era. The difference between the 'haves' and the 'have-nots' has increased as a consequence of this rush to remake the world, increased to the point of having become utterly grotesque. But not only backward peoples or mystic traditions were in trouble because of this. Systems of government were weighed in the same balance and found wanting. The technological revolution spelled the doom of the socialist system – at very least, of doctrinaire socialism among other totalitarian forms of government. By the same token the technological revolution favoured forms of government like the conventional democracies that guaranteed or otherwise promoted freedom of discussion. This was and is so because freedom of discussion is the lubricant necessary to the very process of thinking. Where there is no freedom of discussion, there is no freedom of thought. And where there is no freedom of thought there can be no freedom of inquiry and hence no scientific progress.

The essential importance of freedom of discussion was a regular fetish with Oppenheimer. While setting up Los Alamos he refused the idea of compartmentalization outright and in total when General Groves broached the subject as a basic security measure and hence a matter of course. He also refused to allow political opinion for consideration as a criterion of suitability for scientific work. In a letter to the Rochester *Democrat–Chronicle* concerning his leftist colleague Bernard Peters, he elaborated on the subject:

> Political opinion, no matter how radical or how freely expressed, does not disqualify a scientist for a high career in science; it does not disqualify him as a teacher of science; it does not impugn his integrity nor his honor. We have seen in other countries criteria of political orthodoxy applied to ruin scientists and put an end to their work. This has brought with it the attrition of science. Even more, it has been part of the destruction of freedom of inquiry, and of political freedom itself. This is no path to follow for a people determined to stay free.

The decision to indict Robert Oppenheimer as a security risk was taken as a result of a variety of circumstances and factors. What precipitated the indictment, however, was a letter written by William Liscum Borden, former executive director of the Congressional Joint Atomic Energy Committee, addressed to J. Edgar Hoover, director of the Federal Bureau of Investigation. Borden had been wholly fascinated by the Oppenheimer case during his five-year tenure as executive director. He had made a thorough study of the four-and-a-half-foot stack of reports that constituted the investigative dossier on Oppenheimer. 'The purpose of this letter,' he wrote, 'is to state my own exhaustively considered opinion, based upon years of study of the available classified evidence that, more probably than not, J. Robert Oppenheimer is an agent of the Soviet Union.' William Borden was a strait-laced, gung-ho Yale man, a bomber pilot out of England and over Europe during World War II, and the author of a book published in 1946 under the title *There Will Be No Time: The Revolution in Strategy*. Like a great many other people, Borden had been impressed by German rocketry in the final stage of the war. It was his book that directed legislative attention to young Borden and brought him to Capitol Hill, first as a staff assistant to Senator McMahon of Connecticut.

Borden's letter contained nothing that was not known to all those more or less familiar with the Oppenheimer file. It was the timing that was embarrassing. The Republicans had only recently accused former President Truman of having appointed Harry Dexter White to a new and more important post after receiving an FBI report to the effect that White was a Soviet spy. The accusation against Truman concerning White had been made in a speech by Attorney-General Herbert Brownell and immediately caused a considerable scandal because for the first time the contents of an FBI investigative report had been made public to what looked like a partisan political purpose. It was an unprecedented breach of form that almost boomeranged because it seemingly impugned the loyalty of Truman himself. The real scandal, the fact that Harry Dexter White, assistant secretary of the treasury from 1941 through 1945, was a staff career agent of the KGB, was almost obscured by the controversy surrounding the political dimensions of the charge. As it was, the receipt of Borden's letter in the Justice Department (of which the FBI is a part) put the attorney-general in an extremely embarrassing situation. He had just accused a former president of laxity in ignoring an official warning that a highly placed official was a Soviet spy. His own administration was now in exactly the same dilemma (until a few hours before he wrote his letter Borden was still the executive director of the Joint Committee on Atomic Energy in Congress; the Borden letter was made part of the weekly summary of top-secret events circulated to all members of the Joint Committee). In an article that later appeared in the *Atlantic Monthly*, Washington correspondent Warren Unna reported that Brownell and FBI director Hoover went to Eisenhower 'and demanded that the physicist be ousted from his position as a consultant to the AEC and that his "Q" clearance be revoked'. A few days later, on 3 December, in a meeting with the AEC's chairman Strauss, Attorney-General Brownell and others, Eisenhower opined that since no formal hearing had ever been held on the charges against Oppenheimer, a hearing ought to be ordered. On 9 December the commissioners of the AEC voted 'unanimously to institute the regular procedures of the commission to determine the veracity or falsity of the charges' contained in William Borden's letter to the FBI. On 23 December the AEC sent its 3,400-word letter of charges signed by Major-General K. D. Nichols, the AEC general manager, to Oppenheimer. The letter contained twenty-four allegations, twenty-three of which concerned Oppenheimer's alleged Communist and left-wing connections from 1938 to 1946, which is to say *before* the AEC's unanimous clearance of Oppenheimer on identical charges in 1947. The twenty-fourth charge, however, dealt with events that postdated the 1947 AEC clearance. Beginning with a recitation of Oppenheimer's statements affirming the feasibility of the hydrogen bomb, the charge then cited reports that

> in the autumn of 1949, and subsequently, you strongly opposed the development of the hydrogen bomb (1) on moral grounds, (2) by claiming that it was not feasible, (3) by claiming that there were insufficient facilities and scientific personnel to carry on the development and (4) that it was not politically desirable.
>
> ... that you departed from your proper role as an adviser to the [Atomic Energy] Commission by causing the distribution separately and in private, to top personnel at Los Alamos, of the majority and minority reports of the General Advisory Committee on development of the hydrogen bomb for the purpose of trying to turn such top personnel against the development of the hydrogen bomb.

185

... that you were instrumental in persuading other outstanding scientists not to work on the hydrogen bomb project, and that the opposition to the hydrogen bomb, of which you are the most experienced, most powerful, and most effective member, has definitely slowed down its development.

The twenty-fourth and final charge is a new departure. It is based on the questioning and rejection of Oppenheimer's opinions – even his officially registered and recorded opinions rendered in his capacity as an adviser to the Atomic Energy Commission. It includes the curious and ominous phrase 'by causing the distribution separately and in private . . . of the majority and minority reports' of the GAC to top personnel, implying clandestine activity on the part of Oppenheimer. The twenty-fourth charge predetermined the nature of the hearing itself.

The American government's choice of the hybrid form of official investigation, the hearing, is significant in itself. It was not just a matter of desiring to avoid the political extreme and general spectacle of a legitimate trial for fear – among other considerations – of poisoning the atmosphere in the American scientific community. The hearing was and is the American government's preferred means of dealing with cases affecting national security. It is the official instrument of the government's loyalty programme. It was a kind of pre-trial investigation with few of the powers or attributes of a juridical procedure and fewer of the principles and protections of due process. It could, if need were found and cause given, bind a person over for prosecution by a regular court, say for perjury. Technically, therefore, it avoided the stigma and onus of the political 'show-trial' or 'people's-court' extravaganzas affected by dictatorships of the left and right. But the hearing invests enormous discretionary powers in the person of the hearing board's chairman and the other members of the board. Indeed, the powers of the board members were virtually unlimited save for the charter outlining the duties and objectives of the board which, in turn, were subject to the interpretation of the board itself. In addition to the three board members – the AEC chose Gordon Gray, president of the University of North Carolina and a former assistant secretary of the Army, a Democrat, to lend a bipartisan character to the board as chairman – there was also the role of outside counsel or prosecuting attorney for the AEC (the conduct of the prosecution of the charges was not supposed to be adversarial, as it would have been in a court of law), while the defendant was likewise allowed counsel.

It was in the process of preparation of the defence that Oppenheimer's counsel, Lloyd K. Garrison, an eminent New York attorney, got a good whiff of the cannon shot that was to come. There was the problem of clearance because much of the material supporting the charges was classified. This was not just the investigative reports of the FBI. There were also military and technical data, much classified top secret. When Garrison requested clearance for himself and his two assistants he was told that he alone could be given a clearance – the commission did 'not feel . . . that granting of clearance to additional counsel would be warranted'. For some time Garrison and his assistants wondered whether it would not be wiser to forgo clearance altogether, their rationale being that non-clearance might limit the amount of secret material included in the hearing, while a security clearance might turn out to be of minimal value in the light of General Nichols's assertion 'that the government would reserve the right to decide what documents were relevant, and even what portion of the relevant documents could be examined by Oppenheimer's attorneys'. In the end it was decided that Garrison should apply for clearance to prevent their client's being left alone in the event they were obliged to leave the hearing room on the introduction of classified evidence. In the case of Roger Robb, the attorney appointed by the AEC for the prosecution, an 'emergency Q' clearance was obtained in eight days. In the case of Lloyd Garrison, the commission declared it was not possible to clear him before the hearing had ended and the Gray Board had submitted its report – eight weeks after Garrison had submitted his request. Thus the defence went through the hearing without access to information that was fully available to the prosecution. On three occasions, after his attorneys had been obliged to leave the hearing room for security reasons, Robert Oppenheimer was left as 'unrepresented and alone' as Galileo had been before the Inquisition. The comparison of the two, the hearing of Robert Oppenheimer by the Gray Board and the trial of Galileo by the Inquisition, does not stop there. In a court of law the rules of evidence would have prevented the imposition of any such nonsense as practised by the AEC in the Gray Board hearing of J. Robert Oppenheimer. But precisely because a hearing is not a juridical procedure it provides none of the safeguards of the rights of the defendant that are characteristic of the law. To paraphrase Hegel, the law is there not because it represents an ideal instrument of justice but in order by its presence to preclude the adoption and institution of something worse. The hearing was invented to circumvent the law for the convenience of the state. Like the Inquisition, it is 'an emergency tribunal creating and changing its own administrative law at will'. The hearing is secret because it deals in secrets and pronounces its findings on the basis of secrets which it refuses to divulge to the counsel for the defence or even, to anything like the extent called for, to the defendant himself. This grotesque situation, the conduct of the prosecution on one level and that of the defence on another, forced a parade of character witnesses by the defence and the attempt to caricature them by the prosecution in every instance.

The haunting refrain of the Oppenheimer hearing is the recurring consideration, expressed in various ways – hearsay, letters, official reports, advice, admonitions, appeals and in quiet conversations – by Oppenheimer and his like-minded colleagues, of the necessity to internationalize the bomb, to open (or at least not to foreclose) negotiations with the Soviets for an international agreement establishing co-ownership, co-production and the reciprocal surveillance and inspection of all forms of nuclear and thermonuclear devices and installations. This consideration was of course the basis of the GAC's reluctance, as a body, to build the hydrogen bomb. The bigger and more destructive the bombs became – in production and in projection – the greater the reluctance of the scientists, or the great majority of them, to build the ultimate bomb. As Dr Luis Alvarez, then professor of physics at the University of California, testified during the hearing: '. . . Dr Op- penheimer pointed out to me, there was no apparent limit to the magnitude of the explosion [of the hydrogen bomb], whereas there appeared to be a limit to the magnitude of explosion from what we now call an atomic bomb.' As far as 'Oppie's' opponents were concerned, this was the root-evil of the 'pattern' of his performance as a senior consultant to the American government on nuclear and thermonuclear matters. In the fourth paragraph of a six-paragraph annexe to a GAC report of the time, the position is stated in a lapidary formulation: 'We believe a super-bomb should never be produced. Mankind would be far better off not to have a demonstration of the feasibility of such a weapon until the present climate of world opinion changes.' When the President of the United States, against the advice of the GAC, publicly decreed the expeditious production of the hydrogen bomb as official government policy, the GAC duly accepted the decision and went to work on the project with a will. With a will, but without enthusiasm. Which is to say, without anything like the enthusiasm Oppenheimer managed to infuse into his charges at Los Alamos during World War II. For this Oppenheimer was held strictly to account: indeed, his own record of accomplishment was held up to him as a standard against which all his subsequent conduct and behaviour were measured. Here is Oppenheimer's old friend, the eminent physicist Isidor Rabi, testifying for the defence:

> ... when we first met in 1929, American physics was not really very much, certainly not consonant with the great size and wealth of the country. We were very much concerned with raising the level of American physics. We were sick and tired of going to Europe as learners. We wanted to be independent. I must say that our generation, Dr Oppenheimer's and my other friend that I can mention, did that job, and that ten years later we were at the top of the heap, and it wasn't just because certain refugees came out of Germany, but because of what we did here. This was a conscious motivation. Oppenheimer set up this school of theoretical physics which was a tremendous contribution. In fact, I don't know how we could have carried out the scientific part of the war without the contributions of the people who worked with Oppenheimer. They made their contributions very willingly and very enthusiastically and single-mindedly.

Dr Bradbury, director of the Los Alamos Scientific Laboratory at the time of the hearing, was even more damning with strong praise:

> ... I think that while loyalty is a very difficult thing to demonstrate in an objective way, that Dr Oppenheimer in his direction of Los Alamos Laboratory during the war years did demonstrate such loyalty. I myself feel that his devotion to that task, the nature of the decisions which he was called upon to make, the manner in which he made them, were as objective a demonstration of personal loyalty to this country as I myself can imagine.

This sort of praise for past accomplishments served only to heighten the contrast between the then and the now, between the

189

remote and the recent. Moreover, there was a certain amount of paranoia on both sides. The United States Air Force and more specifically the Strategic Air Command, the big-bomb men who were and still are on perpetual alert, were more upset by the Soviet Union's explosion of an atomic device than anyone else and thirsted after the acquisition of the Super more than anyone else. Unfortunately, people on perpetual alert are easy targets for directed rumours. The big-bomb men were always hearing things. As he testified at the Oppenheimer hearing, the chief scientist of the Air Force, David Tressel Griggs, in an almost plaintive note averred that 'we were told that in the late fall, I believe, of 1951, Oppenheimer and two colleagues formed an informal committee of three to work for world peace or some such purpose, as they saw it. We were also told that in this effort they considered that many things were more important than the development of the thermo- nuclear weapon, specifically the air defense of the continental United States, which was the subject of the Lincoln Summer Study.' Indeed, Dr Griggs swore under oath that he had seen Dr Zacharias, the physicist, colleague and friend of Robert Oppenheimer, write the word 'ZORC' in capital letters on the blackboard during a session of the Lincoln Summer Study. The word 'ZORC' was alleged to be an acronym of the names Zacharias, Oppenheimer, Rabi and [Charles] Lauritsen. In May 1953 there appeared an article in *Fortune* magazine under the title 'ZORC Takes Up the Fight'. The thrust of the article was that, having failed to prevent the test of Edward Teller's thermonuclear device at Eniwetok in late 1952, and having lost their official positions as a consequence, Oppenheimer and his friends formed 'ZORC' in order to achieve their goals by other means. It was apparently an Air Force-leaked story and smacked of cabal. Zacharias denied ever having written any such thing as 'ZORC' on any blackboard or anything else. He also denied ever having seen or heard the word 'ZORC' before it appeared in the *Fortune* article. Of the fifty to a hundred people said to be present by both Griggs and Zacharias only one, a James B. Fisk, was reported by hearsay to have seen Zacharias write anything like 'ZORC' on the blackboard. The hearing could do nothing with the story and it remains a piece of Air Force paranoia. In his book, *The Oppenheimer Case*, Philip Stern adds a footnote describing the extreme sensitivity of the Air Force in its pride of place:

The acuteness of interservice sensitivity was illustrated earlier by the Air Force reaction that was stirred when Secretary of Defense James Forrestal casually cited, before a Congressional committee, a favorite Navy statistic: that two-thirds of the globe is covered by water. Air Force Secretary Stewart Symington heatedly protested that Forrestal had dealt the Air Force a 'death blow'. His passion was dissipated when a Forrestal aide hit upon a diplomatic solution to the crisis: the transcript of the Secretary's testimony would be amended to add that above all the water *and* all the land on earth was *air*. Symington and the Air Force generals were delighted with the proffered amendment.

It must be said, however, that the scientists, too, came in for their share of paranoia. There was the *canard* that Secretary of the Air Force Thomas K. Finletter had said at a luncheon in the Pentagon something to the effect of 'If we had the hydrogen bomb we could rule the world.' It is dismaying and uncharacteristic of Oppenheimer but significant that he clung to the authenticity of this rumour. For the larger point is that the very subject of the Super was a perfect prop for paranoia. Given into the hands of any man or group of men the ultimate bomb warranted the worst and most extravagant speculation. And the reverse proposition was equally true: withheld from the appointed defenders of the republic, that 'last, best hope of mankind', by any man or group of men the ultimate bomb warranted the wildest and most extravagant accusations.

The most extreme accusation that can be lodged against a public servant is the charge of disloyalty. Fittingly, the most telling blow to the board delivered by a witness under oath at the Oppenheimer hearing was the testimony of the doyen of scientific advisers and consultants, Vannevar Bush. It is worth quoting *in extenso*:

> . . . I feel that this board has made a mistake and that it is a serious one. I feel that the letter of General Nichols which I read, this bill of particulars, is quite capable of being interpreted as placing a man on trial because he held opinions, which is quite contrary to the American system, which is a terrible thing. And as I move about I find that discussed today very energetically, that here is a man who is being pilloried because he had strong opinions, and had the temerity to express them. If this country ever gets to the point where we come that near to the Russian system, we are certainly

not in any condition to attempt to lead the free world toward the benefits of democracy.

Now, if I had been on this board, I most certainly would have refused to entertain a set of charges that could possibly be thus interpreted. As things now stand, I am just simply glad I am not in the position of the board.

MR GRAY: What is the mistake the board has made?

THE WITNESS: I think you should have immediately said before we will enter into this matter, we want a bill of particulars which makes it very clear that this man is not being tried because he expressed opinions.

MR GRAY: Are you aware, Dr Bush, how this got in the press and was spread throughout the world?

THE WITNESS: Yes, I know how it was released.

MR GRAY: Do you know who released it?

THE WITNESS: I believe this gentleman on my right [Roger Robb] released it.

MR GRAY: I don't think you can blame the board. We had quite a discussion about that.

THE WITNESS: It was bound to be released sometime when you made your report.

MR GRAY: It might have leaked. I don't think it was bound to be released. I assure you, and I am sure that we are all sure that whatever the outcome, the board is going to be very severely criticized.

THE WITNESS: I am sure of that, and I regret it sincerely, sir, because I fear that this thing, when your report is released, will be misinterpreted on that very basis whatever you may do.

DR EVANS: Dr Bush, you don't think we sought this job, do you?

THE WITNESS: I am sure you didn't, and you have my profound sympathy and respect. I think the fact that a group of men of this sort are willing to do as tough and as difficult a job as this augurs well for the country. It is in stark contrast with some of the things that we have seen going on about us in similar circumstances. Orderly procedure and all of that is good. I merely regret that the thing can be misinterpreted as it stands on the record, and misinterpreted in a way that can do great damage. I know, of course, that the executive branch of the United States Government had no intention whatever of pillorying a man for his opinions. But the situation has not been helped, gentlemen, recently by statements of the Secretary of Defense. I can assure you that the scientific community is deeply stirred today.

A highlight of the month-long proceedings was the appearance of John J. McCloy as a witness for the defence. McCloy, who was assistant secretary of war during World War II and, as such, very much a part of the team that produced the atomic bomb, emphasized positive aspects in security considerations as posed against wartime exigency:

... Indeed, I think we would probably have taken a convicted murderer if he had that capacity. There again is this question of the relative character of security. It depends somewhat on the day and age that you are in.

I want to emphasize particularly this affirmative side of it. The names we bandied about at that time included a number of refugees and a number of people that came from Europe. I have the impression – I may be wrong about it – but I have the impression that a very large element of this theoretical thinking did emanate from the minds of those who immigrated to this country, and had not been generated here as far as it had been in Europe. There were names like Fermi and Wigner and Teller, Rabi, another queer name, Szilard, or something like that – but I have the impression they came over here, and probably embued with a certain anti-Nazi fervor which tended to stimulate thinking, and it is that type of mind that we certainly needed then.

We could find, so to speak, practical atomic physicists, and today there are great quantities of them being trained, and whether we are getting this finely balanced imagination which can stretch beyond the practicalities of this thing is to my mind the important aspect of this problem. The art is still in its infancy and we are still in need of great imagination in this field.

In a very real sense, therefore, I think there is a security risk in reverse. If anything is done which would in any way repress or dampen that fervor, that verve, that enthusiasm, or the feeling generally that the place where you can get the greatest opportunity for the expansion of your mind and your experiments in this field is the United States, to that extent the security of the United States is impaired.

In other words, you can't be too conventional about it or you run into a security problem the other way. We are only secure if we have the best brains and the best reach of mind in this field. If the impression is prevalent that scientists as a whole have to work under such great restrictions and perhaps great suspicion, in the United States, we may lose the next step in this field, which I think would be very dangerous for us.

From my own experience in Germany, although they were very backward in this field, and in that respect there is a very interesting instance which I have seen referred to in print –

At this point McCloy was interrupted by the chairman on the grounds that he was wandering 'too far afield'. In the face of McCloy's polite insistence, the chairman allowed him to continue:

I did want to make one point. I have been asked this recently in New York frequently: Do you think that Dr Oppenheimer is a security risk, and how would I answer that. This is long before I had any idea I was going to be called here. What do you mean by security, positive, negative, there is a security risk both ways in this thing. It is the affirmative security that I believe we must protect here. I would say that even if Dr Oppenheimer had some connections that were somewhat suspicious or make one fairly uneasy you have to balance his affirmative aspect against that, before you can finally conclude in your own mind that he is a reasonable security risk, because there is a balance of interest there; that he not only is himself, but that he represents in terms of scientific inquiry – I am sorry if I rambled on about that and I didn't mean to.

In his current incarnation as a banker McCloy was asked if he would leave anyone in charge of his vaults about whom he had any doubts in his mind. McCloy answered in the negative but went on to elaborate on the 'pat analog of the bank-vault man'. If the man in charge of the vaults, he said, 'knew more about ... the intricacies of time locks than anybody else in the world, I might think twice before I let him go, because I would balance the risks in this connection'. McCloy then related how, as high commissioner in Germany, he had selected for employment in the United States German scientists who 'a few years before were doing their utmost to overthrow the United States Government by violence', many of whom became prominent in the American guided missile programme, one of whom, Wernher von Braun, became famous as the architect of the moon shot, the Apollo programme. It would not have helped McCloy's argument could he have foreseen that some of the German scientists he had invited to the United States in 1945–6 would return to Germany forty years later rather than face the expense of contesting, and the ignominy of enduring deportation proceedings on charges of war criminality of World War II vintage. (This delayed-action – by a

194

full four decades – was possible because there is no statute of limitations for Nazi war crimes.)

Surely the most eloquent explanation of Oppenheimer's youthful delinquencies, a sort of *threnothriambics* (lamentation and triumph combined) of the man, his weaknesses and his works, was provided in the testimony of John von Neumann, physicist and mathematician at Los Alamos. Von Neumann was asked what he made of Oppenheimer's embroiling himself in the attempt to disguise the Chevalier incident in 1943. Here is his answer:

> Look, you have to view the performance and the character of a man as a whole. This episode, if true, would make me think that the course of the year 1943 or in 1942 and 1943, he was not emotionally and intellectually prepared to handle this kind of job; that he subsequently learned how to handle it, and handled it very well, I know. I would say that all of us in the war years, and by all of us, I mean all people in scientific technical occupations, got suddenly in contact with a universe we had never known before. I mean this particular problem of security, the fact that people who looked all right might be conspirators and might be spies. They are all things, which do not enter one's normal experience in ordinary times. While we are now most of us quite prepared to discover such things in our entourage we were not prepared to discover these things in 1943. So I must say this had on anyone a shock effect, and any one of us may have behaved foolishly and ineffectively and untruthfully, so this condition is something ten years later I would not consider too serious. This would affect me the same way as if I would suddenly hear about somebody that he has had some extraordinary escapade in his adolescence.
>
> I know that neither of us were adolescents at that time, but of course we were all little children with respect to the situation which had developed, namely, that we were suddenly dealing with something with which one could blow up the world. Furthermore, we were involved in a triangular war where two of our enemies had done suddenly the nice thing of fighting each other. But after all, they were still enemies. This was a very peculiar situation. None of us had been educated or conditioned to exist in this situation, and we had to make our rationalization and our code of conduct as we went along.

Robert Oppenheimer could not make this defence for himself because he had matured in charge, because it was his responsibility, because it was he who had pulled it all together, because he was Mr Atom Bomb (after the 'trial' André Malraux said that Oppenheimer's defence should have consisted of one statement: *'Je suis la bombe atomique!'*). After the 'trial' all were agreed that Oppenheimer had been his own worst witness. There was the searingly painful, acutely embarrassing scene when Oppenheimer, under cross-examination, pronounced judgement on himself:

ROBB: Now, let us go back to your interview with Colonel Pash [the security officer]. Did you tell Pash the truth about this thing?

THE WITNESS: No.

ROBB: You lied to him?

THE WITNESS: Yes . . .

ROBB: Didn't you say that X [Chevalier] had approached three people?

THE WITNESS: Probably.

ROBB: Why did you do that, Doctor?

THE WITNESS: Because I was an idiot.

These answers, especially the last, were not given with bravado or manly evenness. Robb, in later recalling the scene, said that Oppenheimer was 'hunched over, wringing his hands, white as a sheet. I felt sick. That night when I came home I told my wife, "I've just seen a man destroy himself."' Oppenheimer had become a phantom to himself. That is to say his former self had become a phantom to his present self. He thoroughly disapproved of the phantom.

There is an atomic theory of personality in literature. As Yuri Trifonov put it at the beginning of his novel, *The House on the Embankment*: 'None of these lads is still in this world. Some perished in the war, some died of sickness, others disappeared without trace. And some . . . became other people.' This is more than 'one man in his time playing many parts, his acts being seven ages', although in many cases and particularly in the case of the self-made man some of the acts connected with the ages are as many different people. The urge for self-transcendence in every human being leads to drug addiction, alcoholism, promiscuity or crowd delirium, as Aldous Huxley called it. It is usually a lateral transcendence and more often downward in the end. With Oppenheimer the self-transcendence was upward. He became within a few years, in a perfectly extraordinary period of history, one of the acknowledged and universally admired leaders of the greatest nation on earth.

He hobnobbed with the great personages of American political and public life as a matter of course. He was on a first-name basis with most of the nation's political leaders. When he spoke of 'George' he was referring to George C. Marshall, secretary of state. As a result, some of his old friends had withdrawn their countenances and given him up as a genius destined to consort with kings, statesmen and captains of industry. Just nine years separated the Oppenheimer of the hearing from the Oppenheimer who, at war's near-end, before the bomb had been dropped, assured an apprehensive Teller warmly that there was nothing to worry about. It is well to remember the quote: 'He conveyed to me in glowing terms the deep concern, thoroughness and wisdom with which these questions were being handled in Washington. Our fate was in the hands of the best, the most conscientious, men of our nation. And they had information which we did not possess.' Meanwhile Oppenheimer himself had become one of 'the best, the most conscientious, men of our nation'. And he possessed, in general terms in any case, as much information as any of his peers. Enough information at any event to credit the rumour that Thomas K. Finletter had stated publicly that 'we' could rule the world if 'we' had the hydrogen bomb.

The Oppenheimer who grovelled in the dock, as it were – 'wringing his hands, white as a sheet' – was a throwback to 1943, a cringing clone of his former self who sat condemned by the man he had meanwhile become. But this man, grown wise in the way of governments at the highest level, knew more than he cared to know about 'the best, the most conscientious, men of our nation'. He was being tried by people who did not trust his judgement and whose judgement he did not trust. He had entered a sphere of contest in which the stakes were the highest and the risks were just as high. This was why he chose to stand his ground and make the fight. He could not docilely leave the field to those who, left to their own devices once those devices had become thermonuclear, might blow up the world. This, after all, had been Teller's advice: 'If I were told that the government didn't want me as an adviser any more I would take my hat and go – without a murmur.' Oppenheimer's very sense of responsibility prevented him from taking the easy way out. In fact, of course, there was no easy way out. If he had withdrawn, resigned and returned to teaching there was always the danger that quitting the field under accusation would have served only to add fuel to the fire of suspicion. Since the evidence adduced was all circumstantial, it would have added yet another circumstance – a big one and a fresh one – to the already imposing (on the face of it) pile. Oppenheimer was trapped by history, by the momentum of the development for which he himself was largely responsible.

Edward Teller was also trapped – in much the same way. He knew as well as Oppenheimer what the stakes were. He was both a Hungarian and a Jew, as the former he feared the Russians by tradition, as the latter he knew, especially after the 'doctors' plot', that the lot of the Jews in the Soviet Union was anything but comfortable and was likely to get worse, not better. He was also an immigrant. He knew that the Soviets must not be allowed under any circumstances to gain any sort of definitive advantage over the United States in the article of military prowess. Everything depended on maintaining military superiority or at least parity with the Soviet Union. For an immigrant the fate of his new nation is a very personal thing. Everything that happens in his new home – the home of his choice – affects him directly. That being the case, what a stroke of fortune for an immigrant – to be in a position to influence the fate of nations in favour of his new nation! It is a position pregnant with paradox – as pregnant as the Trojan horse.

Teller's answers to the two questions that summed up the case of Robert Oppenheimer are entirely in keeping with the mentality of the immigrant who finds himself in a position to influence the fate of nations and, most particularly, *the* nation.

MR ROBB: To simplify the issues here, perhaps, let me ask you this question: Is it your intention, in anything that you are about to testify to, to suggest that Dr Oppenheimer is disloyal to the United States?

MR TELLER: I do not want to suggest anything of the kind. I know Oppenheimer as an intellectually most alert and a very complicated person, and I think it would be presumptuous and wrong on my part if I would try in any way to analyze his motives. But I have always assumed, and I now assume, that he is loyal to the United States. I believe this, and I shall believe it until I see very conclusive proof to the opposite.

MR ROBB: Now a question which is the corollary of that. Do you or do you not believe that Dr Oppenheimer is a security risk?

MR TELLER: In a great number of cases I have seen Dr Oppenheimer act – I understood that Dr Oppenheimer acted – in a way which for me was exceedingly hard to understand. I thoroughly disagreed with him on numerous issues, and his actions frankly appeared to me confused and complicated. To this extent, I feel that I would like to see the vital interests of this country in hands which I understood better and therefore trust more.

Oppenheimer and Teller have become symbols in the field of nuclear and thermonuclear armament for the two-party republic America is. In a sense, Oppenheimer paid for the fact that a Democratic administration had remained in office for twenty full years. If Adlai Stevenson instead of Dwight D. Eisenhower had won the presidential election in 1952, Robert Oppenheimer would not have been brought before a board of review. If Dewey instead of Truman had won the presidential election of 1948, while the American monopoly of nuclear weapons still held, Oppenheimer would in all probability have been rotated out of his consultative position in a routine change of administration.

As it turned out, the combination of Oppenheimer and Teller insofar as their influence on the conduct of American foreign policy *vis-à-vis* the Soviet Union was concerned made for a balance between nuclear and thermonuclear preparedness and restraint. Thus the Soviet Union was always provided with the option of entering into serious disarmament negotiations despite the fact of the arms race. The Soviet Union used the option – too well: the Soviets proffered options to the United States in turn. These, however, were always integral parts of the Soviet Union's peace propaganda. They were designed to appeal to the emotional element in the human make-up while ignoring and thereby prejudicing any realistic approach to the complex of problems concerning disarmament. The Soviets answered the challenge presented by the advent of the nuclear age by resorting to their favourite and basic technique: sloganeering. Hence it immediately went to the extreme of demanding and appealing for 'universal disarmament' – surely the most utopian of all goals – secure in the conviction that the very proclamation of the goal ruled out the possibility of making even the most modest beginning in the direction of partial disarmament. As so often, the Soviet Union was using sloganeering as a blocking tactic. In short, the new 'discipline' of global strategy resultant from the development of intercontinental rockets with nuclear warheads was seized upon by the Soviets as a propaganda ploy. This was probably inevitable: mass-communication techniques have reached such a pitch of perfection in the past forty years that the temptation must have been overpowering in a one-party state dictatorship to use them – radio, films and television. As Aldous Huxley put it, 'the objectification of tendentious phantasy' had long since become absurdly easy. The United States and the conventional democracies were forced to respond in kind and after their several fashions. As a result, the nuclear-arms race became perforce a mass-media race: the more frightful the prospect, the more effective the propaganda concerning it. Instead of nuclear exchanges, which are rationally ruled out by the strategy of massive deterrence, there are rhetorical exchanges, Homeric epithets hurled by each side at the other ('evil empire', 'imperialist aggressors'), catchword accusations repeated *ad infinitum* ('cheating on arms control agreements', 'deliberately spreading AIDS as a form of surreptitious bacteriological warfare'). A good many observers have suggested that there should be negotiations between the superpowers to de-rhetorize relations as a prerequisite to negotiations on disarmament ('we will agree to stop calling you war mongers if you agree to stop calling us the evil empire'). Indeed, the elimination of war as the rational–traditional recourse to solving political disputes between nations has clearly served as midwife to the birth of rampant terrorism on the one hand and rampant rhetorization of international issues on the other. It seems that the progeny of this situation is indeed a set of twins. At first blush it would appear that the rhetorization of issues is a step in the right direction – closer to the cause of armament than mere waffle about the dangers of armament in and of itself. Also, rhetorization constitutes an enlargement of the general area of communications, albeit an abusive one. But there is the other, terroristic, twin. While it seems highly likely that rhetorization is a help in coming to rational grips with issues between governments, it seems equally likely that the same process bodes no good for the elimination or containment of terrorism. Rhetorization was part of the machinery for 'sensitizing' publics and republics to prospective physical harm or extinction on an individual or small group scale. This was the other, complementary side of the impairment of moral and political strength as the result of a 'misplaced faith in atomic weapons and strategic bombing' that left the United States and other major Western powers 'not well equipped to deal with problems of limited aggression' – such as 'the extension of the techniques of guerrilla warfare'. By the end of the fifties the age of the urban guerrilla was already in the stage of formation. Of course the softening up of the world public to all forms of physical violence had already been accomplished and continued by a sensationalist press and a film industry concentrating on the spectacular action film featuring the most violent and colourful types of explosion (in every such film at least one such explosion was *de rigueur*, accompanied by a minimum half-dozen automobile rammings or demolitions). Meanwhile there was no lack of major military actions such as the Korean War in the fifties and the Vietnam War in the sixties and seventies to keep violence in legitimate prospect before the world public. In the latter case – the Vietnam War – the effect of close and partisan coverage by the American press on the American and general Western public was devastating. For the first time in history it was not only made clear but emphasized with a drumbeat insistence that the American leadership in its conduct of the war did not know what it was doing.

IX

❧

LYSENKO *REDIVIVUS*: 'A CERTAIN ENGINEER NAMED SAKHAROV...'

World War II or the Great Patriotic War, as it is known in the Soviet Union, curtailed the self-imposed quarantine of the Soviets. After World War II the Soviet Union was not the same: even the granting of three delegations instead of one in the United Nations Organization by Roosevelt served the more to break the quarantine by tripling Soviet representation. In the same way triple member-ship increased Soviet representation in all the various subsidiary organizations of the UNO such as the World Health Organization (WHO), the United Nations Educational, Scientific and Cultural Or-ganization (UNESCO) and the United Nations Industrial Develop-ment Association (UNIDA) by a multiple of three. There were also the international organizations ancillary to the UNO such as the International Labour Organization (ILO) which, in the atmosphere prevailing immediately after the war, the Soviet Union was fairly obliged to join. Then, too, there were the repatriation teams that roamed the displaced-persons camps in Western Europe for years after the war as part of the United Nations Refugee and Resettle-ment Agency (UNRRA). Finally, the number of displaced persons from the Soviet Union (those who refused repatriation) was well over 3 million, most of whom were resettled overseas – in America, Australia, Canada and South America. This was the so-called second wave of Soviet emigration, which swelled the colonies of Russians, White Russians and Ukrainians in the various countries of the Western hemisphere by 100 per cent and often more.

To counteract this dangerous new intercourse with the nations of the world the Soviet Union denounced the American Marshall Plan (the European Recovery Program) as a self-serving instrument of 'dollar-imperialism'. This was one of the most fateful decisions in international affairs ever taken by the Soviet Union. With this denunciation the Soviet Union denied itself and its Eastern European satellites, including the newly won Czechoslovakia, billions of dollars in long-term low-interest loans and outright grants in aid. It effectively excluded itself and its satellites from the international financial machinery of the great industrial nations – such as the Office of European Economic Cooperation (OEEC) and the General Agreement on Tariffs and Trade (GATT) – and rusticated the rouble (with the satellite currencies in tow) to the status of scrip since general convertibility, the hallmark of a currency, was ruled out by virtue of its exclusion from the open international market. By the same token, after having participated in the opening Bretton Woods Conference for the Clarification of Currency, Payments and Trade Questions in 1943 (from which emerged the World Bank), the Soviet Union absented itself from the ratification of the measures decided by the conference in 1945. Thus the whole process was yet another example of Soviet self-mutilation in the name of an ideological phantom.

Thus the true believers in the Communist Party of the Soviet Union found themselves facing a vastly different situation. It was a question of mounting a perpetual offensive on several fronts – scientific, cultural, commercial, athletic (the Soviets decided to participate in the Olympic Games for the first time in 1948 in London) and military (the Soviet Union having acquired by conquest a collection of 'allies' in Eastern Europe and western Asia – the northern half of Korea). So it was that in August 1948, in a session of the LAAAS that came to be known as 'historical' (some scientists suggested that a more apt designation would have been 'hysterical'), the Lysenkoists indulged themselves in an exercise of slander that resulted in the dismissal or demotion of hundreds of scientists, 'the best and most qualified representatives of Soviet biology'. The charges levelled against them were idealism, reactionary views, Morganism, Weismannism, complicity with imperialism and the bourgeoisie, Mendelism, anti-Michurinism, grovelling before the West, sabotage, metaphysics, mechanism, racism, cosmopolitanism, formalism, unproductiveness, anti-Marxism, anti-Darwinism, alienation from practice, etc. The same thing happened to the opponents of the Vilyams grassland system. The crusade culminated in the administrative rout of the classical or conventional scientists. An example was set that lasted as long as Stalin lived and somewhat longer. Nevertheless, the struggle was an unequal one. The international scientific community is rather closely knit. In effect, then, the Soviets had taken the field against all flags: their ultimate defeat was a foregone conclusion. Because of the sheer size of their opposition (almost everybody else) and the velocity of scientific development in the system of free enterprise, it soon became clear that the Lysenkoists were simply not well enough equipped professionally – above all they lacked the general and specific erudition – to compete in scientific debate. And as luck would have it, some of the greatest advances had meanwhile been made in that very branch of biology in which they had chosen to make their main stand: genetics. What was still more disturbing, the advances had been made in America. But even before the 'historical–hysterical' LAAAS session, Lysenko had put his foot into it again. In an article in late 1945 he announced the absence of intraspecific competition in plant life. This extension of Lysenko-ism brought conflict with other scientific groups such as botanists, morphologists, zoologists and evolutionists that immediately re-sponded with criticism. This new stand of Lysenko was somewhat surprising in that intraspecific competition is one of the corner-stones of Darwinism. Undeterred by this or any other consideration, Lysenko branded all those who disagreed with his hypothesis as 'defenders of imperialism'. In 1947, in the *Literaturnaya Gazeta* Lysenko published an article explaining why he insisted on the absence of intraspecific competition. It is worth quoting at length:

How explain why bourgeois biology values the 'theory' of in-straspecific competition so highly? Because it must justify the fact that, in the capitalist society, the great majority of people, in a period of overproduction of material goods, lives poorly.

All mankind belongs to one biological species. Hence, bourgeois science had to invent intraspecific struggle. In nature, they say, there is a cruel struggle for food which is in short supply, and for living conditions, within each species. The stronger, better adapted individuals are the victors. The same, then, occurs among people: the capitalists have millions, the workers live in poverty, because the capitalists supposedly are more intelligent and more able be-cause of their heredity.

We Soviet people know well that the oppression of the workers, the dominance of the capitalist class and imperialistic wars have nothing to do with any biological laws. They are all based on the laws of a rotting, moribund, bourgeois capitalist society.

There is no intraspecific competition in nature. There is only competition between species: the wolf eats the hare; the hare does not eat another hare, it eats grass. Wheat does not hamper wheat. But couchgrass, goose-foot, pastor's lettuce are all members of other species, and when they appear among wheat or *kok-sagyz* (Russian dandelions), they take away the latter's food, and struggle against them.

Bourgeois biology, by its very essence, because it is bourgeois, neither could nor can make any discoveries that have to be based on the absence of intraspecific competition, a principle it does not recognize. That is why American scientists could not adopt the practice of cluster sowing. They, servants of capitalism, need not struggle with the elements, with nature; they need an invented struggle between two kinds of wheat belonging to the same species. By means of fabricated intraspecific competition, 'the eternal laws of nature', they are attempting to justify the class struggle and the oppression, by white Americans, of Negroes. How can they admit absence of competition within a species?

Here Lysenko simply reverses his own motivation and attributes it to the Americans and other bourgeois scientists. But his opposition to competition within a species is belied by his advocacy of intraspecific competition in the sciences. It was a logical and rhetorical mistake to categorize so broadly as to maintain that there were a 'Soviet biology' and a 'bourgeois biology' or, worse still, a 'Soviet science' and a 'capitalist science'. It is a peculiar position and reminiscent of Urban VIII's contention that there was, or could be, a divine physics as well as a physics concocted by the feeble mind of man. But in the middle of the twentieth century this was too much. No one, not after Hiroshima, was prepared to contend that there were two physics, two chemistries or two different sets of laws for thermodynamics. And yet before Hiroshima, precisely this contention was made, and implemented on a scale that proved to be critical for all mankind.

It is perhaps the strangest story in politico–sociological history. In 1932 the director of the Institute of Physics in Dresden made a statement. It was this: 'Modern physics is an instrument of Jewry for the destruction of Nordic science. True physics is the creation of the German spirit. In fact, all European science is the fruit of Aryan, or better, German thought. Statistical laws in physics must be racially understood.' The director was one of an even hundred Nazi professors represented in a book of the time condemning the theory of relativity. Einstein's response was to the point: 'If I were wrong, one would have been enough.'

This ideological fanaticism, which substituted race-hatred for the Soviet–Communist class-hatred, was exemplified by Philip Lenard, the Nobel laureate in physics for the year 1905. Lenard was an arch-anti-Semite, a Nazi Party member from the early days when there were very few scientists in the Nazi movement, a man whose *bête noire* was Albert Einstein, the Nobel laureate in physics, vintage 1921. For Lenard the whole of nuclear physics and the theory of relativity were a 'typical Jewish swindle'. Hitler revered Lenard and trusted his professional judgement implicitly. In his table talk, thoroughly indoctrinated by Lenard as he was, Hitler would occasionally refer to nuclear physics as 'Jewish physics'. This attitude was adopted by Alfred Rosenberg, Reichsminister and party ideologue as well as by other leading Nazi politicians such as the minister for science and education who for this reason withheld his support from German nuclear research. Hence very little provision and only the barest allocation were made for the study and development of the possibilities of constructing a nuclear bomb. When the Americans overran the German nuclear installation in Hechingen and Otto Hahn's chemistry laboratory at Tailfingen at the close of the war – it was Hahn, it will be remembered, whose fission experiment in 1938 had started the race for the atom bomb – they found that German efforts had hardly progressed beyond the most rudimentary stages of research. In other words, the same unreasonable and unreasoning hatred of the Jews on the part of the Nazis was the cause of two simultaneous effects: it moved the Jews to their signal role in the production of the nuclear bomb in America and prevented the Germans, who had discovered nuclear fission, from even so much as seriously addressing the problem of construction of the bomb.

There were voices that were heard, even in the late forties, and articles that appeared in highly specialized scientific publications and they asked the same question: 'If there is only one physics and only one chemistry, how can there be two botanies or even two biologies?' After the L A A A S session V. M. Molotov, the minister of foreign affairs, in a speech commemorating the thirty-first anniversary of the October Revolution, delivered himself of a rousing endorsement of the erroneous thesis of Lysenko concerning genetics. Medvedev cites an example typical of the times. After Molotov's speech, the Soviet geneticist I. A. Rapaport was requested to make a public repudiation of the chromosome theory of heredity. When Rapaport instead attempted to demonstrate the practical value of genetics he was refuted by excerpts from Molotov's speech. 'Why,' asked Rapaport in reply, 'do you think that Molotov knows genetics better than I?' Rapaport's reply, which should go down in history as a question summing up the confrontation of a highly trained specialist with a very loosely trained generalist, resulted directly in the expulsion of Rapaport from the Communist Party and dismissal from his post. He was forced to work for several years as a laboratory assistant in a geological institute. After Stalin's death he was rehabilitated and reinstalled. Nevertheless, the incident ruined his health.

But even before Stalin's death Lysenko was repeatedly if sporadically under fire. One of the main reasons for this change from slavish obedience cum noble passive resistance against a tyranny ferociously jealous of its totality was the explosion by the Americans of the atomic bomb. The bomb magnified at least a thousandfold the present danger, the potential for world-ending catastrophe depending not only on the good or evil intent but even of an innocent wrong move on the part of a head of state – and particularly on the part of the head of a totalitarian state, that is, one without the benefit of democratic safeguards in the system of checks and balances in legislation. If a Thomas K. Finletter could be considered suspect and therefore dangerous by Robert Oppenheimer, what did the same considerations make Lavrenti Beria (in charge of the Soviet nuclear energy programme) look like?

Even so, the consequences of the 1948 LAAAS session were devastating. The Academy of Sciences was the first bastion of rational science to fall. A resolution was passed by the presidium of the Academy supporting without qualification all the decisions of the LAAAS session. A number of the laboratories pronounced 'hotbeds of reactionary Morganism' were abolished (these were the laboratories of cytogenetics, botanical cytology, phenogenesis and others). Then the minister of higher education, S. V. Kaftanov, ordered the country's university staffs to rid themselves entirely of all carriers of reactionary Morganism. The Academy of Medical Sciences followed suit. Kaftanov was especially assiduous. He dug up statements made by N. V. Koltsov twenty-five years earlier and pilloried the eminent biologist with false charges: 'There is no need to comment on these man-hating ravings that smell of Fascist delirium a mile off. This is the kind of wild fanatic that our contemporary Morganist–Mendelists have for an apostle!' Kaftanov also made sport of the idea that there are hereditary diseases in man – what kind of hereditary diseases, he asked, could there be in a progressive socialist society?

Special commissions were created for searching out Morganist–Mendelists in the large biological and agricultural instructional and research institutions and experiment stations. Nearly all scientists in such places of work were obliged to appear before one of the commissions and pledge allegiance to the new faith. 'Within two days alone (23–24 August 1948),' continues Medvedev, 'Kaftanov issued a series of detailed orders published in pamphlet form and sent to every institution of higher learning. Order Number 1208, regarding universities, decreed (Point 2) the dismissal from Moscow University of those who actively fought against Michurinism, including the professor of Darwinism, Shmalgauzen, the professor of developmental biology, M. M. Zavadovsky, the professor of plant physiology, Sabinin, the dean of the faculty, Yudintsev, and Assistant Professors Alikhanyan, Zelikman, Berman, and Shapiro. Similarly dismissed from Leningrad University were the prorector Polyansky, the dean of biological sciences, Lobashev, Professor Svetlov, and Assistant Professors Novikov and Arapetyants. There followed similar lists for the universities of Kharkov, Gorky, Voronezh, Kiev, Saratov and Tbilisi (Tiflis). But that was only the beginning.'

Point 6 of the order read: 'The Central University Administration and the Administration of Cadres are directed to review within two months all departments of biological faculties to free them from all opposed to Michurinist biology and to strengthen them by appointing Michurinists to them.' The order abolished courses and directed the destruction of texts and of books based on Mendelism–Morganism (Sinnot and Dunn, Serebrovsky, Shmalgauzen, etc.), and the elimination of all non-Michurinist research projects.

On the same day, Kaftanov issued a similar order (Number 1210) for zootechnical and veterinary institutes, dismissing Rokitsky, Vasin and many others, while a lengthy order on schools of agriculture decreed dismissal from the TAA alone of Golubev,

Zhebrak, Paramonov, Khokhlov, Borisenko, Konstantinov* and others. This was followed by similar rosters for Kharkov, Omsk, Saratov and other agricultural institutes.

The next day, still another order (Number 1216/525) from the minister of higher education and the deputy minister of public health was sent around the medical institutes. It decreed that 'all courses in such disciplines as anatomy, histology, pathophysiology, pathoanatomy, microbiology, psychopathology, forensic medicine and psychiatry were to shift to a Michurinist basis.'

Of course this last order was absurd: there could be no question of introducing Lysenkoism or Michurinism into any of the disciplines mentioned. What was done, as Medvedev explains, was to eliminate any mention of heredity from the various courses concerned. And again, rosters of dismissed scientists and anathematized textbooks followed. The pogrom continued for several months.

The object of this protracted and painstaking exercise was not only the crushing of all opposition to Lysenkoism. It was also the taking of widespread precautions to ensure that opposition could not rise again in the foreseeable future. Other ministries joined in the chase. The minister of agriculture, I. A. Benediktov, issued order Number 1530, dated 6 October 1948, putting an end to all genetic research in animal-husbandry, announcing that there could not be any such thing as lethal mutations, and closing the experiment station on distant hybridization, run by the famous geneticist, A. R. Zhebrak. The order also prescribed the cessation of all instruction and all research projects not in line with the teachings of Michurin–Vilyams–Lysenko.

This catalogue of castigation is crowned by the 'anecdotal' order Number 543 (7 May 1949) directing the review of all forestry courses to 'ensure their being taught on the basis of the materialistic Michurin–Lysenko doctrine of denial of intraspecific competition and facilitation, and the recognition of interspecific competition and facilitation as the basic factor in the evolution of living matter'.

The victory of Lysenkoism was complete. His monopoly in biology was established. A number of geneticists were even deprived of their academic degrees in 1948 and a ban was placed on genetics of the old school for many years to come. Research in

* Well known if not famous names all.

genetics, plant hormones, cytogenetics, polyploidy, etc., was also banned, with what effect may be imagined. Yet Lysenko was literally idolized: statues were raised to him (some of them remained in place for ten years and more). Busts and bas-reliefs of him were sold and his portraits hung in all scientific institutions. These *'objets d'art'* could still be purchased in 1961, though at triple discount. In the repertory of the State Chorus was a hymn to Lysenko.

At this point, at the height of his fame and influence, Lysenko's undisciplined imagination made another quantum leap in absurdity. He began propagating, via a series of fraudulent experiments, the transformation of one species into another: wheat into rye, cultivated into wild oats and barley, cabbages into turnips, sunflowers into dodder, etc.*

The truth is that Lysenko in his triumph went even further out on the limb of his own eccentricity. Support of his views became increasingly difficult. By the end of 1952 even friends and loyal colleagues had begun to turn against him, his absolute domination having lasted just four years. Thus the first attacks appeared in the Soviet press even before the death of Stalin. Two articles appeared in the December issue of *Botanichesky Zhurnal*. Both dealt with only one of Lysenko's theories, a theory on speciation by saltation distinguished by its especial waywardness. The reaction on the

---

* Shortly before, after becoming professor of genetics and breeding – in addition to his other posts and honours – Lysenko gave his first lecture to his students. It was memorable for his assertion that when different birds were fed hairy caterpillars, cuckoos hatched from their eggs. All these discoveries were published in Lysenko's journal *Agrobiologiya*. In an article entitled 'Species', written by Lysenko for the *Great Soviet Encyclopedia*, the author discloses the inspiration and authority for these experiments: 'Stalin's teachings about gradual, concealed, unnoticeable quantitative changes leading to rapid, radical qualitative changes permitted Soviet biologists to discover in plants the realization of such quantitative transitions, the transformation of one species into another.'

The only basis in Stalin's writings for the teaching attributed to him by Lysenko (and by A. I. Oparin, a biochemist) is to be found in an article entitled 'Anarchism or Socialism', written in 1907. It consists of the following statement: 'The Mendeleev periodic table clearly shows the great significance of qualitative and quantitative changes in the history of nature. This is also shown in biology by the theory of neo-Lamarckism which is supplanting neo-Darwinism.' (Jean Baptiste Pierre Antoine de Monet de Lamarck (1744–1829) was a French naturalist who developed a theory of evolution which contained the view that acquired characteristics are inherited. He died in oblivion and penury; however, interest in his theory was revived toward the end of the nineteenth century because of its tangencies with Darwinism.)

part of the mass of Soviet scientists consisted of several dozen articles to the editors of *Botanichesky Zhurnal* and the general assumption that the discussion had been thrown open again. The Lysenkoists reacted violently, with the result that the discussion was broadened to include all aspects of Lysenkoism. The size and the circulation of *Botanichesky Zhurnal* went up; from a bi-monthly it became a monthly. Not long thereafter the publication of the Moscow Society of Naturalists entered the fray with several critical articles. Research in genetics was resumed: genetics laboratories were set up in the Academy of Sciences and study groups organized. A number of articles demonstrated the practical damage to agriculture caused by Lysenkoism. A petition requesting the removal of Lysenko from the post of L A A A S president and the dismissal of Oparin as secretary of the Biological Section of the Academy of Sciences was signed by more than three hundred scientists. Both requests were met: Lysenko and Oparin were replaced by the conventional scientists Lobanov and Engelgardt respectively.

In desperation the Lysenkoists responded true to form by attempting to invoke administrative coercion. At the plenary session of the central executive committee in December 1958 Lysenko blanketed all criticism against him as merely the intrigues of Western imperialists. But he made one telling point in his *plaidoyer*: 'It is clear that the question is not about me but about the materialistic trend of biology related to collective-farm practices, which I have upheld and still uphold in my articles.' The entire phenomenon of Lysenkoism cannot be separated from the collectivization drive, that began in 1928 with the dispossession of the kulaks and never ended. The neverending Soviet collectivization drive, in turn, cannot be separated from the neverending Soviet agricultural disaster. There certainly was, and just as certainly continues to be, a kind of dialectical determinism operative in the entire chain of events. Fascinatingly, Medvedev is purblind to this aspect of the situation. He accuses Lysenko and his followers of courting disaster out of tactical considerations:

> Deliberately and anti-patriotically they provided grounds for criticism of our country and the Soviet government, and tried to take advantage of the criticism of their own ends, without taking into account that such criticism could do real damage to the socialist

ideal of scientific progress and freedom of scientific discussion. Criticism from abroad, even if justifiable, was desirable for them, because it helped them to fight off criticism from their own compatriot Soviet scientists.

One may marvel at the self-inflicted perversity of this situation. Because of the outlawing of everything foreign, which was pretty much Lenin's doing although it went hand in hand with the traditional excessive Russian xenophobia, it was and remains comparatively easy to turn this paranoia against itself – either by exciting praise or blame of the Soviet Union, that is to say, anything Soviet; praise in the West equating with blame in the Soviet Union and blame equating with praise in the same relationship. This is the basic formula of the cold war situation, but it is one that admits of refinement. If Lysenko and his followers had been capable of earning praise from abroad they could have profited from it simply by styling it 'praise from enlightened, progressive elements in capitalist countries', or – in cases where the praisers were unmistakably reactionary – by passing them off as rascals trying to use the truth for their own fell purposes. But the Lysenkoists were scarcely capable of earning praise from abroad – their talents were modest indeed and often enough simply nonexistent. In the ultimate sense, then, Lysenko and his friends were victims, dupes of a philosophy of class warfare that constrained them to work within the narrow limits and fatal temptations of a sectarian creed. They were not capable of attracting praise and so, in a society expectant of great events and under a regime that demanded great events as a matter of course and a tenet of faith, they were reduced to attracting blame. It was the only thing they could do. To attract blame is the recourse of the inferior. But there is a double compulsion here: blame attracts the inferior as well. All the inferior lacked to work their way was the licence afforded by the basic premise of Communism à la Lenin: 'In the name of the downtrodden anything is fair.' The National Socialists of Germany afforded the same licence, merely inserting the word 'German' before 'downtrodden'. In 1932 Edgar Jung, who was the chief aide of Franz von Papen as Chancellor and then Vice-Chancellor of Germany, wrote a book entitled *Against the Dominion of the Inferior in the New Order for Germany and Europe*. Its publication cost Jung his life. He was liquidated in 1934 in the course of Hitler's putting

212

down the putative Röhm *putsch*. The combination of licence and inferiority renders possible the formation of a cacistocracy, literally 'the rule of the worst'. The National Socialist clique that ruled Germany for twelve years was a cacistocracy, as was the Soviet government under Stalin. After the death of Stalin and the subsequent 'thaw', the Soviet government improved, particularly in the reduction of the ferocity of its repressiveness, but it was and remains a slow and tortuous process.

Indeed and in the event, Lysenko prevailed: his telling point told, the authorities listened and the empire struck back. Administrative reprisal undid almost everything the conventional scientists had finally managed to do. The editorial board of the *Botanichesky Zhurnal* was disbanded and reconstituted for the most part with Lysenko's followers by the end of 1958. The Moscow Society of Naturalists was put on its best behaviour. Engelgardt was removed from the biological section of the Academy of Sciences and replaced by Sisakyan, a Lysenko follower. The Soviet delegation to the Tenth International Congress in 1958 in Canada was changed at the last minute. This was awkward because the delegation as originally constituted had submitted several papers on genetics. These were withdrawn, but the programme announcing the times and order of succession of the papers had already been printed and could not be changed. Thus the entire membership of the congress waited in silence until the time designated for the reading of the undelivered papers expired. The Soviet delegates attended only one of the congress's twenty sections. This was the section on graft hybrids which had been arranged for them especially.

Unhorsed in a skirmish, as it were, Lysenko quickly re-established himself and his kind, recapturing a number of ministerial posts and regaining key positions in the Academy of Sciences biology section, in the LAAAS, the committee on higher degrees, the academies of Union republics, the Znanie [knowledge] Society and in the agricultural section of the Union of Societies for Cultural Links Abroad. In other words the Lysenkoists had retaken the central blocking position from which they could intercept all information on biology and agricultural science. This they did, extending their control of the situation for fully another five years, for a total of fifteen years after the 1948 session of the LAAAS.

Despite this commanding position, the broad variety of facilities and the length of time at their disposal, the Lysenkoists made not one recognizable theoretical discovery, not one in any sense considerable contribution to the furtherance of agriculture in the Soviet Union. But the significance of the Lysenkoists and their tenure lies not in what they did but in what they prevented being done: for some twenty years they prevented the acquisition by the Soviet Union of the greatest agricultural innovation of the twentieth century, namely the hybridization of corn, achieved by the Americans during World War II, with resulting yield increases of up to 80 per cent. It was, in fact, the spectacular success of American agriculture during the war that moved the Soviet government to welcome a total quarantine against any and all agricultural information coming from the United States, for the stupendous fact of the matter was that in just five years the Americans had succeeded in slightly more than doubling their total agricultural production. For the Soviets what was worse than the fact itself was the contrast in which it stood to Soviet agricultural achievement. Nevertheless, the Soviet government would have welcomed the innovation of hybrid corn. As it was, thanks to the Lysenko monopoly in all matters agricultural, they were obliged to wait for the benefit until Khrushchev visited an American farm during his visit in 1959, when the innovation was offered him and his country as a matter of course.

It is impossible to determine the extent of the damage done by Lysenkoism to Soviet agriculture. And yet all the harm was done in the name of a 'fulfilment of a socialist reconstruction of agriculture', which harks back to Stalin's personal initiative for a 're-structuring of the land'. The determination from the beginning and throughout was to do something totally new, departing altogether from the old; the operative words in the Soviet agricultural scientific jargon are 'rapid' and 'radical'. The Lysenkoists were caught squarely on the horns of a dilemma. They could not accept a truce because the struggle against world science was their bread and butter; it was their raison d'être. But neither, on the other hand, could they accept a fair fight: they could not allow a straight-up presentation of two theories of the same phenomena of nature for the purpose of determining which of the two was valid. In this regard it was not surprising that Khrushchev took up the cudgels for Lysenkoism. He expressed the position nicely in his speech to Soviet writers on 8 March 1963, entitled 'Peaceful Co-existence in the Area of Ideology is Treason against Marxism–Leninism and Betrayal of the Cause of Workers and Peasants'. Here he made the issue clear: 'The biological front of the battle,' he said, 'is not only the battlefront of a Soviet scientist to further technical progress; it is the battlefront of Soviet ideology versus bourgeois ideology.' In much the same fashion the Lysenkoite philosopher, G. V. Platonov, had narrowed the choice in a book with the title *Dialectical Materialism and Problems of Genetics*. In it Platonov presented his readers with the alternative: 'either genetics or Marxism and dialectical materialism'. There was no question of having it both ways. Thus the Lysenkoites were reduced to making the fight strictly by resorting to government and Party administrative coercion, that is, by placing blinkers, trammels and hobbles on their scientists, hampering and handicapping them in their struggle with the bourgeois West. In short, the position was perfectly paradoxical. The Soviets had painted themselves into a corner and were vociferously complaining about the laws of geometry. They could neither prevail nor surrender in their struggle with 'world science'.

The first sign of the impending breakdown of Lysenkoism was the resolution passed jointly by the Central Executive Committee and the USSR Council of Ministers restoring medical genetics. Medical genetics consists in large part of the study of hereditary diseases. For this reason it could not be Michurinist, since the Lysenkoist clique which had embraced and embroidered Michurinism denied the existence of hereditary diseases. For the same reason the restoration of medical genetics presupposed the restoration of general genetics. This prerequisite was impossible to ignore. The presidium of the Academy of Medical Sciences sponsored a series of conferences in 1963, the upshot of which was a resolution 'On the state and perspectives of development of research in medical genetics'. This took note of the 'acute lag of the USSR in this area, and of the economic damage connected with the rout of medical genetics in 1937 and 1948'. Moreover the blame for this state of affairs was placed precisely where it belonged – with the school of Michurinist biology.

Thus the way was opened for a return to reason. Practical measures were proposed and carried out for the gradual revival of general genetics. Cooler heads, alive to the dangers involved in continuing neglect, bowed to the discipline of circumstances and prevailed over the ideological zealots in the Central Committee. Thus the official recognition of Morganism–Mendelism was enforced and reinforced. And yet the Lysenkoites could not read the handwriting on the wall. A desperate counterattack was undertaken by S. Pavlenko in an article entitled 'Neopositivism – the Arms of Reaction'. Here the author pilloried the harm caused by the chromosome theory of heredity and castigated Morgan and Mendel, who had 'directed genetics into the riverbed of idealism', etc. To no avail. Medvedev recounts that the attack remained isolated and constituted nothing more than a curiosity against the background of developments. The Lysenkoites were being overtaken by events. In the year 1963 there appeared two books written by native authors, the first texts written in Russia on scientific genetics in twenty-five years. These were Lobashev's *Genetika* and Efroimson's *Introduction to Medical Genetics*. Early the year before, wide circulation was given to a pamphlet issued by the World Health Organization, which was written by an international committee of experts. Of course the circulation of this pamphlet did much to emphasize the question of reintroducing the teaching of genetics in universities and medical schools in the Soviet Union after an absence of fifteen years. 'The First Report of the Expert Committee on Human Genetics' of the World Health Organization was published in English, French, Russian and Spanish and given worldwide distribution. A selection of passages from this report is quoted here because it provides a revealing background to the Soviet genetics dispute in general and to the horrendous aberration of Lysenkoism in particular:

I. THE IMPORTANCE OF GENETICS IN THE MEDICAL SCIENCES

The gene is at the basis of life, and it is self-evident that instruction about its nature and function should be included in the education of those who intend to follow any biological discipline. There are, however, even more cogent reasons for teaching genetics to medical students. Knowledge of the means by which genes influence the development and function of the living organism has advanced to the point where it not only forms an essential background to a proper understanding of disease but has important practical applications of which physicians must be aware if they are to provide high standards of medical care . . .

The concept of molecular disease can be extended to many other variants, be they malformations or metabolic diseases: the 'inborn errors of metabolism', for instance, which are being identified at the rate of about three a year, are characterized by the fact that they show simple Mendelian inheritance, and that each results from a specific enzymatic defect. Thus, when the geneticist establishes the genetic basis for a disease, this is an indication for the biochemist that there is probably an underlying specific biochemical defect. Identification of the defect provides the basis for sound treatment and may also improve the precision of genetic counselling through the biochemical detection of normal carriers of the gene . . .

The committee agreed that students entering medical school should already have a thorough grounding in biology, including the elementary principles of genetics. In many areas of the world this would require a marked improvement in the teaching of biology, and in particular, the inclusion of genetics in the curriculum of biology teachers.

The plenary session of the Central Committee of the Communist Party of the Soviet Union in February 1964 was convened expressly to discuss 'the intensification of agricultural production on the basis of widespread utilization of fertilizers, irrigation, complex mechanization and the adoption of scientific advances and front-rank experience for the attainment of most rapid increase of agricultural production'. This was an opportunity of a magnitude almost consonant with the character of a provocation for Lysenko and his followers. The greater their disappointment and indignation, then, when the Minister of Agriculture Volovchenko, who gave the main report of the session, made only cursory reference to Lysenko and his achievements and refrained from making any mention of 'reactionary Morganism'. Shortly thereafter came Lysenko's turn to speak. He immediately took up the minister's failure to mention the Lysenko method of increasing the butterfat content of milk and his earth-compost fertilizers. 'This is not a mere detail,' he said. 'These methods are of great significance in increasing yields and dairy production throughout the Soviet Union. We have formulated a general law about the life of the species, a law subsuming all other biological and genetic laws.' Lysenko then proceeded to explain how this universal law had enabled him to discover a means of raising the butterfat content of milk. The secret was the crossing of dairy cows with Jersey bulls, and the bull calves were to be had from Lysenko's own experimental farms. At the final session Khrushchev himself spoke. He devoted a great deal of attention to Lysenko, of whom he was fulsome in his praise, calling him the ideal Soviet scientist.

Khrushchev's wholehearted support of Lysenko should have surprised no one. As the author of 'competitive co-existence', the Soviet leader had, as early as 1956, put in prospect the Soviet Union's catching up with the United States in the production of milk, butter and meat within a year – or two at the most. Such claims, like his most famous threat–promise to 'bury' the United States in twenty years, were of course part and parcel of Khrushchev's de-Stalinization policy: he was determined to demonstrate by the production of practical results that the entire miserable showing of the Soviet Union in the arena of international comparisons had been due exclusively to the great blight of 'the cult of personality'. At the time of the plenary session of the Central Committee in 1964 it was already very late in the Khrushchev era. By this time, if not long before, he was grasping at straws. He had to come up with something fast and he knew it. He had acquired the reputation in the Central Committee, which is roughly the size of the American Congress at a poorly attended joint-session, of an unpredictable, eccentric blowhard. There were many reasons for Khrushchev's growing unpopularity in the higher reaches of the Party: his backing away from his own ultimatum in Berlin (1958–60), his withdrawing Soviet rockets from Cuba during the crisis of confrontation with the United States in 1962, but the main reason was his failure to improve the situation in the priority he himself had set: agriculture. It was Khrushchev, after all, who had conceived and tried to implement the ill-starred, tremendous and extremely costly 'virgin lands' project, in which 42 million hectares of new land in the eastern reaches of the Soviet Union were opened to cultivation. Khrushchev had no choice but to push his luck. Much like a field commander, Lysenko saw the strategic necessity for storming the biology section of the Academy of Sciences and making it a stronghold of Lysenkoism – just as Olshansky had done with the LAAAS. On Khrushchev's initiative then, a number of vacancies in genetics were created in the former institution: three full and two corresponding memberships, it being understood that all the new posts would be filled by Lysenkoites. The trouble with this procedure was that in each case the vote of the section concerned had to be confirmed by the vote

of the general assembly of the Academy of Sciences with all sections
– physiology, biochemistry and physics, etc. (all branches of science
in which there was no internal controversy and never had been) –
attending. One of Lysenko's candidates, Remeslo, a plant-breeder,
was rejected resoundingly within the biology section on three
consecutive votes. Another, N. Y. Nuzhdin, a geneticist, was voted
in by the biology section but ran into trouble in the general
assembly. Medvedev supplies excerpts from the stenographic account of the session:

ENGELGARDT: Among the candidates for the vacancies in genetics,
we find the names of people well known throughout the land as
having made contributions of considerable significance to agricultural practice and to breeding. We look at these names with respect,
and their merits raise no doubts in anyone's mind. But also among
the candidates in genetics there is, at least in my opinion, a reason
to depart from the recommendation of the committee and the opinion expressed by the vote of the appropriate section, I have in mind
the candidacy of Nuzhdin. I am here in an embarrassing position:
after all, some ten years ago we elected Nuzhdin as a corresponding
member in the biology section. In the natural course of events his
promotion would be normal. But the question arises, has Nuzhdin
kept pace in this period with the advancement of science? I know of
no practical contributions he has made that are comparable with
those of other candidates in the same category.

It is hence clear that our judgement here must be based on the
theoretical and experimental work of Nuzhdin. The problem of
developing experimental genetics in all its modern aspects is one of
the utmost importance for our country, because at all costs we
have to overcome the essential lag which had developed in this
area in the course of recent times. I see no basis for supposing that
the election of Nuzhdin would aid in the solution of the problem . . .
Thumbing through several annual indexes of the leading journals
in genetics for the last few years, I found no mention of Nuzhdin's
name. And even without indexes, had such work been in existence,
it would have been known to us.

In a word, it is clear that the Academy of Sciences would not
gain, in the person of Nuzhdin, a scientist who could raise the level
of genetical research and turn it in the direction of the main line of
contemporary genetics. I must therefore disagree with the evaluation of the section of general biology, and hence cannot consider
Nuzhdin's candidacy as meeting the requirements expected of the
highest-ranking scientists of our land.

SAKHAROV: I shall be brief. We all recognize that the scientific reputation of a member of the Soviet Academy of Sciences should be above reproach. And now, in discussing Nuzhdin's candidacy, we must approach this issue with great attentiveness. In the document passed around it says: 'Nuzhdin has paid much attention to the problems of the struggle with anti-Michurinist distortions of biology, constantly criticizing various idealistic trends in the study of heredity and variations. His general philosophical works, in connection with the further development of the materialistic teaching of Michurin and other outstanding figures of biology, are widely known not only in our country but also abroad.'

It is a matter of scientific conscience for each of the academicians who will vote as to how to interpret what is really hidden behind this struggle against anti-Michurinist distortion and for the further development of the philosophical works of outstanding figures in biology, and so forth. I shall not read the excerpt a second time.

As for myself, I call on those present to vote so that the only 'ayes' will be by those who, together with Nuzhdin, together with Lysenko, bear the responsibility for the infamous, painful pages in the development of Soviet science, which fortunately are now coming to an end. [*Applause.*]

PRESIDENT KELDYSH: ... I do not think we can approach ... the election from this point of view. It would seem to me inappropriate to open up here a discussion on the problems of development of biology. And from this standpoint I consider Sakharov's speech tactless ...

LYSENKO: Not tactless, but slanderous! The presidium ...

KELDYSH: Trofim Denisovich, why should the presidium defend itself? It was Sakharov's speech, not the presidium's. It is not supported, at least by me; I don't know about the presidium, but think it would not support it, since the presidium discussed the resolution on biology of the CEC and Council of Ministers and will carry on in the spirit of that resolution. I think that, given Trofim Denisovich's protest, we can discuss the incident which just occurred, but this is not the time. I think we should concentrate now on the candidacy.

LYSENKO: At least, if not the meeting as a whole, does the presidium support Sakharov's statement? You said you did not, but what about the presidium?

Lysenko never received an answer to his specific question, but he received an answer to his larger question and forthwith. Of the 150 members present, 126 voted against Nuzhdin. The vacancy remained unfilled and Lysenko remained in shock. The spectacular intervention of Andrei Sakharov was also remarkable for the obvious animus that informed it. In citing the 'document passed around' Sakharov held up both its style and its content to ridicule – and not only once: 'I shall not read the excerpt a second time' (having just given an acid description of the document in question). There was also the element of surprise: who could have expected the quiet, reserved physicist to take so decided, so combative a stand? And then there was the prestige involved. Eleven years before this same Andrei Dmitrievich Sakharov had been elected to the Academy of Sciences at the age of thirty-two, thus becoming the youngest scientist ever to receive this honour. Moreover he was elected a full member of the Academy without ever having been a corresponding member (Sakharov's mentor, Igor Tamm, who was elected to the Academy on the same day, had been a corresponding member for twenty years). No, the Lysenkoites and the Soviet government leadership (or at least a good part of it, since the leadership had begun to split on the issue), were fully expectant but not apprehensive of the opposition of Engelgardt and the conventional biologists, but the sudden appearance of Sakharov on the scene and the pitch of authoritative condemnation in his tone set a signal.

Khrushchev reacted angrily to the signal. He had the president of the Academy of Sciences summoned and a memorandum of explanation to the Central Committee was demanded of Sakharov. Here there was another unpleasant surprise: Sakharov complied, but did so in a very sharp tone. This irritated Khrushchev still further. At a reception Khrushchev accused the Academy of entering politics (whereas, of course, politics had entered the Academy) and vouchsafed his opinion that the Soviet people did not need such an Academy. Indeed Khrushchev went so far as to order a commission formed to look into the possibility of reforming the Academy as a 'Committee on Science'. Likewise a series of plenipotentiary commissions was created to review the work of the biological institutes of the Academy of Sciences.

And yet time was running out for Khrushchev. In the year before, 1963, for the first time in history large amounts of grain had to be bought abroad to feed the population – from the United States, Canada, Australia, the Federal Republic of Germany and other countries. It was the final ignominy of the collectivization programme. But the ignominy of buying grain abroad to make up for shortfalls in Soviet grain production was to become habitual. The summer of 1964 was a bad one for the crops both in Siberia and in the virgin lands. There loomed the necessity of buying grain abroad again, a portent that caused a flurry of reorganizational measures in Soviet agriculture. These measures were all, as usual if not always, to no avail, but they comprised the last report prepared by Nikita Sergeyevich Khrushchev. When he returned from his vacation on the Black Sea in the fall of 1964 at the sharp instance of the Central Committee, he arrived in time to participate in the ceremony of his own ouster by unanimous vote. It was the end of the Khrushchev era.

It was also the end of the Lysenko era (although by no means the end of Lysenkoism). Any painstaking review of the Lysenko era reveals Lysenkoism as a mere symbol, a symptom of a virulent political disease and the entire period as the unbroken causal chain of successive calamities beginning with the collectivization drive or, more specifically, with 'dekulakization' – the dispossession of the more prosperous peasants. The elimination of the individual land-holding peasant farmer in the course of the collectivization drive was followed by his replacement with the institution of central planning and a huge, cumbersome, highly centralized staff of agricultural bureaucrats. This was exactly the wrong thing to do. The whole planning concept of collectivization was a break in the development of the country's agriculture, because in farming decisions have to be made on the spot: the farmer has a very short time to maximize the opportunity nature gives him. The idea of central planning is a stultification of any such initiative.

Central planning, particularly the attempt to coerce success administratively by setting quotas impossible to fulfil, necessitates in turn the falsification of reports to higher authorities in order to create and maintain the appearance of success. In the Lysenko era (but not only then), questionnaires of a set form were sent to all kolkhoz chairmen to be filled out to show crop yields. In effect, these questionnaires were formal invitations to cheat. By exaggerating dairy, meat and crop yields, the kolkhoz chairman could satisfy everyone (except, of course, ultimately the consumer) because there was no danger that the figures he supplied via the questionnaires would be checked. In this way the Soviets deliberately and programmatically deceived each other, as it were, by tacit mutual agreement. Six years after Khrushchev mentions the possibility of catching up with the United States in dairy and meat production he is obliged to buy grain abroad for the first time in the history of the country he serves. Similarly, in the aftermath of the Lysenko era it was discovered that 'a large number' of deceptive and fraudulent methods had been and were being used in the evaluation of experimental results and even in the experimental design of tests of practical application (a sort of second generation in fraudulent methods), both in agricultural chemistry and in animal husbandry. There was deliberate falsification of data in great detail concerning the milk yield of hybrid cows. As a wide series of experiments conducted in American agricultural colleges at the turn of the century had demonstrated, the overall yield of hybrid cows fell as butterfat content rose, so that in sum total there was less butterfat yield per cow. The same result held true for protein and beef production. In the course of its investigation the state review commission discovered that Lysenko had known full well his methods were economically unsound and by 1965 causing serious losses.

After rebuttals by Lysenko and re-rebuttals by the investigating commission, after the debate on the report and the report of the proceedings of the debate on the report had been published, the tentacular hoax of Lysenkoism lay exposed for all to see. But also exposed was the Augean task of cleaning up the mess that had been institutionalized for fifteen years, of undoing the harm that had been done through all the relevant institutions of the country, and of setting the matter of the study and practice of biology in the Soviet Union to rights. In other words, it was a matter of reversing all the measures, both organizational and governmental, that had been taken in 1948: then Mendelism was out and Lysenkoism (Michurinism) was in; now Lysenkoism was out and Mendelian genetics – and with it classical biology – was back in. But the reversal of these measures could not be accomplished with any-thing like the dispatch that had characterized their imposition. There were various reasons for this. Lysenkoism had been defeated and was being dismantled in the name of democracy. The demo-cratic way of doing things is far more complicated, far more pains-taking than its opposite, the dictatorial fiat. Lysenkoism had imposed itself in a matter of days, or a few weeks at most. To reverse the measures imposed and effect a full renovation of the scientific institutions concerned would take not weeks nor months

223

but many years. One of the chief reasons for the sluggish pace of the reform is a circumstance peculiar to the Soviet system. It is the most betitled and bemedalled society in world history. Lysenko, for example, belonged to three academies, was a laureate of many prizes, a Hero of Socialist Labour (the highest non-military distinction), the bearer of nine Orders of Lenin, etc. The complicating factor is that titles, awards and medals in the Soviet Union are interconnected with privileges and positions. The recipient of such titles, awards and medals has a lifetime income and various privileges that are independent of his professional standing. To strip a laureate of his titles, awards and medals is to run the risk of debasing the institution of such awards and titles. The prodigality with which the Soviet government bestows such awards is indicative of the degree of the system's presumption that citizens so lavishly awarded will conduct themselves strictly in keeping with the state's expectations. It is, in fact, a system of a whole series of presumptions, beginning perhaps with that of the binding gratitude of the recipient. The award is a kind of insurance premium from and for the state, paid in advance to the citizen on the basis of a projection of his behaviour, the philosophy of *largesse oblige*. Andrei Dmitrievich Sakharov was awarded the Hero of Socialist Labour three times: he had done the state great service and they knew it. But the state's acknowledgement of services rendered was no greater than its expectations of loyalty to come, and that in the strict but arbitrary interpretation of the Party leadership or leader. The Lysenko era had demonstrated that the Party leadership did not know what it was doing. The semantic bandage applied to the Stalin era and all its savage injustices and horrible blunders – 'the cult of personality' – did not hide but pointedly exposed the fact that the new Party 'collective leadership' did not have or could not give an explanation for what had happened. Medvedev, reviewing the battlefield and recalling all the alarms and excursions, concludes that the Lysenkoites installed themselves in scientific institutions, editorial boards and academic councils 'by the basic method of decrees from ministries, government departments and boards, and by creation of special plenipotentiary commissions – in other words, by a coup', as if the government had lent itself to the enterprise or been duped into collaboration by a group of conspirators. In fact, of course, the coup was practised by the Party leader, using or sanctioning the methods mentioned. When

Khrushchev tried to repeat the coup in 1963–4 he failed because the Party leadership, which is to say the Central Committee, was in the process of turning against him. As the young Trotsky, already so quoted, put it: 'The organization of the Party takes the place of the Party itself; the Central Committee takes the place of the organization; and finally the dictator takes the place of the Central Committee.' In the case of Khrushchev, the Central Committee took its place from the dictator. But the larger point, of course, is that Khrushchev was never anything like the dictator Stalin was for some two full decades of absolute power (1933–53). There can be no doubt that the Central Committee, having learned the hard way that he who is most in harm's way under a dictatorship is the Party member and particularly the prominent Party member, meant to invalidate the conclusion of Trotsky's syllogism in future, preserving primacy as jealously as need be. This consideration in itself enhanced the prestige and independence of the Academy of Sciences, acknowledging it as a non-partisan bulwark against the vagaries of any general secretary or his favourites. The same consideration found in favour of increasing the scope of that institution's foreign contacts since the evidence had accumulated over the decades of the Lysenko era to the effect that any lessening of such contacts inevitably contributed to emphasizing still further the sectarian nature of Soviet society. Sectarianism had been identified as an unfailing accompaniment, if not a cause, 'of the unlimited power of one man', as de Tocqueville's syllogism puts it. The Central Committee itself emerged from the Lysenko era as the main institutional guarantee against at least the worst abuses characteristic of Stalinism.

But agriculture, in the Soviet scheme of things, has always been the great imponderable. Famine, the fear and actuality thereof, runs through Russian and Soviet history like a black thread. From the American point of view the endowment by nature of the Soviet Union with agricultural resources has been niggardly. Something like half of the territory of the Soviet Union lies above the 60th degree of latitude, as does most of Alaska. This also roughly marks the line above which the soil never thaws more than a few inches from the surface and is hence unarable – permafrost. In general, then, the growing season is very much shorter in the Soviet Union than in the United States and there are very few areas in which the average annual rainfall is as high as 20 inches.

When the population of what is now the Soviet Union was less than 100 million, as it was at the turn of the century, feeding the nation was comparatively easy. Over 40 per cent of the exports of Imperial Russia in 1913 were made up of grain. The Ukraine, the Caucasus and neighbouring areas were regarded as the agricultural cornucopia of Europe. But with the doubling and then near tripling of the populations concerned, with the revolution and the convulsions that preceded and followed, the agricultural problem gradually emerged in something very like its original starkness and immensity. For the Americans this explains the 'dramatic efforts' that have been made since the revolution to reclaim vast areas for agriculture, to implement programmes for reforestation and create huge irrigation projects. The solutions proposed or carried out were on the same scale of magnitude as the problems nature posed. But only apparently. In actuality the Soviets never invested more than half of what was necessary to achieve the goal they had set themselves. Soviet agricultural policy has always been based on achieving maximum agricultural output at minimum budgetary cost. In a sense this is no more of a contrast than a conformity between the size of the problem and the means applied to solve it. But was there ever really a choice? In order to solve the problem the Soviets would have had to reverse their whole system of priorities and give precedence to agriculture over heavy industry and armaments. This, as Soviets, they could not do.

In any case, when in the mid-fifties Khrushchev mentioned the possibility of the Soviet Union catching up with the United States in the production of milk and meat 'within a year or two', he was speaking of production areas where the Soviets had done better than anywhere else. In grain yields, for example, the Soviets had never managed to produce half as much as the Americans. But in the late fifties the Soviets produced almost two-thirds as much milk as the Americans (on state farms, as distinct from the more numerous collective farms, milk yield per cow reached almost 90 per cent of the American), 85 per cent as much pork and 70 per cent as much beef. Within these areas, then, there was some hope. Otherwise the yawning discrepancies between needs and means merely served to heighten the desperation with which the Soviets proceeded to deal with the agricultural problem. Moreover, it was a desperation that grew with the subconscious realization that an extremely thorny problem was being complicated immeasurably by the fixed idea of collectivization. But Marx was a city boy, and so was Lenin. And there was the immemorial inability of the Russian city-dweller to understand the Russian peasant. And there was, finally, the great, fundamental ideological taboo of private property. Now, the primordial idea of private property is the possession of land. Indeed, the possession of land belongs to the strongest of animal instincts, 'the territorial imperative' as Robert Ardrey called it in a book of the same title. The Communists could not grant more than one acre (0.45 hectare) to each kolkhoznik without forswearing the system and renouncing the faith. The Soviets are stuck with collectivization.

X

THE METAMORPHOSIS: FROM CONFORMIST TO DISSIDENT

I

The emergence into the public domain of Andrei Sakharov during a plenary session of the Academy of Sciences in 1964 marked a change in the attitude of the Academy as a whole. In a newspaper account of the session Sakharov was referred to as an 'engineer', as though he were an obscure figure who had somehow blundered into the Academy. In a sense Sakharov was a progeny of the atomic bomb. For it was the explosion of the atomic bomb by the Americans that had shocked Stalin profoundly with the knowledge that the Americans were far more powerful than he had taken them to be. The Soviets had always been awe-struck by America; now they feared it. Stalin directed that every effort be made to duplicate the new weapon as quickly as possible. This of course meant giving first priority to military engineers in general and physicists in particular. In the Soviet Union, in the last eight years of Stalin's dictatorship, the *virtuosi* came into their own again with a vengeance. There was no time for non-essentials: 'Don't bother our physicists with political seminars,' Stalin told a Party functionary; 'let them use all their time for their professional work.' In this same spirit he did not hesitate to release Lev Landau – a physicist who later became a Nobel laureate and who was arrested in 1938 as a 'wrecker, spy and enemy of the people' – when Peter Leonidovich Kapitsa made Landau's release the *sine qua non* of his, Kapitsa's, cooperating in work on the Soviet atomic bomb.

But it did not come to the cooperation of Kapitsa in the Soviet atomic weapons programme. Kapitsa had a falling out with Beria, 'on humanitarian and not political grounds', as Kapitsa himself put it in a conversation with Medvedev. Beria demanded Kapitsa's head, Stalin demurred, merely 'rusticating' Kapitsa instead (it was said that Stalin did not want to prejudice relations with the British, who held Kapitsa in high regard: the Soviet physicist had worked for some twelve years in England under Rutherford). After a year and a half Kapitsa was back at work but sidetracked in the Institute of Crystallography. It was not until after the death of Stalin that he managed to return to the Institute for Physical Problems which he himself had founded before the war. But all the more did Kapitsa's steadfastness set an example of the independent scientist who refused to bow to political pressure.

When Otto Hahn split the atom in Germany in 1939, the significance of the discovery was recognized just as quickly in the Soviet Union as it was elsewhere. Igor Tamm, the great theoretical physicist, is reported to have told his students, 'Do you know what this new discovery means? It means a bomb can be built that will destroy a city out to a radius of perhaps ten kilometres.' Accordingly, Russian physicists began working to produce a chain reaction. Two of them, G. N. Flerov and I. G. Petrzhak, discovered spontaneous fission under the general direction of Igor Kurchatov, one of the most energetic and enterprising Soviet physicists. The Soviets cabled a description of this discovery to the American scientific *Physical Review*, where it was duly published in the 1 July 1940 issue. The lack of any American reaction whatever to the news of this discovery helped convince the Soviets that the Americans were hard at work building a bomb on the principle of an atomic chain reaction. It was a good example of secrecy needlessly advertising itself.

Germany's invasion of the Soviet Union forced Soviet physicists to address themselves to the more immediate problems of weaponry and defence. But in February 1943 Igor Kurchatov was encharged with the programme to produce an atomic bomb. It was a much smaller effort than the American Manhattan Project: there were apparently not more than twenty physicists (including Y. B. Zeldovich and Kurchatov's younger brother, Vladimir) assigned to the programme, while the total complement at the main laboratory never exceeded fifty people. Here Igor Kurchatov ruled as monarch. A forty-year-old with a bad heart (he was dead at the age of fifty-seven) Kurchatov affected a foot-long beard in the shape of a flange (he was known among his colleagues as 'the beard') and a proclivity for urinating in laboratory sinks regardless of the rank or sex of those present.

When Harry Truman told Stalin at the Potsdam Conference in July 1945 that the United States had developed an atomic bomb, Stalin reacted in character. He told Marshal Zhukov and Foreign Minister Molotov, according to the former's memoirs, that 'they [the Americans] simply want to raise the price. We've got to work on Kurchatov and hurry things up.' As a result, the Soviets increased their efforts in something very like American earnest. They set up an engineering council under the chairmanship of Boris L. Vannikov, a full general in the army who had been in charge of all munitions during the war. Vannikov's deputies were Kurchatov and M. G. Pervukhin, commissar of the chemical industry. The council comprised engineers, industrial managers and scientists. Colonel-General Avraamy Zavenyagin of the NKVD was put in charge of security and administration. It was Zavenyagin rather than Vannikov who approximated the role of General Groves in the American programme, taking part in the preparation and assembly of the first Soviet bomb (as likely as not, however, the reports of General Zavenyagin's active participation in the actual work on the bomb is Party propaganda for the NKVD). The first Soviet atomic bomb was exploded on 29 August 1949 near the town of Semipalatinsk in Kazakhstan. A passage from the official biography of Igor Kurchatov by his colleague Igor Golovin describing the explosion provides insight into the Soviet attitude on the occasion:

When the physicists who had created the bomb saw the blinding flash, brighter than the brightest sunny day, and the mushroom cloud rising into the stratosphere, they gave a sigh of relief. They had carried out their duties. No one became frightened like the physicists in the USA, who had gathered from everywhere and had made the weapon for the army of a country that was foreign to many of them and whose government used it against the peaceful populations of Hiroshima and Nagasaki.

The Soviet physicists knew they had created the weapon for their own people and for their own army which was defending peace. Their labour, their sleepless nights and the huge effort that had constantly increased in the course of those past years had not been in vain: they had knocked a trump card from the hands of the American atomic diplomats.

The term 'atomic diplomats' is Soviet diplomatic usage for atomic blackmailers. The statement containing the term is entirely in keeping with Stalin's comment that 'they simply want to raise the price' – of the political concessions the Soviets would be required to make in the face of American atomic blackmail. For the same basic reason, the physicists in the USA became frightened, that is, they could not be sure for what purposes the Americans might put the bomb to use. They could not be sure because America was not really their country, the implication being that America is not really anybody's country – except, of course, the Indians. America is, before and after all, a continent ruled and regulated by an idea. That idea is anathema to Soviet Communism. It is the idea of the Stamp Act pamphlet of 1766 as enlarged upon by Thomas Jefferson, the idea of private adventurers establishing themselves in an uninhabited country on the basis of a right, 'which nature has given to all men, of departing from the country in which chance, not choice, has placed them, of going in quest of new habitations, and of there establishing new societies, under such laws and regulations as to them shall seem most likely to promote public happiness'. The idea is a standing invitation to anyone who is dissatisfied with his lot for any reason and it is obviously not affixed or restricted to any place, including the sovereign territory of the United States of America. In fact, the idea is a formula for permanent revolution: 'going in quest of new habitations, and of there establishing new societies . . .' need have no topographical relevance whatever. It may, indeed, form the foundation of the peculiarly American anti-historical mentality. The idea has certainly to do with the federation of the American states and just as surely led to the confederation of American states and the right of secession (which happens to be anchored in the Soviet constitution) as when men 'departing from the country in which chance, not choice, has placed them', take the country – or a piece of it – along with them, as it were (and as it was). As it is, Americans seem to be 'in quest of new habitations, and of there establishing new societies' without leaving the continent but by legislation establishing 'such laws and regulations as to them shall seem most likely to promote public happiness'. This accounts, presumably or at least in part, for the sheer velocity of change in American institutions and American society.

The diametric opposition between the United States of America and the Soviet Union can be converged to a burning focal point:

refugees (using the word in its broadest sense). The Soviet Union and the Soviet Union's satellites produce refugees; the United States absorbs refugees, refugees comprise the stuff of its physical constitution. As Franklin Delano Roosevelt confirmed in his address to the Daughters of the American Revolution in 1934: 'Fellow immigrants!' For the Soviet Union this focal point is particularly neuralgic for a wide variety of reasons. As the seat of the first Marxist revolution and the first Communist state in being, the Soviet Union proclaims itself as the homeland of socialism. The most important word in internal political use in the Soviet Union is *rodina* (literally 'birth-land'). In sharp distinction from those whom the Soviet state deports (like Solzhenitsyn) or forces to emigrate, every individual who leaves or signals the desire to leave the Soviet Union belies the proudest claim of the Union – to be the paradigm of social order in the modern world – and constitutes in fine a threat to the stability of the state. Despite this sensitivity, the Soviet Union has been forced or obligated to suffer two mass emigrations since the October Revolution and its aftermath. There were the 3 million plus displaced persons lodged in Germany and Western Europe at the close of World War II (most of whom left the Soviet Union as forced labour during the war and refused to return) and the 250,000 and more Soviet Jews who were allowed to leave the country within the terms of the Jackson–Vanik Amendment in the mid-seventies. There are anywhere from 1.5 to 3 million Jews in the Soviet Union. Some 40,000 of these have actively indicated their desire to emigrate and risked their livelihoods in so doing (the first repressive measure of the state in such cases is usually the denial of the applicant's right to work in the Soviet Union). It is estimated that ten times this number would follow suit if any real prospect of emigration existed. The Volga Germans, who also number about 3 million, are in approximately the same situation as the Soviet Jews.

In 1943 Stalin dissolved the Comintern as a gesture of conciliation to the Western Allies. At the same time the GRU (Glavnoe Razvedochnoe Upravlenie – Chief Intelligence Directorate), the military Intelligence organization of the Soviet Union, was reorganized to absorb most of the Comintern's Intelligence assets, including files and dossiers. A strategic Intelligence arm was built into the organization to handle the GRU's expanded foreign espionage network as a whole. One of the communications clerks seconded to service

232

the new network was Lieutenant Igor Gouzenko. Gouzenko's first (and last) post was the Soviet embassy, military attaché's office, in Ottawa. As Gouzenko learned in the two years in Ottawa before he defected in 1945 (to escape his imminent recall to Moscow), the most important agent run by the GRU in Canada was Dr Alan Nunn May, a noted British experimental physicist working on atomic research in Montreal. May was also a member of the British Communist Party or corporant, to use the jargon of Soviet Intelligence. He was selected in July 1944 to head a research group at the Montreal Laboratory for the joint British–Canadian Atomic Energy Project. He thus had clearance for the most sensitive information in the project.

The equivalent of Dr Alan Nunn May in New York and at Los Alamos was the skipping-stone immigrant, the naturalized British subject and former refugee from Nazi Germany Dr Klaus Fuchs whose sister Kristel was an American immigrant, resident in Cambridge, Massachusetts. Fuchs's contact in the United States was Harry Gold, whose real name was Heinrich Golodnitsky and who had immigrated from his native Switzerland. When Fuchs was arrested in England on charges of conducting espionage for the Soviets he confessed, implicating his contact Harry Gold. Gold, in turn, implicated David Greenglass, whom Gold had serviced on a single occasion as the result of an oversight by his Soviet case officer, Yakovlev, who worked out of the Soviet Consulate in New York. Yakovlev had inadvertently crossed his lines, thus connecting through Gold two networks that should have been kept strictly separated. David Greenglass, a draughtsman at the Los Alamos workshops and a member of the Young Communist League (a fact that is itself a sad commentary on American security measures), was the brother-in-law of Julius Rosenberg, who had recruited him. Greenglass implicated Julius and Ethel Rosenberg, who were executed in 1953, two years after having been found guilty of treason. (The Rosenbergs refused to turn state's evidence by implicating any of the members of their ring: Morris and Lona Cohen fled the country immediately the Rosenbergs were arrested, assuming, as they had to, that they would be implicated by the Rosenbergs. Cohen had come to the United States from Russia as a child with his parents.) The Rosenbergs were both long-standing members of the Communist Party of America. They had gradually slipped into Intelligence work for the Soviet Union as a result of this affiliation. Neither was an immigrant.

233

The question poses itself: how valuable was the information gathered by Soviet Intelligence to the Soviet nuclear programme? The experts in the matter calculate that it saved the Soviets at least five years of research and development work. This much can be said of the information supplied by Klaus Fuchs alone. In his two years at Los Alamos Fuchs worked his way into a key position: he became a member of the coordinating council, the top leadership at the installation. His grasp and overview of the most advanced work on-going at Los Alamos was second only to Oppenheimer's and the division chiefs'. He provided atomic information to the Soviets seven times through Harry Gold, reported on the production of plutonium, supplied a wealth of detail on the plutonium bomb and the implosion lens that acted as a trigger. His notes were always well ordered and meticulous. At his final meeting Fuchs gave Gold detailed information on the size of the plutonium bomb, the dimensions of its component parts, its structuring and firing device. All this was done before the Trinity test at Alamogordo on 16 July 1945.

Even more important than the atomic bomb, with Soviets as with Americans, was the Super, the hydrogen bomb. In 1947 Andrei Sakharov took his doctoral degree, having had Igor Tamm as his supervisor. Part of his doctoral thesis provided the material for the paper he published in the same year under the title 'Generation of the Hard Component of Cosmic Rays', a subject germane to the phenomenon of thermonuclear fusion. In 1948, as already indicated, he was chosen by Tamm to work on thermonuclear fusion. In 1950 the team of Tamm and Sakharov obtained a controlled thermonuclear reaction through 'the application of an electrical discharge in a plasma, placed in a magnetic field.' Sakharov had discovered the secret of the solar phoenix. This was hailed as 'the theoretical foundation of the use of thermonuclear energy for peaceful purposes'. In 1953 the Soviet Union tested its first nuclear device using the thermonuclear fusion of the hydrogen bomb. Less than a year before, on 1 November 1952, the Americans had detonated a massive thermonuclear device, described as 'the predecessor of the hydrogen bomb'. But the Soviets, well within a year, had the real thing, a bomb that could be made compact enough for delivery by plane. Thanks to Tamm and Sakharov, for a time they led the arms race.

In the same year Sakharov was elected a full member of the

Soviet Academy of Sciences and received his first of three Orders of Hero of Socialist Labour. In the mid-1960s most of Sakharov's published work in science was concerned with the origin and structure of the universe. In early 1965 he published a hypothesis 'on the creation of astronomical bodies as a result of gravitational instability of an expanding universe'. This appeared under the title *The Initial State of Expansion of the Universe and the Appearance of Nonuniformity in the Distribution of Matter*. In 1966 Sakharov and Y. B. Zeldovich collaborated in the publication of a hypothesis on the quark phenomenon under the title *Quark Structure and Masses of Strongly Interacting Particles*. In early 1969 Sakharov's last published contribution to theoretical physics appeared under the title 'Antiquarks in the Universe'. This last book can be regarded as a sort of aftermath of Sakharov's long period of grace and favour with the Soviet government. That period ended with the publication abroad of his essay, 'Progress, Coexistence and Intellectual Freedom', first in the *New York Times* (July 22) and then, under the title *Reflections on Progress, Coexistence and Intellectual Freedom*, in book form later in 1968. When the book appeared Sakharov lost his security clearance and was demoted. Thereafter, as he persisted in his dissidence, repressive measures by the Soviet government grew in number and intensity, always stopping short of formal indictment or an expulsion by vote or otherwise from the Academy of Sciences. The Soviet government remained mindful of the perils of poisoning the atmosphere of the Soviet scientific community.

II

It took Sakharov ten years to reach the point of openly criticizing his government. As he said to the American journalist, Jay Axelbank: 'I developed a moral consciousness gradually in the 1950s. I suppose the turning point came when I sent a letter of protest to the government against our atomic tests in 1958 – and again in 1961.' Between the two series of Soviet atomic tests conducted in 1958 (23 January to 22 March and 30 September to 25 October) Sakharov wrote a paper with the title 'Radioactive Carbon from Nuclear Explosions and Nonthreshold Biological Effects', in which he estimated the amount of genetic damage caused by tests already conducted and destined to appear in the future even if no further

235

testing took place. 'The continuation of tests and all attempts to legalize nuclear weapons and their tests are contrary to humanity and international law,' he wrote. The paper, which was published in the December issue of the Soviet journal *Atomnaya Energiya* (*Atomic Energy*) answers the author's question, 'What moral and political conclusions should be drawn from the figures cited?' The following quote is interesting generally as an expression of Sakharov's moral stand and particularly against the background of the genetics controversy in the Soviet Union. It had become known by the mid-1950s that radiation exposure could alter the genetic code of cells, causing mutations:

> One of the arguments advanced by the proponents of the theory of the 'inoffensiveness' of tests is that cosmic rays cause doses of radiation larger than doses from tests. But this argument does not alter the fact that the suffering and deaths of hundreds of thousands of victims, including those in neutral countries and in future generations, are additional supplements to the suffering and death already occurring. Two world wars also added less than 10 per cent to the death rate in the twentieth century, but this does not make war a normal phenomenon.
>
> Another argument disseminated in the literature of many countries reduces itself to this: that the progress of civilization ... causes the sacrifice of human life. Casualties of the automobile are frequently cited as an example. But the analogy here is not precise, and not legitimate. Automobile transportation improves the condition of people's lives; it is the cause of accidents only in individual cases due to the carelessness of individuals, who are thereby criminally liable. But accidents caused by tests are the inescapable consequence of each explosion. In the author's view, the unique specific in the moral aspect of the given problem consists of the complete impunity from crime, because it cannot be proved that radiation is the cause of death of the individual in each specific case, and likewise because our offspring are totally defenceless against our actions.
>
> The cessation of tests will directly preserve the lives of hundreds of thousands of people and will have a far greater indirect importance by helping to reduce international tension and decrease the threat of nuclear war – the basic threat of our era.

Sakharov also sent a letter of protest in the autumn of 1953 to Igor Kurchatov against the holding of the October tests. Kurchatov agreed to intervene and flew to see Khrushchev, who was then on

236

vacation at Yalta. To no avail. Sakharov also went to see Mikhail Suslov, member of the Politburo and chief ideologist of the CPSU, telling him that he was 'haunted by the complete defencelessness of our descendants with regard to our actions'. Posterity, he reminded Suslov, was also at stake. But Sakharov's opposition went further back in time. In 1955, one year after the Oppenheimer hearings, he had voiced his concern to Marshal M. I. Nedelin, chief of the Soviet strategic rocket forces. It would be a catastrophe, he said, if thermonuclear weapons were ever used. Nedelin told Sakharov that such matters were no business of scientists, that these were matters for the Central Committee. In 1957 Sakharov became strongly influenced by the works of Linus Pauling, Albert Schweitzer and others. He felt himself, as he wrote in *Sakharov Speaks*, 'responsible for the problem of radioactive contamination from nuclear explosions'.

In the summer of 1961 Sakharov tried again to interrupt Soviet atomic testing. The occasion was an assemblage of scientists at Khrushchev's behest to receive the announcement of the need for a new series of tests. Sakharov passed a note to Khrushchev during the proceedings. In it he insisted that the tests were unnecessary technically and that to break the three-year moratorium on atmospheric tests would inevitably reactivate the arms race. He added that this would be 'a far more serious matter than building a wall in Berlin'. Khrushchev replied that political decisions, including the matter of testing nuclear weapons, were the prerogative of the Party and government leaders, and did not concern scientists.

In September 1962 Sakharov tried yet again to prevent the wholly unnecessary testing of a thermonuclear device. After pleading in vain for several weeks, Sakharov telephoned Yefim Slavsky, the Soviet minister of medium machine building (his ministry was responsible for the Soviet nuclear-weapons programme), and threatened to resign if the test, scheduled for the next day, were carried out. Apparently Slavsky assured Sakharov that the test had been cancelled. Sakharov then telephoned Khrushchev, who was in Ashkhabad, for confirmation. Khrushchev recalled in his memoirs, *Khrushchev Remembers*, that Sakharov appealed to him 'to cancel the scheduled explosion and not to engage in any further testing, at least not of the hydrogen bomb'. Sakharov then added 'As a scientist and as a designer of the hydrogen bomb, I know what harm these explosions can bring down on the head of mankind.'

Khrushchev temporized, adding that he would consult with Frol Kozlov. When Kozlov talked with Sakharov the next day the test had already taken place.

The Soviet leaders had clearly led Sakharov by the nose, an experience that Sakharov himself, ten years later, described as a kind of psychological turning-point in his life. In an interview with *New York Times* correspondent Hedrick Smith, Sakharov remembered his feelings of frustration: 'I had an awful sense of powerlessness. I could not stop something I knew was wrong and unnecessary. After that, I felt myself another man. I broke with my surroundings. It was a basic break. After that I understood there was no point in arguing.' He went on: 'The atomic question was always half science, half politics ... a natural path into political issues. What matters is that I left conformism. It is not important on what question. After that first break, everything later was natural.'

III

But 1958 was the year of Sakharov's public debut, as it were. He also appeared for the first time in the mass media, as the co-author along with Y. B. Zeldovich of an article in the 19 November issue of *Pravda*, commenting on Khrushchev's proposed education reforms. The latter proposed that pupils in their final year of secondary education should spend one-third of their time in factory or farm work (making shift to relieve the growing Soviet manpower problem). Sakharov and Zeldovich countered with the proposal citing 'the need to create a network of special schools with a bias in the natural sciences and mathematics'. The co-authors regarded the ages of fourteen and fifteen as critical for pupils with a talent for mathematics and physics, brooking no interruption in their education: 'Many major discoveries and valuable research are effected by talented scientists at the ages twenty-two to twenty-six ... To delay the training of such people means ... to harm the development of science and technology.' They also called for a 'radical revision' of the entire school system, especially in the fields of natural science and mathematics, and demanded the introduction of subjects relevant to the modern world, like the theory of probability, analytical geometry, vector analysis and computer principles.

Sakharov put his signature for the first time to an open group appeal on the eve of the Twenty-third Congress of the Communist Party of the Soviet Union. This was in February 1966. Copies of the appeal were circulated in samizdat under the title 'Letter of Twenty-five Cultural Functionaries to Brezhnev on the Tendency towards the Rehabilitation of Stalin'. Andrei Sinyavsky and Yuri Daniel had been tried, found guilty and sentenced shortly before. The Twenty-third Congress did not rehabilitate Stalin, but – as though in reaction to the Sinyavsky–Daniel trial – Articles 190–1 and 190–3 were added to the criminal code of the Russian Soviet Federated Socialist Republic (RSFSR) by a decree of 16 September (corresponding articles to the codes of the other republics of the Union were added *pari passu*), Article 190–1 treating deliberate fabrications defaming the Soviet state and social system and Article 190–3 group activities disturbing public order. Again, Sakharov was one of the twenty-one signatories of an open appeal to the deputies of the RSFSR Supreme Soviet not to approve the decree. Both the appeals were signed by the academicians Igor Tamm and M. A. Leontovich. Sakharov's erstwhile co-author, Y. B. Zeldovich, signed the second appeal in which the signatories argued that the articles were 'contrary to Leninist principles of socialist democracy' and 'if approved . . . might be an obstacle to the realization of the liberties guaranteed by the USSR Constitution'. Articles 190–1 and 190–3 were approved.

On 11 February 1967 Sakharov sent an appeal to the Party's Central Committee, asking that the Galanskov–Ginzburg case be closed. (Yuri Galanskov and Alexander Ginzburg were arrested on charges of conducting anti-Soviet propaganda, tried and sentenced to seven and five years in the labour camps respectively. Galanskov died in the camps for lack of medical treatment in 1973.) Sakharov's intercession followed the arrests of Galanskov and Ginzburg by some few weeks but preceded their trial. It was his first attempt to rectify the violation of the civil rights of individual citizens. It also marks his overt break with 'conformism'. Up to the time of the Galanskov–Ginzburg arrests Sakharov had perhaps stretched the bounds of 'conformism', that is remained more or less within the confines of what was expected of a Soviet citizen of his prestige and achievements, but he had not overstepped those bounds. Protesting the arrest of Galanskov and Ginzburg put Sakharov squarely in the dissident camp and presented the Soviet Party-government with an unprecedented problem.

The year 1968–9 formed the great caesura in Sakharov's life. For twenty years Sakharov had worked on secret projects for the Soviet government. During the last eighteen years, from 1950 to 1968, he 'resided and worked in a remote, secret city' while keeping his Moscow apartment. 'I have not done theoretical work for twenty years,' he told the journalist Jay Axelbank in 1968, 'because I was involved in practical defence work.' All this came to an end in August 1968 when his security clearances were withdrawn after the publication of his essay 'Progress, Coexistence and Intellectual Freedom' in the 22 July issue of the *New York Times* and, shortly thereafter, in the Russian *émigré* publications *Russkaya Mysl* in Paris (a weekly newspaper) and *Possev* (a monthly magazine) in Frankfurt am Main under the title 'Reflections'. Sakharov returned to Moscow and was called to account before the Academy of Sciences Party committee, even though he was not and never had been a Party member. (In the Soviet Party-state the Soviets have never succeeded in clarifying definitively the relationship between Party and state.) In the 30 April 1969 issue of the samizdat publication *Chronicle of Current Events* there appeared the following announcement: 'The ministry of medium machine building, at which Sakharov was a consultant, has dispensed with his services. Now Sakharov holds a post only at his own institute [Lebedev], where no security pass is required.' Zhores Medvedev recounts this exchange between Dmitri Skobeltsyn, the institute director, and Sakharov:

SKOBELTSYN: We are taking you in the hope that you will stop making political statements.
SAKHAROV: I will not speak out if there are no serious reasons for doing so.

Sakharov told Axelbank that the seminars he attended at the Lebedev Physics Institute were 'more passive than active' and that the authorities 'had to provide me with some work because they didn't want any scandals involving me'. In 1969 Sakharov's wife, the mother of his three grown children (two daughters who were already married and a son), died of cancer. In 1970 Sakharov married Elena Georgievna Bonner, the daughter of two holocausts, as it were – properly the daughter of Gevork Sarkissovich Alikhanov, an Armenian, and of that same Ruth Grigorievna Bonner, the construction engineer who built prisons while in prison, herself the daughter of Tatiana Matveyevna Bonner, the bookkeeper who sorted out and assessed the Kremlin treasure for the Bolsheviks during the revolution, both of them – mother and daughter – born in the offical tsarist exile village of Nikolayev in Siberia. Ruth Grigorievna recounts that Sakharov's children did not approve of his 'public service' nor of his marriage. Neither disapproval is in the least surprising: the marriage to Elena Bonner followed within a year of the death of his wife and their mother; his 'public service' threatened the position of the children among their peers in the Soviet scientific élite and, worse still, it made them objects of the officious solicitude of the KGB. Sakharov lost no time in turning over his official apartment – assigned to him as a member of the Academy of Sciences – to his children and in moving into the apartment of Ruth Grigorievna, which consisted of two rooms, where he lived with his wife and her two teen-age children. Ruth Grigorievna relates that the family of Elena Georgievna Bonner became Sakharov's family, her children became his children, that he was surrounded by respect, tenderness and loving care and, most important, by a deep understanding of his innermost problems, the solution of which had become the purpose of his life. Thus the break that Sakharov herewith made with his past could not have been greater. He lost – or gave up – everything he had, and what he had was – for a Soviet – a great deal indeed. 'I had money ... title and everything which my work bestowed upon me,' he told Axelbank, 'but I had a very tragic feeling.' All he kept was the tragic feeling, but at least he had turned his back on 'conformism' and the 'conformists' – specifically on the Great Russian majority. In so doing Sakharov joined the minorities in the Soviet Union (and everywhere else): the Jews, the Armenians, the Georgians, the Crimean Tartars, the Chechens – any one or more of a hundred different 'national minorities' within the Soviet empire. In sum, Sakharov had a new wife, a new family, a new apartment, a new philosophy and a new world. Like the clouds and cranes in Berthold Brecht's poem 'The Lovers', he had flown 'aus einem Leben in ein anderes Leben' (from one life into another life).

When he broke with his past and the Soviet ideal of 'conformism' Sakharov made certain basic assumptions in plotting his course as a full-time dissident in the Soviet Union. The evidence from which he drew in making these assumptions was provided by both personal and hearsay experience in the course of the long struggle against Lysenkoism. Sakharov's first assumption was based on the following calculation: where there is no freedom of discussion, there is no freedom of thought. Where there is no freedom of thought, there is no freedom of inquiry. Freedom of inquiry is the cardinal prerequisite to scientific progress. And, meanwhile, the world has been overtaken by the technological revolution, making scientific progress the cardinal prerequisite to economic sanity. Sooner or later, as Sakharov saw it, these facts would simply compel the Soviet government to permit freedom of discussion as the cornerstone of the structure that would comprise freedom of inquiry. In short, in Sakharov's eyes the struggle against Lysenkoism had been a sort of pilot operation conducted to prove a larger, overall hypothesis. The second basic assumption Sakharov made rested on the idea of solidarity within the international scientific community. This too was an inference drawn from the experience with Lysenkoism – as he himself had put it, under the heading of 'The Responsibility of Scientists': 'In the contemporary world scientists, by virtue of the international character of science, constitute the only really existing international society.' The third and final basic assumption of Sakharov was a corollary of the first. It was that the Academy of Sciences had emerged from the thirty-year struggle with Lysenkoism strengthened to the point where, in its hard-won professional independence, it would act as a kind of counterweight to the political arbitrariness of the Central Committee. The posing or counter-posing of the professional integrity of the Academy of Sciences against the vagaries of the Soviet leadership was not an idealist or romantic pipe-dream, but rather Sakharov's conviction that détente was essential to disarmament and that internal reform in the Soviet Union, that is, respect for human rights, was essential to détente. Behind this conviction was Sakharov's strong apprehension, based on his experience as a scientist, of the danger of a closed society. The reason for this apprehension is perhaps best expressed in Robert Oppenheimer's statement that 'there was danger in the fact that such decisions had to be taken secretly, not because the people who took the decisions were not wise, but because the very need, the very absence of criticism and discussion tended to corrode the decision-making process'. Sakharov came to see the Soviet practice of 'democratic centralism', in which as few as possible decide as secretly as possible, as a fetish corroding the decision-making process.

Andrei Sakharov's education as a dissident began in earnest only with his marriage to Elena Bonner and his acquisition of a family with a tradition of opposition to the state going back six generations. The Bonners, mother and daughter, were encyclopaedias of Soviet dissidence, the two of them together knowing perhaps the large majority of dissidents in Moscow and Leningrad personally. But mother and daughter Bonner were also something else, namely fair game for Soviet organs of suppression. Sakharov expressed his concern for his new family to the journalist Axelbank: 'I am just worried about the consequences of my actions for those near to me, my family.' He then added, as if to explain the situation, 'They are afraid to touch my children or me because of my position, but they go after Tanya and Elena.' In this case the reference was to the daughter and granddaughter of Elena Georgievna. At this point Ruth Grigorievna was seventy years old. The fact of her age spared her some of the indignities and humiliations reserved for dissidents and members of minorities by the Party-government and, often enough, by the public as well. Elena Bonner, in her turn, had one advantage regarding the Soviet state and society. This was her status as a war invalid-veteran. Elena Georgievna had been invalided out of the Red Army in 1945 as a lieutenant in the medical corps (she had volunteered for service as a nurse in the Red Army immediately after the German invasion of the Soviet Union in June 1941). She had lost most of the sight of her right eye and suffered increasing loss of sight in her left eye as a result of being wounded and buried in a bomb crater at the front. She was classified as an invalid of the second category, a status that carries with it various minor but none the less important privileges such as the right to purchase in special stores. In 1947 Elena Bonner was accepted as a medical student in the First Leningrad Medical Institute after having been twice rejected because of her invalidity. She graduated as a general practitioner six years later and went on to specialize as a paediatrician. Elena Bonner married her fellow student at medical school, Ivan Vassilievich Semeonov, and bore him two children, a daughter, Tanya, in 1950, and a son, Alexei, in 1956. The couple divorced in 1965, whereupon Elena moved to Moscow with her two children and her mother, Ruth Grigorievna. Elena had spent some six months in Iraq in the late fifties working for the Soviet ministry of health. She also engaged in a considerable amount of

243

literary activity, writing for the medical newspaper *Medrabotnik*, the *Literaturnaya Gazeta* and the magazines *Neva* and *Yunost*. In addition she collaborated on the collection, *Actors Who Fell at the Front during the Great Patriotic War*, and acted as publisher of the book, *Vsevolod Bagritsky: Diaries, Letters, Poems*. She also worked as an editor in the Leningrad section of the Medical State Publishing House. Elena Bonner's political affiliations were complicated by her status as the daughter of two convicted traitors. A member of the Komsomol since 1938, she was nevertheless unable to reconcile her status with membership in the Communist Party and decided to wait until her parents were cleared of all charges before submitting her application. The exposé of Stalin as a criminal at the Twentieth and more especially at the Twenty-second Party Congresses brought with it the rehabilitation of both Elena Bonner's parents. Nevertheless it was almost ten years before she became a full member of the Communist Party of the Soviet Union, in 1965. The Soviet invasion of Czechoslovakia in 1968 for the purpose of crushing the reform efforts of the Prague Spring and combining with the rising tide of dissent in the Soviet Union gradually convinced Elena Georgievna that she could not be a Communist. She resigned her membership in the Party in 1972. It had been an agonizing ordeal, and yet the real struggle was only just beginning.

The year 1972 saw the dawn of the general realization in the Soviet Union that a systemic catastrophe was in the making. The crushing of the Prague Spring in 1968 was followed by the uprising of Polish workers in 1971. Something else was happening that was far more alarming: the Soviet population was beginning to lose its fear of Soviet power, which is to say the fear of the Soviet state as a coercive machine.

XI

❧

GLASNOST AND PERESTROIKA WRIT SMALL

The impact of the exposé of Stalin by Khrushchev in the course of an hour-long speech at the Twentieth Congress in February of 1956 can be gauged only by contrasting its polemically denunciatory nature with a quarter-century's well-nigh unbridled official adulation. On the front page of one issue of *Pravda*, Stalin's name appeared well over a hundred times. Mention of Stalin in all branches of the media and in Soviet literature was an incantation by repetition. There were tens of thousands of statues and busts erected and placed in every official building in every township throughout the Union and the Eastern European satellites. Probably the most representative examples of socialist realism in the creative arts – music, painting, sculpture and literature – were those devoted to the apotheosis of Stalin. There is the huge neo-classical portrait by V. Komar and A. Melamid from the series *Nostalgic Social Realism* entitled *Stalin and the Muses* and depicting the dictator in his white dress uniform as generalissimus (the white greatcoat with turquoise lining visible as the bottom hem is turned up by a gust of wind) presenting the muses with a volume of his works.

Khrushchev's speech was never published in the Soviet Union. It was nevertheless widely circulated in samizdat (and, of course, in Party circles) and Sakharov, like many if not most of his colleagues, was thoroughly familiar with it. Khrushchev's denunciation of Stalin and Stalinism is massively reflected in Sakharov's first publication abroad, his essay, 'Thoughts on Progress, Peaceful Coexistence and Intellectual Freedom' published on 22 July 1968 in the *New York Times*. The *New York Times* gave Sakharov's essay three full pages, including photographs and explanatory boxes. The essay is couched in the style and form of at once a declaration, a warning and an appeal:

> The views of the author were formed in the milieu of the scientific and scientific–technological intelligentsia, which manifests much anxiety over the principles and specific aspects of foreign and domestic policy and over the future of mankind. This anxiety is nourished, in particular, by a realization that the scientific method of directing policy, the economy, arts, education and military affairs still has not become a reality.
>
> We regard as 'scientific' a method based on deep analysis of facts, theories and views, presupposing unprejudiced, unfearing open discussion and conclusions. The complexity and diversity of all the phenomena of modern life, the great possibilities and dangers linked with the scientific–technical revolution and with a number of social tendencies demand precisely such an approach, as has been acknowledged in a number of official statements.
>
> In this pamphlet, advanced for discussion by its readers, the author has set himself the goal to present, with the greatest conviction and frankness, two theses that are supported by many people in the world. These theses are:
>
> The division of mankind threatens it with destruction. Civilization is imperiled by: a universal thermonuclear war, catastrophic hunger for most of mankind, stupefaction from the narcotic of 'mass culture' and bureaucratized dogmatism, a spreading of mass myths that put entire peoples and continents under the power of cruel and treacherous demagogues, and destruction or degeneration from the unforeseeable consequences of swift changes in the conditions of life on our planet.
>
> In the face of these perils, any action increasing the division of mankind, any preaching of the incompatability of world ideologies and nations is madness and a crime. Only universal cooperation under conditions of intellectual freedom and the lofty moral ideals of socialism and labor, accompanied by the elimination of dogmatism and pressures of the concealed interests of ruling classes, will preserve civilization.
>
> The reader will understand that ideological cooperation cannot apply to those fanatical, sectarian, and extremist ideologies that reject all possibility of rapprochement, discussion and compromise, for example, the ideologies of Fascist, racist, militaristic and Maoist demagogy.
>
> Millions of people throughout the world are striving to put an

end to poverty. They despise oppression, dogmatism and demagogy (and their more extreme manifestations – racism, Fascism, Stalinism and Maoism). They believe in progress based on the use, under conditions of social justice and intellectual freedom, of all the positive experience accumulated by mankind.

The second basic thesis is that intellectual freedom is essential to human society – freedom to obtain and distribute information, freedom for open-minded and unfearing debate and freedom from pressure by officialdom and prejudices. Such a trinity of freedom of thought is the only guarantee against an infection of people by mass myths, which in the hands of treacherous hypocrites and demagogues, can be transformed into bloody dictatorship. Freedom of thought is the only guarantee of the feasibility of a scientific democratic approach to politics, economics and culture.

There is little in these opening paragraphs to disturb or alienate the Western reader, although phrases like 'the lofty moral ideals of socialism' might have made many an American right-wing Democrat wince even if ever so slightly. On the other hand, for the Soviet reader the effect was simply earth-shaking. The equation of Stalinism with Nazism alone was enough to infuriate approximately half of the membership of the Communist Party of the Soviet Union. But there were other equations that were equally painful and pointedly made:

'The usual practice is the use of demagogy, storm-troopers and Red Guards in the first stage and terrorist bureaucracy with reliable cadres of the type of Eichmann, Himmler, Yezhov and Beria at the summit of the deification of unlimited power.'

The naming of Beria of course recalled the painful fact that the Georgian hangman-bandit had been, as head of the security forces, Politburo member and Stalin's deputy, in charge of all nuclear and thermonuclear development in the Soviet Union until his arrest and summary execution in December 1953, nine months after the death of Stalin. But more important, particularly for the Soviet readership, was the use of the word 'deification'. Here the Soviets had clearly outdone the Germans in their glorification of Hitler. In continuing, Sakharov made it clear that deification of Stalin had been practised for a set purpose:

Fascism lasted 12 years in Germany. Stalinism lasted twice as long in the Soviet Union. There are many common features but also certain differences. Stalinism exhibited a much more subtle kind of

247

hypocrisy and demagogy, with reliance not on an openly cannibalistic program like Hitler's but on a progressive, scientific and popular socialist ideology.

This served as a convenient screen for deceiving the working class, for weakening the vigilance of the intellectuals and other rivals in the struggle for power with the treacherous and sudden use of the machinery of torture, execution and informants, intimidating and making fools of millions of people, the majority of whom were neither cowards nor fools. As a consequence of this 'specific feature' of Stalinism, it was the Soviet people, its most active, talented and honest representatives, who suffered the most terrible blow.

Sakharov's singling out of the aspect of fraud in the Soviet system is surely the most telling point of all. For it was precisely the idea of the 'convenient screen for deceiving the working class ... who suffered the most terrible blow' as a consequence 'of this "specific feature" of Stalinism', namely the reliance 'on a progressive, scientific and popular socialist ideology'. For the perpetration of the fraud by Stalinism turns on the claim to be the very thing it most glaringly is not: scientific.

'At least 10 to 15 million people perished in the torture chambers of the N.K.V.D. from torture and execution,' Sakharov then writes in his comparison of Stalinism and Nazism, 'in camps for exiled kulaks and members of their families and in camps 'without the right of correspondence.'*

People perished in the mines of Norilsk and Vorkuta from freezing, starvation and exhausting labour, at countless construction projects, in timber cutting, building of canals or simply during transportation in prison trains, in the overcrowded holds of 'death ships' in the Sea of Okhotsk and during the resettlement of entire peoples, the Crimean Tatars, the Volga Germans, the Kalmyks and other Caucasus peoples ...

Just as notorious as the mines of Norilsk and Vorkuta is the Byelomorski Canal from Lake Vyzgero to the Beloye More, the construction of which in the twenties and early thirties exacted the lives of tens of thousands of Soviet prisoners. Assignment to work on the Byelomorski Canal was tantamount to a death sen

---

* Which were in fact the prototypes of the Fascist death camps, where, for example, thousands of prisoners were machine-gunned because of 'overcrowding' or as a result of 'special orders'.

tence. The writer Maxim Gorky drew perhaps eternal opprobrium down on his head by lending himself to the official encomium of work on the Byelomorski Canal at the head of a group of writers seconded to the task. Gorky himself could not be 'seconded'; his was too big a name. He therefore did not have the excuse of the writers placed in his charge. Readers of the literary journal *Novy Mir* could recently read for themselves a description of the 'road of death' between Norilsk and Igarka, in northern Siberia.

> Temporary masters were replaced (Yagoda, Molotov, Yezhov, Zhdanov, Malenkov, Beria), but the antipeople's regime of Stalin remained equally cruel and at the same time dogmatically narrow and blind in its cruelty. The killing of engineering and military officials before the war, the blind faith in the 'reasonableness' of the colleague in crime, Hitler, and the other reasons for the national tragedy of 1941 have been well described in the book by Nekrich, in the notes of Maj. Gen. Grigorenko and other publications – these are far from the only examples of the combination of crime, narrow-mindedness and short-sightedness.

This was putting it mildly. When Stalin decided to purge the Soviet general staff in 1937 he sent an agent, a former tsarist general, to Berlin with information implicating several German generals in a *complot* with the Soviet generalcy. The Germans, particularly Reinhard Heydrich, chief of the SS Security Office, hatched a plan to turn the information around to implicate the Soviet generalcy. The information was then passed to Eduard Beneš, President of Czechoslovakia, who gave it to Stalin as the Germans were certain he would. It was just what Stalin had wanted all along: proof supplied by the Germans that the generals and staff officers he suspected were indeed traitors. Thus Stalin's paranoia was satisfied by the Germans, who likewise served their own purpose of decimating the Soviet general staff. The total achievement of this joint Soviet–Nazi operation was 82,000 Soviet officers executed summarily – from Marshal Tukhachevsky down to battalion commanders.

> Stalinist dogmatism and isolation from real life was demonstrated particularly in the countryside, in the policy of unlimited exploitation and the predatory forced deliveries at 'symbolic' prices, in the most serf-like enslavement of the peasantry, the depriving of peasants of the most simple means of mechanization and the appointment

of collective farm chairmen on the basis of their cunning and obsequiousness. The results are evident – a profound and hard-to-correct destruction of the economy and way of life in the countryside, which, by the law of interconnected vessels, damaged industry as well.

The inhuman character of Stalinism was demonstrated by the repressions of prisoners of war who survived Fascist camps and then were thrown into Stalinist camps, the antiworker 'decrees', the criminal exile of entire peoples condemned to slow death, the unenlightened zoological kind of anti-semitism that was characteristic of Stalinist bureaucracy and the N.K.V.D. (and Stalin personally), the Ukrainophobia characteristic of Stalin and the draconian laws for the protection of socialist property (five years' imprisonment for stealing some grain from the fields and so forth) that served mainly as a means of fulfilling the demands of the 'slave market'.

This section shows how greatly Sakharov was concerned with the entire collectivization drive and its consequences. He puts it in the centre of the whole phenomenon of economic ribaldry quintessential to the Marxist–Leninist system. Against this backdrop he hardly need have mentioned that the Soviet Union is the only industrialized country in the world with a death penalty for 'economic crimes'.

... Our country has started on the path of cleansing away the foulness of Stalinism. 'We are squeezing the slave out of ourselves drop by drop' (an expression of Anton Chekhov). We are learning to express our opinions, without taking the lead from our bosses and without fearing for our lives.

The beginning of this arduous and far from straight path evidently dates from the report of Nikita S. Khrushchev to the 20th congress of the Soviet Communist party. This bold speech, which came as a surprise to Stalin's accomplices in crime, and a number of associated measures – the release of hundreds of thousands of political prisoners and their rehabilitation, steps toward a revival of the principles of peaceful coexistence and toward a revival of democracy – oblige us to value highly the historic role of Khrushchev despite his regrettable mistakes of a voluntarist character in subsequent years and despite the fact that Khrushchev, while Stalin was still alive, was one of his collaborators in crime, occupying a number of influential posts.

The exposure of Stalinism in our country still has a long way to go. It is imperative, of course, that we publish all authentic documents, including the archives of the N.K.V.D., and conduct nationwide investigations. It would be highly useful for the international authority of the Soviet Communist party and the ideals of socialism if, as was planned in 1964 but never carried out, the party were to announce the 'symbolic' expulsion of Stalin, murderer of millions of party members, and at the same time the political rehabilitation of the victims of Stalinism.

In 1936–39 alone more than 1.2 million party members, half of the total membership, were arrested. Only 50,000 regained freedom; the others were tortured during interrogation or were shot (600,000) or died in camps. Only in isolated cases were the rehabilitated allowed to assume responsible posts; even fewer were permitted to take part in the investigation of crimes of which they had been witnesses or victims.

From this section emerges, very roughly, the dimensions of the extent of the damage done and of the compromise of the Party by Stalinism. There emerges, too, something of the nature of the dilemma facing the whole of the Soviet establishment. Sakharov calls for no less than a full-scale investigation. By whom, one wonders. In a totalitarian state there is no opposition – loyal or otherwise – to which to turn over the awesome task of cleansing the Augean stables. With no opposition, without even an independent judiciary, the 'Party' is constrained to purge itself. Not only 'self-criticism' but also 'self-purgation'. No wonder the Party could not bring itself to expel Stalin 'symbolically' and formally rehabilitate the millions of Stalin's victims. In so doing the Party would be denouncing and renouncing itself. The Party purging itself in any effective way or measure is impossible on the face of it. It would be far better for the Party simply to abdicate. But again, there is no one to whom to abdicate. It gradually becomes clear how horribly involved the Soviet situation really is. The Party is not really a 'Party', by reason of the absence of other parties. The Party has not been a 'Party' since the Tenth Party Congress in 1921, when all other parties and even factions within the one remaining Party were abolished. Of the National Socialist German Workers' Party – NSDAP – Franz von Papen said that it was the Nazis' 'unbridledness' that caused them to destroy themselves. It was likewise the 'unbridledness' of the Communist Party of the Soviet Union that has forced the Party into a situation where it cannot live and cannot die. What are we witnessing, then – the slow, agonizing break-up of the Communist Party of the Soviet Union?

The primacy of freedom of thought is the leitmotiv of Sakharov's essay. In this connection he goes on to switch the focus of his commentary to the People's Republic of China:

> In recent years, demagogy, violence, cruelty and vileness have seized a great country that had embarked on the path of socialist development ... It is impossible without horror and pain to read about the mass contagion of antihumanism being spread by 'the great helmsman' and his accomplices, about the Red Guards who, according to the Chinese radio, 'jumped with joy' during public executions of 'ideological enemies' of Chairman Mao.
>
> The idiocy of the cult of personality has assumed in China monstrous, grotesquely tragicomic forms, carrying to the point of absurdity many of the traits of Stalinism and Hitlerism. But this absurdity has proved effective in making fools of tens of millions of people and in destroying and humiliating millions of more honest and more intelligent people.

Once again the theme of coercive deception on a mass scale is struck: those who are silly enough are misled; those who are too intelligent to be misled are murdered or forced to recant publicly.

> The greatest damage from Maoism is often seen in the split of the world Communist movement. That is, of course, not so. The split is the result of a disease and to some extent represents the way to treat that disease. In the presence of the disease a formal unity would have been a dangerous, unprincipled compromise that would have led the world Communist movement into a blind alley once and for all.

This is likewise a theme that Sakharov uses repeatedly to great effect: formal unity with a diseased body politic on the basis of unprincipled compromise results only in contagion, not harmony.

> Actually the crimes of the Maoists against human rights have gone much too far, and the Chinese people are in much greater need of help from the world's democratic forces than in the need of the unity of the world's Communist forces, in the Maoist sense, for the purpose of combating the so-called imperialist peril somewhere in Africa or in Latin America or in the Middle East.

There can be no doubt at this point that Sakharov is holding Stalinism responsible as a deviative example for the Chinese deviation into Maoism. Equally unmistakable is the primacy accorded to human rights.

This is a threat to the independence and worth of the human personality, a threat to the meaning of human life.

Nothing threatens freedom of personality and the meaning of life like war, poverty, terror. But there are also indirect and only slightly more remote dangers.

One of these is the stupefaction of man (the 'grey mass', to use the cynical term of bourgeois prognosticators) by mass culture with its intentional or commercially motivated lowering of intellectual level and content, with its stress on entertainment or utilitarianism, and with its carefully protective censorship.

Another example is related to the question of education. A system of education under government control, separation of school and church, universal free education – all these are great achievements of social progress. But everything has a reverse side. In this case it is excessive standardization, extending to the teaching process itself, to the curriculum, especially in literature, history, civics, geography, and to the system of examinations.

One cannot but see a danger in excessive reference to authority and in the limitation of discussion and intellectual boldness at an age when personal convictions are beginning to be formed . . .

Modern technology and mass psychology constantly suggest new possibilities of managing the norms of behaviour, the strivings and convictions of masses of people. This involves not only management through information based on the theory of advertising and mass psychology, but also more technical methods that are widely discussed in the press abroad. Examples are biochemical control of the birth rate, biochemical control of psychic processes and electronic control of such processes.

This discussion of the 'more technical methods' is *Zukunftsmusik*: the danger looms but is not yet present, and yet the looming in itself imposes urgency – hesitation will forfeit everything.

Such a danger will become quite real in a few decades if human values, particularly freedom of thought, are not strengthened, if alienation cannot be eliminated.

Let us now return to the dangers of today, to the need for intellectual freedom, which will enable the public at large and the intelligentsia to control and assess all acts, designs and decisions of the ruling group . . . Now the diversity and complexity of social phenomena and the dangers facing mankind have become

253

immeasurably greater; and it is therefore all the more important that mankind be protected against the danger of dogmatic and voluntaristic errors, which are inevitable when decisions are reached in a closed circle of secret advisers or shadow cabinets.

Here Sakharov supplies the explanatory linkage between disarmament and détente on the one hand and an open society on the other. These considerations are the seeds of a wider recognition, that of the spectral similarity between the secretive totalitarian state – 'As few as possible to know as little as possible as late as possible,' as Hitler lapidarily put it – and the clandestine terrorist group that arrogates to itself the status and function of a state, imposing 'death sentences' and carrying out 'executions', demanding acquiescence and exacting concessions while its effectiveness and, indeed, its very existence depends entirely on its continuing clandestinity.* Sakharov's recognition is that the body politic cannot tolerate either one of these phenomena – that, indeed, the secret organization masquerading as a state is the most dangerous political phenomenon in history, particularly when it possesses the means of universal destruction and thus becomes a threat to mankind as a whole. This is the pass to which Lenin's cadre of professional revolutionaries has led. For decades (and here the Stalin era seems as much coincidence as consequence) the twist of Leninism, like the trick that has to be practised in Plato's *Republic* – secrecy at the top, the hermetic sealing off of the leadership from the body politic – seemed to be an all powerful, perfectly foolproof arrangement. In a totalitarian regime the 'public domain' becomes not the province but the preserve of the state (hence the extreme sensitivity to 'outside interference in internal affairs'). This was the closed society *par excellence*, enabling the leadership to exclude whole categories of issues and problems and to deal with those problems which they considered important in good time and undisturbed by public clamour. But it was in foreign policy that the system proved itself invaluable. While the Western democracies struggled despairingly with mass peace movements and insistent demands for unilateral disarmament in almost daily demonstrations, the Soviets stood comfortably by, feeding the flames of foreign public opinion to suit their own strategic purposes. They had no problem with public opinion at home: it was entirely under control. The strata-

* What is the difference between the clandestine terrorist group masquerading as a state and the state that conducts itself like a clandestine terrorist group?

gem of eliminating public opinion at home while exacerbating public opinion abroad was essential to Soviet foreign policy. They relied on it, fully expecting, for example, that West German public opinion allegedly expressed in frequent mass demonstrations against the stationing of Cruise and Pershing missiles in West Germany would force the Bonn government to desist from its – and NATO's – declared policy. When West German opposition to the stationing of medium-range missiles proved too weak to be representative the Soviets were taken by surprise – and forced to change their policies accordingly. It was not a good gamble; the Soviets have more than ordinary difficulty in recognizing the odds. When the Soviets adopted the policy of refusing to let private opinion organize itself into public opinion they deprived themselves of any way of knowing what their citizens thought or how deeply they felt on any issue. There was no way of telling how representative anyone was of anything. And the Soviets' lack of experience in such matters at home did not contribute to their expertise in judging such matters abroad. The fiasco in judging the issue of stationing the missiles in West Germany was a classic example of the unscientific approach to a problem. Of course, the insistence on secrecy is fundamentally unscientific. It was this feature of Soviet Communism, which Sakharov in *Reflections* apostrophizes as 'Stalinist' but which is actually Lenin's doing, that impelled the confrontation between the Soviet scientific community and the Soviet Party-government. It is the core of the deception. Soviet Communism bases its claim, as does Marxism, to the right to rule uninterruptedly and unsharingly on the principle of the scientific approach to all problems. The claim is thus demonstrably unfounded. It is for this reason that the Soviet Party-state has no choice but to introduce *glasnost* – the essential meaning of which is freedom of speech.

Humanity's alternative to annihilation Sakharov sets forth in four stages. 'In the first stage,' he writes,

> a growing ideological struggle in the socialist countries between Stalinist and Maoist forces, on the one hand, and the realistic force of leftist Leninist Communists (and leftist Westerners) on the other, will lead to a deep ideological split on an international, national and intraparty scale.
>
> In the Soviet Union and other socialist countries, this process will lead first to a multiparty system (here and there) and to acute

255

ideological struggle and discussions, and then to the ideological victory of the realists, affirming the policy of increasing peaceful coexistence, strengthening democracy and expanding economic reforms (1960–80). The dates reflect the most optimistic unrolling of events.

The author, incidentally, is not one of those who consider the multiparty system to be an essential stage in the development of the socialist system or, even less, a panacea for all ills, but he assumes that in some cases a multiparty system may be an inevitable consequence of the course of events when a ruling Communist party refuses for one reason or another to rule by the scientific democratic method required by history.

In the second stage (1972–85 – the various stages overlap) the two systems begin to converge. In the body of the essay Sakharov bases his expectation of convergence on the observation that capitalism has already adopted and absorbed many of the features of socialism, thereby saving itself through the process of adaptation. He now expects the socialist countries to adopt and absorb some of the features of capitalism, particularly in terms of the market economy and the uses of democracy, primarily freedom of speech.

In the third stage (1972–90) the Soviet Union and the United States 'solve the problem of saving the poorer half of the world' by levying a 20 per cent tax on the national incomes of all developed countries in order to finance the industrialization and modernization of backward countries. 'Giant factories will produce synthetic amino acids, and synthesize proteins, fats and carbohydrates.' Meanwhile, too, disarmament will proceed apace.

In the fourth stage (1980–2000) the 'socialist convergence', as Sakharov calls it, will reduce differences still further and promote intellectual freedom, leading to the creation of a world government. (It would seem that the levy of a 20 per cent tax on the national income of developed countries mentioned in stage three presupposes the existence of a world government or an international mechanism for the enforcement of the tax – which comes to the same thing: 'No taxation without representation!') In this stage Sakharov also foresees the international development of nuclear energy and the expansion of space exploration. He likewise mentions the synthesis of materials into superconductors, a development that will 'completely revolutionize' electrical technology, cybernetics, transportation and communications. Finally, he touches upon progress in biology. This will make possible the control and direction of all life processes 'at the levels of the cell, organism ecology and society, from fertility and ageing to psychic processes and heredity'. Thus genetic engineering is only part of this extremely ambitious (ambitious not least in the timing) programme. Sakharov sums up the preconditions of such a programme:

If such an all-encompassing scientific and technological revolution, promising uncounted benefits for mankind, is to be possible and safe, it will require the greatest possible scientific foresight and care and concern for human values of a moral, ethical and personal character . . . Such a revolution will be possible and safe only under highly intelligent worldwide guidance.

Specifically, Sakharov's proposals presuppose worldwide interest in such a programme, which is to say, in a truly scientific approach to politics, economics and culture. His proposals also presume the disappearance of contradictions and differences between the two systems by virtue of their convergence. These, as he is well aware, are big 'ifs'. But he is also aware that the general situation of mankind in the world is already critical. By no means the least of the factors comprising this crisis is the state of ecology – particularly in the industrial countries. Sakharov's *Reflections* were written twenty years ago. Meanwhile they have become all the more relevant.

'The problem of geohygiene [earth hygiene],' as he calls it,

is highly complex and closely tied to economic and social problems. This problem can therefore not be solved on a national and especially not on a local basis. The salvation of our environment requires that we overcome our divisions and the pressure of temporary local interests. Otherwise, the Soviet Union will poison the United States with its wastes and vice versa. At present this is a hyperbole. But with a ten per cent annual increase of wastes, the increase over 100 years will be 20,000 times.

The fundamental calculation of this plan, then, is not that there will be at least a scintilla of good will on each of the two sides as a result of which the necessary cooperation will ensue and save the day. Nothing so euphoric as that. No: Sakharov is counting on nothing more than the animal instinct of self-preservation once the dilemma becomes so clear as to be unmistakable. The only

257

question is: will these threats that emerge from the increasing and increasingly compounded scientific and technological interventions in the natural process be recognized for what they are soon enough to allow for the necessary counter-measures? 'Solutions cause problems' – so runs the homely wisdom in the south and west of America. Humanity's course has been set in the direction of scientific and technological intervention. More and more of it. There is no turning back. The harm that has been inflicted on nature by science can be cured only by more science. This is a fact that may well prove to be an intolerable burden on humanity's ability to cope with a technology that is so high as to be sublime – or so insidious as to be infernal. What is beyond doubt is that a revolution will be required the likes of which are hardly imaginable since there is no precedent, a revolution that will of necessity involve the whole of mankind, in short – a 'world revolution', no less. As Sakharov puts it, 'Such a revolution will be possible and safe only under highly intelligent worldwide guidance.' This guidance can come only as a result of the convergence of the United States of America and the Soviet Union, their allies and satellites, their systems, uses and interests. The comparative merits and demerits of the two systems, their outright failures and absolute shortcomings, their traditions bad and good, do not change the imperative nature of some effective form of convergence. The whole process, then, is indeed a race against time. The apparent naïveté of Sakharov's *Reflections* disappears against the background of urgency that impelled him to make them.

Thus Sakharov is calling for 'world revolution', although he is careful not to use the term, and for at least two reasons. It is not the Communist model so widely and persistently proclaimed that is indicated here. Instead he is telling the Communists that their model, as it currently exists, is not fit for export:

> The situation involving censorship (Glavlit) in our country is such that it can hardly be corrected for any length of time simply by 'liberalized' directives. Major organizational and legislative measures are required, for example, adoption of a special law on press and information that would clearly and convincingly define what can and what cannot be printed and would place the responsibility on competent people who would be under public control. It is essential that the exchange of information on an international scale (press, tourism and so forth) be expanded in every way, that we get to

258

know ourselves better, that we not try to save on sociological, political and economic research and surveys, which should be conducted not only according to government-controlled programs (otherwise we might be tempted to avoid 'unpleasant' subjects and questions).

The prospects of socialism now depend on whether socialism can be made attractive, whether the moral attractiveness of the ideas of socialism and the glorification of labour, compared with the egotistical ideas of private ownership and the glorification of capital, will be the decisive factors that people will bear in mind when comparing socialism and capitalism, or whether people will remember mainly the limitations of intellectual freedom under socialism or, even worse, the fantastic regime of the cult [of personality].

In one of the most interesting and significant parts of his *Reflections*, Sakharov comes to the general area of economic competition of the two systems. He breaks the bad news gently:

I am placing the accent on the moral aspect because, when it comes to achieving a high productivity of social labour or developing all productive forces or insuring a high standard of living for most of the population, capitalism and socialism seem to have 'played to a tie'.

But Sakharov immediately qualifies this statement. He compares the United States and the Soviet Union to two skiers, one of whom is following exactly in the tracks of the other. The leading skier, the United States, must break the snow, must make way while the following skier, the Soviet Union, profits from the benefit. He can follow along closely behind while expending less energy than the leader. He then makes the usual and valid excuse of the hardships and devastation caused by the German invasion of the Soviet Union and the Soviet invasion of Germany, and adds that 'some absurdities in our development were not an inherent aspect of the socialist course of development, but a tragic accident, a serious, though not inevitable, disease'. But then he gives the quietus to the hopes of the hardline Soviet Communists:

On the other hand, any comparison must take account of the fact that we are now catching up with the United States only in some of the old, traditional industries, which are no longer as important as they used to be for the United States (for example coal and steel). In some of the newer fields, for example, automation, computers, petrochemicals and especially in industrial research and development,

259

we are not only lagging behind but are also growing more slowly, so that a complete victory of our economy in the next few decades is unlikely.*

That was putting it very mildly. In his letter, written jointly with Valery Turchin and Roy Medvedev, in April 1970 and addressed to Brezhnev, Kosygin and Podgorny (the leaders of the Central Committee, the Council of Ministers and the Supreme Soviet, respectively), Sakharov denies authorship of a letter addressed to Brezhnev which appeared three months earlier over Sakharov's signature and contained a graphic description of the state of the Soviet economy (for this reason, regardless of the origin or the purpose of this letter – Sakharov and company describe it as a fabrication distributed as provocation – it is excerpted here):

At closed Party assemblies they read your letter aloud, Leonid Ilyich, addressed as it is to all members of the Soviet Communist Party.

In this letter are set forth certain details unknown to the lowest strata of society, but in general a picture is herewith drawn which is already known to Party members and the people by and large.

We have long known that we have not only lost the race to the moon but also the economic competition as a whole, that work productivity in this country is piddling, that our country is becoming a raw materials supplement of Europe, that we are able to maintain ourselves only thanks to the legendary natural resources and traditional patience of the peasantry of this country. Everyone sees that no one among us desired to occupy himself with real work, but only throws dust in the eyes of his superintendents, that such fictional events as jubilees and anniversaries have become more important for us than the real events of economic and social life.

All this comes as the result of the fact that for many years now we have lived in a make-believe world, that we deceive each other and do not have the courage to look truth in the face while other governments do not float in the air but go about their business here on earth and for this reason outstrip us and leave us further and further behind.

At present not one friendly get-together takes place but that people talk about this stage of affairs. After all, everybody knows that the ensnaring device of collective self-deceit leads to catastrophe. Every-

* Sakharov wrote his *Reflections* on the eve of the Soviet crushing of the Prague Spring in which he, like many another Soviet intellectual, had placed such high hopes.

where in Russia they talk about it. And in the midst of all this your letter appears.

This is a bold, right-minded move on your part, and history will ascribe it to you as a service. But history will not forgive you if this signal is not followed by salutary measures. And these are very simple. The cure is suggested by the diagnosis. The all-pervasive, ever-present living-by-the-lie can be cured only by freedom of speech. How much initiative, wit, enthusiasm will release itself and come to the surface if, finally, they cease to stop our mouths. In the editorial offices of magazines there are dozens of articles, there are dozens of books already printed and just out of the machines, in all of which our life here is analysed thoroughly and honestly. All these they do 'not let pass'. The pride of Russian literature, Solzhenitsyn, has been driven out of the Writers Union. Parliament, which costs so much money, has become nothing more than a rubber stamp.

Freedom of speech and only freedom of speech can put Russia on the road to recovery. [signed] Sakharov.

This letter was widely distributed in the form of samizdat throughout Moscow and later appeared in the foreign press. Despite its inelegancies the forgery epitomizes the letter under triple authorship that followed three months later, which set forth the complaint point by point over fifteen pages. In the light of the mass of detail and the solemn march of arguments in the latter document, it is small wonder that the authors were intent on disowning the much shorter version as a fabrication and provocation. The genuine letter reads like a manifesto of failure. Here, by way of sample, is one of its paragraphs:

In the course of the last decade the economy of our country began to evidence threatening signs of dissension and stagnation, although the roots of these difficulties reach back to an earlier period and run deep indeed. The rate of growth of the national income decreases unremittingly. The gap between what is necessary for the normal development and the actual introduction of new productive forces is growing. We are faced with a large number of mistakes in the determination of technical and economic policy, of inadmissible delay in the solution of urgent problems. Defects in the system of planning, accounting and incentives often lead to contradictions of the local and district interests with those of the commonwealth and with those of the government. As a result the reserves of the development of production do not accrue in the necessary way and are not put to use; instead technical progress slows down markedly.

By dint of these causes the natural resources of the country are frequently and uncontrollably destroyed without anyone being brought to account: forests are cut down, reservoirs are polluted, large tracts of rich, fertile land are inundated, erosion occurs as well as the salination of soil, etc. The chronically critical situation in agriculture and especially in livestock-breeding is well known. In recent years the real income of the population has hardly increased at all, food production, medical care and general service improve very slowly and sporadically. The number of unavailable products is on the increase. Signs of inflation are clearly in evidence. Especially alarming for the future of the country is the slowing down in the development of education: in fact, our expenditures for education considered in all its facets are less than those in the USA and are growing more slowly. There is also the tragic growth of alcoholism and the beginnings of drug addiction. In many areas of the country the crime rate is increasing systematically [sic] as it does among teenagers and the youth in general as well. In the work of scientific and scientific–technical organizations bureaucracy administrative provincialism, lack of initiative and a purely formal relationship to one's assigned task are increasingly widespread.

This catalogue of shortcomings and abuses is followed by a general conclusion:

The decisive, summary factor in the comparison of economic systems, of course, is labour productivity. And here the matter stands in the worst case of all. Our labour productivity remains as before many times lower than in the developed capitalist countries and its growth has slowed down markedly. This situation appears especially critical if it is compared with the situation of the leading capitalist countries and, in particular, with that of the USA.

But the catalogue does not stop there. There follows an explanation of how the capitalist countries have managed to avoid destructive crises – by introducing into their economies elements of government control and planning, by being flexible in their approach to economic problems, in short. And also, of course, by introducing modern methods of management such as the shortening of the working day as a means of combating unemployment caused by the introduction of new, highly technical labour-saving devices. And here the three authors add a particularly bitter comment:

In comparing our economy with that of the USA, we see that our economy lags behind not only in quantity, but also – and this is the saddest thing of all – in quality. The newer and more revolutionary any aspect of the economy, the greater the gap between us and the USA.

Here the three authors broach the matter of computer technology, the introduction of which into the national economy is a phenomenon of decisive importance, 'radically changing the face of the system of production and the whole culture'. This phenomenon, they add, has been rightly called 'the second Industrial Revolution'. And how stands the comparison here?

> The magnitude of our inventory of computers is *one hundred times* less than that of the USA meanwhile, and as far as the utilization of computers in the national economy is concerned – well, here the gap is so great that it is impossible to measure it. We are simply living in another epoch.

What must be constantly kept in mind in evaluating these statements and their effect on the authorities is the position from which they are made. It is a position not only of prominence and prestige but above all of access to information such as that enjoyed only by the Soviet élite. It is more than that, because these are scientists pronouncing judgement, men who not only have long experience in gathering and evaluating information but are also, on the evidence of the distinction they have attained, extraordinarily gifted in doing so. Thus the fact that none of the three authors is an economist by profession takes little if anything away from the weight, the specific gravity of their findings. They pass, and they pass with distinction, as adepts in the general field of acquiring and evaluating knowledge. This, too, is *glasnost*. And with it the authors enter their home territory in the course of their epistolary disquisition. On home ground the three scientists make the bitterest and most telling point of all:

> In the sphere of scientific and technical discoveries the matter stands no better. Here again there is no visible growth of our role. Rather to the contrary. At the end of the fifties our country was the first country in the world, having launched the Sputnik and sent a man into the cosmos. At the end of the sixties we had lost that leadership, and the first people to land on the moon were Americans. This fact is only one of the surface appearances of the substantial and ever-growing difference along the broad front of scientific and technological work between us and the developed countries of the West. In the twenties and thirties the capitalist countries went

through a period of crises and depressions. In this same period we, making use of the surge of national energy born of the revolution, created an industry with a speed and dispatch never before seen. Then we brought out the slogan: 'Catch up with and overtake America!' And indeed we did catch up with her within the course of a few decades. And then the situation changed. There began the second Industrial Revolution. And now, at the beginning of the seventies, we see that not even having caught up with America we are falling further and further behind her.

What is the matter? Why is it that we have not only not become the front-runners of the second Industrial Revolution, but have even shown ourselves incapable of entering that revolution on even terms with the more developed capitalist countries? Is it indeed because the socialist form of government presents fewer and lesser possibilities than the capitalist system for the development of productive forces, is it because in the competition between capitalism and socialism capitalism is the conqueror?

The answer to this painful question is a thundering 'of course not!' The source of their trouble has nothing to do with socialism, but – quite the contrary – is foreign to it, goes against its grain and is to be found in those specialities (specialities of the house, as it were), in those conditions of 'our' life which run athwart socialism and are inimical to it. This source is the anti-democratic traditions and norms of social life that were formed in the Stalinist period and have not been definitively liquidated to this day. The non-economic constraints, limitations on the exchange of information, limitations placed on intellectual freedom and other manifestations of the anti-democratic perversions of socialism that took place under Stalin were accepted in the Soviet Union as part of the cost of the process of industrialization. It is considered that they had no serious influence on the economy of the country although they certainly had the most serious consequences in political and military areas, affecting the fates of wide strata of the population and whole nationalities. As a consequence of the enlargement of the scope and the intricacy of economic systems there arose new problems of organization and management. These problems cannot be solved by one person or a few persons standing at the apex of the 'pyramid of power', regardless of his or their putative omniscience. No, these problems demand the creative participation of millions of people at every level of the economic system. They demand a wide exchange of information and ideas. Herein lies the difference between a modern economy and the economies, let us say, of the countries of the ancient East.

There follow the standard justifications offered by the Soviet authorities for the cultural and sociological privations they visit upon the Soviet population. Any negative information about Soviet conditions is suppressed because its disclosure would provide aid and comfort for the enemy in the form of food for their anti-Soviet propaganda. By the same token the exchange of information with foreign countries is limited out of fear of the 'infiltration of an inimical ideology'. Theoretical generalizations and practical proposals alike which strike someone as too daring are nipped in the bud, without any discussion whatever, under influence of the fear that they might 'undermine principle'. These examples betray the authorities' blatant mistrust of creative thinkers, of critical, active personalities. In this state of affairs the conditions are created for the ascent on the bureaucratic ladder not of those who distinguish themselves as highly qualified professionally but of those who pay lip-service to the cause of the Party and in the event distinguish themselves only by devotion to their own narrowly conceived personal interests or by passive instrumentality.

This is the most fundamental disadvantage of any totalitarian order. There follows, however, a more insidious drawback that is generic to both Soviet Communism and Nazism. The authors of the letter to Brezhnev point out that not only control for supervisors as well as individual initiative are made more difficult by the limitation of freedom of information, but also that the middle managers suffer accordingly. But in the end the top management suffers even more by dint of receiving incomplete information edited to the taste of the recipient, making it impossible for him to use the power of his position effectively. All this amounts to the stultification of the political process as a whole. (The resultant situation is strongly reminiscent of the headlessness of the Third Reich. By ruthlessly applying the *Führerprinzip* or leadership principle, the Nazis reduced the German state to the paradoxical absurdity of a total lack of leadership.) With this in mind the authors avow that purely economic reforms – such as the much-heralded but abortive reform of 1965 – are of no avail because the measures they propose cannot be put into effect without political reform, namely in administration, information and openness in discussion and publicity.

Once again the key to the entire cure for the ills besetting Soviet society and the Communist system is *glasnost*, which has the double meaning of freedom of discussion and access to information. There can be no talk of scientific approaches to anything without the establishment of the principle of free discussion and full access to information. In this connection the letter touches on the problem of the relationship between the Party-state and the intelligentsia. The freedom to communicate and create, write the authors, is prerequisite to the intelligentsia by the very nature of its activity, of its social function. The striving of the intelligentsia to enlarge this freedom is both legal and natural. The Soviet government, however, counters this striving by well-nigh every possible means, such as administrative coercion, dismissal from employment and even court action. This opens up a gap and causes mutual distrust and a deep lack of understanding between the Party-state and the most active, that is, the most valuable strata of the intelligentsia, a situation that renders any sort of meaningful cooperation extremely difficult. And this is the very heart of the matter, because in the conditions of a modern industrial society in which the role of the intelligentsia is constantly growing, this gap, this lack of cooperation between the Party-state and the intelligentsia, 'cannot be characterized as anything other than suicidal'.

The overwhelming majority of the intelligentsia and the youth of the country understands the ineluctable need for democratization, and likewise understands the need for proceeding cautiously and gradually in this matter, but it cannot understand and justify actions of a patently anti-democratic character. And indeed, how is one to justify the confinement in prisons, labour camps and psychiatric clinics of persons who, while in opposition, nevertheless represent an opposition that lies well within the legal limits, in the sphere of ideas and convictions?*

* There is something unspoken here that is of crucial importance. This is the studied avoidance of any form of violence on the part of Soviet dissidents. Considering the scope and intensity of the provocations and repression practised by the Party-state in this connection, the record of dissident non-violence is a constant source of astonishment. To be sure, their avoidance of violence is of great strategic significance. They are intent on making it clear that the Soviets live in fear of ideas, not of force. Bukharin, speaking of Stalin, said that there was no need to fear his ideas because he did not have any. The same, by and large, can be said of the Soviets particularly in terms of the civil statute. Whatever else, Soviet society without *glasnost* was the dullest and dreariest in creation: boredom frozen by fear.

266

It is just this aspect, the Soviet phobia of ideas, of innovation, that moves the Soviet Party-state to oppose everything that is worthwhile and commendable, to mistake the striving to achieve excellence for opposition, to misconstrue the simple and honest urge to acquire knowledge and information, the attempt to participate in enlightening discussion of socially important problems as deep, dark conspiracies directed against the Soviet state and the Communist system. The only opposition in the Soviet Union is that mounted by the Soviet Party-state itself against the spectral projections of its own psychopathic fear. It can fairly be said that the Soviet system opposes itself at every turn out of sheer panic. The bureaucratic, ritualistic, dogmatic, hypocritical and totally unimaginative style of Soviet officialdom is by far the greatest danger to one and all in the Soviet Union today.

It is for this reason that the process of democratization must come and will brook no very long delay. The course of democratization will evoke an avalanche of enthusiasm comparable to that of the twenties. The best intellectual forces in the country will be mobilized for the solution of national economic and social problems. And yet the introduction of democratization will not be easy. The normal course of such a process will be threatened on the one hand by individualist and anti-socialist forces and on the other by advocates of 'strong government' – demagogues of the Fascist mould who may try to exploit for their own purposes the economic difficulties of the country, the mutual lack of understanding and the distrust between the intellectuals and the Party-state apparatus, the existence in certain strata of society of low-minded and nationalistic tendencies. But there is no other way out of the mess; the mission, difficult as it is, must be accomplished. The introduction of democratization on the initiative and under the control of the highest authorities will make possible the implementation of this process according to plan, blazing a trail so that all levels of the Party-state apparatus succeed in re-structuring (this is the first appearance of *perestroika* in the form of the reflexive verb *perestroitsa*) in accordance with the new style of work, which will distinguish itself from the old by greater *glasnost*, openness and broader discussion of all problems.

The authors then submit, by way of example, a programme of measures to be taken, a programme it would be possible to carry out within the course of four or five years. There are fourteen points:

1. The announcement by high Party-state authorities of the necessity of further democratization, of the time-limits and methods of implementation of the same. The publication in the press of a series of articles containing discussions of the problem of democratization.

2. The limited distribution, through Party and Soviet offices, enterprises and institutions, of information concerning the situation in the country and theoretical work on public problems which, for the moment, it would be expedient to make the object of wider discussion. The gradual enlargement of access to such materials to the point of complete removal of all limitations.

3. The cessation of the jamming of foreign radio broadcasts. The free sale of foreign books and periodicals. The entrance of our country into the international system of copyright for authors and editors. The gradual (three to four years) broadening and facilitation of international tourism in both directions, the facilitation of international correspondence, and also other measures for the broadening of international contacts, with emphasis on the development of such tendencies in relation to the countries of Comecon.

4. The establishment of an institute for the study of public opinion. This would begin with the limited publication and then go on to the full publication of materials showing the attitudes of the population to the most important problems of domestic and foreign policy, and also of other sociological materials.

5. The amnesty of political prisoners. A decree declaring obligatory the publication of the full record of all court proceedings of a political character. Public investigation of the places of confinement and psychiatric institutions.

6. The implementation of a series of measures calculated to improve the work of the courts and the public prosecutors, their independence of the government executive, of local influences, of prejudices and connections.

7. Abolition of the designation of nationality in passports. A uniform passport for the inhabitants of the cities and villages. Gradual discontinuance of the visa system in passports to be carried out simultaneously with the equalization of territorial dissimilarities of economic and cultural development.

8. Widespread organization of complex industrial corporations (firms) with a high degree of independence in questions of production planning and technological process, of sale and supply, in financial and personnel questions, and the extension of these rights to smaller production units. Scientific determina-

tion after careful research of the form and extent of government regulation.

9. Reforms in the domain of education. An increase in the allocation of funds for primary and secondary schools, and improvement in the material situation of teachers, their independence and their right to experiment.

10. The passage of a press and information law. The guarantee of the possibility of creating new organs of the press by public organizations and groups of citizens.

11. Improvement in the training of managerial cadres showing promise of executive ability. The establishment of the practice of employing probationers. Improvement of the access to information of managerial cadres at all levels, the guarantee of their rights to independence, to experiment, to defence of their opinions and to regular checks on their work.

12. The gradual introduction of the practice of presenting several candidates for an office in the election of Party and Soviet authorities at all levels, including general elections.

13. The broadening of the rights of Soviet authorities. The broadening of the rights and responsibility of the Supreme Soviet of the USSR.

14. The restoration of all rights of the nation, which were removed by force under Stalin. The restoration of the national autonomy of exiled peoples. The gradual reservation of the possibility of return transmigration (in those cases where this has not already taken place).

The authors are convinced that the only realistic policy in the era of the thermonuclear weapon is to follow a course of increasing international cooperation, particularly in the article of the persistent search for avenues to a possible *rapprochement* in scientific–technical, economic, cultural and ideological areas and in the principle of the renunciation of weapons of mass destruction. But the prerequisite of such *rapprochement* is the democratization of the Soviet Union. And this not least because it would lead to fuller explanations and discussions of Soviet foreign policy, thus removing a great deal of misunderstanding as well as 'negative features' from the policy itself. The other great bugaboo, the mutual lack of understanding between the Party-state and the intellectuals, would disappear in the first stages of democratization.

There is the final question: 'What awaits our country if the course of democratization is not taken?' And there follows the catalogue of catastrophe. Falling behind the capitalist countries in the process of the second Industrial Revolution and the gradual transformation into a second-rate provincial state (history knows similar examples, they add); increasing economic difficulties; increasing tension in relations between the Party-state apparatus and the intelligentsia; the dangers of upheavals to right and left; a gathering crisis in the nationalities problem because the movement toward democratization in the national republics, coming from below, will inevitably assume a nationalistic character. This prospect becomes particularly threatening if we take into account the present dangers from the quarter of 'Chinese totalitarian nationalism' which, regarded historically, can be discounted as temporary, but will constitute a serious threat in the years to come. 'To confront this danger is only possible by increasing or at least maintaining the existing technical and economic gap between our country and China, while increasing the ranks of our friends in the world at large and offering the Chinese people the alternative of cooperation and aid.' This course becomes obvious if they take into account the numerical superiority of their potential opponent and his clamorous nationalism as well as the great extent of their southern border and the sparsely populated Eastern regions of the Soviet Union. Therefore a stagnant economy, a decrease in the rate of growth and development in combination with an insufficiently realistic, too often over-ambitious foreign policy on all continents may lead their country into catastrophic consequences.

XII
※

INTERVIEWS AND INTERROGATIONS:
THRUST...

On 6 June Sakharov addressed a letter to Leonid Brezhnev alone, protesting the forcible lodging of his colleague and friend Zhores Medvedev in a psychiatric clinic:

> I am deeply troubled by the lawlessness indulged in by authorities in the Public Health Service in respect of my friend Zhores Alexandrovich Medvedev. On 29 May a detachment of militia accompanied by two doctors broke into his apartment and, without presenting a warrant for his arrest, removed him by force to the city of Kaluga for psychiatric examination. He remains there at the present time in a general hospital for psychiatric diseases.
>
> This entire incident, from beginning to end, constitutes an absolutely lawless act. There was not and there is not in the possession of the health authorities any sort of instructions based on data suggesting the psychic abnormality of Zhores Medvedev or, more seriously, describing his condition as dangerous to the public. Z. Medvedev is an absolutely healthy human being. He is widely known to Soviet and foreign scholars for his work in the fields of gerontology, genetics and his history of biology in the Soviet Union, and his public service, carried out on a strictly lawful basis in the interests of international cooperation, and in the interests of Soviet democracy. It is possible that the activity of Medvedev runs counter to the interests of some people, in particular, of those former members of the widespread clan of anti-scientific orientation in Soviet biology, who, by dint of their provocations, mistakes and fly-by-night projects did such harm to our country . . .

To judge from the tone of indignation and the sense of outrage expressed in this letter, this was Sakharov's introduction to the

Soviet government's use of psychiatric hospitals – the long since infamous *psychushka* – as a means of dealing with particularly bothersome dissidents who are legally non-accountable. The first case of the use of the *psychushka* on dissident record is that of Viktor Fainberg who was arrested while demonstrating against the Soviet invasion of Czechoslovakia in 1968 on Red Square in the centre of Moscow. Natalya Gorbanyevskaya, another partici- pant in the Red Square demonstration in August 1968, was released soon after her arrest (as the mother of two small children) but later re-arrested and confined to a *psychushka* for a full two years. The arrest and 'hospitalizing' of Zhores Medvedev was ten- tative. Instead of being committed under criminal procedure as were Gorbanyevskaya, Fainberg, General Grigorenko, Vladimir Bukovsky and company, Medvedev was committed under the civil statute, a less serious charge and more amenable to appeal. Even so, the commitment of an eminent scientist to the *psychushka* was a slap in the face for the scientific community. Unforgettable is the scene of Medvedev's arrest, in his own apartment, by a full colonel of the militia (at the head of the detachment of four men plus two doctors, all of them in Medvedev's apartment: the Soviet Party- state does not stint in the use of rank in such cases – the officer in command is often a major and never less than a captain). 'How dare you break into my apartment?' shouted Medvedev in a tower- ing rage. The colonel of militia shouted back at Medvedev: 'What do you mean *your* apartment? This apartment belongs to the state!' Seldom has the essential connection between privacy and property so forcefully been put.

The commitment of dissidents or even dissenters (the latter within the ranks of the Party) to the *psychushka* is a shift by the Soviet government to avoid due process and an open trial even *à la* Soviet – for whatever reason. In this regard it bears a resemblance, *mutatis mutandis*, to the American governmental security shift of the closed hearing and to the special commission of the Inquisition as 'an emergency tribunal creating and changing its own adminis- trative law at will'. (There is also the parallel of the unique instance of an American government's commitment to a psy- chiatric clinic – however makeshift – of a political prisoner; in this case a Fascist sympathizer-cum-traitor during World War II in the person of a universally acknowledged major poet: Ezra Pound. His confinement lasted thirteen years.) But the practice of committing politically embarrassing dissidents to special clinics for psychiatric examination and treatment goes back a good deal further than the demonstration on Red Square in 1968. Soviet abuse of forensic psychiatry seems to have emerged gradually, on an *ad hoc* basis, in the thirties and almost certainly as an exemplary alternative to the death sentence. The Soviet authorities have shrouded the subject in secrecy. In 1955–6, in the throes of de-Stalinization, a commission of the Central Committee conducted an extensive investigation of such abuse. The commission, headed by Sergei Pisarev, himself a victim of the practice (he spent two years in a mental institution after sending a report to Stalin criticizing the KGB as having fabricated the 'doctors' plot'), reported that 'hundreds of absolutely healthy persons' had been confined in mental institutions for years. The report of the commission was suppressed.

The persistence in the practice of this abuse points to considerable embarrassment on the part of Soviet authorities in their routine but exacting task of upholding their sectarian standards of behavioural rectitude. In the brothers Medvedev's book, *A Question of Madness* (the Russian edition's title is blunter: *Who's Crazy?*), the story of Zhores Medvedev's commitment is told in detail. The action against Medvedev began with the school-board sponsored psychiatric examination of his seventeen-year-old son, who had begun to assume the characteristics of a 'hippy'. But this was only a front. The actual target of the operation was the father, Zhores. He was called to an interview with a disguised forensic psychiatrist on the pretext of the necessity of discussing his son's case. In the reproductions of the interviews between Medvedev and various Soviet authorities the paternalism of the Soviet system comes unmistakably to the fore. He is treated as a child – *in loco infantis* – to the point where the original pretext of taking the child for the father becomes the reverse symbol of the real purpose of taking the father for the child.

The paternalism of the pretext of the psychiatric examination and treatment of the Soviet people has two faces. As a convenience the use of psychiatric institutions as houses of correction is of especial value in cases where the prestige and standing of the client is particularly great. This was the case with General Grigorenko, a man of exceptional probity with an impeccable record of public and patriotic service – *integer vitae scelerisque purus.* A huge, craggy mountain of a man, Grigorenko eagerly gave evidence of the stuff he was made of. At a Party meeting in 1941 he criticized Stalin as a military bungler. He came away with a reprimand. Twenty years later he gave vent to his dissatisfation with the 'unreasonable and often harmful activities of Khrushchev and his team', as he put it in an open letter to Moscow voters. On this occasion he was merely demoted and transferred to Ussuriysk near Vladivostok. In this remote region Grigorenko not only continued to write and send out pamphlets but also went on to organize a group with the resounding title of 'the Union for the Struggle of the Revival of Leninism'. For this he was arrested in 1964 and confined in a *psychushka* in Leningrad in order to avoid the publicity of a trial. Grigorenko had already made a name for himself – particularly among his colleagues in the Soviet Army. What made Grigorenko's case especially difficult for the Soviets was the general's steadfastness: there was never any question of recanting. Rather the opposite. He was confirmed in his criticism of Krushchev by the Central Committee itself when that body, in the process of ousting the Soviet leader, made the same indictment as had Grigorenko. (The identical charade took place with the Ukrainian mathematician Leonid Plyushch, who was arrested after he criticized the Ukrainian Party leader, Sherlest. While the public prosecutor was building a case against Plyushch the Party chief was ousted by Party decree, based on the same arguments as those advanced by Plyushch. This made it impossible to proceed against Plyushch in a court of law, so recourse was taken to confinement in a mental institution.) Grigorenko was deprived of his rank, his pension and his Party membership and confined for fifteen months, eight of them in a *psychushka* where he was diagnosed as suffering from 'sluggish schizophrenia', a conceptual concoction of the Soviet psychiatrist Andrei V. Snezhnevsky, who has enlarged the definition of schizophrenia by including the mildest of neuroses. Snezhnevsky's neuroses manifested themselves in such symptoms as social withdrawal, confrontations with authorities, philosophical concerns and the desire to reform society. These are admittedly 'symptoms that merge into normality'. Snezhnevsky has done the Soviet state great service in providing catch-all conceptions of psychiatric disorders that lend themselves to application by 'an emergency tribunal creating and changing its own administrative law at will'. And yet the 'laughing house', to use the American vernacular, is no laughing matter. For a psychically normal detainee to be confined among mentally disturbed patients is a frightening and often traumatic experience; worse, by several cuts above the mark, than the lot of the political prisoner confined at close quarters with common criminals. But this is not the sum of the experience of the political prisoner in the psychiatric clinic. There is also the treatment – particularly the practice of giving injections of tranquillizing or benumbing drugs that reduce the 'patient' to something like the vegetable state. The spectacle of the defiant strongman in custody is likely to bring out the masochist in any seconded tormenter. As Grigorenko's doctors in Leningrad told him: 'We have had sane people here before. But never before was a person officially recognized as mentally ill punished without any court order, and especially as savagely as you have been.'

In many ways the application of 'Punitive Medicine' – to quote the title of a book on the subject by one of its victims, Alexander Podrabinek – to political deviants is a more damnable aberration of statecraft than its opposite extreme, the outlawing of a whole branch of medicine, as in the case of hereditary diseases in the genetics controversy. But its practice by the Soviet Party-state bears witness to a kind of ecclesiastical quixoticism that is utterly impervious to the whole realm of historical precedents, comparisons and associations. These, on the heels of the phantasmagoria of the Nazi experience, crowd in. Solzhenitsyn drew a comparison in an open letter, a comparison that will already have forced itself upon the reader:

> It is time to understand that the imprisonment of sane persons in madhouses because they have minds of their own is spiritual murder, a variation of the gas chambers and even more cruel; the condemned suffer torments more frightful and prolonged ... In lawlessness and evil-doing one must always remember the boundary line beyond which man becomes a cannibal.

The expectations of the Soviets that they could continue their membership in the World Psychiatric Association in the teeth of these practices, without being called to account, found guilty as charged and excluded, was simply foolhardy. They were, after all, on the judges' bench together with the Western Allies at the Nuremberg Trials (as a Russian proverb has it; 'Victors are not judged'). Among the 'crimes against humanity' condemned at Nuremberg was the Nazi programme for the physical destruction of various categories of the mentally ill which involved psychiatric 'special examinations' by qualified physicians – with results that are well known throughout the world. In 1977, at its annual meeting, the World Psychiatric Association officially condemned the 'systematic abuse of psychiatry for political purposes in the Soviet Union'.

As for his part, Andrei Sakharov did not leave his intervention on behalf of Zhores Medvedev at letter-writing. Along with his colleague Peter Kapitsa he joined a number of other friends of Zhores Medvedev at a meeting with government officials on 12 June at the Soviet ministry of health. In the book *A Question of Madness*, Roy Medvedev describes an incident at the meeting:

'Enumerating the various kinds of mental illness that demand hospitalization, Snezhnevsky spoke of "obsessive reformist delusions", and at this point he shot a penetrating professional glance at Sakharov. "I found it comic," Sakharov commented, "but of course I know it is not very funny for people who land up in a mental hospital after being diagnosed like that."'

This assemblage of professionally prestigious friends of Zhores Medvedev – Solzhenitsyn was very much one of their number – was too much for the advocates of psychotherapy as a political instrument in this case. Kapitsa and Sakharov were very big guns and they were – still – members of the Establishment, members of the Soviet Academy of Sciences, to be exact, and as such representative of that institution. In short, their appearance lent a note of formality to the protest and with it the inchoate impression of a split in the Soviet Establishment. An attack on Zhores Medvedev – and most particularly because it was an attack based on pseudoscientific pretensions against a scientist who had fought long and hard against such pretensions as manifested in Lysenkoism – was an attack against the Soviet scientific community. It had not been a good idea. According to Roy Medvedev, Snezhnevsky himself remonstrated with Alexander Lifshits, the chief doctor at Kaluga, on this point: 'In a year's time there's going to be an international psychiatric congress in Mexico. How do you think this is going to make our delegation look?' Zhores Medvedev was released five days after the meeting at the ministry of health. He had spent just nineteen days in the *psychushka*.

But the Soviet Union refused to cease and desist in the practice altogether: the sheer expedience of the method in the face of the appalling 'case-load' of bureaucratic intervention at every level of intellectual pursuit was simply too great. The great disadvantage of political psychotherapy, of course, was that those subjected to it lived to tell the tale. Thus, the greater the number of victims of this Soviet form of *selektion*, the greater the number of witnesses willing and able to testify against it. The Soviets once again manoeuvred themselves into the vicious circle of seeking to counteract anti-Soviet slander and thereby producing material that can and will be held against the Soviet state by the international community. By 1984 (the right date for the action) the World Psychiatric Association, after having issued its warning in 1977 against the abuse of psychiatry for political purposes and meanwhile confronted with a mass of new evidence on the persistence of the practice in the Soviet Union, took steps to expel the offending government from its ranks. To forestall the expulsion the Soviet Union cancelled its membership in the organization.

On 11 November 1970 Sakharov signed a letter conjointly with nine colleagues (among them the academician Mikhail Leontovich as well as Valery Turchin and Valery Chalidze) addressed to the chairman of the Supreme Court of the RSFSR, protesting the sentencing to five years' exile of their colleague, Revolt Pimenov, and the puppet-theatre actor, Boris Vail. The two had been charged with having passed to close friends a few typewritten texts which the court in Kaluga found libellous of the public and political order of the Soviet state. The body of the letter is germane to this account:

> Such court cases in recent years have called forth protests from many citizens. Each new trial of this kind increases the concern of the general public, all the more so since despite repeated appeals the legislature has not particularized the formulations of Article 190–1 of the criminal code of the RSFSR, and the more so since in these trials the factual violation of the principle of free speech has become habitual. Because they showed interest in critical articles on public themes, because they took part in the exchange of information which is essential to society, two men will be torn away from creative work, from normal life in accustomed surroundings, for five years.

The letter ends with a plea that the Supreme Court study the fact of legal prosecution for an act that in a democratic society must be considered a normal manifestation of citizenship. But the Kaluga trial itself was so colourfully apposite as to warrant scrutiny. Fortunately one of the defendants, Boris Vail, produced the following account of the occasion:

Like a great many other Soviet citizens I heard of the Academician Sakharov for the first time in the year 1968. Foreign radio stations broadcast selections from his essay, 'Thoughts on Progress, Peaceful Coexistence and Intellectual Freedom', in their Russian-language programmes. But soon I had the essay itself in hand in the form of the samizdat typewritten sheets. It was still difficult for me to believe that a highly placed Soviet academician could think so independently and freely, could openly come to the defence of political prisoners and, finally, put the question as to an all-world government. But one of my friends assured me that the author of this unusual composition was really the atomic physicist Sakharov whom my friend had just met at a scientific conference in Tiflis.

Two years passed. In the autumn of 1970 I happened to be in a rather strange situation. I had been arraigned on charges of distributing samizdat, but while awaiting trial I was not kept in custody but remained at liberty on the strict understanding that I was not to leave the city – that was the strange thing about it, you don't get that sort of situation very often in the Soviet Union. And even the restriction to the city was strange because I lived in one city, Kursk, while the venue for the trial had been set in another city, Kaluga, and I was trying to find a lawyer for my defence in a third city, Moscow. So it was not quite clear which city I was confined to.

In any case I learned from friends that the Academician Sakharov was planning to attend our trial (I had been arraigned along with the mathematician Revolt Pimenov). But my Moscow friends told me Sakharov had just had a heart attack and would not be able to travel to Kaluga unless accompanied by a doctor. I didn't meet Sakharov in Moscow and went straight to the trial by inter-urban train, but without my lawyer – he happened to be busy at the time with another trial.

In the corridor of the Kaluga regional courthouse someone pointed out a tall, plainly dressed individual to me. He was leaning against the wall. This was the Academician Sakharov! I walked over to him and asked if he were really Sakharov. He confirmed it. I thanked him for his engagement in our case. He looked tired. My friends told me then that the authorities were very much against Sakharov travelling to Kaluga to attend a political trial. For this reason, on the eve of his departure for Kaluga, the shock absorbers were removed from the car he was to use for the trip.

Among other things, in the corridor of the regional courthouse I told Sakharov that in my home town Kursk a typist had lost her job because she had typed copies of his essay, 'Thoughts on Progress, Peaceful Coexistence and Intellectual Freedom.' 'Yes,' he said, 'I know of such cases. But apparently no one has yet been brought to trial because of the essay.'

The authorities allowed Andrei Dmitrievich to attend our trial – the first trial connected with the distribution of the *Chronicle of Current Events* and the first trial attended by Sakharov, who wanted to know how such trials were conducted. But he was not allowed in the courtroom of the numerous political trials that followed.

On that day, however, the trial did not take place – because of me. I announced that my lawyer could not be present for good and admissible reason and that I did not want another lawyer. However, I said, I would agree that Valery Chalidze defend me. He was standing at the entrance of the courthouse along with other friends of mine whom the authorities refused attendance at a formally open trial. (As usual they filled the courtroom through a back passage with specially selected public and then announced that there were no seats available.)

The judges consulted and decided to postpone the trial for a few days. 'But the next time,' said the judge to me, 'you come here with a lawyer.' I understood that, perhaps, this delay would be turned against me. The presence of Sakharov had given me courage; but the next time – suppose all of a sudden he would not be able to travel to Kaluga? In the corridor I saw Andrei Dmitrievich again and approached him: 'Please excuse me for interrupting the trial. I suppose it will be difficult for you to come here again?' 'Never mind,' he said. 'You did the right thing – and I'll be here next time.'

And indeed a few days later we met again in the same narrow corridor. In the courtroom there was the mixture as before – the same carefully selected public, including operatives of the KGB (in civilian clothes, of course), close relatives of the accused and Andrei Dmitrievich Sakharov. I knew that before the trial began our judge, who is the chairman of the Kaluga regional circuit court, summoned Sakharov to his chambers where they spent half an hour talking about something or other. Now I understand that the judge told Sakharov he would allow him to attend the trial, but only under certain conditions. (More about this later.)

In the evening they declared a recess and it was necessary to make arrangements for spending the night. As far as witnesses summoned by the court from out of town are concerned, usually the local authorities pay their travel expenses and book them rooms in hotels. But as for the accused, like me, nobody bothered: to travel to the place of trial and from there to prison I myself was obliged to pay and meanwhile make my own arrangements for spending the night. My wife and I canvassed several Kalugan hotels. And what did we expect to find? Everywhere, just as in all other cities – 'From Moscow to the very borders' – there was no room at the inn: the same plaque everywhere – 'No room'. We took a look at the local militia station where I showed the duty officer my summons as the accused and requested that he put a room of some sort at our disposal. For some reason the militiaman was not very much surprised, saying only: 'Well, you won't want it, but come along – I'll show you the room.' He brought us to a room in which snoring drunks lay side by side, taking up most of the floor space.

We had no friends or acquaintances in Kaluga, and the situation seemed to be completely hopeless. Only the intervention of Elena Georgievna Bonner – the future wife of Sakharov, who had also come to Kaluga to attend our trial – and, it would seem, of Andrei Dmitrievich himself, opened the doors of one of the main hotels in Kaluga to us. There was a room available after all – in spite of the legend on the plaque.

The next morning we listened to the speech of the state prosecutor. In the introductory part there was nothing at all interesting: 'At a time when the whole Soviet people . . . under the leadership of our own Communist Party . . . at a time when the imperialists . . . there are certain individual people . . . bourgeois propaganda . . . slandering our achievements . . . the construction of Communism . . .' It was terribly close in the courtroom and the windows were thrown wide open. The prosecutor spoke in a loud voice and, even though the courtroom was situated on the second floor, our friends, who had been standing in the courtyard near the entrance for the last two days, were apparently able to hear his accusatory speech. Suddenly into the courtroom strode the convoy commander and whispered something into the judge's ear. I was sitting only two steps away from him in the dock and clearly heard how in answer to the whispered alarm of the convoy commander the judge uttered a single word as an order: 'Motor!' I could not understand what the matter was and yet everything was very simple: the convoy commander started the motor, that is, the engine of the Black Maria parked near the entrance of the courthouse. In this way they drowned out the speech of the prosecutor so that our friends could not hear it. (I was immediately reminded that in Stalinist times they shot people under the cover of the noise of running automobile and truck engines . . .) Now they were drowning out by the same means – not some bourgeois propaganda or other – that would still have been understandable – no, they were drowning out the speech of the representative of the Soviet government.

It was exactly then, during the speech of the prosecutor, that there occurred a remarkable incident involving Sakharov. Somebody in the audience interrupted the state prosecutor – just imagine, what insolence! – and addressed himself to the court: 'Comrade judge, that citizen there [with a gesture at Sakharov] is taking notes!'

SAKHAROV: Do you assume that it is prohibited to record the speech of the state prosecutor? Do you forbid me to take notes?

JUDGE: No, I do not forbid it; I *request* it of you.

The prosecutor resumed his speech, but within a few minutes the judge interrupted him again and turned to Sakharov: 'Comrade Sakharov, I request you not to take notes . . . After all, whatever you record here will appear later in the reactionary Western press.'

SAKHAROV: Somehow that doesn't bother me.

And then for the third time the judge said that he himself *personally* very much requested Sakharov not to take notes, and he emphasized the word 'personally' especially. 'Remember what you and I talked about.' Only after this very insistent request and reference to their talk before the trial did Sakharov cease to take notes of the speech of the prosecutor. It is possible that they would have removed him from the courtroom if he had not yielded.

On the same day sentence was pronounced – five years' exile for each of us. The sentence – let us say this straightaway – was a mild one, especially considering the fact that we did not plead guilty. I consider that the mildness of the sentence is attributable to the presence at the trial of Andrei Dmitrievich Sakharov.

And although they took me from the courtroom straight to prison, I felt happy. In the first place because from prison I shall go into exile and not to a camp, and exile is almost freedom, and in the second place I carried with me the sensation of happiness – happiness over meeting with such people, with such a person as Andrei Dmitrievich. And no one can take this sensation away from me.

On 28 December 1970 Sakharov joined a group of Soviet scientists who were, like himself, also members of the American Academy of Arts and Sciences, in writing an open appeal to the President of the United States, Richard Nixon, and to the Chairman of the Presidium of the Supreme Soviet, Nikolai Podgorny. That part of the letter addressed to the president was a plea for the protection of the life and rights of Angela Davis, then on trial in California for terrorist activity. The section addressed to Podgorny was a plea to spare the lives of Mark Dymshits and Eduard Kuznetsov, both of whom were condemned to death by firing squad for the attempted hijacking of an airplane at the Leningrad airport (nine other Soviet Jews involved in the action were sentenced to lengthy prison terms: the action was conceived as a protest against Soviet refusal to allow the emigration of Jews to Israel). Within a few days Sakharov received an answer to his appeal to Nixon by telegram from Martin Hillenbrand of the American State Department, assuring him that the full rights of Angela Davis would be observed by the California court concerned, in open session with full access to the American and foreign press. No answer was received to that part of the letter addressed to Podgorny, although Dymshits's and Kuznetsov's death sentences were commuted to fifteen years at hard labour in the camps under the pressure of international public opinion not long thereafter. The symbolic hijacking of a Soviet aircraft (on the ground, with no harm to anyone, as the group letter points out) had the desired effect: it marked the beginning of the exodus of Soviet Jews to Israel and other Western countries.

Earlier, some time in September, Sakharov had joined Valery Chalidze, Alexander Volpin and Pyotr Yakir in an appeal to the Presidium of the Supreme Soviet for the release of Olga Iofe and Valery Novodvorskaya, both of them nineteen years old when arrested on a bagatelle charge for which others involved had already been released. The appeal also included Anatoly Marchenko and former Major-General of the Soviet Army Peter Grigorenko. Marchenko, a writer of the purest proletarian background, wrote several accounts of life in Soviet prisons, the best known of which are included in his book, *My Testimony* (New York, 1969). Between then and his death in 1986 Marchenko established the all-time record for time spent in Soviet prisons not involving the sentence of life imprisonment – twenty-five years. He was serving his fifth sentence when he died. While he lived he remained perhaps the chief individual subject of Sakharov's public concern.

During the next two and a half years, from the beginning of 1971 to August 1973, Sakharov took part in a double dozen of various public protest actions – articles, letters, appeals, declarations and statements – as author, co-author or co-signatory and, in addition, took part in various small or even individual demonstrations simply by appearing at dissident trials or hearings or visiting dissidents in various stages of custodial or house arrest for the purpose of informing himself. The strategy behind this activity is clear enough: by publicly marking and emphasizing as many occasions of Soviet illegality as possible, Sakharov and his friends drew both public and official attention to the frequency and nature of these often deliberate miscarriages of justice as well as to the fact that these miscarriages were attracting public protest – the worst and best of it being that Sakharov's prestige and that of some of his colleagues made up for the lack of numbers involved. Not that any of this deliberate marking made the protests or their matter any less important; indeed, some of them pointed to generic flaws in the Soviet system. At the end of May 1971, for example, Sakharov addressed another letter to Nikolai Podgorny, protesting the sentencing of the religious writer, A. E. Levitin-Krasnov, to three years' confinement in a labour camp for the distribution of written material ('mendacious fictions') libellous of the public and political order of the Soviet state (Article 190–1 of the Criminal Code of the RSFSR again). But Levitin's articles, Sakharov points out, merely

> express the point of view of a religious man as to the moral and philosophical significance of religion, give opinions on current inner-Church questions and also discuss from loyal and democratic positions problems of freedom of conscience, and in this connection adduce, naturally, concrete examples of violations of that freedom in individual cases. Expressing his religious convictions, analysing events that have actually taken place, Levitin-Krasnov by that very fact cannot be accused of the distribution of mendacious fictions and even less of what he knows to be (that is to say, from his point of view) mendacious fictions. In criticizing certain aspects of existing legislation in questions of religion and of the practice of his application of it, he can in no way be accused of calling for the non-observation of laws insofar as he is appealing for their perfection by legislative means. I attended the trial and am convinced of the absence of any violation of the law in all the cited activities of Levitin. I appeal to you to take steps to ensure the restoration of justice in this matter. Levitin is no longer a young man and he is weighed down with illness. For this reason I ask you to make use of your constitutional rights and influence to ease the burden of his

fate out of considerations of humanity should you find yourself unable to accept the arguments I have adduced above, attesting to the lawful character of his actions.

It is clear from this relatively short letter – perhaps clearer than when the document is a fifteen-page analysis of the state of the nation, complete with an outline of a prescription for its reform – that the strategy of Sakharov and his colleagues in this undertaking is not simply one of marking and emphasizing human-rights violations. There is a strong didactive strain in all these communications. It is as if the scientific community, or part of it, had taken upon itself the task of educating the Soviet leadership and Party apparatus in the art and science of democratic government, in a two-pronged presentation consisting of a demonstration of the need for reform (*perestroika*) on the one hand and a demonstration of the prerequisite of reform, namely freedom of every form of open communication (*glasnost*) on the other. Some of these missives, then, loaded with ideological and political meaning must have seemed rather like highly explosive missiles lobbed into the seigniories of the Party great. A good example of such an epistolary projectile is the open address to the members of the Presidium of the Supreme Soviet of the USSR. It is dated 20 September 1971.

Court trials in recent months bring to mind once again the tragic collisions occurring in connection with the difficulties of citizens desiring to leave the USSR and move to another country, and the legal, social, psychological and political aspects of this problem.

Soviet citizens such as Jews and many another nationality – Russians, Ukrainians, Germans, Armenians, Lithuanians, Latvians, Estonians, Turkmen and others aspiring to exodus for personal, national or other reasons – receive unexplained rejections in answer to their applications for years on end, a fact that turns their lives into an uninterrupted torment of expectation.

There is also another side to the problem. One cannot remain unmoved by the fate of those who, having lost all hope of satisfaction in their attempts to leave the country by legal means, decide to achieve their goal by breaking the law in some way or other. Many of these people are sentenced to long periods of confinement in camps and prisons or are doomed to the horrors of enforced psychiatric care in places of detention with such severe regimens as the special psychiatric hospital in Dnepropetrovsk and the like. The desperate thrashing about of these citizens is interpreted by the courts for the most part as high treason, a crime that entails the most severe punishment.

Here Sakharov buttresses his account with a number of examples, among them the commuted death sentences of Kuznetsov and Dymshits, who led the hijacking attempt on an aircraft in Leningrad, and the desperate deed of a Lithuanian sailor who swam across New Orleans Bay and climbed aboard an American battleship to ask for political asylum. Unaccountably, the Americans returned the Lithuanian to the Soviets (which is ironic, to say the least, since the United States has never recognized the Soviet annexation of Lithuania or that of the other two Baltic states). The Soviets charged the Lithuanian with high treason and sentenced him to ten years' imprisonment. Sakharov then continues with the essay in statecraft:

Finally, there is yet another side to the problem. Persons attempting (usually without success) to leave the country legally, by virtue of existing prejudices, traditions and conformism, are regarded because of this as though they were in the position of second-class citizens insofar as the realization of a number of their rights are concerned. This exclusionary pressure is brought to bear on the possibilities of continued study, of finding and keeping a job and even in the item of prosecution by the courts. The recent trials of Palatnik in Odessa and of Kukuyem in Sverdlovsk are examples from my point of view of this sort of prejudiced, obviously unjust proceedings.

Considering the aspects of the problem here enumerated, I should like to emphasize that the humane, just resolution of the questions touched upon would be very important for the further democratization of our country, for the definitive removal of her international isolation, for the mutual exchange of people and ideas, for the defence of human rights – that primary and basic value in the socio-political structure of a state. Freedom of movement from country to country, which in reality is enjoyed by very few of our citizens, constitutes the indispensable condition of spiritual freedom for all. A free country cannot resemble a cage – even if it is a golden cage and full of good food.

Most respected members of the Presidium of the Supreme Soviet of the USSR, I call upon you, I call upon everyone who desires that our citizens should feel themselves to be truly free to take all necessary measures to bring about a resolution of the questions here mentioned. In particular, I call upon you personally to take the initiative in the following:

1. It is imperative to achieve the passage of legislative acts resolving the problem of exiting the country in a democratic spirit – everyone who so desires must have the right to leave, and if he changes his mind, to return without hindrance – in accordance with universally recognized human rights.

2. It is imperative, further, to achieve the amendment of the formulation of the articles of the criminal code concerning high treason, to preclude the inequitable extension of the concept such as exists in our juridical practice today.

3. It is imperative to amnesty all citizens who have been tried and sentenced for having attempted to leave the country and to free all such persons as have been committed to special psychiatric hospitals for enforced treatment on the same charges.

This letter is signed, for the first time in Sakharov's series of missives to various offices of the Soviet Party-government (it cannot be called a 'correspondence' since there was never any epistolary response from the government), with the title 'Member of the Human Rights Committee' in addition to his title of academician. The Moscow Human Rights Committee was founded in November of 1970 by Sakharov, Valery Chalidze (it was his initiative) and Andrei Tverdokhlebov who were joined some time later by the mathematician Igor Shafarevich and the geophysicist Grigory Podyapolsky. These men were lay jurists and they conceived of the committee as a consultative council, the purpose and function of which were set forth in their statement, 'Principles of the Human Rights Committee', dated 4 November 1970. As listed, they were:

Advisory assistance to state agencies in creating and applying safeguards for human rights, such assistance to be initiated either by the committee or by interested governmental authorities;

creative help for persons occupied with constructive investigations of the theoretical aspects of human rights and the study of the specific character of this problem in a socialist society;

the furtherance of legal education and, in particular, the dissemination of documents of international and Soviet law concerning human rights.

On 15 November 1972 Sakharov addressed an open appeal to the psychiatrists of the world:

The young psychiatrist, Semeon Gluzman, has been sentenced to seven years' confinement in a labour camp of strict regimen and three years of exile according to Article 62 of the Criminal Code of the Ukrainian Soviet Socialist Republic. A search of Gluzman's living quarters revealed nothing incriminating. The charges were made on the basis of the testimony of those suborned to the purpose. In particular, Gluzman was accused of distributing my work on the Czechoslovak question, but I have not written any such work. The conviction of Gluzman should attract especial attention not only because of the severity and unfoundedness of the sentence in a trial conducted behind closed doors, but also because of the profession of the condemned. The world public should react attentively to the communication of the fact that Gluzman is the author or one of the authors of an anonymous expert opinion prepared in absentia in the matter of Grigorenko, a document proving the insubstantiality of the official expert opinion according to which Major-General Grigorenko has been confined for more than three years in the most onerous conditions of a psychiatric prison-hospital.

I consider that there is a basis for the following affirmation: Gluzman was convicted because of his professional honesty. I call upon qualified psychiatrists throughout the world to come to the defence of their young colleague, I call upon them to demand an immediate international investigation of all the facts in the practice of psychiatric repression.

Sakharov had told the journalist Axelbank a month earlier that Khrushchev had once 'ordered the authorities to find compromising material on me ... He told them "Sakharov is against testing the bomb, he pokes his nose into politics. He must be given a lesson."' This story goes back to the summer of 1964, in the last stage of the battle over Lysenkoism. The order had apparently disappeared with Khrushchev.

But now the battle had been joined again, and in a field that bore a sinister similarity to the genetics controversy, in that here again the spectral projection of 'the new Soviet man' was abroad to punish deviants and reformers of any and all kinds. But there was also a sinister contrast, that of the Soviet practice with the vagaries of American forensic psychiatry, particularly in California in the late seventies, in which convicted murderers were released as 'cured' only to kill again. Most sinister, as evident in both similarity and contrast, was the use of the conceptual elasticity of a new, developing science in the preparation of a more effective equation of political reform with psychic deviation.

On 14 February 1973 Sakharov was criticized for the second time in his career in the Soviet press by the *Literaturnaya Gazeta*.

The sense of Sakharov's mentioning the use of his name in the text of the charge brought against Gluzman was to signal the apparent preparation of a case against him by the KGB. This would not have been the first time the KGB had taken such action. In his 'Reflections' Sakharov mentions that his appeal of 11 February 1967 to the Central Committee, that the case against Galanskov and Ginzburg be closed, remained unanswered. 'Only much later' did he learn that 'there had been an attempt (apparently inspired by Semichastny, the former chairman of the KGB) to slander the present writer and a number of other persons on the basis of instigated false testimony . . . Subsequently the testimony of that person – Dobrovolsky – was used at the trial as evidence to show that Ginzburg and Galanskov had ties with a foreign anti-Soviet organization, which one cannot help but doubt.'

In much the same way, during the investigation in preparation for the trial of the poet Anatoly Ivanovich Lupynis two witnesses testified that Lupynis had given them works by Sakharov to read. Sakharov cited the case in his 'Afterword' of June 1972 as one of several 'new facts of psychiatric repression'. Lupynis was diagnosed as schizophrenic in the Serbsky Institute of Forensic Psychiatry in Moscow, returned to Kiev, tried and sentenced to treatment in the prison psychiatric hospital in Dnepropetrovsk. His crime was that of reciting poetry in the Ukrainian language at the Shevchenko Memorial in Kiev in celebration of the centennial of the return of Shevchenko's remains from St Petersburg to Kiev.

The *Literaturnaya Gazeta*'s attack on Sakharov was written by Alexander Chakovsky in an article entitled. 'And What Next? Reflections on Reading Harrison Salisbury's New Book'. The new book referred to was Salisbury's *Many Americas Shall Be One*, published two years earlier. The article discusses East–West détente at a point in time between the first and second series of Brezhnev–Nixon talks, which resulted ultimately in the SALT agreements. The passages dealing with Sakharov warrant quotation:

[Salisbury] examines several suggested 'prescriptions', including the so-called 'declaration' by the Soviet scientist Sakharov.

At one time I read this concoction published in the Western press. It seemed to me to be a naïve conglomeration of selected passages from the Gospel, Rousseau's *The Social Contract*, the Soviet and American Constitutions, and one's own wishful thinking . . . I found nothing new in the ways Sakharov proposes to achieve peace on earth, or, in particular, in the main 'way' – the establishment of a 'world government' to which 'everyone' so to speak would be subject: Soviet workers and kolkhozniks and Texan oil kings . . .

This Sakharovian utopia, already long since used in the West for anti-Soviet purposes, disgusts me not because of its 'goodness', but because of the demonstrative coquettishness and pose of a man who stands majestically 'above the battle', waves an olive branch fanlike, and benignly accepts compliments from that very military-industrial complex which regards the harmless political idiocy of saints with condescension, but . . . on the other hand simply destroys everyone who really threatens its power.

For the sake of justice it must be said that Sakharov's 'prescription' evokes an ironic sneer from Salisbury, although he cannot refrain from complimenting its author.

In a sense Sakharov had forestalled this criticism in an interview he granted Jay Axelbank which appeared in the 3 December 1972 issue of the British Sunday newspaper, the *Observer*. (The interview – it was the first major interview given by Sakharov – was published in a full-page spread with a six-by-eight inch photograph of Sakharov and his wife, Elena Bonner, relaxed and smiling. As such it constituted a provocation the Soviet establishment could not ignore.) During the interview Sakharov picked up a copy of his manifesto, *Reflections* (which had since appeared in book form), and said to Axelbank:

'When I wrote this book I was a little idealistic. Remember that Czechoslovakia had not yet been invaded. I wrote from what you call a position of abstraction. Now I know many more things and am a much more disappointed man. I called myself a socialist then, but now I have modified my beliefs. What I stand for now is contained in the postscript to the Memorandum which became known this summer. I would no longer label myself a socialist. I am not a Marxist–Leninist, a Communist. I would call myself a liberal.'

He explained that in the past four years he had come to realize that the practice of socialism in Russia, and everywhere else it has been tried, had proved 'a grave disappointment' and that even the theory of socialism, he felt, did not offer the solution for mankind's ills.

'The redeeming aspects of Soviet society,' he said, 'do not come from anything peculiar to our system but from the nature of society itself. The same benign aspects of life can be found in the capitalist system. That is why I stood for, and still stand for, convergence' . . .

When I asked him . . . what kind of society he would like to see in this country, he replied . . . 'I would like more human-ness here, the freedom to write and read what one pleases. I would like to see emotional rights, and the absence of chauvinism' . . .

Sakharov said he did not know enough about the US, England, France, West Germany or other Western democracies to say whether he favoured similar institutions here. 'You,' he said . . . 'can compare both. You have lived in both places. We only know what we read, which isn't much, or hear things from visitors. We are in the dark. We only know really what has to be changed here.'

I asked about the future of the dissident movement – decimated by repressions and also by the emigration of many 'democrats' of Jewish persuasion to Israel. Sakharov's wife replied: 'Our struggle is really useless and senseless. If you look upon our struggle as a political activity, then nothing will change.'

Sakharov said: 'One cannot be inactive when people are perishing from increased repressions. Recently in the Western press there was a statement of 55 Soviet citizens [including Sakharov] about an amnesty for political prisoners here and abolition of the death penalty. These appeals need popular support. The defence of freedom of conviction, saving people from cruel repressions have no less importance for mankind than, for instance, the very important problem of the freedom to emigrate, which has attracted attention of legislative organs in the United States' . . .

Since President Nixon's visit last February, he said, 'things have got worse. The authorities seem more impudent because they feel that with a détente they can ignore Western public opinion, which isn't going to be concerned with the plight of internal freedoms in Russia.' He went on to express an opinion that I have heard stated by almost all dissidents I have talked to in the past few months: 'The movement has never been in worse straits.' He was referring to the imprisonment of two of the most active dissenters, Vladimir Bukovsky earlier in the year and the arrest last summer of Pyotr Yakir. 'When Bukovsky was tried, there were 70 people outside the courthouse. For Lubarsky there was just a handful.'

I asked him how active and influential was the Committee on Human Rights. 'Active?' he said in pained surprise. 'I don't know. Is it active to stand outside the courthouse all day as we did? Is that being active? We stand outside courthouses and we write protest letters. But who listens?'

Sakharov said that the group – there are three others besides himself [Valery Chalidze had meanwhile emigrated to the United States] meets once a month to support such causes as that

290

of the Buddhist scholar in Central Asia who is being persecuted for his religious beliefs, or a psychiatrist in Kiev imprisoned for several years on charges of anti-Soviet activity. Sakharov suffers the most anguish over two men confined in a Leningrad mental asylum: art critic Viktor Fainberg who was seized after demonstrating in Red Square in 1968 against the invasion of Czechoslovakia, and engineer Vladimir Borisov.

'These people have the true courage because, unlike me, the authorities put them in prison. They are not immune. And now they may be near death after going on a hunger strike. The Fainberg–Borisov case is the worst blot on our record.'

'What about ten years from now, fifty years from now?'

'In ten years nothing will change. This country could perish, but it still would be the same. We know we cannot change anything really, despite all the things I write. We would be grateful if only the authorities would only follow the laws, like freedom of speech, and open trials, that are supposed to be guaranteed to us in the Constitution. I used to be allowed into trials because I'm Sakharov, but now even I can't get in.'

'Why, then, do you struggle, if you think it is so futile?'

'Because for us it is not a political struggle, and I must emphasize I really know nothing about politics or political theory. It is a moral struggle for all of us. We have to be true to ourselves.'

'You are a pessimist, then?'

'No, I am not a pessimist. I am a born optimist. I am just making an objective analysis of the situation.'

Lest this foregoing bout of crêpe-hanging leave too strong an impression of humility on the part of Sakharov, a passage occurring earlier in the same interview is here quoted as an offset:

At times we sat on a double bed that serves as a couch. Above Sakharov were only a handful of scientific books. 'A theoretical physicist,' he explained, 'doesn't need books, or a laboratory, or equipment. He needs a brain.'

A Soviet Communist functionary reading this passage would feel his blood run cold. He would see or hear this statement against the background of the ritualistic repetition of Party slogans that takes the place of reasoned debate and has made the official rhetoric of the Party-state hardly more than an expansion of authorized slogans. He would hear it as a knell or a battle-cry (which is the original meaning of the word 'slogan') of the scientific and technical intelligentsia, laying claim to the leadership of the country by virtue of intellectual superiority – in short, as a thunderous answer to the question, 'Who is going to do the thinking around here?'

The *Memorandum* and *Afterword* which Sakharov mentions in the Axelbank interview were written with a separating interval of more than a year while Sakharov waited in vain for an answer from his addressee, Leonid Brezhnev. He then wrote the 'Afterword' in June 1972 and gave it over for publication along with the 'Memorandum'. The two together run to sixteen typewritten pages and form an addition and expansion of the letter dated 13 March 1970 written in collaboration with Valery Turchin and Roy Medvedev. Of the points added the most interesting are, under the heading of foreign affairs, a plea for a change of policy on Berlin (by way of improving relations with the Federal Republic of Germany); a plea for a review of Soviet policy in the Middle East; in domestic affairs, a plea for the liquidation of 'elections without choice' or replacement with elections with a plurality of candidates from which to choose (in Russian 'election' and 'choice' are the same word, *vybor*: the phrase is thus reminiscent of Milovan Djilas's description of a Communist election as 'a horse race with only one horse'); in agriculture a call for the extension of agricultural production to the private plots of the kolkhozniki through enlargement of the same, grants in aid, etc.; under the heading of the exchange of information, a call to encourage freedom of conviction and the spirit of inquiry into 'commercial restiveness'; under the heading of ecology, a whole series of requests to mount an organized struggle against pollution and wastage, and a special plea for noise reduction; finally a plea for the reform of medical services and facilities plus a reform of the pharmaceutics industry as a whole.

In the 'Afterword' there is an air of impatience and misgiving. As Axelbank notes in the interview, Sakharov here uses unprecedentedly strong language: 'Our society,' he wrote, 'is infected with apathy, hypocrisy, narrow-minded egotism and hidden cruelty.' But there is also something else: a deadly accurate description of the fraudulence permeating Soviet society:

> Free health service and free education are nothing more than an illusion in a society in which the whole of the national income is expropriated and allocated by the state. In the health service and in education especially is the hierarchic class structure of our society with its system of privileges most perniciously reflected. The nature

of education and health service for the people – this is the poverty-stricken condition of the generally accessible hospitals, the beggarliness of village schools, overcrowded classrooms, the poverty and exhaustion of the average teacher, the state-paid hypocrisy in pedagogy, the inculcation of the younger generation with the spirit of indifference to moral, artistic and scientific values.

A special place in the catalogue of conditions prerequisite to the recovery of society is the abolition of prosecution for political reasons whether it leads to the prison cell or the psychiatric ward or takes place in any other form of which our sluggish bureaucratic system is capable (termination of employment, exclusion from higher education, denial of a passport, limitation of promotion prospects, etc.).

It was clear to all the spectators of this drama that some kind of crisis was approaching. There was, of course, a great deal of speculation as to what the fate of Sakharov would be: some tipped in the direction of the psychiatric ward, others guessed that the Party-state would steel itself to a regular, old-fashioned prison sentence with exile to follow, à la Article 70 of the Criminal Code, with seven and five years respectively for first offenders (ten and five for second offenders); still others thought that the Soviet government would prefer to deport Sakharov, strip him of his citizenship and leave him to the lot of the émigré. (This last speculative foray was particularly wayward: as obsessed with secrecy as the Soviets are, how could they conceivably bring themselves to send abroad 'the father of the Soviet hydrogen bomb', a man who, by any security reckoning, had to be placed at the very pinnacle of the 'bearer of state secrets' category? The speculators – Soviet style – did not have to wait very long.)

On 23 January 1973 Sakharov and Elena Bonner addressed a letter to Yuri Andropov, then chairman of the KGB, appealing for the release of their friend Yuri Shikhanovich. Shikhanovich was a former Moscow University mathematics teacher, the warrant for whose arrest had stated that 'for a number of years he has systematically saved, reproduced and disseminated anti-Soviet literature'. He was, of course, charged under Article 70 of the RSFSR Criminal Code ('anti-Soviet activity'). He had been held incommunicado in Lefortovo Prison since his arrest four months earlier. Sakharov and other friends of Shikhanovich arrived at his flat while the KGB search was still in progress, but they 'were not allowed into the flat nor permitted to say goodbye to him'

293

(*Chronicle*, No. 27). Samizdat copies of the Sakharovs' letter to Andropov on behalf of Shikhanovich were made available to Western correspondents in Moscow on 11 February.

On 14 March Decree Number 138, which heralded Soviet accession, effective 27 May, to the Universal Copyright Convention of 1952, was published. The decree came just twenty-one years too late, the delay having cost the Soviet Union an indeterminate sum of money in lost copyrights over the two decades. Soviet champions of human rights immediately assumed the decree might be used as an instrument of censorship abroad – to restrict publication in the West of 'anti-Soviet' literature. On 22 March Sakharov and five other dissidents addressed an open letter to UNESCO welcoming Soviet accession to the convention as a 'substantial contribution to the cause of the free exchange of information, the reduction of mutual distrust and . . . cultural *rapprochement* among peoples', but warning that the 'international understanding of authors' rights assumes that these rights are profoundly personal, which an author can transmit to any publishing house, theatre, film company or the like'. The five authors then point out that this is not so in the Soviet Union:

> In the special circumstances obtaining in our country the law on the [government] monopoly of foreign trade can be used to restrict or even to suppress entirely the international copyrights of Soviet citizens. Ideological and aesthetic censorship has always been extremely rigorous in our country, and in recent years it has become all the more severe and arbitrary . . . This censorship must not be allowed the possibility of functioning on an international scale by virtue of its accession to the Geneva Convention.

The authors of this letter need not have worried: the Soviet government cannot have it both ways. The 'profoundly personal' (which is to say 'private') rights of the individual author preclude the concept of an operative state monopoly of literary production when that monopoly refuses to recognize works not conforming to the hootenanny standard set by the Party-state. Samizdat by its very nature cannot come under either the protection or the restriction of the copyright convention. When a samizdat work appears in the West it is 'first come, first served' as far as publishers are concerned. The American film producer, Lester Cowan, bought the rights to the novel *Dr Zhivago* from a Western publisher in the mid-sixties without a penny being paid to the Soviet Union, because the Party-state could not bring itself to acknowledge *Dr Zhivago* as a Soviet work. Cowan went on to produce the film, which did very well at the box office, among other reasons 'as a lesson to the Soviet Union'. The lesson was learned: the same thing could not happen today; there is now a great deal of talk concerning a forthcoming publication in the Soviet Union; *Dr Zhivago* has finally been recognized by the Party-state as a Soviet work.

On 23 March Sakharov was called to his first interview with the KGB. The reason given for the call was the letter Sakharov and Elena Bonner had written to Yuri Andropov about Yuri Shikhanovich, but on query the KGB made it clear they did not want Elena Bonner present at the hour-long interview, which was conducted by two KGB officers, General Frolov (exact rank indeterminate) and Lieutenant-Colonel Galkin, and concerned what they described as Sakharov's 'personal activities', meaning his private initiative in the public domain. Sakharov was informed that he was 'not morally sound' and that his membership in the Moscow Human Rights Committee in itself constituted 'slander' against the Soviet Union, since its very existence questioned the cause of human rights in the Soviet Union. Sakharov was also criticized for attempting to attend political trials (whereas he had first been admitted to such trials, he had been barred from attendance beginning with the trial of Vladimir Bukovsky on 5 January 1972) and for his interviews with foreign correspondents.* Sakharov was accordingly advised by his KGB interlocutors that Westerners were interested in him 'only for anti-Soviet purposes'.

Scholars, such as the samizdat specialist Peter Dornan, have dwelt on the KGB's use of the phrase 'not morally sound' in the first interview with Sakharov and have read into it the intimation that the psychiatric clinic was ready and waiting if he persisted in his 'personal activities'. Sakharov himself, in his press conference of 21 August, recalled being told in March 'that Shikhanovich had also been warned without drawing the appropriate conclusions'. By warnings, Sakharov added, the KGB apparently meant the

---

* The interview with Axelbank at the end of 1972 had been widely reprinted in the West and translated back into Russian by the 'anti-Communist' *émigré* monthly magazine *Possev* in West Germany. Since *Possev* is the journalistic flagship of the National Workers Union, the only Russian political organization outside the Soviet Union, anything it does is regarded with particular misgiving by Soviet authorities.

searches of Shikhanovich's home. But this is taking 'sound' to mean 'healthy' and 'morally' to mean 'mentally', so that 'not morally sound' becomes 'not mentally healthy' and ready for the psychiatric clinic. Such an interpretation is in keeping with the Soviet practice of using code words or metonyms where one word stands in for another, for example the use of 'anti-Zionist' for 'anti-Semitic'. But this is scarcely necessary: taking 'not morally sound' to mean not morally sound is in keeping with the absolute claim of Marxism–Leninism to a monopoly of the cause of the proletariat, the cause that transcends all morality and hence monopolizes it too. The new morality is what the Party leadership or leader (when the cult supplants the collective) says it is. In telling Sakharov that he was 'not morally sound' the KGB was more probably addressing Sakharov's then recent statement in the Axelbank interview in which he protested that he knew nothing about politics and stressed the moral nature of his protest. In such a case the use of the phrase 'not morally sound' would simply be a calling of Sakharov to order, reminding him that in a Communist society he had no right to a personal moral stand or position of any kind. It is instructive in this connection to compare Sakharov's interview with the KGB to Oppenheimer's interview with the Manhattan Project's security officer, Colonel John Lansdale, Jr. Lansdale, addressing Oppenheimer, began the interview with a statement: 'You are probably the most intelligent man I have ever met.' Lansdale performed a deferential interrogatory minuet with Oppenheimer for two hours on 12 September 1943, but for all his courtliness, did not manage to extract the name of Haakon Chevalier from Oppenheimer. And this was in wartime and concerning the most secret project the American nation had ever known. The blow fell only ten years later, after the advent of another political administration. The American Army security officers concerned with Oppenheimer concluded more or less by consensus that Oppenheimer was 'deeply concerned with gaining a worldwide reputation as a scientist, and a place in history' and added that 'the Army is in the position of being able to allow him to do so or to destroy his name, reputation and career, if it should choose to do so'. At least one American Army security officer, Captain Peer de Silva, who is here quoted, went on to express the opinion that the Army's option in this matter, 'if strongly presented' to Oppenheimer, would change not only the latter's attitude to security but that of 'the lower echelons of employees'. The option of ruining Oppenheimer's career and name was never presented. When the blow did fall, it was much too late. In delivering the blow, the new administration managed only to expose itself and make something of a martyr of Oppenheimer as the noble victim of a hapless bureaucracy.

The KGB in dealing with Sakharov had no such option. Sakharov's reputation was long since made, the nation's highest honours already bestowed. Stripping Sakharov of his medals and distinctions would have hurt the nation more than Sakharov. All the nation could do to Sakharov was martyr him, thereby contributing to his international fame and detracting from that of the Soviet Union. In treating Sakharov as a 'living machine' (Bukharin's term), a unit in the 240,000,000 coordinated human beings that made up the mass of production relations at that time in the Soviet Union, the KGB was informing Sakharov, as it was bound to do, that he was *vehementer suspectus* of heresy, of having believed and held a doctrine that is false and contrary to the sacred and divine scriptures of Marxism–Leninism. It was the sentence of Galileo all over again and, what was more, infinitely more, it was – in the attitude of the Soviety Party-state – the fulfilment of the prediction made in connection with 'the crime of Galileo', namely the mechanization of all life and pre-eminently mankind with it – that the attempt to make machines very much like men would result in the attempt to make men very much like machines. According to Bukharin's *The Theory of Historical Materialism: A Popular Manual of Marxist Sociology*, which was used for many years (beginning in 1921) as a basic text in the theoretical training of Party cadres: 'Production relations are simply the coordination of human beings, considered as "living machines", in the labour process' (Kolakowski). It was the ultimate reduction of the human being to the status of a mere cog in the magnificent machine of the Party-state, capable of doing anything, achieving any goal in the service of humanity.

As part of the KGB's 'treatment', Sakharov received a letter from Pyotr Yakir on 13 April. Yakir, a prominent dissident, had been in Lefortovo Prison since 21 June 1972. The letter, which can only be described as a crude forgery (an anonymous postscript circulating in samizdat pointed out the many spelling errors in the original), is merely a variation on a very familiar theme, namely that anti-Soviet organizations in the West are forever lying in wait for any sort of expression of opposition from within the Soviet Union which they then exploit to the hilt. The forgery dwells on the role of the NTS (the National Workers Union) in this connection. There was the comic-opera effect of the forged letter's being delivered by a 'man in the uniform of a counsellor of justice from the procuracy' but it was followed by a tragic denouement when Yakir and his fellow dissident Viktor Krasin were tried behind closed doors on 27 August. Both men had been broken under interrogation, implicating several scores of people as well as themselves. For their cooperation they were given comparatively light sentences – three years' imprisonment plus three years' exile.

Meanwhile, however, at the end of June Sakharov granted an interview to the Swedish correspondent Ole Stenholm, his second interview with a foreign correspondent, and his first with a television reporter. In the context of events, this was an answer to the letter forged over the signature of Yakir. For Sakharov was fully aware that Andrei Amalrik, Bukovsky and Yakir had appeared on Western television as interviewees. And all three were now in prison or in labour camps. To be sure, this was Swedish television and Sweden was neutral, but the text of the interview was published in the Swedish daily, *Dagens Nyheter*, and then translated for publication in *The Times*, the *New York Times*, the German magazine *Spiegel*, the French magazine *L'Express*, the Russian language daily in New York *Novoe Russkoe Slovo* and in the Russian *émigré* magazine, *Possev* (NTS). It was also picked up by the various Western wire services. In short, the interview with Stenholm received a broad play in the Western media.

It was, moreover, in the interview with Stenholm that Sakharov made public his final, definitive break with socialism. He begins by explaining the naïveté of his *Reflections on Progress, Peaceful Coexistence and Intellectual Freedom*, written in 1968:

> And I, as it were, found myself at a great distance from the basic problems of the whole people and the country in its entirety. I happened to be in an extraordinarily privileged position in material terms and I was isolated from people ... but after that life changed somehow, on a personal psychological level and the process of development simply continued ... Well, what is socialism? I began by thinking that I understood it and reckoned that it was a good thing. Then gradually I ceased to understand very much. There arose in my mind an incomprehension of the very bases of the

economy, an incomprehension of whether – apart from mere words or propaganda – there was anything there of value for internal or international use. Certainly the thing about the government that fairly jumps out at you is the extraordinary concentration of economic, political and ideological power, that is to say, the extreme monopolization. One can look at it in this way, that – as Lenin said at the beginning of our revolution – it was simply state capitalism, that is, the state assumes the monopolistic control of the whole economy. But then, in such a case, this socialism is nothing new at all. It is simply a limited form of the same capitalist development that is taking place in the United States and in other Western countries, only with extreme monopolization added. Then we must not be surprised that we have qualitatively the same problems, the same criminality, the same alienation of the individual that they have in the capitalist world. It is just that our society is a limited case, as it were limited in its lack of freedom, limited by its ideological corseting . . . and beyond that certainly the most characteristic feature of our society is its pretentiousness, which is to say that not being a better society it nevertheless pretends to be far better than the others.

Talking to Stenholm on camera, Sakharov describes the Soviet Union's greatest lack as the lack of freedom. In second place he names the inequality of Soviet society and goes on to describe, without naming it as such, the New Class, the *nomenklatura*, the privileged, the Party members who buy their food, clothing, household effects, tools and automobiles and suchlike in special stores, whose salaries run from ten to fifty times as much as the average wage and who enjoy a wide variety of non-material privileges, preferences and priorities in employment, housing and unrestricted movement (here Sakharov mentioned the plight of the farmworker whose categorical lack of a passport bound him as if by chains to his locale of habitation), who have access to special sanatoria and hospitals and a whole special service of medical care. He went on to name a number of the Party privileges: the fact that, with very few exceptions, a man cannot be the director of a factory or the chief of a section without being a Party member, the fact that there is a 'cadre tradition' of insurance in adversity – when a member of the *nomenklatura* fails he can count on the help of his peers to bail him out and find him another job at the same salary and with the same perquisites. In this connection he went on to describe special 'supplementary' salaries paid in envelopes passed under the table, as it were. This system of 'supplementary' salaries he describes as coming and going, cropping up and then disappearing to crop up again in another place. He made mention also of a system of 'supplemental prices', in which the privileged get more quantity and better quality for the same price. All these hidden privileges and perquisites make it extremely difficult to judge what the real amount or actual buying power of a given salary is. Here Sakharov touched on the extraordinary isolation of the Soviet Union from every outside entity and influence and the equally extraordinary obfuscation in the internal life of the country. He judged that there was a movement afoot to break the country out of its international isolation. This could only come to good, even if only in the sense of making known the history of the Soviet Union to serve as a cautionary tale to the rest of the world. It was in this interview that Sakharov made public mention for the first time of the great danger that lay in the possibility of other countries – 'the outside world', as he put it – accepting or adopting the Soviet 'rules of the game'. On the contrary, it was desirable in his view to publicize Soviet mistakes so that other countries could be forewarned.

At this point Stenholm puts a key question to Sakharov:

But if you are of the opinion that socialism in the Soviet Union has failed to show its advantages, does that mean that you think that in order to correct the situation here it will be necessary to re-do completely the whole state [*perestroika*] or do you think that it is possible to do something within the present system in order to improve [it] and remove its greatest deficiencies?

SAKHAROV: That is certainly a question that is beyond me, because to completely reconstruct a state is unthinkable – there always has to be some sort of priority and some sort of gradualness, otherwise there will be once again the same sort of terrible destruction through which we have already passed several times – where everything goes to pieces. So that I, quite naturally, aspire to gradualness, I am a liberal, I am . . . a gradualist, so to speak.

STENHOLM: So what should be done to begin with?

SAKHAROV: What is to be done? Well, I understand that our present system in its internal nature is not capable of doing anything, or is capable of doing something only to a very small degree. What is to be done? It would be necessary to liquidate the ideological monism of this society. Well, the ideological structure which is anti-democratic in its very essence is a great tragedy for a state. The isolation from the outside world, for example the absence of the right to leave the country and return, works itself out in a very pernicious way for the internal life of the country. It is, in the first place, the greatest of tragedies for all those who wish to leave for personal or national reasons. But it is also a tragedy even for those who remain in the country, because a country which it is impossible to leave freely and to which it is impossible to return freely is already for this very reason a country that lacks the necessary respect, it is a closed area in which all processes develop in a radically different way from that of an open system.

STENHOLM: Well, you know that the right to free exit . . .

SAKHAROV: . . . is one of the most important conditions for returning, for a free return.

STENHOLM: And what else?

SAKHAROV: . . . With us here extreme state socialism has brought matters to such a pass that in those areas where individual or personal initiative plays an effective role – there, too, the area is closed off, as in the case of heavy industry, and of transport where perhaps the state system of direction is reasonable. Beyond this, the personal initiative of the citizen is closely bound up with the personal freedom of the individual. This fact has an adverse bearing on the standard of living and simply makes life far more boring and melancholy than it need be for a great many people. This is also a matter of free initiative in the consumer sector, in the service sector, in education and in the field of medicines. All of this would certainly have a very positive significance for the marked weakening of the extremely monopolistic structure of the state. There are things which relate to the monopoly of management and administration, that is, concerning the party monopolization of management that have gone to such lengths, to such an extent that it has become clearly visible even to that stratum [of monopolist managers] that this is an impermissible business in itself. This certainly has an influence on the effectiveness of management.

Well, what needs to be done? We need, certainly, to open up to the public view, to ventilate publicly the workings of the whole management apparatus [glasnost again]. Probably the one-party system is all too much given to senseless brutality. Even within the conditions of a socialist economic structure it is possible to do without the one-party system. Why, even in the countries of peoples' democracy certain, so to speak, elements of a multi-party system exist – to be sure, in a somewhat caricatured form and style.

We need elections to government office with a plurality of candidates. Indeed there are a whole series of measures, each of which taken separately would have very little effect, but which taken altogether might be able to shatter such a monolith as has been created here and the nature of which is so petrified that it weighs heavily on the life of the whole country.

The press must change its character. As it is now, the press is so infected that it has already lost a significant part of its informational value. And if indeed facts are reflected in the press then only in such a way that they are decipherable only to the initiate, but otherwise distort the true picture of real life in the country, and as far as intellectual matters are concerned – they simply are not there, so that it is impossible to distort it especially – there is no variety of intellectual life.

And especially do we need to take note of the role of the intelligentsia in society. With us the intelligentsia has been suppressed out of all proportion. In material terms our intelligentsia has been very badly provided for. Even if we do not except people who do manual labour in the comparison, our intelligentsia comes off badly. But especially, of course, do they suffer in any comparison of living standards if Western countries are regarded, particularly those whose general level of economic development is the equivalent of ours. Thus the suppressed situation of the intelligentsia is also an economic suppression, which signifies in addition an ideological suppression; indeed a kind of general anti-intellectual atmosphere is created in our country when the professions, say the profession of the pedagogue and that of the physician, do not enjoy the esteem that ought to be accorded them. And this anti-intellectualism is also manifested in the fact that the intelligentsia itself has already begun to seek refuge either in narrow professionalism or in leading a double life at home and at work, in the narrow circle of their acquaintances people begin to think differently, and the bifurcation of thinking leads to hypocrisy and the further decline of the ethical and the creative in people. This is grievously borne out, of course, not in the technical but especially in the humanitarian intelligentsia. And there, in the humanitarian disciplines, there is already a sense of being at a complete loss. As a result the literature that comes to the surface in this country is terribly grey and institutional, in general our literature and art are dull . . .

Stenholm concluded the interview with a question about Sakharov's fears for his health and freedom when following so active a course of opposition. In what had become almost a refrain in his interviews, Sakharov replied that his fears did not concern himself, but rather his family and, specifically, his wife's family. The authorities had already made it clear that they were in no wise minded to accord the same privileges, respect and solicitude to his second wife as they had to his first. The matter was even more at variance when it came to Sakharov's own children and those of Elena Bonner. Elena's daughter, Tatiana Ivanovna Semeonova (born 1950), was expelled from the evening department of the faculty of journalism at Moscow University (where she had been a student in good standing) in October 1972. Elena's son, Alexei Ivanovich (born 1956), was expelled in the winter of 1973 from a special school for physics and mathematics. In July 1973 Alexei was refused admission to Moscow University. In the fall of the same year, however, he was allowed to enter the Lenin Pedagogical Institute, where Sakharov's father had taught physics. As for Elena Bonner herself, the evidence of discrimination against her was overwhelming. Suffering from a malfunction of her thyroid gland she had tried to arrange for a thyrotomy in late 1973. (It should be remembered that as a practising physician she had her own professional connections in this regard.) However, the young surgeon selected to perform the operation refused to do so, saying such an act would prejudice his chances of getting a Ph.D. As a substitute she persuaded an old doctor, a friend of hers who was already in retirement, to operate on her. Her old friend had managed to find a clinic in an outlying part of Moscow where he could do the operation with the help of a trusted assistant. The two men performed the operation in three hours under what might be described as 'cloak and scalpel' circumstances. Elena Bonner later described the operation as 'not particularly successful'. She told this writer that her friend had really been too old to undertake such work, so that despite his courage and the best intentions he had not been able to perform as he should have. There was also some courage displayed by the sponsors of the clinic accommodation, since a thyrotomy usually requires a post-operative bed-rest convalescence of several days. Sakharov had good reason for concern over the welfare of his new family.

XIII

❧

INTERVIEWS AND INTERROGATIONS:
... AND PARRY

The interview with Stenholm was broadcast 2 July 1973. Ten days later the press-agency TASS replied with an article entitled 'Purveyor of Slander' by its political commentator, Yuri Kornilov. The article was published six days later in *Literaturnaya Gazeta*. In it Kornilov stated that 'the entire activity of Sakharov as a purveyor to the reactionary press of calumny against the Soviet Union is dictated by a ... desire to slander his own country'. The interview 'merely confirms that [Sakharov's] "ideological baggage" ... contains nothing but grovelling before the capitalist system and a collection of malicious fabrications about the Soviet system'. The article also contained the charge that Sakharov discussed 'questions about which he is utterly ignorant'.

The text of the interview on Swedish television was published in the August issue of *Possev*, which appeared in late July. It was clear to all who watched that the issue of Andrei Sakharov versus the Soviet government was heading toward a climax. The suspense was heightened when on 4 August Vladimir Maximov directed an open letter to Heinrich Böll in which the outside world was called upon to save Sakharov, 'the honour and conscience of contemporary Russia', before it was too late.

On 15 August Sakharov received a telephone call from the deputy prosecutor general of the Soviet Union, Mikhail Malyarov. In the telephone conversation the deputy prosecutor simply stated that this was to be 'a talk of a decent human being with a decent human being'. On 16 August at high noon Sakharov went to the office of the deputy prosecutor general, where he was received by Malyarov and another official who was not introduced but merely described as Malyarov's assistant. The 'talk' lasted seventy minutes and was reproduced from memory by Sakharov and given to foreign correspondents. It is cited here in full:

MALYAROV: This talk has the character of a warning, wherefore not all assertions will be provided with exhaustive proofs, but you can rest assured that we dispose over such proofs. I ask you to hear me out attentively and insofar as is possible not to interrupt me.

SAKHAROV: I am ready to hear you out.

MALYAROV: When you began a few years ago to take part in that activity which you call public, we followed your actions attentively but considered it possible not to take any measures whatever. At that time it was possible to interpret your actions as those of a concerned Soviet citizen moved by occasional defects and mistakes [in our society], as you understood them, but not acting against the Soviet system of social and governmental order as a whole. To be sure, even then your public appearances were published in the foreign, anti-Soviet press and caused perceptible harm to our state. Most recently your activity and public appearances have taken on a still more harmful and openly anti-Soviet character, and the procurator's office, always watchful of the laws and interests of our society, can no longer stand idly by. You meet with foreigners and give them material for anti-Soviet publications. In particular this refers to your interviews. In the interview with the Swedish television you come out against the socialist order in our country, calling it an order of maximal unfreedom, undemocratic, closed, deprived of the possibility of [developing] initiative in the economic sector, decaying.

SAKHAROV: I did not say 'decaying'.

MALYAROV: You meet with such reactionary journalists as, for example, the correspondent of the Swedish television, Stenholm, and give them your interviews which are used for subversive propaganda, used by the publishing arm of the NTS, *Possev*. You must know that the programme of the NTS demands the violent overthrow of the Soviet state. It is precisely *Possev* that publishes the great bulk of your material; in your interview you proceed essentially from the same anti-Soviet, subversive positions.

SAKHAROV: I am not acquainted with the programme of the NTS. If there is such a demand [in their programme], then it is absolutely contradictory to my views and particularly as they were expressed in the interview with the Swedish television. I spoke there of the desirability of gradual changes, of democratization within the framework of the existing order. It is another matter, that

305

I point to what are, in my view, substantial faults of the system and make no attempt to hide my pessimism as to the possibility of such changes taking place within the near future. With regard to publication: I never gave any sort of material whatever to the NTS or to *Possev* and my material was published in many foreign editions of the mass media apart from *Possev*, among them such as, for example, *Spiegel*, which the Soviet press up to now has adjudged to be rather progressive.

MALYAROV'S ASSISTANT: But you never protested against the publication [of your material] in *Possev*. We have confirmed that the great bulk of your material has appeared in such publications as *Possev*, and *Grani* and the White-Guardist newspaper *Russkaia Mysl*.

SAKHAROV: I would be very glad of publication in the Soviet press. For example, if in addition to the critical article of Kornilov in the *Literaturnaya Gazeta* my interview had been published alongside it. In such a case Kornilov would have been forced to proceed without distorting the interview. But such is not the reality of the situation. I regard publication, *glasnost*, as very important. I consider that the text of a publication is far more important than where it happens to be published.

MALYAROV'S ASSISTANT: Even if that publication takes place in anti-Soviet journals with an anti-Soviet purpose? In *Possev*?

SAKHAROV: I consider the publishing activity of *Possev* to be very useful. I am grateful to that publishing house. I reserve the right not to identify *Possev* with the NTS, not to share the programme of the NTS, which may be regarded as a provocation . . .

MALYAROV'S ASSISTANT: We weren't talking of that, that was long ago.

SAKHAROV: To return then . . . You called Stenholm a reactionary journalist. That is unjust. He is a social democrat, he is far more of a socialist or a Communist than I am, for example.

MALYAROV'S ASSISTANT: Social democrats murdered Rosa Luxemburg. But this 'Communist' of yours interpolated into your interview [the statement] that our system is 'falling apart', if indeed no such thing was in your version.

SAKHAROV: I am convinced that Stenholm accurately transmitted my interview.

MALYAROV: I continue. I ask you to follow my words with especial attention. By the nature of your former work you had access to government secrets of especial importance. You signed an undertaking not to publish anything by way of a government secret and to the effect that you would not meet with foreigners. But you do meet with foreigners and communicate to them information which could be of interest to foreign Intelligence organizations. I ask you to ponder the full seriousness of this warning and to draw your own conclusions.

SAKHAROV: What information are you talking about? What precisely do you have in mind?

MALYAROV: I have already said that this meeting has the character of a warning. The information is at our disposal, but we do not consider it possible to go into detail.

SAKHAROV: I attest that I have never published military or military–technical secrets known to me by the nature of my work in the years from 1948 to 1968. I shall never do this in the future. I also direct your attention to the fact that I have not participated in any sort of secret work for more than five years.

MALYAROV: But your head remains with you. And also your obligation not to meet with foreigners is still in force! Not only are anti-Soviet forces, forces antagonistic to our state, beginning to use you, but also foreign Intelligence services.

SAKHAROV: With regard to meetings with foreigners. I know many people who find themselves in the same situation as I do, and now they meet freely with foreign scholars and with ordinary citizens. I have indeed met with some foreign journalists, but these meetings had no relationship whatever to state, military and military–technical secrets.

MALYAROV'S ASSISTANT: These meetings were of the greatest convenience to our enemies.

MALYAROV: We have given warning. It is up to you to draw conclusions.

SAKHAROV: I repeat that I would prefer publication in the Soviet press, that I would prefer contacts with Soviet institutions. But I see nothing unlawful in meeting with foreign journalists.

MALYAROV'S ASSISTANT: But after all you are still a Soviet citizen. Your signed undertaking binds you, as does your basic relation to our system.

SAKHAROV: Soviet institutions ignore my letters and other forms of appeal. If I am to be limited [in my actions] by the prosecutor's office, then I wish to remind you that in May 1970 [17 May, it would seem] I directed a surveillance complaint along with other persons to the address of the general procurator of the USSR, Comrade Rudenko, in the matter of Grigorenko. In this matter there were a great number of grievous violations of the law. To this day we have received no answer whatever to this complaint. In the great majority of cases I do not even receive an acknowledgement of receipt of my letters. The recently deceased member of the Presidium of the Supreme Soviet of the USSR, Academician Petrovsky, promised me that he would explain the case of the psychiatrist, Semeon Gluzman [sentenced in Kiev in 1972 illegally]; this was the only instance when they promised me to elucidate the truth. But Petrovsky died! And the case of Amalrik? The man was unjustly sentenced to three years' imprisonment, lost his health, contracted meningitis, and now he has again been sentenced by a camp court to another three years! This is a case that cries out for justice. In fact he is now being sentenced for the same thing, for his convictions, which he refuses to renounce, but which he has never imposed on anyone. But as for the camp court – what sort of *glasnost* do we have here, what sort of justice?

MALYAROV: This Amalrik is a student who never finished his studies. He was never of any use whatever to the state, he is an idler, a parasite. But Böll writes about him as though he were an outstanding historian, and where does Böll get such information?

SAKHAROV: Böll and very many others evidence a great deal of interest in the fate of Amalrik. A camp court is in fact a closed court.

MALYAROV: And in your opinion it was necessary to bring him to Moscow?

SAKHAROV: Considering the great public interest in this matter, I think it would have been reasonable. If I had known that Amalrik could be tried again, I'd have travelled to the venue of the trial.

MALYAROV: Amalrik has caused great harm to our society. In his work he tried to show how Soviet society was doomed to destruction in 1984 and in the same breath he called for violent action. Every society has the right to defend itself. Amalrik broke the law and he had to suffer punishment. In camp he broke the law again. You know that law and I am not going to try to persuade you. Abroad they wrote that Amalrik had been deprived of a lawyer, but that was a lie, Shveisky went to the trial and you know that.

MALYAROV'S ASSISTANT: In contrast to that dropout you have done great service to society.

MALYAROV: Who gave you the right to doubt our jurisprudence? After all, you were not present at the trial. You act on rumours and they are often lies.

SAKHAROV: When there is in fact no such thing as freedom of speech, when systematically in political trials conditions are created for the violation of *glasnost*, there are also created grounds for doubting the justice of the court. I consider that prosecution according to the Articles 190–1 and 70 is anti-democratic. Everything I know about them confirms me in this opinion. An example of recent date is the case of Leonid Plyushch. In this matter the court without corroboration accepted the most severe of three conflicting expert psychiatric opinions. And although the court commuted the sentence, when the prosecutor protested it was restored. Plyushch is in a special hospital, and his wife has not had a meeting with him for more than a year and a half.

MALYAROV: You are occupying yourself with juridical matters, but, apparently, not profoundly enough. The court has the right itself to choose the form of obligatory cure without regard to the decision of the commission.

SAKHAROV: Unfortunately, I know that that is true. And therefore, even if the commission designates a general hospital [instead of a 'special' or psychiatric hospital] it is necessary to fear something worse. You say that I act on rumours all the time. That is not accurate. I try to receive authentic information. But in general in our country it is more and more difficult to find out what is going on. There is now a publication with full and accurate information concerning violations.

MALYAROV'S ASSISTANT: You mean the *Chronicle*?

SAKHAROV: Of course, the *Chronicle*.

MALYAROV'S ASSISTANT: Yes, we will soon talk about the *Chronicle*. Do you know what I have in mind? But now we are dealing with something else, with another theme.

MALYAROV: You don't like the fact that in our codex there exist the Articles 190–1 and 70. But they are there. The state has the right to defend itself. You render account to yourself for your actions and I shall not try to convince you of anything. I know that that is useless. But you must understand what this whole business is all about. And who supports you, who needs you? Yakir, who is well known to you, did not disappear from the pages of the foreign press while he was the purveyor of their propaganda. But when he changed his position they forgot about him.

SAKHAROV: To say that he is well known to me is not accurate. I hardly know him at all, as a matter of fact. The interest [abroad] in his court trial is still great. I know that for a fact. Everyone is asking when the trial will take place. Is the time set for the trial known to you?

MALYAROV'S ASSISTANT: No, we do not know. When the trial date is set you will probably know about it yourself.

MALYAROV: Your friend Chalidze was a famous man in the West when he appeared publicly to make anti-Soviet statements, but when he stopped doing that everybody forgot about him. Anti-Soviet circles have need of such as Telesin, Telnikov, Volpin, who uninterruptedly slander their former home-country.

SAKHAROV: I do not consider that Chalidze has ever engaged in anti-Soviet activity. The same goes for the others. You said something about Volpin; as far as I know he is working in mathematics in Boston.

MALYAROV: That may be, but we have authentic reports on his anti-Soviet activity.

SAKHAROV: You say that no one supports me. Last year I participated in two collective appeals – concerning an amnesty and the abolition of the death sentence. These appeals were signed by more than fifty people.

MALYAROV: This was in the order of a formal question put to the government?

SAKHAROV: Yes, but we were very much saddened that the amnesty was strictly limited and the death penalty was not abolished.

MALYAROV: I don't think that you counted on the laws being changed in accordance with your wishes. The death penalty we cannot possibly abolish at this time. Murderers and violent people who perpetrate serious crimes we cannot possibly let go without punishment.

SAKHAROV: We are talking about the abolition of the institution of capital punishment. A great many thinkers consider that this institution cannot be preserved in a humane society, that it is amoral. Serious crimes are perpetrated in this country even in the face of the existing death penalty, the death penalty does not help to make a society more humane. I have heard that even in our judicial circles here the question of abolishing the death penalty has been discussed.

MALYAROV: No. One lawyer raised the question, but no one supported him. This is not the proper time.

SAKHAROV: This question is being discussed now all over the world. In many countries the death penalty has been abolished. In what way are we worse than they?

MALYAROV: In the United States they abolished it, but now they are forced to reinstate it. You have read about the crimes that took place. We have nothing like that here. You like the American way of life – but there they have the free sale of weapons, they kill their presidents, and now this demagogic hocus-pocus with the Watergate affair. Sweden takes pride in its freedom, but there on every street corner there are pornographic pictures. I saw them myself. So what about you – are you for pornography? For that kind of freedom?

SAKHAROV: I don't know the American and Swedish ways of life. Probably they have their difficult and painful problems, too. I don't want to idealize. But just now you mentioned the Watergate affair. It is a good example of American democracy.

MALYAROV: Everything is done and calculated for show. Nothing will come of the whole business, it is just a matter of Nixon taking a hard line. Such is their democracy, nothing but hocus-pocus.

But we must finish our conversation. I wanted to ask you one more question – you have spoken well of Belinkov. Do you know that name?

SAKHAROV: I consider that Belinkov is an outstanding publicist; I have an especially high regard for his letter to the PEN Club.

MALYAROV: Do you know that Belinkov was arrested and convicted of distributing leaflets that called for the killing of Communists?

SAKHAROV: I know nothing about that. Probably it was a long time ago, in Stalin's time. Is it worth taking that sort of thing seriously? After all, *then* all convicts were 'terrorists'.

MALYAROV: No, Belinkov was convicted twice. That was a long time ago. And this Daniel of yours? After all, in *The Day of Open and Legalized Murders* he openly called for the murder of leaders of the Party and the government. And Amalrik – in what way is he any better? That is what you ought to be thinking about.

SAKHAROV: *The Day of Open and Legalized Murders* is a work of art, an allegory, and with all its force it was directed against the Stalinist terror. Then, in 1956, that was still so very close. Daniel explained all this at his trial. *1984* is also an allegory. You know that this date was taken from a story by Orwell.

MALYAROV: We must come to a close. I want you to draw conclusions from these serious warnings. Any government has no choice but to defend itself. The articles of the law stand, and no one will be allowed to infringe them.

SAKHAROV: I have attentively heard you out, I have committed to memory all that you have said – I have, so to speak, taken it as 'a shot across the bow'. But I cannot agree that I have broken the law. In particular, I cannot agree with your assertion that my meetings with foreign correspondents were against the law, or that they represented in themselves a threat to divulge state secrets. Goodbye [*Do svidania*].

MALYAROV: *Do svidania.*

By way of emphasizing his final statement to the deputy prosecutor general of the Soviet Union, Malyarov, Sakharov invited twelve foreign correspondents to a press conference in his Moscow apartment on 21 August, having first provided them with his transcript from memory of the 'talk' on 16 August. In his opening statement Sakharov asked the correspondents to consider that record an introduction to the conference. He followed with a series of detailed comments on the institution of KGB 'warnings' to dissidents and cited the two opposite extreme consequences that sometimes followed such 'warnings': arrest or the issuance of permission to leave the country. There were more severe types of warning than those he had as yet received: some persons had been informed that their fate depended on their behaviour as witnesses at forthcoming trials – if it should not be that desired of them, then they would not 'leave the courtroom'. But the worst was yet to come: 'Even more ominous,' continued Sakharov, '– resembling the institution of hostages – were the widely rooted warnings that for every future issue of the *Chronicle* [*Chronicle of Current Events*], appropriate people would be arrested, and that those already under arrest would be sentenced to long terms.' Articles about himself which had appeared in the Soviet press, he said, were also probably meant as warnings. In general, Sakharov summed up, warnings were intended as reminders that there existed a force based on the supposed 'right of the state to defend itself' that did not allow any deviations from the desired line. If this interpretation of the 'warnings' was correct then such an institution was symptomatic of the type of thinking of police agencies but had no relation whatever to democracy, or to the right of one's convictions, or to the law, or to humanity.

In the second place Sakharov went into the Party-government's fixation on the NTS (People's Labour Front) and its flagship publication, the monthly magazine *Possev*. (The publishing house of the NTS bears the same name.) Said Sakharov: '. . . accusations that writings or appeals are being used in the anti-Soviet publications of *Possev* for anti-Soviet, subversive purposes have become the main bogyman of the KGB and their like, the principal accusation and the principal means of intimidating or exerting pressure on public opinion. Even accidental possession of any one of the *Possev* publications is considered criminal.' Clarity on this point, continued Sakharov, is therefore very important.

In the third place, Sakharov turned to the deputy prosecutor general's statement that his meetings with foreigners were not compatible with his previous pledges:

In 1950 when I went to work in a secret institution I did, in fact, sign a commitment making me responsible for any meetings with foreigners 'in an extra-legal matter', that is, outside of office duties. The maximum extra-legal penalty is dismissal from work. And yet, I was dismissed from work as early as 1968 after publication of my *Reflections on Progress and Coexistence*, long before I met with any foreigner. I can only repeat here what I told Malyarov, namely, that meetings with foreign journalists have nothing to do with any violations of state secrets and that I never, and under no circumstances, would regard such violations as permissible.

Sakharov described his interview with Stenholm of Swedish television as 'the straw that broke the camel's back' (and brought him the warning from the deputy prosecutor general). But it was this warning from Malyarov that proved to be the straw that broke the camel's back as far as Sakharov was concerned. He called the 'mass' press conference in order to deliver his most stunning indictment of the Soviet state and system. His chance came late in the conference with the question of whether his views had changed since he published his book on progress and coexistence of socialism and capitalism in 1968. Said Sakharov:

The deadlines I fixed were allegorical. The lines of convergence, or the lines of stronger confrontation, the increase of the danger of nuclear war; this opposition between the two lines still exists, and as before, I think the crucial point is the suppression of the confrontation of two worlds. The reality happens to be more shrewd in the respect that we are now facing very concrete problems, whether in the process of *rapprochement* there will be democratization of Soviet society or not . . .

Détente without democratization, a *rapprochement* when the West in fact accepts our rules of the game in the process of this *rapprochement*, such a *rapprochement* would be very dangerous in that respect, and wouldn't solve any of the world's problems, and would mean simply a capitulation to our real or exaggerated strength. It would mean an attempt to trade, to get from us gas and oil, neglecting all other aspects of the problem. I think it's very dangerous.

By liberating ourselves from problems we can't solve ourselves, we could concentrate on accumulating strength, and as a result, the whole world would be disarmed and facing our uncontrollable bureaucratic apparatus. I think that détente without any qualifications, accepting our rules of the game, would be very bad.

That would be cultivation and encouragement of closed countries, where everything that happens goes unseen by foreign eyes behind a mask that hides its real face. No one should dream of having such a neighbour, and especially if this neighbour is armed to the teeth.

I suppose most Western politicians understand this and it has already been confirmed at the Helsinki conference, that détente has to take place with simultaneous liquidation of isolation.

The adoption of the Jackson Amendment looks like the minimum step, which is important not only by itself, but as a symbol of the fact that détente with the Soviet Union does not preclude some kind of control on this country so that it could not become a danger for its neighbours.

In studying the last twenty years and more of Soviet history one is struck again and again by the resemblances with the American Revolution, its basic conditions and even its atmosphere. The situation of the Soviet people or peoples towards their own government is very much like that of the American colonists towards the mother country, Great Britain, in the first three-quarters of the eighteenth century: the American colonists were just as much British as the Soviet 'colonists' are Russian. That the Russian people were, and very largely still are, *in statu colonorum* seems obvious. What the Atlantic Ocean did for the colonies in terms of separating space, the October Revolution has done for or to the Soviet people or peoples in terms of a separating caesura, a break in time, an almost unbridgeable gap interrupting historical continuity. The Soviet people (with and without quotation marks) is emerging from its colonial status, having raised the banner and adopted the demand of 'no taxation without representation!' But the Soviet citizen pays no taxes, one may protest. Correction: the Soviet citizen pays nothing but taxes. As Sakharov pointed out, the state confiscates his wages and then doles out driblets to him in the form of a pittance instead of wages (an average of 160 roubles a month, or some $250 at the Soviet official rate – and there is no other official rate because the rouble is not a currency, strictly speaking, but rather a fractional currency or scrip), in the form of 'free' housing, 'free' education and 'free' medical care, all of it of indifferent if not of inferior quality unless destined for the élite, or *nomenklatura*. With the gradual recognition of the exactive nature of the Soviet system the determination is growing to gain a truly democratic representation.

Examination of the record reveals a continuing and growing

314

embarrassment on the part of the authorities in the face of Sakharov's admonitions. This is clear in the example of the offer of Sakharov and his wife to be guarantors in the case of Yuri Shikhanovich. The Soviet Party-government was obviously not used to being openly and publicly challenged and lectured and did not know how to react. It is almost a question of 'it cannot be if it is not permitted', to paraphrase Christian Morgenstern. Sakharov's attempt to intervene from a position of loyal opposition took place in a system that made no allowance whatever for any opposition whatever. The consternation of the Soviet authorities from case to case and over the whole twenty-year period is palpable. The other salient feature of the record is Sakharov's persistent and calculated use of *glasnost*. Instead of being able to silence Sakharov by any of the routine methods of intimidation, all that the authorities achieved was greater publicity abroad for their use of such methods. In this sense, Sakharov's strategy and tactics constituted a continuing lesson by example in the new science of electronic mass communications, in the applications of *glasnost*, in fact.

The press conference with foreign correspondents became Sakharov's chief instrument in his tutorial campaign against the Soviet Party-state. Curiously, the entire campaign was directed at a chink in the custodial armour of the Party-state, which was the triple isolation of the citizen, first from his government, second from his fellow citizens (through the use of the collective as a control system of random informers) and finally and most strictly from the outside world. The chink in the custodial armour was the gap between Soviet law and Soviet propaganda. In effect, Sakharov, particularly in the twelve-man press conference of 21 August 1973, was publicly challenging the Office of the Public Prosecutor to declare private contacts between Soviet citizens and foreigners illegal. This, of course, the Soviet Party-government could not do. There is a Soviet law which prohibits Soviet citizens from putting up foreign guests overnight in their private quarters. But further than this the Soviet government, as distinct from the Communist Party of the Soviet Union, could not go. To be sure, the law was backed and would-be extended by a 'bodyguard of lies', of propaganda that frowned severely at all except official contacts between Soviet citizens and foreigners. But propaganda is basically the Party's business; the Party, *qua* Party, cannot legislate. (Then, too, the Soviet government ratified the Covenants on Political and Civil

Rights this same year.) Sakharov, having found the chink in the custodial armour of the Party-state, drove a wedge between the Party and the state by announcing to the world the existence of an opposition that demanded to be heard and insisted on its legality. It was, in essence, a citizen's initiative, as was the Soviet human-rights movement overall.

There can be no doubt that the combination of measures taken by Sakharov – all of them counter-measures to initiatives of the state – his interview with Ole Stenholm, his publication of his transcript of the 'talk' with the deputy prosecutor general and finally his press conference with twelve foreign correspondents – was also a kind of watershed. It marked the beginning of his main struggle with the Soviet establishment, the point where the battle was joined head-on, as it were. This period was to last seven years. Beyond what has already been cited, the press conference brought the news that Sakharov received a salary of 350 roubles a month as a senior research worker in the Institute of Physics of the Academy of Sciences (which was the minimum rank they could give him) plus 400 roubles a month status emolument as a member of the Academy. Here he also repeated an earlier statement to the effect that he had given all the savings he had to the State Fund in 1969, to the Red Cross for the construction of a hospital. He named the sum involved as 'very large, 139,000 roubles, to be exact'. When asked why he had done this he replied that he had come to consider this action incorrect, that he did not think it was right to do it and so would not give his reasons for doing so.

Sakharov's branding the 'institution of warnings' as symptomatic of the type of thinking of police agencies characterized accurately the atmosphere that surrounded his own and his family's case for a long while after his press conference of 21 August. Just seventy-two hours later the Moscow evening edition of *Izvestia* featured a TASS report of a *L'Humanité* article critical of the statements Sakharov had made during his press conference three days earlier. At seven o'clock the same evening the Radio Moscow press review carried an article and a letter to the editor in the *Volksstimme*, the official newspaper of the Austrian Communist Party, which were likewise critical of Sakharov's statements at his recent press conference. The following evening *Izvestia* and Radio Moscow made much of a letter of indignation over Sakharov signed by forty members of the Soviet Academy of Sciences. All these salvoes decried Sakharov as an opponent of détente, defamer of Soviet state structure and distorter of Soviet reality. The campaign ceased on 8 September with a TASS article entitled 'To be a Soviet Scientist Means to be a Patriot', featuring a survey of letters protesting Sakharov's statements as received by Soviet press and broadcast media.

In response there were a number of statements in Sakharov's defence by prominent dissidents, among them a proposal by Igor Shafarevich, Alexander Galich and Vladimir Maximov recommending Sakharov for the 1973 Nobel Peace Prize. (The chairman of the Nobel Institute, August Schou, announced on 10 September that nominations for the 1973 prize had been closed on 1 February.) Solzhenitsyn made the same proposal at about the same time in an article, 'Peace and Violence'. A number of statesmen and scholars in the West seconded the proposal.

Far from intimidating Sakharov, the campaign merely spurred him on to greater activity. He returned to Moscow from vacationing in Georgia in early September and granted interviews to foreign correspondents almost daily. On 8 September at a press conference to which fourteen foreign correspondents answered his call, Sakharov characterized the main theme of the campaign in progress against him, that he was opposed to détente, as 'an unscrupulous play on the anti-war feelings of the nation which suffered the most from the Second World War'. Thereafter the Soviet media campaign against Sakharov stopped abruptly. There was, perhaps, the sensing on the Soviet side that enough, at least for the moment, was enough. But there was also, almost certainly, the first general understanding that Sakharov had become or was well on his way to becoming established in the international public consciousness as something very much like if not quite like a cult figure – his name, as the American phrase has it, had become a household word. In early September the Austrian chancellor, Bruno Kreisky, had described Sakharov as a symbolic figure in the struggle for scientific freedom while the Swedish foreign minister, Krister Wickman, had roundly charged that the campaign against Sakharov and Solzhenitsyn 'did not serve the cause of détente'. And then, on 8 September, the president of the American National Academy of Sciences, Dr Philip Handler, sent two telegrams to his Soviet counterpart, Mstislav Keldysh. The shorter telegram stated that 'harassment or detention of Sakharov will have severe effects upon the relationships between the scientific communities of the USA and the USSR and could vitiate our recent efforts toward increasing scientific interchange and cooperation'. The second telegram was even more explicit:

It is with great dismay that we have learned of the heightening campaign of condemnation of Sakharov for having expressed, in a spirit of free scholarly inquiry, social and political views which derive from his scientific understanding . . .

Were Sakharov to be deprived of his opportunity to serve the Soviet people and humanity, it would be extremely difficult to imagine successful fulfilment of American pledges of binational cooperation, the implementation of which is entirely dependent upon the voluntary effort and good will of our individual scientists and scientific institutions. It would be calamitous indeed if the spirit of détente were to be damaged by any further action taken against this gifted physicist.

The Soviet letter-writing campaign was replaced by a series of pot-shots at Sakharov by the Soviet press. Sakharov first presented himself as a target for the journalistic sniper's bullet when he joined Alexander Galich and Vladimir Maximov in an open appeal to the new Chilean government to safeguard the freedom of the poet Pablo Neruda (the military junta in Chile had overthrown Salvador Allende's leftist government on 11 September). For a while it looked like the Marxist poet might be in danger. 'The violent death of this great man,' read the the appeal, 'would darken for a long time what your government has proclaimed to be the era of the rebirth and consolidation of Chile.'

The French Communist Party organ, *L'Humanité*, and its Italian equivalent, *L'Unita*, seized upon this sentence as an indication that the authors themselves expected the junta to introduce this era. TASS carried this distortion while omitting any mention of Galich and Maximov. *Pravda* then published the TASS dispatch three days later, on 25 September. (The time lag in Communist press pick-ups should bother no one: the effect of such a release is the same in a Communist country regardless of the delay, and propagandists are not interested in timeliness for its own sake.) When a foreign correspondent telephoned for clarification, Sakharov explained that he could not comment on the junta, because 'Chile is too far away.' The appeal, he said, had been motivated 'strictly by humanitarian considerations'. There were foreign correspondents who wished he would explain his explanation.

On 11 October Sakharov gave an interview to an unidentified Lebanese correspondent in which he stated that Egyptian and Syrian military action had started the 1973 Arab–Israeli war. This was in conflict with Soviet policy, which claimed that Israel was the aggressor. But the real trouble started when Sakharov was asked what he thought the United States and other Western countries could do to end the war. Replied Sakharov: 'Call upon the USSR and socialist countries to abandon the policy of one-sided interference in the Arab–Israeli conflict, and take retaliatory steps if this policy of interference continues.'

Pravda, in a distortion of this passage, accused Sakharov of 'calling on imperialist states to "take retaliatory steps against the Soviet Union" because it is giving aid to Arab states in repulsing the Israeli aggression'. *Pravda* then quoted *L'Unita* to the effect that 'Sakharov always sides with imperialism. Yesterday he sided with the Chilean insurgents, today with Israel ... But this time the case is far worse: it is an open call to foreign states "to take steps" against his own country in order to make it change its policy.'

At this point his own country did change its policy: instead of another press campaign it sent 'Arabs' (in Russian slang the word 'Arab' also means a petty swindler or impostor; in this sense alone the two worthies concerned were true 'Arabs') who, after they had insinuated themselves into the Sakharov apartment, where they held Sakharov, his wife and his stepson hostage for well over an hour, claimed to be members of the Palestinian Black September organization. The 'Arabs' cut the telephone wire and barred the door, forbidding the Sakharovs to answer the doorbell. They then accused Sakharov of being 'under the influence' of his wife and roundly demanded that he cease supporting the Jews and start supporting the Arabs. Although Sakharov was described as 'badly shaken' by the incident, he was by no means shaken badly enough to change his views on the Arab–Israeli conflict and neither was his wife. When news of the incident reached Solzhenitsyn he wrote a letter to Sakharov stating that 'with blanket physical and telephone surveillance put on you such an assault is impossible without the knowledge and encouragement of the authorities'. According to a footnote in Peter Dornan's account of this series of events, Sakharov on 28 November showed correspondents a letter addressed to him from Beirut in which he was threatened with another visit by Palestinians if he continued his 'policy of confrontation with Arab countries'.

On 13 November the KGB returned to the classic method of intimidation, the summons for interrogation. This time it was Elena Bonner's turn, as Sakharov had all along feared. (This fear, as pointed out, had become the refrain of his press conferences and interviews. The fear of bringing harm down on one's family is, of course, the standard fear in all cases of dissidence with the Soviets. It also serves as the standard excuse on the part of conformists for doing nothing, for not taking any sort of stand: 'Of course, I was against this policy but what could I do? I have a son [or a daughter – or both] who is about to graduate, you know.') It is ironic and, of course, highly significant that the dissidents' only link, their only form of contact, with their own government was the KGB interrogation while the counter-measure Sakharov and other dissidents had devised was the interview with foreign communications media.

The pretext for the summons of Elena Bonner for KGB interrogation was Sakharov's offer of 28 October in a letter to KGB director Yuri Andropov to stand surety for Viktor Khaustov who was accused, along with Gabriel Superfin, of transmitting the prison diaries of the would-be airplane hijacker, Eduard Kuznetsov. The series of interrogations of Elena Bonner, begun by one Sokolov and continued by Colonel Syshchikov, KGB investigator from the Orel region, are on the level of broad, peasant-theatre farce. Both Sokolov and Syshchikov pulled all the stops in the KGB claviature of threats and attempts at entrapment, revealing themselves as incompetent or poorly briefed or both – although it must be admitted that it is extremely difficult to deal with a charge of transmitting private papers, a diary, in a system that claims to be open but desires to be closed and is gored on the horns of the ensuing dilemma. At the second interrogation on 19 November Bonner asserted that she, too, had transmitted the documents in question. 'I believe and still believe it to be my duty,' she said. 'What would the world know of our life if no one did this?' At the same time Sakharov and Podyapolsky made a similar statement. In three consecutive sessions, on 20, 23, and 27 November, Colonel Syshchikov tried to trap Bonner, first as an accomplice, then as a witness, finally as a sympathizer. The fates of Superfin, Khaustov and Kuznetsov, whose original death sentence could be reimposed, depended on her, Syshchikov warned. As a mother she should consider the fate of her children. When she refused to give testimony (it was not clear whether it might be used against her) she was told that 'the guards can be called' and that possibly she was mentally sick. He continued that she would have to speak anyway and not as a witness; moreover, she was only harming her husband. On the twenty-seventh, when she declared that she would not appear for the next day's session because there was no point in the interrogations, Syshchikov threatened to send a truck for her and 'all your anti-Soviet friends and foreign correspondents'.

(Dornan)

At this point Sakharov intervened with an open letter to Andropov on 28 November. He described Syshchikov's antics in interrogating his wife as 'a form of pressure' on himself and added: 'I object to her being summoned . . . and I assume full responsibility for her non-appearance.' Sakharov advised Andropov 'to explain to your subordinate' the illegality of interrogating his wife as a witness if he considered her to be an accomplice, pointless if she had good reason not to testify and 'immoral to subject a sick person who is a war invalid to many hours of exhaustive interrogation accompanied by threats'. As to the accusation itself – the keeping and transmitting of the diaries – Sakharov stated, 'This can in no way be considered a crime by generally accepted legal standards and in accordance with the Declaration of Human Rights.'

But from all these examples the position accepted and assumed by Sakharov as the leader of the opposition in the Soviet Union becomes unmistakably clear. Meanwhile Elena Bonner had not idly suffered her exposure to the KGB interrogatory panoptikon. She called a press conference on 21 November to give a current account of the proceedings. In so doing she also gave Sakharov the opportunity to answer questions as to the meaning of the repeated interrogations of his wife. A Reuter's dispatch cited Sakharov as viewing 'the sudden interest shown by the KGB in his wife as part of the general campaign against him for his outspoken criticism of Soviet society'.

On 7 November Roy Medvedev's samizdat article entitled 'The

Problem of Democratization and the Problem of Détente' appeared. It was dated October 1973. In the article Medvedev took issue with Sakharov on a number of counts. In the first place, détente was important in itself and no conditions should be set before agreeing to it (Sakharov had urged that the West set minimal conditions before agreeing). Further, although détente had not yet brought any extension of the democratic freedoms, these would undoubtedly come because through détente the influence of world public opinion on the internal policies of the superpowers would increase. Still, 'the basic impulses' for democratization would have to come from within Soviet society and that included its leaders. On the other hand the adoption of the Jackson–Vanik Amendment and the denial of most-favoured-nation status to the Soviet Union were forms of outside pressure that would worsen relations between the two countries and the prospects for emigration from the Soviet Union. Finally, appeals to the West should be addressed to groups on the left, not on the right, because the right was intent on using 'arbitrary acts' by the Soviet regime for the purpose of discrediting their own left opposition and Communism and socialism in general. Roy Medvedev, like the good Marxist he still was, was concerned about the planet and not just about the Soviet Union.

Sakharov's answer to the Medvedev article was characteristic and to the point. 'By their pragmatism,' he wrote,

the Medvedevs have set themselves against those who are waging a moral struggle for the right of man to live and think freely. The release of political prisoners, freedom to emigrate and freedom of convictions – these are demands of a purely moral nature. On their implementation depends the spiritual health of society, the economic and political conditions of life of the entire people. I can in no way agree, in particular, with the belittling by the Medvedevs of the role of the question of free emigration. I am convinced that free emigration is not only important for those who leave, but also and no less important for those who stay. I consider, with reference to our tragic problems, that we must speak openly and loudly, appealing to all decent people, regardless of their political convictions. This is our duty to our country and to the whole world. The position of the Medvedevs that one should appeal only to so-called left-wing political forces seems to me to be mistaken.

Roy Medvedev's insistence that appeals should be directed only to the left, as Sakharov perceived, was a red herring of the first order. The nature and the colour of the fish he drew across the landscape was predetermined by the fact that between East and West the political fronts in confrontation are reversed, which is to say that the traditional concepts cannot be applied straightforwardly: in the Soviet Union left is right and right is left, a fact that has wrought untellable confusion in political discussions since the October Revolution. Why this is so has been explained cogently by Lev Timofeev in his book *The Peasant Art of Starving*. 'The Soviet system,' writes Timofeev,

> is the dictatorship of the untalented, the dictatorship of the fear which the untalented experience when confronted with talent. It is precisely the fear in the face of the conditions of the open market, the fear of losing [money or being cheated] at the market. It is precisely this fear that feeds throughout the world the socialist idea. In our country this victorious fear has taken on the properties of statehood.

On 29 November Sakharov disclosed to foreign correspondents that he had taken the first step required of a Soviet citizen applying for an exit visa for travel abroad. This was a request for a character reference from his place of work (the Lebedev Physics Institute), which he made on 21 November, the date of Elena Bonner's press conference. Foreign correspondents following the Sakharov story noted that Sakharov had not mentioned his application then and assumed he had not done so in order to avoid the impression that he was acting under KGB pressure. When queried by correspondents as to when he arrived at the decision to travel abroad, Sakharov gave a date that fell shortly after he, his wife and his stepson had been held hostage in their own apartment by the two 'Arabs' representing the Black September organization. Sakharov had a whole series of invitations from Princeton University, the latest extended by Professor Marvin L. Goldberger, chairman of Princeton's department of physics. In informing reporters of his decision, Sakharov stated that he had 'decided it was time to do something. The situation here has become very critical.' He envisaged delivering a series of unpublished lectures on the theories of gravitation and elementary particles over a period from three to six months at Princeton. He realized, of course (Sakharov is always straightforward with journalists: he will either discuss a subject or he won't) the risk that he would be deprived of Soviet citizenship while abroad, but he made it clear that he meant to return: 'My place for moral, social and personal reasons is in my native land.'

On 21 November, Sakharov revealed, he had received a personal invitation for himself and his family from Professor Herman Feshbach of the Massachusetts Institute of Technology. He added that he had decided to make use of it. The invitation was endorsed by Henry Kissinger, then secretary of state, and so might meet Soviet official requirements. In his account, Peter Dornan cites the reaction of Veniamin Levich, corresponding member of the Soviet Academy of Sciences, who said he believed that the Soviet authorities' response 'will be interpreted by many as a sign of what is the actual way of further [scientific] development of international co-operation'.

But Sakharov's was not a good test case. He was, after all, 'the father of the Soviet hydrogen bomb'. He was therefore in the highest possible security category, 'first bearer of official secrets'; he was and is the bearer of the greatest secret in the world (for those who object that Sakharov could not have told the Americans anything they didn't already know, the answer is he could have told them what the Russians didn't already know). But he was also the country's leading dissident and this outstandingly so: he was the rallying point. Moreover, the head-on collision between Andrei Dmitrievich Sakharov and the Soviet state was in full progress. It was not the time and Sakharov was not the man for such a test.

Lest it be forgotten: the Americans were edgy about Robert Oppenheimer's travels abroad and especially to Europe in the late forties and early fifties for fear that he might be entrapped and spirited to the Soviet Union. With the Russian historical record of obsessive secrecy and the Soviet conspiratorial compounding of that urge, it is hard to understand how anyone, least of all a Soviet citizen, could have expected that Sakharov – of all possible people – would receive an exit visa. The idea of Sakharov leaving the Soviet Union, even for a short while, was utterly illusory. But this categorical veto (for as such it must be regarded) only heightened the dilemma of the Soviet state by reducing its traditional option of sending undesirables either East (to exile in Siberia) or West (by deportation) to the bare choice of sending him East or leaving him in relative peace (with maximum publicity for every form of state-inspired chicanery assured). By the same token the veto strengthened the stand of Sakharov as a fighter's back is strengthened by being placed squarely against a wall. Sakharov had no way out. He had no choice but to see the fight through. Again, the fact of no escape played an extremely important role in determining the ultimate outcome of the struggle. The same consideration that underlay his enormously privileged position, that gave him so much leverage and a certain immunity in his struggle against the Soviet state, also forced him to bear a disproportionate personal responsibility for the positions he asserted, and robbed him of the escape-hatch enjoyed by most prominent dissidents.

There can be no doubt that Sakharov, at one point or another in his long ordeal, would have left the Soviet Union if he could have and that he would have stayed in the West if he should have, that is, if convinced that his return to the Soviet Union portended death or disablement. During another November, fourteen years after this event, in Sakharov's apartment in Moscow, this writer broached the subject of the death the year before of Anatoly Marchenko, adding that he had always had a bad conscience for not helping Sakharov's favourite and most tragic charge, although he, the present writer, had no idea what he might have done to help. 'You needn't have a bad conscience,' said Mrs Sakharov sternly: 'Tolya Marchenko could have left the Soviet Union if he had chosen to; he chose not to.' There is a kind of angry love that speaks out of the mouth of 'Lusia', otherwise known as Elena Bonner. Sakharov tacitly agreed (when he does not agree he unfailingly speaks up).

Late in December 1973 in Paris there was detonated a literary bombshell that shook the Russian-speaking world and resounded throughout the world at large. It still resounds. This was the publication in Russian of Alexander Solzhenitsyn's monumental *The Gulag Archipelago*, in which the author compares the Soviet penal system and its network of concentration camps and prisons to a giant sewage system. He then describes the waste of human life that enters and travels the system. The work is the greatest single blow ever dealt the corpus of Communist theory. It coined and set in universal circulation the acronym GULAG (*Gosudrastvennoe Upravlenie Lagerei* – State Directorate of Camps). It branded the letters GULAG on the body politic of the Soviet Union.

Sakharov lost no time in coming out in defence of Solzhenitsyn's right to publish abroad. In a statement made on 5 January 1974, he and four other Moscow intellectuals asserted that 'the right of an author to write and publish what his conscience and duty as an artist dictate is one of the most basic in civilized society. This right cannot be limited by national frontiers.' On 20 January Sakharov gave an interview – among many others – to the *Tribune de Genève*. Said he: 'I would like to believe that the book *The Gulag Archipelago* will be widely read not only in the West but also in the USSR, and will become the stone that will finally crack the ice of mistrust and lack of understanding created by lies, wickedness, cowardice and stupidity. This stone has been cast by a powerful and sure hand.' Solzhenitsyn was arrested on 12 February and forcibly deported the next day. On the day of Solzhenitsyn's deportation Sakharov, his wife and eight other Soviet intellectuals issued a 'Moscow Appeal', which made four demands of the Soviet authorities;

1. Publication of *The Gulag Archipelago* in the USSR and making it available to all our countrymen.
2. Publication of the archival and other materials which would give a full picture of the activity of the Cheka–GPU–NKVD–KGB.
3. Formation of an international public tribunal to investigate the crimes that have been committed.
4. Protection of Solzhenitsyn against prosecution and the opportunity for him to work in his native land.

      We reject in advance the attempts to declare an international collection of signatures in answer to our appeal interference in the internal affairs of the USSR, the more so since not only citizens of the USSR but also hundreds of thousands of citizens of other countries have been victims of this same terror. The truth about what happened in USSR must be made known to all people on earth. We ask all mass-information media to disseminate our appeal. We also ask all public and religious organizations to form national committees for the collection of signatures.

Among those who signed this appeal were Vladimir Maximov, Mikhail Agursky, Anatoly Marchenko (by way of exception out of jail) and his wife Larissa Bogoras. If these demands seem extravagant under the circumstances it should be noted that the aspect of 'making book' or establishing a public precedent plays an important role in a struggle that depends so much on publicity. Human interest has everything to do with human rights. Indeed, one week later in a telephone interview to the *Sunday Times* Sakharov explained that the aim of the signatories was to produce not a 'pragmatic document' but rather 'a moral appeal'. He believed that such an appeal 'showed the approach of a live democratic movement in the USSR for the defence of moral values of all mankind'.

On 27 February Elena Bonner underwent a second thyrotomy, this time under normal medical conditions in a regular hospital in Leningrad. At the same time Sakharov was troubled over the fate of his stepchildren, Alexei and Tatiana Semeonov, and Tatiana's husband, Efrim Yankelevich. The last named had been offered a position as instructor at the Massachusetts Institute of Technology. All three had submitted visa applications early in 1973 and in May of the same year 'authoritative Soviet representatives', as Sakharov put it in an open letter to the academician V. A. Engelgardt, 'including the Soviet ambassador to the United States, had promised the president of MIT to resolve the question of their being allowed to make the trip'. Almost a year had passed since then. The trip was all the more necessary, as Sakharov explained, because Tatiana Semeonova-Yankelevich had been deprived of the possibility of receiving a higher eduction in the USSR.

Sakharov's concern over the fate of his wife and her family was well founded. In the separate trials of Khaustov and Superfin (6 March and 13 May respectively), the name of Elena Bonner came up in connection with the transmission of the Kuznetsov diaries. The charge of her complicity was made within the context of Khaustov's sentence while Superfin denied similar charges levelled by the prosecutor at his trial and asserted that he alone had transmitted the diaries. Nevertheless, three weeks after his wife's operation, seated at her bedside in their Moscow apartment, Sakharov told foreign correspondents that since Solzhenitsyn's deportation he had 'given up thoughts of taking his family to the United States' (thereby saving Soviet authorities the embarrassment of denying him an exit visa).

On 20 March Sakharov and Igor Shafarevich presented foreign correspondents with the samizdat volume, *Live Not by Lies*, a 194-page compilation of Soviet press and radio attacks on Solzhenitsyn and of letters and documents supporting him. The two academicians contributed a foreword to the volume in which they made an important assertion: 'The great number of voices, among them people who have no protection from prosecution, shows how illusory were the hopes of those who thought Solzhenitsyn's influence on the country's spiritual life would diminish.' Here Sakharov was echoing his statement some three weeks earlier to the *Corriere della sera*: 'Solzhenitsyn had and will continue to have a very important role [to play] for our cause. His moral conceptions deserve great respect.'

It was therefore with all the more consternation that the dissident and Western publics registered and read Sakharov's critique of Solzhenitsyn's *Letter to the Leaders of the Soviet Union*. And yet Sakharov's critique needn't have done anything of the sort. It was short (scarcely twelve pages) and to the point. Above all, Sakharov's critique was inevitable. In his letter to Engelgardt, already cited, Sakharov gave a good capsule version of his credo: 'I always openly express my position on various questions of public life, with no pretension of having found the definitive answer to complicated questions I call for their open and public discussion.' As a scientist devoted to his calling, Sakharov could not but disagree with much of what Solzhenitsyn had to say in his seventy-five-page disquisition. To begin with, Sakharov could not agree with Solzhenitsyn's singling out of the Russian people for his compassion and consideration to the virtual exclusion of the many other peoples caught in the same Communist-statist trap. Secondly, he could not agree with Solzhenitsyn's combination of 'back to the land', 'small is beautiful' and 'Old Russia was best' points of view, in stark preference to the Industrial Revolution which he considers a Western invention and holds responsible for ravaging the Russian countryside and pillaging its natural resources. Said Sakharov: 'The very classification of ideas as Western or Russian is incomprehensible to me. In my view, a scientific and rational approach to social and natural phenomena is only compatible with a classification of ideas and concepts as true or false.' Sakharov and Solzhenitsyn also parted company diametrically on the subject of ideology. Sakharov could not agree that the 'various anomalies' and 'costly absurdities' in the internal affairs and foreign policy of the Soviet Union were generated by ideological causes. To the contrary: Sakharov saw Soviet society marked by ideological indifference. In his view, the ideological rituals of the Soviet system were merely the substitute for an 'oath of allegiance'. It was another example of an 'expedient absurdity generated by the system'.

I find Solzhenitsyn's treatment of the problem of progress particularly misleading. Progress is a worldwide process, which must not be equated, certainly not in times to come, with the quantitative growth of large-scale industrial production. Given universal scientific and democratic management of the economy and of the whole of social life, including population growth, this, I am quite convinced, is not a utopia but a vital necessity. Progress must continually change its immediate forms according to need, in order to meet the requirements of human society while preserving at all costs the natural environment and the earth for our descendants.

Here Sakharov's basic calculation is speaking – his view, derived from his scientific understanding, of what generally must come sooner or later. Progress is not a linear improvement: it is humanity coping as it goes on, with the single assurance that as it goes on life will become increasingly complicated. And life is already complicated enough. This is why, as he puts it in the critique, he is convinced,

unlike Solzhenitsyn, that there is no really important problem in the world today that can be solved at the national level. Disarmament in particular, so essential in order to eliminate the danger of war, can obviously be undertaken only in conjunction by all the major powers on the basis of treaty obligation and trust. The same is true of birth control and the limitation of industrial growth, and of the transition to a technology harmless to the environment, which will inevitably be more expensive than our present technology . . .

In short, then, a strategy for the development of human society on earth, if it is to be compatible with the continuation of the human species, can only be worked out and put into practice on a global scale.

Sakharov could no longer agree (he might well have done five years earlier) with Solzhenitsyn on the problem of China. By this time he considered Solzhenitsyn's 'dramatic' view of the danger downright melodramatic. China was industrially and technologically too far behind to contemplate a 'large-scale aggressive war against the USSR' in the foreseeable future. There was also the distinct possibility that exaggerating the Chinese threat was a political ploy of the Soviet leadership. (In Russia, not surprisingly, the fear of China has a long tradition: it is 'in the bones' of the Russian.) In any case, emphasizing the Chinese threat was anything but conducive to the democratization and demilitarization of the Soviet Union, which was what everyone so badly needed.

In his answer to Sakharov's critique, Solzhenitsyn noted in passing that Sakharov agreed with a great many of the points in his *Letter to the Leaders*, among them the demand for the 'separation of Marxism from the state', hinting – at least by the formal inclusion of the item – at a certain inconsistency in Sakharov's argument that the ruling ideology of Communism was of no great consequence. For the rest, Solzhenitsyn added a spirited defence of the importance of ideology and an expression of his indignation at being called a 'Great Russian nationalist'. He supported this last point with the assertion that the Russian and Ukrainian peoples had borne the brunt of the blows dealt by Communism in the Soviet Union and continued to do so and hence were worthy of demanding equal rights in terms of national rebirth after so dreadful a firestorm of suppression.

By any standards this was a gentlemanly exchange. There is, moreover, one sentence in Solzhenitsyn's reply that is important to this account. In chiding Sakharov for making a mountain out of a molehill on the nationalism question, Solzhenitsyn commented: 'This is a vehemence not of Sakharov personally, but of a broad stratum of the educated class, whose spokesman he has involuntarily become.'

In this connection the late poet and political folk-singer Alexander Galich told a story that is characteristic of Sakharov. When the scientist became a public spokesman some of his friends, knowing their man, grew concerned lest he lend his name all too readily and generously, lest he espouse the causes of all possible and some impossible dissidents and so waste his influence and authority. His friends thus asked Sakharov to exercise discretion, reserving his support for the most important and representative dissidents. In answer to this adjuration Sakharov turned to Galich who had been deputized to broach the matter: 'How can I know when a case is important or unimportant? Every breach of human rights, every injustice inflicted on anybody is important in my eyes. So I have no choice but to take seriously and make public every case that comes to my attention.'

The exchange which came to be known as the Solzhenitsyn–Sakharov debate became a kind of watershed in its own right, setting forth on either side the arguments that characterized the two main camps in the Russian political emigration. There took place also during this time – over a period of something more than five years – a gradual shift of dissident activity from East to West, from the Soviet Union to western Europe and the United States of America. Valery Chalidze went abroad in 1972 and was stripped of his Soviet citizenship shortly after arriving in New York (his Soviet wife was not). Zhores Medvedev left in 1973. Solzhenitsyn was deported in early 1974 and Vladimir Maximov 'voluntarily' went to Paris at about the same time, as did Sinyavsky, Nekrassov, Galich, Golem-Stock, Joseph Brodsky and other lesser lights. Chalidze founded the *Chronicle of Current Events* in New York in 1973 and Vladimir Maximov founded the magazine *Kontinent* in Paris and Berlin (seats of the Russian and German editions respectively) in 1974.

For almost seventy years the elaborate controls over information in the Soviet Union forced anyone trying to communicate freely to take recourse to the corps of foreign correspondents in Moscow. This was true even if the person concerned was interested in practising *glasnost* only within the borders of the USSR. The information had to get out in order to get in – by foreign radio broadcast (primarily Radio Liberty, the Voice of America and the BBC). This explains the attraction of the non-Soviet world to the Soviet dissident and the disapproval of the Soviet authorities, who regarded contacts between Soviet citizens and foreigners as most objectionable if not indeed criminal. Thus Soviet citizens maintained a precarious balance between interrogation at home (usually the dissident's only form of contact with his own government was through the institution of the KGB interrogation) and interview or press conference with foreign correspondents for publication abroad – by any account a curious reversal of the generally accepted practice in which the citizen is interviewed by his own government and interrogated (if at all) by foreign governments. This novel system of alliances across, and misalliances within national boundaries reflected not only alienation but downright estrangement between citizens and government of the Soviet Union.

So the dissidents and non-dissidents turned to the Western world and the Western world responded after its fashion: Solzhenitsyn won the Nobel Prize for literature in 1970 and Sakharov won the Nobel Prize for peace in 1975, and Joseph Brodsky – who was arrested and sent to prison and then thrown out of the country as a *tuneyadets*, a fainéant, a do-nothing and a parasite – in 1987 won the Nobel Prize for literature.

In 1977 Sakharov's stepdaughter, Tatiana Yankelevich, and her husband, Efrim, with their two children, received their exit visas and left for America. At the same time Elena Bonner received an exit visa for travel to Italy to consult an eye specialist. This trip had been preceded by an attempt to undergo ocular surgery in Leningrad. After having been prepared for surgery for the better part of a week and already under sedation, Bonner was informed by the surgeon designate the day before the operation was scheduled that he would not perform the operation for fear of ruining his career. Sakharov's stepson, Alexei Semeonov, received his exit visa in 1980 and emigrated to the United States (he joined his sister, Tatiana, in Newton, a township on the outskirts of Boston). Alexei was promised by the Soviet authorities that his fiancée, Lisa Alexeyeva, would be allowed to follow him within a few weeks. When, after several months of waiting and protesting in vain, it became clear that the Soviet authorities had no intention of redeeming the promise of an exit visa for the fiancée, Sakharov went on his first hunger strike to force the issue. Not a few dissidents could not understand why Sakharov went to such an extreme for what seemed a purely personal reason and not a general cause. But for Sakharov the right to leave the country had always been – or at least since his political awakening – one of the most important general causes. In the end, at no little cost to his health, he won through: Lisa Alexeyeva was allowed to emigrate in 1981.

XIV

THE SAKHAROV HEARINGS: AN EXILE APPEALS TO THE WORLD

The Sakharov hearings, beginning with the hearing in Copenhagen on 17, 18 and 19 October 1975, were a direct result of the 'Moscow Appeal' of 13 February 1974 signed by eight Soviet dissidents including Sakharov and Elena Bonner. This effort was characterized by Sakharov as not a 'pragmatic document', but rather 'a moral appeal', asking that the truth about 'what happened in the USSR must be made known to all people on earth'. As the Introduction to the report published by the Sakharov Hearing Committee put it, the 'Moscow Appeal' might well have gone unnoticed, like many other appeals coming out of the Soviet Union, had it not been taken up by Øjvind Felsted Andresen, a Dane who had fought in the Danish underground army during World War II. Andresen had turned to the Hungarian Ernö Eszterhazy, the then president of the United Committee for Refugees from East European Countries, to organize a series of hearings on the problems of the violation of human rights in the Soviet Union. The Danish parliament building itself was to serve as venue. It required several months to collect the necessary funds, select a jury of personages from various countries and to locate and invite particularly knowledgeable witnesses. Meanwhile the Danish government received a number of official warnings from the Soviet government not to allow the hearings to take place. When these failed to have any effect, the Soviet government took recourse to a well-worn artifice: three days before the scheduled opening of the Sakharov hearings, uninvited and unheralded, an official delegation of Soviets descended upon Copenhagen and arranged an 'anti-hearing' under the title, 'Is Sakharov right in his criticism of the USSR?' The delegation was headed by an editor of the *Literaturnaya Gazeta*, Alexander Chakovsky, and featured one Professor Vul, who claimed to be a personal friend of Sakharov. Another member of the delegation was styled as a rabbi, but speedily exposed as an impostor by the chief rabbi of Copenhagen. Yet another member was a professor of psychiatry who had the great misfortune to find himself confronted at the press conference by one of his victims. The delegation was completed by a well-known Soviet jurist whose one contribution to the charade was his abrupt breaking off of the press conference to avoid further embarrassing questions. As it developed, the Soviet 'anti-hearing' served only to give much-needed publicity to the Sakharov hearing itself.

The First International Sakharov Hearing in Copenhagen featured a collection of witnesses whose testimony was given under four headings: the persecution of dissidents, psychiatric hospitals and experiments on people in the USSR, the persecution of religion and the curtailing of the rights of nations and national minorities. Twenty-six witnesses were called. They included (under the first heading) Boris Shragin, who spoke 'concerning the crimes of the Soviet regime against human rights in the world process', Maria Sinyavskaya (Mrs Andrei Sinyavsky) – 'the fate of the wife of a political prisoner', Dmitri Panin – 'lawlessness and despotism in the Soviet Union'; (under the second heading) Marina Fainberg – 'the committing of dissidents to psychiatric hospitals under the civil statute', and Viktor Fainberg, whose subject was 'the committing of dissidents to psychiatric hospitals under the criminal code'; (under the third heading) Anatoly Levitin-Krasnov spoke on 'the situation of believers in the USSR'. Nine witnesses gave testimony under the fourth heading and their subjects merit recording and remembrance: 'the persecution of the Lithuanian people, the persecution of Ukrainian national culture, the violation of the national rights of the Armenian people (Eduard Oganessian), the persecution of the German people in the USSR, the annihilation of Jewish culture in the USSR, the violation of the right to leave the country, the policy of the CPSU is the policy of russification, the fate of the Crimean Tatars, the national–patriotic movement of the Crimean Tatars. These subjects and their headings were suggested by Sakharov himself. This is clear from his message to the Sakharov hearing published in the committee's report. Here Sakharov writes:

334

'I am grateful for the possibility offered me to express myself at this "hearing" and also for the fact that it bears my name. I regard this as an acknowledgement of just deserts – not only my own, but of all those in my country who strive for *glasnost*, for the implementation of the rights of man, and especially of those who have paid dearly for this with the loss of their freedom.' Sakharov then went on, as was and is his wont, to demand a general amnesty for all political prisoners in the Soviet Union.

The twelve members of the jury included such notables as Eugene Ionesco, the Reverend Michael Bordeaux, Cornelia Gerstenmaier, Viktor Sparre and Simon Wiesenthal. Wiesenthal's statement, which is included in the committee's report, requires some scrutiny here: 'Above all,' he writes,

> I want to explain why I immediately and unconditionally put myself at the disposal of the committee for the Sakharov hearings.
>
> Thirty years ago, at the time of my liberation from a concentration camp, I dedicated my life to the struggle for justice. I never returned to my former profession as an architect. With the foundation of the Jewish Document Centre I tried to warn the world against forgetting the events of the Nazi era, the murder of millions of people. I dedicated myself to the search for those who were responsible for this – the executioners who took part in this tremendous catastrophe.
>
> During the long period of my active career I succeeded in discovering many until then unknown actors in the European tragedy during the Nazi era and I bound over many criminals for prosecution by the courts.
>
> Immediately after the year 1945, at the Nuremberg Trials and other trials, the crimes of National Socialism were brought to account and branded as such. For me this was not enough. Because I knew that these crimes, the victims of which ran into millions, were not the work of a few dozen people. The Hitlerian machine of destruction was serviced by many thousands of assistants. I considered that these assistants should also be made to pay for their part in these crimes. I succeeded in bringing more than 1,100 of them before a court. I wish to say that in everything that happened not only Hitler and his closest associates were guilty. That totalitarian regime was the fruitful soil of a plurality of sadists and provided them with the possibility of satisfying their criminal inclinations, to torture and kill innocent people with impunity. These were sadists whose place, in normal conditions, is in prison – but as prisoners, not as jailers.

335

I discovered very early what was going on in the Soviet Union with regard to the suppression of the human personality. As of 1939 I spent twenty-one months in the Soviet Union and was able to observe personally the omnipotence of the secret police and the ignoring of even the most elementary spirit of justice. Later, in German concentration camps I met Russian prisoners of war ... Everything they told me broadened the impressions I had already received.

After the war I discovered that my friends who had fled to the Soviet Union to escape German Nazism had been arrested on suspicion of espionage. In prison they were informed that they had been sentenced to many years' confinement – without trial and, of course, without the possibility of defending themselves against the accusation. I learned of the inhuman labour camps, of the despotism of the camp commandant and his deputies, of the outrages committed by the common criminals who had been placed in privileged positions so that they could amuse themselves at the expense of the political prisoners ... And when the reports of those people who had survived the camps were published, I saw that there existed a great similarity between the two totalitarian systems – the Nazi and the Soviet – with regard to their treatment of prisoners.

Involved as I was in activity directed against National Socialist crimes, I had no opportunity to devote myself to the crimes committed in the name of a so-called socialism.

Wiesenthal's chance to do so came in 1961, several years after Khrushchev's exposé of Stalinism at the Twentieth Party Congress. The occasion was the trial of Eichmann in Jerusalem. At a press conference Dr Friedrich Kaul of East Berlin accused the Israeli government of ignoring other Nazis at large. In answer to this charge, Wiesenthal made a statement:

Now we know of the crimes of Stalin. We cannot be sure that we know everything. But, as in the case of Hitlerism, it is known that there were thousands of accomplices involved. There were secret courts – the so-called *troiki* – that sentenced people to many years' imprisonment without so much as having seen or heard the accused. There were inhuman camp commandants who dealt with prisoners in a criminal fashion. They refused medical attention to sick prisoners. They beat people and caused them to die of starvation. World public opinion did not find that it was enough to try and sentence to death the leadership of the Nazi government and party. Those who took part in the mechanism of annihilation directed against millions of people in the Third Reich were hunted down and brought to justice. The same thing is also expected of the Soviet Union after de-Stalinization. Until such time as Dr Kaul or another representative of the East European countries can inform us that, in addition to Beria and Abakumov and, perhaps, a half dozen others, court action has been initiated and thousands upon thousands of officials of the NKVD tribunals, labour-camp comm- ands and other organizations involved in outrages against innocent people, have been brought to trial – until such time the represent- atives of the Eastern bloc do not have the right to accuse Germans.

Dr Kaul, Wiesenthal writes, was livid with rage at this statement because 'the powers in the East reserve unto themselves the right to decide what constitutes the violation of human rights'. And at that time Communists were not used to being measured by the general rule. They claimed exemption from all bourgeois rules and standards and demanded that the claim be honoured. Wiesenthal was one of the first to dispute this claim and insist that the Communists be held to the same account as everyone else.

Indeed, Wiesenthal quickly became a leading *spiritus curator* of the Sakharov hearings and the general complex of movements, trends and initiatives more or less connected with Sakharov. As a member of the international jury co-presiding over the first hearing he had much to do with the proceedings which, not entirely by coincidence, came just two months after the signing of the Helsinki Accords. The Helsinki Accords were the culmination of a political process that began with the Soviet suppression of the Prague Spring. For it was in reaction to the reform movement in Czecho- slovak Communism that the so-called 'Brezhnev doctrine' was born, which stipulated the intervention of the Soviet Union in any country of the Soviet bloc where socialist order was threatened or appeared to be threatened. Over and above the immediate concern of giving the 'Brezhnev doctrine' an international contractual framework, there was the need to formalize diplomatically the consolidation of Soviet territorial gains in World War II plus the revised borders of its Eastern European satellites. This in lieu of a peace treaty, which could not be negotiated because the chief belligerent of World War II had disappeared, to be replaced by two German states in cold-war confrontation with each other. Negotia- tions among thirty-six states, at the instance of the Soviet Union, for a treaty of 'Security and Cooperation' in Europe were begun in earnest in early 1970. There was from the beginning strong opposition in the West to such a treaty or series of treaties, such opposition resting basically on the consideration that an agreement would sanction and seal the division of Germany and with it the division of Europe, including the Soviet Union's annexation of the Baltic states. Thus Western diplomats were under pressure from the beginning to negotiate an offsetting improvement in the quality of the relationship between the two blocs. Since the course of negotiations between the two blocs ran simultaneously with that of the human-rights struggle in the Soviet Union and Eastern Europe, it was natural that the diplomats take their cue from the dissident cause. Thus to the two 'baskets', security and cooperation, was added a third – human rights – and, indeed, a fourth, which provided for a plenary session of the signatories every two years for the purpose of verifying the observance of the agreements in the interim. The 'third basket' quickly became famous in the parlance of international journalists, but the 'fourth basket', scarcely ever mentioned as such, has resulted in a series of Helsinki Accord meetings in various capitals at two-year intervals since the signing in 1975: Belgrade, Madrid, Ottawa, Vienna. However, each of these sessions has gone on for several months, the Soviets learning too late that the concession they made in allowing for a third and then of necessity a fourth 'basket' had placed them in a sort of permanent *statu pupillari* as far as human rights were concerned. And human rights, moreover, in view of the nature of the Soviet system, are always concerned: the Soviets found themselves permanently on the defensive – structurally, as it were, since if they raise objections similar to those being raised against them they are merely invited 'to come and see' for themselves, an invitation they could not and would not reciprocate.

Almost as if by chance, then, the human-rights struggle in the Soviet Union and in the satellites took on an official international aspect, it became a *res diplomatica* overnight. Hardly had the ink dried on the signatures of the thirty-six states when Helsinki Watch Committees sprang up out of the ground in Moscow and in other Communist capitals. These were all more or less speedily put down, but not before their presence and activities and the fact of their suppression were noted and designated for discussion at the current or next scheduled full assembly of the Helsinki Accords group of nations. Of course, these Helsinki Watch Committees had no official status whatever, but they provided material for discussion and deliberation in various councils of the United Nations or the Council of Europe and the like. In any case it is impossible to understand or assess the human-rights struggle in general and the fate of Sakharov in particular in isolation from the Helsinki Accords and the resultant periodic follow-up conferences to verify the observance and progress of human rights in the countries concerned. In short, the follow-up conferences that sprang out of the 'fourth basket' were in themselves, lasting as long as each one has, a kind of official Helsinki Watch Committee.

The object of the exercise of the first Sakharov hearing was to generate as much publicity as possible in the West concerning the cause of human rights in the Soviet Union. The Copenhagen hearing had the advantage of novelty and a plethora of fresh material to draw from – thanks especially to the flow of Soviet Jews out of the Soviet Union as the Jackson–Vanik Amendment entered into force. (The flow increased in the second half of the seventies to the high watermark of 51,000 in 1979, whereafter it ebbed drastically.) The press coverage of the Copenhagen hearing was more than good enough to warrant a repeat performance. Accordingly, a Second International Sakharov Hearing was held two years later in Rome, with Simon Wiesenthal presiding.

The International Sakharov Hearing in Rome from 25 to 28 November 1977 expanded the scope of the hearings to include the Eastern European satellites of the Soviet Union. There were twenty-two witnesses in all, ten of them representing the Soviet Union, one from Bulgaria, two from Romania, two from Poland, three from Czechoslovakia and four from East Germany. Also various religious denominations under persecution were represented – Pentecostalists, Baptists, Lutherans and Catholics. The hearing was opened with a showing of a videotape interview with Andrei Sakharov. In the interview Sakharov listed areas in the Communist bloc where human rights had been most blatantly violated. He asked his audience to investigate the cases mentioned. Sakharov singled out the Czechoslovak human-rights organization Charter 77 for special mention, saying that it 'is close to me because of its constructive and legal spirit'. He went on to point out that 'the hearing is taking place during the Belgrade Conference and this fact increases its importance'. (The Belgrade Conference was the first of the Helsinki Accords follow-up conferences. As luck and careful planning would have it, the second Sakharov hearing took place while the first follow-up conference was still in session. The coincidence provides a good example of the strategy followed by both the dissidents and the diplomats.)

Easily the most spectacular incident of the second hearing was the surprise appearance of Josef Cardinal Slypy, the spiritual leader of 4 million Ukrainian Catholics, himself a political prisoner in the Soviet Union for eighteen years before his release in 1963, and the model for the novel by Morris West, *The Shoes of the Fisherman*, on which a film was based, starring Anthony Quinn. At the time of the Sakharov hearing in Rome the prelate was eighty-five years old. He entered the conference hall in flowing white robe and vestments, accompanied – as befitted a prince of the Church – by a large entourage of Vatican priests. While the cardinal stood at ease, his secretary read out his message: 'All of our bishops, with the sole exception of myself, died in prison or in exile. Hundreds of thousands of believers were taken to prison camps: 1,500 Ukrainian Catholic priests died. I still bear the scars of that terror on my body.' Then Slypy compared that persecution of his Church to that of the early Christian martyrs. There was another comparison. It was 340 years and more since Galileo was found guilty before the Inquisition in Rome and sentenced to indefinite imprisonment. Now there was a perfect reversal of positions. Instead of atheists, agnostics and apostates or those *vehementur suspectu* as such in Galileo's time being prosecuted by the Church, here was the spectacle of the Church being prosecuted by self-avowed atheists, agnostics and apostates, who had since assumed the properties of statehood. Josef Cardinal Slypy never became Pope, but his brother in Christ, Karol Cardinal Wojtyla of Cracow in neighbouring Poland, did. As John Paul II, Wojtyla threw himself into the struggle against the statehooding (as it were) of atheists, agnostics and apostates in his own country and throughout the Communist bloc. The attempted assassination of Wojtyla soon thereafter bears witness to the effectiveness of his struggle.

Perhaps the most interesting aspect of the Sakharov hearing in Rome in 1977 was provided by the session set aside for lawyers, on the last day. Probably the boldest stroke of Sakharov and the dissidents as a whole was the cutting of the Gordian knot comprised of the Soviet taboo against any unauthorized communication with foreigners. The connection of the Western democracies to the cause of the Soviet dissidents had proceeded so far afield by 1977 that prominent lawyers from Western countries had undertaken the defence of arrested members of the human-rights movement in the Soviet Union. Several of these were invited to the Rome hearing: Edward Bennett Williams (USA) as counsel for Alexander Ginzburg; Daniel Jacoby (France) as counsel for Anatoly Shcharansky; John MacDonald (Great Britain) as counsel for Yuri Orlov; Ramsey Clark (USA) for Mikola Rudenko and Burton Hall (USA) for Alexander Sergienko, to mention only the more prominent. Clark and Williams sent associates to the hearing – in both cases lawyers of considerable standing (Melvin Wolff and Andrew Craig).

In addition to the Western lawyers there were former Soviet lawyers, particularly Dina Kaminskaya, then recently emigrated from the Soviet Union, who had defended a number of dissidents. Mrs Kaminskaya pointed out that Soviet lawyers were not free, in effect, in the performance of their professional services. By way of example she mentioned Boris Zolotukhin, Alexander Ginzburg's lawyer in 1968. Zolotukhin argued his client's innocence and asked for a verdict of not guilty. He was thereupon disbarred. (An excellent example of the Soviet difficulty in procedural practice under existing legislation: there is nothing in Soviet law that prohibits a defence counsel pleading the innocence of his client; in practice, however, by so doing he runs the overhanging risk of losing not only his job but his calling by disbarment. The point, of course, is that there is nothing in Soviet law that protects a defence counsel in pleading his client's innocence.) This being the case it was not surprising that Mrs Kaminskaya went on to mention the near impossibility of finding a lawyer with the necessary clearance who would agree 'at a political trial' to plead the innocence of the defendant. Consequently, more and more defendants were refusing counsel. Mrs Kaminskaya mentioned the trial of Sergei Kovalev in which the distinguished biologist, whose work on the electrophysiology of muscles and the control of the heartbeat had secured him an international reputation, refused the services of A. I. Rozhansky because the latter could not support the plea of not guilty (even though Rozhansky himself believed Kovalev to be innocent). Rozhansky had since emigrated to the West and was present at the hearing to corroborate this evidence.

Nor was it surprising that the Soviet Union flatly refused (by simply ignoring all requests to the effect) to permit foreign lawyers to attend political trials as observers – let alone as defence counsels. But once again: the object of the hearing was not justice – it was publicity. Even so, the exercise went so far as to include the organization of a 'preparatory defence' for Yuri Orlov by his counsel, John MacDonald. This included MacDonald's cross-examining seventeen witnesses in the presence of reporters and diplomats from countries signatory to the Helsinki Agreements, including Soviet representatives from TASS and the Soviet Embassy. All witnesses agreed in writing to go to Moscow to give testimony or be questioned at a Soviet consulate in any country. These statements plus the witnesses' testimony were then sent to the prosecutor general of the Soviet Union. Since under Soviet law investigative authorities must examine evidence from all sources and MacDonald failed to hear from the Soviet prosecutor general for the six months intervening between his action and the Rome hearing, he concluded that 'the Soviet authorities do not respect their own laws'.

But meanwhile another force was gathering – slowly, insidiously, implacably – a force stronger than any other in the field because it includes and involves them all. For this reason the economic process is an exceedingly complex phenomenon. It was high time the Sakharov hearings focused on this all-important aspect of life in general and Soviet life in particular. The Third International Sakharov Hearing did just that, making working conditions in 'the workers' state' its dominant theme. Convened in Washington, DC in the Dirksen Senate Office Building from 26 through 29 September 1979, it boasted a star-studded cast of dissident witnesses to give testimony on working conditions in the Soviet Union – Amalrik, Bukovsky, Chalidze, Ginzburg, Grigorenko, Litvinov, Maximov, Natalia Solzhenitsyn (Mrs Alexander Solzhenitsyn) and Sinyavsky among at least a dozen others. The members of the commission that heard the testimony were at least equally imposing: former Supreme Court Justice Arthur Goldberg, historian Arthur Schlesinger, Jr., the Danish Nobel laureate in biochemistry Dr Christian Anfinsen, Simon Wiesenthal, British playwright Tom Stoppard, the International Ladies Garment Workers Union President Sol Chaikin and AFL/CIO Secretary–Treasurer (now President) Lane Kirkland, who presided. Kirkland's presidency was appropriate: the AFL/CIO, again most fittingly in view of the subject matter, was the sponsor of the Third Sakharov Hearing.

Despite the large number of personages present and the intrinsic value of the material produced, in terms of publicity the Washington hearing was the least successful of the entire series. For the most part the American media simply ignored the event. This was ironic. In the special message sent to the hearing Sakharov emphasized that non-violent methods – 'namely openness and publicity [read *glasnost*]' should be 'the main weapon'. The trouble with this principle is that in the West, publicity doesn't flow from non-violence. Not as a rule – indeed quite the contrary. But there was a more important motive-force involved. At the beginning of the Sakharov hearings in Washington, the committee in charge was informed that the *Washington Post* editors had decided in conference that the hearing was not news. (While the hearing was in progress, a rather modest story on it appeared in the society section of the *Post*.) The decision was reached not because the majority of editors of the *Post* are leftist but because the categorical alignment of the Soviet and East European dissidents with the American government lumps the dissidents with the American establishment and hence renders them and their doings unacceptable to the American media. As contradistinct from the Soviet media, the American media are out to criticize the American government – whatever it does – not to praise and popularize it.

And yet the broad effect of the hearings – the support accorded Sakharov in the West in general – was growing. More important still was the fact that Sakharov's cause, the cause of human rights – in a complex of parallel tendencies and initiatives on an international scale – was institutionalizing itself. In a desperate attempt to counter and bid halt to this progress, the Soviet leadership came to a decision typical enough of the Party-state. On 17 January 1980 Sakharov was called to the Prokuratura where a colonel, with curt ceremony, read him the official decision to strip him of all medals and awards (including the thrice-awarded Order of Hero of Socialist Labour), and exile him to the town of Gorky, 130 miles due east of Moscow and off limits to all foreigners, to Apartment 3, Gagarin Avenue, 214. He was to be alone, without a telephone, with only his wife permitted to visit him and a KGB sergeant posted in the corridor outside his door day and night. His exile had begun.

*

343

The fourth session of the Sakharov hearings took place in Lisbon, Portugal in October of 1983 under the honorary presidency of Mario Soares, the prime minister of Portugal, and supported by all political parties of the country with the exception of the Communists and extreme right-wing monarchists. The hearing consisted of contributions presented by witnesses late of the Soviet Union under four thematic heads: the situation of Andrei Sakharov (in the light of his exile in Gorky), the suppression of intellectual freedom in the Soviet Union, the situation in Poland, the situations of workers in the USSR. Of these the most important to the present purpose is the last since it continues the examination of 'the workers' paradise' on its own terms begun at the Sakharov hearings session in Washington four years earlier.

Appearing at the Lisbon hearing as a witness was the general practitioner Semeon Badash, who had emigrated from Moscow the year before. Badash gave a thorough account of the conditions of medical workers in the Soviet Union. There was the wage scale for qualified physicians which has remained unchanged to this writing: for the first five years of practice a doctor receives 110 roubles a month, for the next five years 120 roubles a month, for the third pentad 130 roubles, for the fourth and fifth pentads 140 roubles which is the maximum wage. For a registered nurse the scale runs from 80 to 125 roubles a month over the same period of service. To put this in perspective, Badash quoted some current consumer prices: a pair of women's boots costs 130 roubles, a pair of men's shoes 45 to 50 roubles, the price of a coat runs from 120 to 200 roubles. Because of creeping inflation and the permanent wage-freeze, doctors and nurses are obliged to work at half wages for another three hours a day, that is, for nine hours instead of six hours (half-time instead of time and a half for overtime). But worse still this growing discrepancy between wages and prices has worked the drastic diminution of non-skilled or semi-skilled help in the hospitals and clinics. The women beyond retirement age who used to supplement their meagre pensions by helping out at the hospital no longer do so, for lack of incentive. This has affected the already catastrophic labour shortage in the public health service most adversely. There is no help to be hoped for from the fact that by Soviet law a physician may practise privately in his free time, because there is no place to house or shelter his practice (he cannot maintain a practice in the cramped conditions of his apartment and the law prohibits his using state premises and facilities to this purpose).

Badash also dwelt upon the notorious chronic shortage of medicine in the Soviet Union. He described a monthly 'list of unavailable medicines' issued to doctors by pharmacists which contained more than 150 items, mainly antibiotics and strong medicines for arteriosclerosis and the like. Badash also made a point of the almost ubiquitous lack of Röntgen plates. The list was always growing. He cited an article that had appeared a few years ago in the *Literaturnaya Gazeta* reporting a lack of the simplest medicines for heart disease in the Tartar Republic capital of Kazan, while some of these medicines – such as validon – remained plentifully stocked in warehouses. The Soviet minister of health reacted to this crisis in the most typical Soviet fashion, sending an order to all pharmacies to note the names of all doctors prescribing unavailable medicines for penalty and possible prosecution.

In answer to the question of why it was that the Soviet Union was unable to provide an ever-increasing list of needed medicines in satisfactory quantity, Badash replied that the Soviets manufactured penicillin in great quantity but that the mass of Soviet patients had long since developed immunity to penicillin. Whereas in Western countries research had produced and continued to produce a wide variety of antibiotics to overcome such immunity, the Soviet pharmaceutical industry had failed to do this. This was a chief reason for the fact that the infant mortality rate in the Soviet Union is three times higher than in Western countries.

Finally Badash touched upon the sorest point of all. There existed, he said, within the ministry of health yet another ministry called the fourth chief directorate. This directorate has its own unlimited budget, its own network, closed to the public, of poly-clinics, hospitals and luxurious rest-home-sanatoria. This ministry-within-a-ministry was established to serve the Soviet élite. It disposed over all the necessary medicines, its installations were provided with every comfort – single rooms with telephones and colour televisions and instead of the usual tasteless hospital fare there were menu-cards with a restaurant selection of delicacies.

In stark contrast to this the final section of Badash's reports also dealt with 'professional diseases', that is, those caused by exposure of workers to gases, irradiation, excessive noise, chemicals and to generally unsatisfactory factory and workshop conditions. These, as described, were so bad that Jean-François Revel, the eminent French publicist and member of the hearing's jury, proposed making available the reports just heard to the International Labour Organization. Badash's report was one of an even dozen on the subject, but it was central to the discussion because it dealt with the physical and psychological consequences of primitive or distorted working conditions throughout the Soviet labour scene.

The Fifth Sakharov Hearing took place in London in April 1985 under multiple sponsorship (there is a small galaxy of human-rights organizations and Sovietological study groups in London) and concentrated on 'The Development of the Human-Rights Situation in the USSR in the Ten Years Since the Signing of the Helsinki Final Act'. Of the thirty contributions made during the two-day conference three are of special interest to this account. The first has to do with the 'rising mortality rate in the USSR'. The author, Dr Allan Wynn, points out that the death rate from all causes has been rising progressively in the USSR since 1966.

Accordingly, in a characteristic reaction to this embarrassing state of affairs, the Soviet Union in 1972 stopped publication and transmission of its mortality data to the World Health Organization. Even so, by using isolated and scattered Soviet sources it has been possible to reconstruct a record over the intervening years with, presumably, high accuracy. The picture that emerges has been accepted by both Western and Soviet samizdat experts. It shows the life expectancy of men in the USSR falling from sixty-six years in 1966 to sixty-two years in 1983 as compared with seventy-one years for men in the USA. Particularly worrisome is the consistently regressive trend in the USSR and Eastern Europe, which contrasts with positive stability in Western Europe and a progressive trend in the United States. The great killer in the Soviet Union in the twenty-two-year period under scrutiny was heart disease (hypertension) where the incidence of deaths therefrom increased from 24.7 in 1960 to 55.1 in 1982, an increase of 125 per cent. During the same period the incidence of such deaths in the United States decreased by 25 per cent. 'A joint Soviet–American study has shown that in European Russia more than 30 per cent of the male population have high blood pressure compared with 11 per cent in a comparable population sample in the USA, and that the proportion receiving adequate medical care in the USSR is below 10 per cent, far fewer than in the USA.' Dr Wynn then sums up:

The relation of these data to human rights issues is indirect. The standard Soviet response to alleged violations of human rights in the USSR and the socialist countries is that their peoples have surrendered individual rights for collective economic and social rights – the right to work, housing, education, medical care, etc. This argument cannot, in my view, be sustained: human rights are indivisible. The data concerning mortality in the USSR suggest that if indeed a bargain has been made, it is a very poor one.

The second contribution concerns 'Soviet Postal Restrictions' by Vladlen Pavlenkov, and throws a revealing light on the lengths to which the Soviet authorities were prepared to go in order to hold contacts between Soviet citizens and the rest of the world to an absolute minimum. 'In 1979–82, due to a series of measures implemented by the authorities,' reported Pavlenkov,

very few things could be sent through the post from the USSR to the rest of the world ... Limitations were placed on the sending of records and books, by the levying of export duties and the necessity of receiving special approval from the authorities; many books were completely excluded from mailing permission. When posting any package abroad, the sender must present his passport, and he is limited to sending only one parcel per year. In addition, the package can only be sent from the postal agency closest to the sender's place of residence.

In order to limit the parcels sent to their citizens as of 1 August 1984, the Soviet authorities have refused to accept duty-prepaid packages. This had been allowed since 1956, when agreements were made between the Vneshposyltorg Agency and private Western companies located in various parts of the world. This action resulted in serious losses of convertible currencies by the USSR (as much as $10–15 million according to our estimates; some estimates are two to three times higher), and demonstrated the importance that they place on limiting foreign contacts.

The USSR, however, has not had the effrontery to terminate completely direct mailing of parcels. (This would violate agreements between governments, as opposed to those made with private companies.) But steps have been taken by the authorities to limit such activities even more. In September 1983 the Soviet Union significantly increased customs duties for the recipients of international parcels. The fees for most articles were increased by two to three times, thereby becoming too excessive a financial burden for the receiver and forcing him to request that his friends and relatives

347

stop sending these parcels. (For example, duty on new corduroy trousers – 50 roubles; sheepskin coat – 250 roubles; 1 kg of instant coffee – 15 roubles.)

In addition the Soviet authorities have demonstrated an increasing tendency towards flagrant violations of postal regulations, such as theft of articles, or returning parcels to the sender without due cause. This is particularly directed at those individuals whom the authorities have designated as 'untrustworthy', i.e., dissidents, 'refuseniks', relatives of political prisoners and so on. These are also the people who are the first to have their letters intercepted. But in the last two or three years this tendency has affected the average citizen as well . . .

On 13 August 1985 Leonard Sussman, the director of Freedom House, sent a registered letter to the exact address of Andrei Sakharov's exile residence in Gorky as part of a campaign to break through Sakharov's isolation. On 30 June 1986 Sussman filed an 'inquiry about a registered article' with the United States Postal Service (such claims must be filed within one year from the date of mailing). On 9 July 1986 Sussman received an advice from the USPS informing him that American postal authorities were required by international agreements to allow up to five months to respond to an inquiry on a registered article. On the same date Sussman received a letter from the general manager of Freedom of Communications, Vladlen Pavlenkov, who is identical with the author of the contribution on postal restrictions in the USSR at the Fifth Sakharov Hearing in London cited above. To judge from its masthead, Freedom of Communications is predominantly concerned with the mysteries and vagaries of the Soviet postal system. From the correspondence involved it is obvious that Freedom of Communications was the organizer if not the originator of the letter campaign to Andrei Sakharov. In his letter Pavlenkov informed Sussman that despite the existence of a return receipt signed 'A. Sakharov' in Cyrillic under the English words 'Thank you', Sakharov had never received the letter. The signature was a forgery. Proof of this was a letter from Elena Bonner to that effect (photocopies of the forged receipt of Bonner's letter were attached).

The dilemma of the Soviet postal system in connection with mail addressed to prominent dissidents was great. Even without benefit of an organized campaign the Sakharovs received several thousands of letters a year over the last decade at least. The Party-state, which allowed itself so much and denied itself so little, could not allow itself to interdict Sakharov's incoming correspondence. There was always the constraint to make some sort of shift to comply with international postal regulations. With outgoing correspondence, of course, it was a different story. But even here restraint of some kind was indicated. Igor Ogurtsov, the conservative nationalist dissident who spent some twenty years in camps and exile, wrote an average of five letters a day – it was his chief occupation for years on end – in answer to his own selection of those he had received. And in some cases, at least, he was able to determine that his letters had been received.

This dilemma, like many others inherent in Soviet policy, was treated comprehensively in the third contribution selected from those made at the Sakharov hearing in London, a contribution concentrating on the development of the human-rights situation in the USSR in the forty years since the founding of the United Nations. This was 'The Sakharov Case and International Law' written by Paul Sieghart, an eminent British jurist, and is worth quoting:

> Every society, large or small, must have laws in order to be able to conduct its affairs. Every modern nation-state therefore has its own internal laws, sometimes called 'national', 'domestic', or 'municipal' laws. But the world's nation-states also constitute a society among themselves, and that society too needs laws of its own. So, for many centuries there has been a system of 'international' law, designed to regulate the relationships between sovereign states. But for most of those centuries, international law consistently refused to take any cognizance of national laws, or of the relationships between the public authorities of a state and its individual inhabitants. Indeed, the whole concept of national sovereignty meant that all such things were matters for the exclusive determination of each sovereign state, and could not be the concern of any other state or of international law.

This meant that something had to be done about national lawlessness. 'The essential characteristic of the atomic bomb is that it is national.' So spoke Couve de Murville in 1958 when France, with little or no help from its major allies, invented its own atomic bomb. This statement meant two things: one, that the possession of the atomic bomb had become the signal of national sovereignty and two, that any possessor-nation would do anything in its power

349

to keep its atomic secrets to itself. But the statement also had a disturbing corollary: should the atomic bomb come into the hands of a group of terrorists, that group would automatically acquire the attributes of nationhood in terms of its own capability – of lawless nationhood capable of blackmailing any nation with the threat of an atomic strike. More than a decade before the Fifth Sakharov Hearing terrorist groups had already succeeded in black-mailing governments merely by taking a few hostages. This meant that Colonel Gadaffi, for example, would not be allowed to come into possession of the atomic bomb by whatever means. Suspicion of his imminent acquisition of the same would trigger his annihilation. Even without such suspicion the continued machinations and terroristic forays of the Libyan revolutionary councils resulted in the infliction of disciplinary punishment in the form of the American air-strike on Tripoli and Benghazi. But it also meant that the United States of America and the comity of industrial nations could not accept the Soviet Union in its Stalinist form or even – *à la longue* – in its post-Stalinist form.

All this came about because the semantic thrust of the discovery of the atomic bomb was that still more terrible bombs could be invented (bacteriological bombs, for example) by any industrial nation. The question of the Super, the hydrogen bomb, was posed almost simultaneously with that of the atomic bomb: Oppenheimer's fate was sealed by the very fact of his success. The race for the Super compelled the foreclosure of international tolerance (or what little there was left of it) of the lawless, eccentric, unpredictable aggressor nation equipped with 'final-solution' weapons. In 1952 Senator Brian McMahon, Democrat of Connecticut, co-chairman of the General Advisory Committee, 'secretly proposed a peace of widening deserts: the United States must get the Super first, then progressively destroy each nation about to do so' (*Lawrence and Oppenheimer*, by Nuel Pharr Davis). Here there was no need to resort to the secret proposals of Senator McMahon. On 21 May 1947 the senator had proposed most publicly a world assembly of all peace-loving nations to adopt the American (Baruch) Plan for international control of atomic energy. He declared then that any nation refusing to accept the plan after a certain period of grace would be 'denominated an aggressor'. He went on to assert that 'for the first time in human history the failure to agree to a sane, effective and righteous control of a weapon of war constitutes in and of itself an act of aggression.'

This is not lastly the significance of Sakharov. His fate was also sealed by the very fact of his success. For the fact of his success impelled him to ponder its meaning, and the magnitude of his achievement set the dimensions of his concern – necessarily about humanity as a whole. Sakharov became concerned about the planet. This was the sense of his warning that a *rapprochement* with the Soviet regime before it had adopted meaningful measures of democratization would be a danger for mankind.

At the Fifth Sakharov Hearing Paul Sieghart calls it ironic that the doctrine of international tolerance of absolute national sovereignty was finally toppled by Adolf Hitler and Josef Stalin. 'The atrocities which they perpetrated against millions of their own citizens,' he writes,

> truly 'shocked the conscience of mankind', and helped to precipitate a world war of hitherto unprecedented dimensions and ferocity. But those atrocities also made the absolute doctrine of national sovereignty untenable in international law ... Something had to be done to ensure that, in future, mere national *legality* could not be enough to validate even the most monstrous Acts of State. Somehow an international standard of legitimacy had to be installed, by which one could assess the conduct of a national government not only in its external affairs, but in its domestic ones also.

This, unfortunately, is noble nonsense. World War II was precipitated by the rapacity afield of Adolf Hitler. It began only when he upset the comity of nations by annexing Austria, destroying Czechoslovakia by incorporating the Czech lands in a protectorate and setting up a puppet Slovakian Republic (after the Munich agreement had betrayed Czechoslovakia into releasing the Sudetenland to Germany in order to secure 'peace in our time') and finally – the last straw – by invading Poland. The outbreak of World War II had nothing whatever to do directly with the atrocities the Nazis inflicted on their own citizens. And what finally moved the Allies to act in terms of international legislation was the evident interplay between lawlessness at home and lawlessness abroad after this home truth of political science had been thrown into an entirely new light by the advent of the ultimate weapon, the nuclear bomb. Without the atomic bomb, the vaccination provided by the syllogism of the Nuremberg judgement, namely, that individual accountability predicates individual rights, would not have taken.

'And so, in the course of a few brief decades,' continues Sieg-hart,

> there was emplaced in the world's international legal order an elab-
> orate structure of what we now call 'human-rights law', comprising
> the Charter of the United Nations and the Universal Declaration of
> Human Rights; the twin International Covenants; the European
> and American Conventions; and a whole mass of more specific and
> detailed treaties dealing with different aspects of human rights,
> several of them establishing international organs with jurisdiction
> to interpret and apply them, either generally or in specific cases . . .
> What human rights now *are* is conclusively determined by the
> content of the international code, and any violation of that code by
> the public authorities of a nation that is bound by it becomes a
> matter of *legitimate* concern for all other nations and their inhabi-
> tants, so that their interests can no longer be dismissed as 'an
> illegitimate interference in the internal affairs of a sovereign state'.

There can be no doubt that Sakharov was risking his life in
making such a statement when he warned against a *rapprochement* with an undemocratized Soviet Union. But only just. The
Party-state could have charged him with high treason, tried him
according to Soviet law, found him guilty and had him executed.
But in order to pursue such a course the Soviet government would
in effect have had to overturn the whole of the international
human-rights legislation, renounce its still-fresh signature of ratification of the relevant covenants; re-declare the cold war, that is,
and accept all the consequences of such an act – first and foremost
the abandonment of all hope of credits, trade or any sort of economic cooperation from the West. And it was late: by this time,
1973, the Soviet economy was already critically diseased. Finally,
such an act would have signalled the Soviet Union's determination
to proceed on the path of world conquest by the use of arms or the
threat of the use of arms. In other words, by taking such a course
the Soviet Union would have branded itself as just such a lawless,
unpredictable aggressor nation which the existence of the atomic
and hydrogen bombs has made internationally intolerable.

On the domestic front such a course would have meant the re-
introduction of Stalinism, a policy that would have been more
painful to the Central Committee than to the scientific community,
as outraged as the latter would have been by a like turn of events.
It is improbable in the extreme that the Soviet Union would have

chosen to risk a show trial under such circumstances, and a secret trial would have whipped world indignation into a fury. Thus the risk Sakharov assumed by taking his stand was minimal – theoretically. To such an extent had Soviet power meanwhile been circumscribed.

And yet this very impotence led to extremes of harassment by the Party-state against Sakharov. During his near seven years' exile in Gorky, Sakharov spent 294 days alone in hospital (only ten of these – one treatment – were 'voluntary'). He suffered the horror and humiliation of force-feeding during his two hunger strikes (here, ironically, the government's *raison d'état* solicitude for his survival degenerated into brutality). Sakharov emerged from this ordeal with his health broken. He would have suffered less had the Soviets felt free to dispose of him in classic Stalinist fashion.

XV

※

BEFORE THE FALL:
ODDMENTS AND ENDINGS

The Soviet Union invaded Afghanistan on 27 December 1979. By the end of the year Sakharov was granting rapid-fire interviews to foreign correspondents in Moscow in which he condemned the invasion unconditionally. On 17 January of the new year he was stripped of his medals and awards and exiled to Gorky. This, like the decision to invade Afghanistan, was a Politburo decision. The opening of a hot war with Afghanistan brought back the cold war with the West in a rush. Within three months the Americans announced their boycott of the Olympic Games in Moscow, scheduled for that summer, and asked their allies and other nations to follow suit. Thirty-six nations did so, among them the Federal Republic of Germany – not among them Great Britain. Moscow's action in Afghanistan sealed the fate of the Soviet Union as far as its receiving 'most-favoured-nation' status from the United States was concerned and with it – via retaliation – the fate of the great majority of Soviet Jews who had applied for an exit visa for the purpose of emigration.

The exile of Sakharov was totally illegal according to Soviet law. There was no trial or any other form of court action. Sakharov was exiled by decree – as he could have been under the tsar. The only regular communication Sakharov had with the outside world was through his wife, Elena Bonner, who thereafter until her arrest, trial and sentencing on 10 August 1984 to five years exile in Gorky, acted as a courier shuttling between the apartment in Gorky and the apartment in Moscow. She held press conferences in Sakharov's stead in the apartment until the Soviet authorities refused correspondents access. Thereafter she met Western correspondents on street corners, handing them Sakharov's statements and answering questions. Among the first of such statements was Sakharov's announcement of solidarity with the boycott of the Moscow Olympic Games, together with his expression of deep sympathy in connection with the unsuccessful attempt of the Americans to liberate the hostages in Iran. By the fall of 1982 as she records in her book, *Alone Together*, Elena Bonner had made over one hundred round-trips between Moscow and Gorky. It was, in fact, in the fall of 1982 – 25 September to be exact – when she made a special trip from Gorky to put her Moscow flat at the disposal of Anatoly Shcharansky's mother, Ida Milgrom (the purpose was a press conference to announce the beginning of Shcharansky's hunger strike on 27 September), that she discovered the apartment was no longer available for press conferences or interviews of any kind. The militia were there to block access to all except residents of the building.

In the autumn of the preceding year, 1981, both Bonner and Sakharov had gone on a seventeen-day hunger strike that worked the release for travel outside the Soviet Union of Lisa Alexeyeva allowing her to join her husband in Boston. Lisa had married Elena Bonner's son Alexei by proxy that summer.

As for relations between the American and Soviet scientific communities, the president of the American National Academy of Sciences had sent telegrams, as already noted, on 8 September 1973 warning the Soviets that 'harassment or detention of Sakharov will have severe effects upon the relationships between the scientific communities ... and could vitiate our recent efforts toward increasing scientific interchange and cooperation'. With the coincidence of the invasion of Afghanistan and the exile of Sakharov to Gorky, the Soviets made it easy for the Americans: the exchange programme between the two academies of science were suspended forthwith. But hardly more than four years later, in the spring of 1984, a representative of the American National Academy of Sciences was in Moscow negotiating the resumption of the exchange with the Soviet Academy. It is important to note that meanwhile nothing had changed. The Soviet invasion army was still laying waste to Afghanistan and Sakharov was still in exile in Gorky. How came this? Here are the basic elements of the calculation made and acted upon by the Soviets: the practice of systematic deception while relying on the short memories and greed of investment bankers and businessmen, and the political frivolity of nonce majorities in popularly and frequently elected governments. The point is that the notoriously short memories of the Western democracies are institutional. An equally important point is that the 'wasteful shifting tendency of short immediate policies under a system of government by bodies elected for short terms' (Galsworthy) is made to order for the sensationalist Western media. So the Soviet government was about to pocket the gain of resumption of the scientific exchange only four years after the indignant American rupture of the same. 'In the fullness of time' (four years) the American scientific community simply came around to accepting the new status quo (as the Soviets – who never budged – had been certain they would).

But no sooner was the resumption of the exchange announced than Sakharov went on a hunger strike – this time to move the Soviet authorities to allow Elena Bonner to leave the Soviet Union for badly needed medical treatment abroad. The American National Academy of Sciences was acutely embarrassed by the timing of these events (as well it might have been) and announced a month or so later that the exchange just negotiated would be postponed until the Sakharov case (by this time a full-blown international scandal) had been clarified.

In exiling Sakharov the Soviet Party-government had only one purpose in mind, that of breaking Sakharov's contact with the outside world, specifically with foreign correspondents (they no longer needed to be 'Western' correspondents: a Hungarian, a Polish or a Yugoslav correspondent would have done just as well). This, of course, was a one-way break in communications: Sakharov could receive, but not send. He had a radio, a television set, but no telephone. He received, even in Gorky, a good deal if not a great deal of mail. But his letters, cards and telegrams from Gorky – as a rule – were carefully screened. In this regard as in others Sakharov's exile can be compared to Galileo's genteel imprisonment in embassies, palaces and villas – *toutes proportions gardées*. To compensate for the lack of splendour, Sakharov enjoyed more freedom of movement, although he was closely watched at all times; he had his automobile and pretty much the run of the city, at least in the first few years of his exile. But what Sakharov had not had, of course, was a trial: he had not been given the benefit of due process of any kind. Galileo had received the full treatment –

he had been duly tried by the highest court of the highest authority in the land he had chosen to live in (or *almost* duly tried: as recounted, the propriety of the procedure against Galileo is still under contention). And Oppenheimer had had his 'review'.

In the period immediately following the exile of Andrei Sakharov to Gorky the KGB unit in charge of the operation was not so well organized as it might have been. Because of this, the physician and long-time friend of the Sakharovs, Natalya Hesse, arriving in Gorky within a week after Andrei Dmitrievich, managed to spend a full month with the Sakharovs (Elena Bonner coming and going the while) in their new 'home'. Of course, all concerned assumed, correctly, that the Sakharov apartment in Gorky was a veritable sound studio, where every breath and sigh would be distinctly audible through the microphones concealed throughout the premises. One of the tasks undertaken by Natalya Hesse was that of sorting the voluminous mail that followed the Sakharovs to Gorky, several hundreds of letters having already accumulated in the apartment. When she had completed her task, Hesse, without thinking of her concealed audience, blurted out: 'Listen – this is terribly interesting: 70 per cent of these letters are favourable, 17 per cent are neutral or puzzled and only 13 per cent are abusive!' As of the next day the favourable or otherwise supportive letters were no longer found in the deliveries: only the abusive and defamatory letters continued unabated.

But perhaps nothing else (certainly not the Soviet invasion of Afghanistan) could have demonstrated so starkly the obtuseness of the Soviet leaders and the nature of the political entity they represented as their decision to exile Sakharov to the 'forbidden city' (to foreigners) of Gorky. The Soviet Party-state acted not by due process of law but, as usual, arbitrarily and by coercion. For extended periods no one – aside from a few Soviet officials – knew where the Sakharovs were. The son of Mrs Sakharov, Alexei Semeonov, publicly offered a reward of $10,000 to anyone who could manage to contact the Sakharovs or establish their whereabouts.

In his article 'Russia and Reality', dated 8 November 1978, Sakharov describes the human-rights movement in the Soviet Union and its Eastern European satellites. 'I note,' he writes,

> that one of the forms of reaction by the powers that be of these countries to the absolutely lawful and constructive position [of the

human-rights movements] is the infringement by these powers themselves of their own laws, especially in court trials and in the increasingly broad use of underground methods of provocation and even of terrorist methods directed against individuals inside and outside the country. In their turn the anti-legal actions of the powers that be strengthened the legalist orientation of the dissidents.

Seen in this light the abduction of Sakharov by the Party-state was merely the crescendo of the forms of reaction by the powers that be in the Soviet Union to the unrelenting pressure of the human-rights movement, strengthened in turn by that reaction. But the fact that the dissidents in the Soviet Union were able to put the Party-state in a position in which it was forced to defend itself by resorting more and more to illegal means is highly significant in itself. It could not have happened if Soviet legislation had not been unlawful or unlawlike in the first place. This account has shown how such cornerstones of traditional jurisprudence as formal rules of evidence and uniformity of legal procedure were simply jettisoned during the October Revolution in the course of the general rejection of due process as a bourgeois relic. In effect, the whole body of the law was dismissed as a figment of the economically determined concept of the ruling class, as a mere class concept – and was replaced by a new class concept. Article 5 of the Bases of Civil Legislation (1968) states that 'civil rights are maintained by law with the exception of cases in which their realization stands in contradiction with the designation of such rights in a socialist society during the period of the construction of Communism.' This is a purely political basis of judgement. It has nothing to do with legality.

What this comes down to, then, is that everything not expressly permitted (or ordered) is forbidden – law takes on the form of a specific obligation. In Roman law, as in natural law, everything not expressly prohibited is permitted. The aspect of specific obligation – the concept of law as a framework of specific obligations outside of which everything is forbidden – is extraordinarily restrictive. It is all the more restrictive being in common with the concept of central planning, which is a highly selected set of economic goals and time frames of an exclusively obligatory nature – outside of which every initiative is forbidden. It would be more relevant to reverse the comparison: 'Soviet law' is the central planning of human conduct overall. The codification of 'economic crimes' in the Soviet Union is a consequence of the anathematization of private enterprise following the seizure by the state of the means of production.

The basic concept of human rights, namely that a human being has rights by virtue of being human – regardless of the society he lives in or the state of which he is a citizen – is foreign to both the Soviet and the Russian way of thinking (and not only to the Soviet and Russian way of thinking). Valery Chalidze makes the point in his report to the Human Rights Committee that in a despotic form of government, of which the Russians and their neighbours have had so much experience, the citizen or subject is liable to perceive even the most natural action on his part as something permitted, particularly when it is regarded, as it must be, against the background of an enormous slate of prohibitions. This is a point that adds a whole new dimension to the confrontation of the ideas of a command economy and of free enterprise. With such an inborn attitude the command economy may look like safe haven; and free enterprise, on the other hand, may look like a hopelessly unfair challenge or perhaps simply as an evil, dishonest way of life. The Russian psyche is associative, but the *Weltanschauung* that emerges is not one of free but of set associations.

In one of his last acts as Soviet foreign minister, Andrei Gromyko requested an audience with Pope John Paul II in 1985. Gromyko's purpose was to plead with the Pope to persuade Ronald Reagan to cease and desist from his stated purpose and fixed policy of constructing a defence against rockets and ballistic missiles in space. When John Paul, astonished, protested that he had no such powers of persuasion, Gromyko contradicted him with the words: 'You can do it if you really want to do it!' Here, in Gromyko's adjuration, was the admission of defeat, of the breakdown of Communism that was taking place all around him. How far a cry from Stalin's famous question – 'How many divisions has the Pope?' – of only forty years earlier. Here was Andrei Gromyko, hat in hand, begging the Pope to intercede with Ronald Reagan because the mighty Soviet Union could not keep up with the mightier United States of America in establishing an anti-nuclear defence system in space – an attempt to eliminate the nuclear bomb by making it obsolete. The Strategic Defence Initiative (SDI) was the last straw because it threatened to remove the one weapon that made the Soviet Union, for all its faults and third-world backwardness, the military equal of the most powerful nation on earth. The Soviet Union has already lost 'the struggle going on for the hearts and minds of billions of people on our planet', to use the phrase of Yuri Andropov. In the Soviet Union as in the Third Reich the separation of Church and state led to the fusion of Party and state. In both cases, Russian and German, the Party failed as an institutional support and inspiration for the state. And now Sakharov, Solzhenitsyn and many another dissident were demanding the 'separation of Marxism from the state'. (The demand for the separation of Party from state is tantamount to a demand for the abolition of the one-party state.)

'A lazy nation,' wrote Thomas Carlyle, 'may be changed into an industrious, a rich into a poor, a religious into a profane, as if by magic, if any single cause, though slight, or any combination of causes, however subtle, is strong enough to change the favourite and detested types of character.' By any such reckoning the Communist experiment in the Soviet Union has been a disastrous failure. In this sense there is an affinity between the figures of Josef Cardinal Slypy and Raoul Wallenberg as towers of moral strength on the one side and the figures of Stalin and Pavlik Morozov (the eleven-year-old boy who denounced his parents as traitors and in so doing delivered them over to the executioner) as monsters on the other. Stalin, as a figure, had to be rejected by the Party on grounds of its own survival and Morozov, as a 'favourite' type of character, stood and fell with Stalin. (In recent years a large number of schools in the Soviet Union have refused the name and rejected the tradition of Pavlik Morozov.) And with Morozov, as a 'favourite' type of character, stood and fell the *stukach*, the secret informer, the denunciant false friend on whom the whole system turned. The *stukach* is not to be compared with the bourgeois stool-pigeon, long since reduced to the function of a police-informer and, as such, not an exclusively detested figure, at least not outside the underworld (see the semi-affectionate abbreviation 'stoolie' – there is no abbreviation for *stukach*). But Pavlik Morozov was a police-informer in the bosom of the family and set against the family; he was, in fact, the dire destructant of the family, an impossible figure conceivable only against the background of unadulterated utopia, a *Schlaraffenland* in which everything is perfect (only such a vision could justify the *raison d'être* of Pavlik Morozov), a material situation so idyllic as to advertise at each turn the cause it represents as the holy of holies, overriding every other conceivable consideration. This was an utterly illusory pre-condition. One is reminded unerringly of Sinyavsky's definition of socialist realism as in need of a religious art 'of pure invention and fantasy within agreed forms'.

But the same idyllic precondition, the same presupposition of utopia immanent and ultimately achievable was the only possible justification for Stalin. When Stalin died his system died with him. There was no candidate for the succession capable of assuming the role he played. There could have been no such candidate. Stalin himself had created his role and the conditions that made it pos-sible. By the same token there could have been no regency or remission of intra-Party blood-letting against the advent of a suit-able candidate. It was here, in the second instance, that the Central Committee of the Party rejected Stalinism out of hand. There were 500 men or so at the helm of the Soviet state who were determined not to work and live in fear of the knock on the door at midnight. That determination was the beginning of some kind of democratic process in the Soviet Union. For it was then that the denouement, the unravelling of Stalinism and its ancillary suppositions began. Where the unravelling began, precisely, is of critical significance. Philosophy, for example, had ceased to be the 'handmaiden of theology' only to become, under Stalin, a mere instrument, un-deserving of the adjective 'theoretical', for the justification and indoctrination of ideology. This, in turn, under the label of *partinost* or Party spirit, was anything the Party leadership said it was. It was, in fact, the demiurge which created or abolished facts that conferred existence on men and events or else annulled them in the making and remaking of history. There were no criteria of any kind, a vacancy most obvious in the area of jurisprudence and more especially in the criminal code, where any point could be stretched to cover any requirement in Stalin's 'broad punitive policy', as Chalidze in his report to the Committee of Human Rights calls it. Thus it was here that, after 1953 (the year of Stalin's death), many of the features of Stalin's punitive policy were removed by the state, aware as it was that far greater atten-tion would have to be paid to the norms of procedural practice. In other words, the post-Stalin reform in the Soviet Union was begun most urgently in the field of criminal law to introduce or re-introduce the principle of due process.

Although much was done, much remained to be done; the criminal code and punitive procedural practice remained the Augean stables of the Soviet Union. After the fall of Khrushchev in 1964, his successor as secretary general, Leonid Brezhnev, set out to quash the dissident movement that had come with Khrushchev's reforms. The criminal code, for all its remaining faults, was pressed into service again as the campaign of dissident-prosecution went into full swing. It was only natural, then, that the *pravozashchitniki* (literally 'defenders of the law' but perhaps better rendered as 'defenders of due process') should spring up in various quarters. The insistence on due process was the informing spirit of the Moscow Human Rights Committee founded by Sakharov, Tverdo-khlebov and Chalidze in 1970, but the insistence of the committee did not stop there. 'The purpose of the committee,' wrote Chalidze,

is not to expose and demand but to study and recommend, and that means an activity which includes the consideration of tradition as well as the reality of existing difficulties ... In the face of this the committee must be prepared for the fact that its pious wishes will have to wait years for realization. The recognition of this fact should not become the source of a sense of frustration and use-lessness because the purpose of the committee is above all to make a contribution to the development of juridical culture in society: intensive progress in the area of the defence of human rights can be hoped for only as a consequence of the growth of juridical culture among the people, including those who wield power.

Part and parcel of the *pravozashchitniki* or due process movement was the samizdat publication of the *Chronicle of Current Events*. The first issue of this remarkable publication appeared on 30 April 1968. It ran fifteen typewritten pages and contained, exclusively, information on people recently or long since arrested along with their presumed or known place of incarceration, the conditions of incarceration, the articles of the criminal code according to which the arrests had been made, etc. The *Chronicle of Current Events* was the unofficial journal of the human-rights movement. It sprang into being, as its first editor, Natalya Gorbanyevskaya, has said, because the idea of such a journal 'was in the air', the idea of keeping book on the excesses of the regime in its application of the criminal code. It was only fitting, then, that in New York in 1974 Valery Chalidze should become editor and publisher of the *Chronicle of Human Rights in the USSR*, an English-language counterpart of the Moscow *Chronicle*.

It must be said that the Soviet Party-state went to great lengths to suppress the *Chronicle*. There was good reason for this: the *Chronicle* had become something like the life-blood, the circulatory system of the democratic movement. By 1972 it had grown from some fifteen pages to more than fifty pages and included reports from all over the Union. By the same token its scope had expanded; the journal had become a mirror of the struggle between the Soviet regime and the democratic movement; the KGB's efforts against the *Chronicle* were duly reported in succeeding issues of the *Chronicle*. The KGB developed a good deal of imagination in trying to crush it. Anyone found with a copy on his person or in his or her apartment was as good as bound over. Indeed, the KGB made a practice of threatening to take hostages among the close relatives of those concerned or suspected of being concerned (the effect on those actually concerned was the same) for every number of the *Chronicle* that appeared after delivery of the threat. Also on the cover page of every issue was a quote from Article 19 of the covenant of civil and political rights: 'Every man has a right to the free expression of his opinion; this right includes the freedom to seek, receive and distribute all kinds of information and ideas without regard to government borders by word of mouth, in writing or by means of the press or artistic forms of expression, or other means according to his choice.' In January 1974, when it looked like the democratic movement had indeed been crushed (the *Chronicle* had not appeared in almost two years), Tatyana Velikanova, Sergei Kovalev and Tatyana Khodorovich issued a statement describing the KGB's attempt to suborn their cooperation. In May – this time at a press conference held in Andrei Sakharov's apartment – the same trio handed Issues 28, 29 and 30 of the *Chronicle of Current Events* to assembled Western correspondents, and made a statement:

> Since we do not consider, despite the repeated assertions of the KGB and the USSR court instances, that the *Chronicle of Current Events* is an illegal or libellous publication, we regard it as our duty to ensure as wide a circulation for it as possible.
>
> We believe it is essential that truthful information about violations of basic human rights in the Soviet Union should be available to all who are interested in them.

By the end of the seventies the *Chronicle* had attained a volume of some 200 pages. It had long since served as a model. The Ukrainians had their own *Chronicle* and so did the Lithuanians. There were national movements to match these publications and national movements without publications among the Volga Germans, the Crimean Tartars and the Jews as a supra-territorial nation. And this was what the Kremlin feared most. (Sergei Kovalev was tried in Vilnius as a founder of the *Chronicle of the Lithuanian Catholic Church* on 9 December 1975. Sakharov was outside the Vilnius courthouse trying to attend the trial. It was the day before he was awarded the Nobel Prize for peace.) Quite clearly forces were gathering – national, moral, traditional; all clamouring for basic changes in the Soviet system. That part of the system under constant fire from the opposition precisely because it was the chief weapon of the system in times of peace was its legislation – Soviet law. Ironically, it was the nuclear bomb, as Oppenheimer predicted, that enforced a world peace over several consecutive decades – forty-four years at this point of narration, a span of time so great as to make the periodical reproclaiming of a state of ideological emergency in the Soviet Union implausible. A basic Soviet stratagem was the identification of the enemy outside (the capitalist–imperialist antagonist) with the opponent inside (the dissident). This stance was inevitable in view of the absolute Leninist intolerance of opposition, a fact that not only provided but protruded the linkage of the internal opposition with the foreign enemies of the state. In short, it was a self-fulfilling prophecy, a catch-all for the counter-revolution. It made a matter of course of the outright damning of any dissidence as espionage and treason. A society stripped for combat looks all the odder as time goes by and no combat is forthcoming. In this sense the protracted peace was debilitating for the Soviet Union: it turned the machine against itself. It made for doldrums that excited both the internal opposition and the state security forces. And so the stand-off continued. But it continued until it became a state of transition: transitions do not last.

It is difficult for a Westerner to comprehend the totality of Soviet domestic control. The collective, which involves every place of employment, is the government's supreme instrument of control. One does not have to be a government spy or a member of the KGB, or an informer by mission, commission or cooptation.

Members of the collective are government spies by virtue of their membership in the collective. Soviet administrative law (Paragraph 2, entitled 'The Classification of Soviet Government Employees') authorizes the ministry of the interior and the KGB to enlist the cooperation of any person working in a state enterprise. Since all enterprises in the Soviet Union were owned by the state, this meant everybody. Every employee in the Soviet Union could be called upon at any time to divulge anything the government wanted to know about any colleague, friend or relative. And what an employee did not already know he or she could be forced to find out. If an employee was discovered to have wilfully withheld any information wanted by the state, he or she could be reprimanded and prosecuted accordingly.

The practice of enlisting the entire population as active or passive spies, and most especially when choosing citizens for the high privilege of travel abroad, formed the official attitude to the reverse phenomenon, namely travellers to the Soviet Union. In the Soviet Union all tourists are spies. In Western democracies the situation is exactly the opposite. There the profusion of freedom makes clandestineness look like privacy. It is easy to carry out espionage in the West because clandestineness receives the same sanction as privacy. Precisely because they are so much involved in it, few citizens of genuine democracies have any clear notion of the extent, significance or consequences of the great freedom they enjoy. In the American–Soviet cultural exchange programme the American authorities have never protested actions of the Soviet participants. These actions would certainly come under the heading of espionage in the Soviet Union, but they are not regarded as espionage in the democratic West. In America all spies are tourists.

Not only did the Soviets shun an open exchange of information with all foreign countries but, as a fundamental means of establishing total control over their population, they placed their own country in something like a permanent communications quarantine. Sacrificing the general concept of currency in its entirety, the Soviets sought to control the flow of all information, going and coming: going, in order to influence public opinion in foreign countries; coming, in order to receive whatever intelligence they deemed necessary from foreign countries (by means of espionage). This practice was modelled on the barter system in trade, barter in its simplest form being a closely controlled bilateral exchange. The

Soviets use espionage to compensate for their lack of an open exchange with the outside world (to make up for the absence of the market – be it the market of goods and services or the market of ideas); in short, they give and get information without the embarrassment of free communications, which the system would not tolerate.

In fact, the Soviets had expanded the concept and systematized the practice of espionage into the field of communications at large. By way of this substitution, espionage became the basic principle of Soviet intercourse in every respect – commercial, cultural, scientific as well as military. Witness the frequently occurring group expulsions of Soviet diplomats in the late seventies and early eighties from other countries on charges of conduct not in keeping with their diplomatic status. This was why Anatoly Shcharansky was a spy (to name one for many), like the foreign journalists with whom he was in contact). It is why Stalin arrested and executed stamp collectors whether or not they were in correspondence with stamp collectors abroad ('guilty by analogy'). It was why, statutorily, any Soviet author receiving royalties from abroad was guilty of a currency violation. It is why, for that matter and as already mentioned, the rouble is not a currency. Finally, it was why the Soviets had such an obsession with espionage. Espionage was the Soviet way of life.

The above exposition will help, it is hoped, to point up the extraordinary role and importance of the KGB in Soviet society. The Jesuits, when they became the 'thought-police' of the Roman Catholic Church, inevitably took on some of the attributes and adopted some of the attitudes of a police force. Conversely the KGB, proceeding from the opposite pole and assuming 'the priest-like task/Of pure ablution round earth's human shores', took on some of the attributes and adopted some of the attitudes of a priesthood. The KGB interrogation became, or was meant to become, in its psychological and sociological function a form of confession. The result in the Soviet Union is perhaps best described as a priest-ridden society in which the priests were particularly meddlesome and given to conniving and intrigue. In both cases – Church and Party – those concerned were more or less convinced that what they were doing was for the best. Particularly so, perhaps, when they intervened – as they constantly did – in family matters. The popular acceptance of Party (KGB) intervention in family matters was surely the underlying sense of the myth of Pavlik Morozov. But it is just this meddling in the most basic of social units that makes it impossible to assess or analyse social relations among dissidents, their families and friends with any hope of reasonable accuracy. To be specific: it is sometimes said that the children of Sakharov's first wife, Klavdia Vikhireva, rejected the entire Bonner family as interlopers after the marriage of Andrei Dmitrievich and his Lusia. Certain it is that the children and relatives of Sakharov's first wife were KGB targets to at least the same extent as were the children and relatives of Elena Bonner, and that enmity with the Bonner family was the main thrust of the KGB's intervention with the former. It is also averred that the children and relatives of Sakharov's first wife, in stark contrast to those of Elena Bonner, have no interest whatever in the human-rights struggle. Certain it is that this is the version of the KGB, which must have gone to some lengths to ensure that no interest was shown by Sakharov's first wife's children and relatives. They can have had no easy time of it – which is probably the reason for Sakharov's deliberate screening of this part of his life ('We have very little contact; but that is my fault, not theirs'). For this reason no attempt has been made in this account to delineate and assess the relationships between Sakharov and his own relatives and those of his first wife unless these appeared to be of overriding importance.

There is only one incident on record in which Andrei Sakharov, the mildest and most good-natured man one can imagine, lost his temper and resorted to force. His opponent and tormentor was the official 'writer' Nikolai Nikolaievich Yakovlev, the author of the book *The CIA Against the USSR* and similar works. The book was serialized in the Soviet magazine *Man and Law* (circulation 8.7 million) and later in the magazine *Smena* (circulation over a million), in both publications passages concerning Sakharov and more especially those concerning Elena Bonner, were carefully selected and emphasized. It was an out-and-out hatchet-job in which Sakharov was portrayed as the naïve victim and Bonner as the corrupt and avaricious CIA agent. ('Sakharov's entire holdings in the USSR have long since been appropriated by Bonner.') Hereupon the Sakharovs brought a libel suit against Yakovlev and the magazine *Smena*.

One day during his exile in Gorky while Sakharov was alone, two total strangers, a man and a woman, appeared at his apartment. Under the prevailing circumstances Sakharov at first assumed that the two were a pair of physicians who had come to examine him. He consequently asked them in and offered his hospitality. At this point the man introduced himself. 'I am Nikolai Nikolaievich Yakovlev. As you know, I am a writer – or perhaps you don't know. I have brought you my books as a gift, and if you like, I'll write a dedication in them for you.' Sakharov was thunderstruck. When he recovered his wits he said, 'I don't need your presents,' and gestured so violently that he swept all the books, which had been stacked on the table, to the floor. Nevertheless Yakovlev continued, 'Well, you know, I have written several articles and we have received a lot of questions as a result, and I can't answer them. So I have come here to put some questions to you so that we can pass the answers on to our readers.'

Sakharov answered that he would not so much as speak with Yakovlev until the latter apologized in writing for slandering Elena Bonner. 'How could you perpetrate such slanders, write such libel? How could you call our children "dropouts" when they have all completed their university studies?' Yakovlev answered that he was aware of this. 'How could you dare to write that my wife beats me?' asked Sakharov. 'Well,' replied Yakovlev, 'that's what they told me in the office of the public prosecutor.' Finally, after the altercation had reached an impasse, Yakovlev said, 'I will not apologize in writing. If you consider that what I have written is libel, go ahead and sue me. And would you try to understand that we are defending your interests?' At this Sakharov said, 'I don't need your protection, and I won't sue you. I am simply going to slap your face.'

When Sakharov said this Yakovlev tried to cover the left side of his face. But Sakharov struck him on the right side of his face with his left hand. Thereupon Yakovlev and his companion fled the scene, overturning a chair in the process. When Sakharov told this story to Natalya Hesse he compared Yakovlev in his moral degradation and meanness with Smerdyakov, the sycophantic servant-murderer in Dostoyevsky's novel, *The Brothers Karamazov*.

*

Beginning on 24 August 1984 the West German tabloid *Bild Zeitung* released the first of eight videotapes of the Sakharovs (usually of Sakharov alone) made secretly by the KGB in Gorky. The series soon became known as the Gorky Tapes and was sold for hard currency to the *Bild Zeitung* by Viktor Louis, a veteran globe-trotting special-assignment courier for the KGB. The object of the exercise on the part of the KGB was to spike rumours that Sakharov was sick, starving (as the result of a hunger strike), miserable or maltreated. He was sometimes shown being treated in a hospital, often shown eating (with considerable gusto), sometimes at the post office telephoning (with his wife when she called from the States), sometimes conversing with one or another of a husband-and-wife team of doctors. The Gorky Tapes are valuable as an example of Soviet public relations. Indeed the public-relations aspect of the Sakharov case is perhaps the most important of all its aspects. Public relations as a concept includes publicity (good or bad). As far as Andrei Sakharov was concerned, there was no such thing as bad publicity. He had every confidence that the cause would speak for itself regardless of the circumstances. For the Soviet Party-state the opposite was true – there could be no such thing as good publicity. This, of course, was simply the other side of the Sakharov calculatory coin.

Thus the Gorky Tapes were purely a defensive measure, an attempt to disprove the contentions pullulating in the Western press. That these contentions were the inevitable result of the exiling of Sakharov in and of itself never seems to have occurred to the Soviets. Nor does it seem to have occurred to the Soviet leadership that not bringing Sakharov to trial would inevitably put the entire operation in the worst possible light. To be sure, it was an unfortunate time for the leadership: three successive general secretaries died in three successive years – 1983, 1984, 1985 – all of them old, all of them sick, the first of them, Leonid Brezhnev, virtually incapacitated over the longest period – from 1980 at the latest. Thus for some five years the Soviet leadership was headless. The spectacle of three dying men, one after the other, trapped in the public view, tottering from door to chair, waving stiff-armed and glassy-eyed, illustrated as nothing else could have done the dilemma posed by the Soviet succession problem. Perhaps so ludicrous a pratfall as the Gorky Tapes – done in the best tradition of terrorist extortioners and complete with prominently displayed publications to establish the date of the filming – could only have occurred during a time of crisis in the leadership. In any case, the last of the Gorky Tapes was released on 18 June 1986, some fourteen months into Mikhail Gorbachev's tenure as general secretary. In some ways it is the most scurrilous of them all. On this occasion the KGB bugged the Sakharovs' apartment in Gorky and recorded conversations between Sakharov and his wife, who had just returned from a six-month sojourn in the United States, where she had undergone a six-channel by-pass operation. Included on the tape is Bonner's reproach of Sakharov for allowing himself to be drawn into conversations with the KGB for the video camera. This was reproduced as 'sound-over' on the video film of the Sakharovs taking a walk in Gorky. It is to be noted that this last of the Gorky Tapes was made after, and some of it perhaps, during, the Chernobyl catastrophe. Thereby hangs a tale.

XVI

CHERNOBYL

Early in April 1986 Sakharov, who was alone in Gorky, decided to devote himself exclusively to science for a full month and more. During this time he read no newspapers, heard no radio and watched no television. Sakharov was therefore oblivious to the disaster at Chernobyl until members of the Academy of Sciences and the government came to get his opinion and ask his advice (only reasonable since Sakharov is one of the world's leading authorities on the peaceful uses of atomic energy). It was several days after the meltdown of one of the reactors at Chernobyl before anyone came to see Sakharov (a full day lapsed after the accident before the Soviet leadership was informed: at least another day went by before the leadership realized the general dimensions of the tragedy).

Sakharov estimates today that the Chernobyl catastrophe was approximately one hundred times worse than the American incident at Three Mile Island in 1979. 'I spent most of my time in talking to these people, trying to calm them down. They were extremely upset. But the last time one of my colleagues [from the Academy] came to see me was on 23 May, which happened to be the same day the KGB was making secret movies of me. They made me look like a complete idiot!' But this, of course, was a double irony, an irony within an irony. While scientists, Party and government officials were consulting earnestly if not half-hysterically with Sakharov over Chernobyl, the KGB was filming Sakharov relaxing; the secret police working as industriously and as secretly as ever – not for Soviet television by way of showing the nation's greatest authority on the peaceful use of atomic energy in discussion with colleagues during the worst crisis in the Soviet Union since World War II, but rather for foreign consumption only, to show the outside world that the exiled champion of human rights was well fed, well dressed and well disposed, despite a host of ugly rumours to the contrary. The larger irony was that by taking such pictures and purveying them abroad, the KGB was merely adding insult to injury. The better the pictures the worse their reception by the free-world public. And this while Elena Bonner was being received with sympathy and understanding by heads of state, including the Pope, throughout Western Europe. The contrast between the two public-relations styles could not have been greater. The KGB method was tantamount to selling pornographic pictures on street corners to prove a point of statecraft.

And yet the meltdown of one of the reactors at Chernobyl was the greatest and most devastating public-relations coup in peacetime history. It was the fulfilment of the collective nightmare of all those throughout the world who incline or fully subscribe to the anti-humanist point of view. The anti-humanist camp had been poised in anticipation of just such an event ever since the invention of the atomic bomb and the realization of the energy potential of nuclear fission and fusion.

On 22 March 1975 the two nuclear-power reactors at Browns Ferry, Alabama, were forced into emergency shutdown procedures when a fire broke out in the walls of the electrical-cable spreading room located directly under the central control room for the two plants. Here are two excerpts from the book *The Arrogance of Humanism* by David Ehrenfeld, published in 1975:

A look at the tables of 'dominant accident sequences' for the two types of reactors in common use shows that 22 accident sequences are listed for one and 28 for the other. Although some of the failures that occurred at Browns Ferry (such as the failure of the emergency core cooling system) are listed, nowhere is there a mention of the possibility of fire in the spreading room, smoke in the control room, or anything remotely like the combination of failures that actually occurred. 'Common mode failures', multiple failures that result from a single event – as happened so dramatically at Browns Ferry – are supposedly taken into account in the report, but somehow they seem to have gotten lost in the statistics and logic. The report states: 'In general, single system failure probabilities

dominated the probability of an accident sequence and single component failures dominated the system probability.' Yet it is safe to say
that at Browns Ferry almost every system that could have failed did
fail – at least one of the reactors came perilously close to melt-down,
which could have caused a release of radio-active gas over an
unevacuated and unsuspecting population. To those who say, 'Yes,
but it did not melt down and nobody was killed,' we can only
answer that blind luck, not human forethought or action, prevented
a slapstick comedy of errors from turning into a calamity.

Later the same year the US Nuclear Regulatory Commission
published a report entitled 'Reactor Safety Study: An Assessment
of Accident Risks in US Commercial Nuclear Power Plants' which,
to save time and breath, is generally known as the Rasmussen
Report. Ehrenfeld is fiercely critical of the report. He writes:

... In the case of the Rasmussen Report, in addition to ignoring the
risk of insulation and other fires in the spreading room, the danger
from earthquakes was underestimated and sabotage was not even
considered. This did not bother the authors of the Rasmussen
Report, secure in their belief in the almighty power of their logic.
They wrote:

While there is no way of proving that all possible accident sequences which
contribute to public risk have been considered in the study, the systematic
approach used in identifying possible accident sequences makes it unlikely
that an accident was overlooked which would significantly change the
overall risk.

But it is not theoretically possible to judge the importance of things
that have been left out. How can anybody assess either the probability or consequences of an unknown event? And even if this were
possible, how many low probabilities does it take to sum up to a
high probability? Once again we find logic being asked to perform a
miracle, and again we find that logic has its limits.

G. H. Lewes, the husband of Marianne Evans (George Eliot), in
his book *Physical Basis of Mind*, comments on 'the inevitable tendency of analysis to disregard whatever elements it provisionally
sets aside'. In the same book he makes mention of the opposite
tendency: 'Materialism in attempting to deduce the mental from
the physical puts into the conclusion what the very terms have
excluded from the premises.' Basically, however, Ehrenfeld is
confronting the authors of the Rasmussen Report with the same

conundrum that Barberini and Bellarmine used to confound Galileo: the problem of negative proof. The variation in this case would be that 'there is no way of proving that all possible accident sequences which contribute to public risk have been considered in the study' – or in any study. With all agreed on this point, anyway, Ehrenfeld proceeds to a very popular conclusion:

> Nuclear reactors are very complex machines built and operated by human beings. Any unequivocal guarantee of their safety must automatically be suspect, and every week fresh evidence adds to our suspicion and uncertainty about nuclear power. Uncertainty rightly generates emotion, and more and more people, including scientists, are deciding that a rejection of nuclear power based on a general fear of it is the proper course of action. Indeed, the Rasmussen report itself is a response to that fear, and as such its very existence, regardless of its contents, is a sign of danger. Not only is nuclear energy an unknown, but it is a powerful unknown: powerful in terms of the absolute magnitude of its actual and potential effects; powerful in terms of the pervasiveness of these effects; powerful in terms of the duration of its effects and its activity; and powerful in the sense of the secrecy of its action (radioactivity is not seen, smelled or touched, and one or two generations must pass before the cancers and genetic defects that it can cause begin to be noted). This power only enhances our fear of the unknown, and again we are right to be afraid.

Sakharov estimated the dimensions of the Chernobyl catastrophe as approximately one hundred times worse than that of the reactor accident at Three Mile Island in 1979, which was worse than the slapstick calamity at Browns Ferry but did not involve a meltdown or an explosion and left no fatalities or dire consequences as yet discernible. But Chernobyl was a calamity of awesome dimensions. Thirty-one people were killed either outright or as a protracted result of exposure to searing heat and radioactive charges. But hundreds of thousands and perhaps millions of 'an unevacuated and unsuspecting population' in the Ukraine and beyond were more or less severely irradiated by clouds of strontium emanating from the meltdown of the reactor in Chernobyl and drifting over Scandinavia and virtually the whole of Europe – to what possibly dire effect there would be no way of knowing for the next several years. But the damage inflicted upon humanity by the Chernobyl catastrophe was a thousand times greater than any statistic connected with it could possibly show. Chernobyl was the confirmation of the second Fall from grace. It was the end of mankind's innocence – the banishment forever from a second, relative Eden of unknowing bliss. The panic of the population of Western Europe is well documented in the European press, that of Eastern Europe necessarily less so. But overnight tens of thousands of Bavarians, Austrians and northern Italians were in possession of Geiger counters which they used on virtually everything, but especially food – fruit, meat, vegetables, milk and water – to determine the degree of irradiation. The word 'becquerel' (after the French physicist Henri Antoine Becquerel, who discovered the radiation emanating from uranium combinations), introduced as a term for the unit of degree of irradiation, became a household word in Europe. The members of the European Economic Community (EEC) debated the amount of becquerels to be standardized as the allowable limits for food and drink in the Community. For months and even years after Chernobyl, European radio and television broadcast regional incidences of high becquerel counts in venison, fish, fruit, vegetables and milk. A trainload of irradiated milk powder was shunted successively on to half the sidings of the German railway system for months on end before it was finally disposed of. The entire 1986 snail crop bound for France from Poland and Hungary (the chief suppliers) was refused at the border by French authorities because the countries of origin had been too long under a cloud of strontium drifting west from Chernobyl. Prevailing easterly winds in the summer of 1986 wrought havoc in Western Europe, causing the interruption and outright cancellation of tourist and business trips. Tourism especially was hit hard because people were afraid to eat the food of regions they didn't know or knew less well than their own. There were daily announcements in the media calculated to alarm families with children: 'Parents! Do not allow your children to play in the sand!' (France); 'Parents! Do not allow your children to drink milk until further notice!' (Germany). Even tapwater was put on the public suspect list in some areas of Western Europe.

The truth, as it emerged in the Soviet report on Chernobyl submitted by the Soviet authorities to the International Atomic Energy Agency (IAEA) at the end of August in Vienna, was stranger than fiction – if the speculations and alarmed reactions of the European press may be so characterized. The basic cause of the

tragedy, ironically, was a scheme to improve the operational security of the atomic power plant. This involved the test of a procedure
for the extraction of emergency electrical power from one of the
station's two turbo-generating sets. The same test had already
been performed at Chernobyl on two occasions, in 1982 and
1984. This time the test was to be carried out on 25 April 1986
during a routine maintenance shutdown of one of the reactors,
Number 4. The object of the exercise was to bridge a gap that
would occur if a reactor should become accidentally isolated from
the power grid.

One of the most important aspects of atomic-energy production
is the constant need for a properly functioning cooling system.
This is because even shut down reactors need cooling: heat from
the radioactive-fission products accumulates in the fuel. It takes
energy to circulate the water in the system to carry off the heat. In
Chernobyl there was an emergency power plant but it would have
sufficed only to keep the instrumentation control panels and systems operating. It would not have produced enough power to
operate the cooling pumps.

The idea of the test was to use the energy coming from a
decaying turbine set to make up the difference. The difficulty lay in
maintaining sufficient voltage at a constant (6 kV). As desirable as
a solution for such an emergency would be, there is, according to
the Soviet report, 'much discussion in the Soviet Union as to the
necessity of these tests'.

In the event, everything that could go wrong did go wrong.
Beginning at 0100 on 25 April the thermal power was reduced by
half (1,600 MW) by 1400. At that point the Kiev regional con-
troller asked for a delay of the shutdown to meet an unexpected
demand for electric power. The delay lasted nine hours, long
enough to bring in a new and apparently less capable control crew
on the succeeding shift. The test began at 2310 on 25 April with
the aim of reducing power to a range of 700 to 1,000 MW of
thermal power as called for by the plan. To achieve this the
operators switched from the automatic system of regulation to a
local control system, normal procedure under the circumstances.
But then, according to the Soviet report, the first mistake was
made: the operator failed to reset the gauges of the automatic
control system correctly. The result was that the control crew
undershot the power target level to such an extent (less than 30

MW) that the reactor was on the verge of a shutdown. At this point they should have broken off the test. Their failure to do so, says the Soviet report, was a violation not only of standard operating procedures but also of the written test plan.

In their attempts to increase power the operators again switched off automatic control and went back to manual control. This involved withdrawing most of the 211 neutron-absorbing control rods from the reactor – which was another violation of regulations. Regulations specify that the operators should not operate the equipment when there is less than the equivalent of thirty control rods of potential reactivity in the reactor without referring the matter to the chief engineer. This they failed to do, even though the reserve of reactivity was far below this limit. In fact, station regulations also warn that never under any circumstances should operations be conducted with less than the equivalent of fifteen control rods of reactivity at their disposal. At Chernobyl there was at most the equivalent of six to eight control rods of reactivity. 'Nobody,' said the Soviets at Vienna, 'not even the prime minister of the country' could give permission to do such a thing.

And yet the thing was done. The sequence of mistakes that followed include the operators disabling the safety devices that would have prevented a loss of pressure in the cooling system by automatically shutting down the reactor. A few minutes later the staff shut off a set of steam safety valves for the purpose of preventing a further decline of steam pressure. This must have seemed to be a good idea at the time, but the ultimate consequences were calamitous. What the crew accomplished by persisting with the test was the progressive disabling of the entire control system of the reactor. By 0123:20, basically but not only because the control rods at their disposal were too few and too far withdrawn, the men had lost all effective control of the machine. Not only that: they had also deprived the installation of its facilities for automatic shutdown in case of danger. When they pressed the panic button twenty seconds later, the only result was that the cooling water could no longer carry off the heat generated in the fuel. As the heat mounted, the water began to boil and, irony of ironies, the whole water content of the cooling system turned into steam. The tremendous head of steam thus gathered either triggered two successive chemical explosions that blew the roof off the reactor vault and spewed chunks of red-hot graphite and pieces of uranium-oxide fuel on to surrounding buildings and countryside or itself constituted the first explosion and perhaps both, to the same effect. The Soviets say they do not know and the logbook of the power station was contaminated. The exact nature of the explosion, originally described by the Soviets as coming from hydrogen, was very much under contention in Vienna, with the view that the sudden and massive generation of steam was the real culprit in the end prevailing. This opinion raised the question of the reliability of water-cooling for reactors in general.

The record of Soviet authorities in terms of the timely evacuation of the population immediately affected was better than it seemed at first glance. As early as 0600 on 26 April local and neighbouring members of the Komsomol, the Communist youth organization, began distributing potassium-iodide tablets to the 49,000 inhabitants of the town of Pripyat, which borders on Chernobyl, instructing them to stay indoors and not to drink milk. A team of managers from the nuclear industry was formed in Moscow and sent to Chernobyl, arriving there at 2000 on 26 April. One hour later the decision was taken to evacuate Pripyat. One thousand buses were assembled during the next two days to that purpose. The decision to evacuate all 135,000 people from a zone thirty kilometres in diameter centred on Chernobyl was taken only ten days after the explosion. The delay is explained by the continuing release of radioactivity and with it the realization that the rural population was more exposed than city-dwellers were. The children from this zone were taken to summer camps and sanatoria where continuing medical supervision was assured. Of the thirty-one people who ultimately perished from the effects of severe contamination, seventeen died within six weeks. Another 200 were more or less seriously injured. But despite such bright spots as the heroic effort of a brigade of firemen, insufficiently protected from radiation and poorly briefed as they were, in containing and then extinguishing the fire in the fourth reactor, the overall impression made by the Soviets in this crisis was a poor one.

This was not least because the Soviet authorities, as is frequently the case, were much laxer in keeping their own citizenry informed of the tragedy, its course and consequences than they were in informing the outside world. The trial of those supervisors held responsible for the disaster (the trial was held on 30 July in Chernobyl with the victims and their families present as spectators

– the clothing and shoes of each and every one of them having been checked by instruments for radiation before they entered the courtroom) was reported hours after the event by a five-line TASS release destined only for export – not a word of it appeared anywhere in the Soviet press. Nor did Soviet television carry the story.

But indignation broke out in another area of public life in the Soviet Union as a result of Chernobyl: the theatre. With the writing and simultaneous performance by various groups in various cities throughout the Soviet Union of the play *Sarcophagus*, a practice begun with revolutionary élan and ended by bureaucratic pressure in the twenties – that of committing a historical event to drama immediately after its happening – was renewed. But with a difference: this time, in contradistinction to the previous, revolutionary practice of unstinting encomium, the heroic tone so common to Soviet works was missing. Instead the tone was sombre, even funebrial. The purpose of the production was clearly critical.

In the end the head of the power station, the chief engineer and the deputy chief engineer were tried, found guilty of gross negligence and sentenced to ten years in a prison camp. Some of the editorial staffs of official Soviet newspapers were beginning to show independence of mind. This was and is especially true of the *Moskovskye novosti* (*Moscow News*) which was the first member of the Soviet media to carry the results of the trial. But other organs of the press were soon using their more audacious colleagues as references in enlarging upon news items hitherto taboo. There took place a kind of cross-pollination of courage in the official Soviet press. In terms of the democratization of the Soviet media there was still not a mountain but a mountain-range of obstacles to be removed. Even so, the Chernobyl explosion had blasted a pass through the sierra.

One of the themes studiously avoided by the Soviet media was the cost of the Chernobyl tragedy – at home and abroad. The Soviets estimated (for foreign consumption only) the cost of eight billion roubles. This included the continual medical supervision of 600,000 inhabitants of the danger zone around Chernobyl for the next several decades. Dr Robert Gale predicted, as a maximum estimate, that some 75,000 cancer cases (predominantly leukaemia) would result over the next fifty years from the Chernobyl fallout. Forty per cent of these victims would be in the Soviet Union. Clearly enough, no reasonably accurate estimate could be made of the cost to the Soviet Union in terms of their energy production programme or in such imponderables as the loss of prestige internationally and, of course, more particularly at home. In the case of Sakharov's particular nightmare, that is, genetic mutation caused by radiation, the estimate ranged between zero and 5,000 victims.

In terms of foreign damage, Italy paid the equivalent of $441 million in damages to farmers whose crops were ruined by the fallout from Chernobyl. The Federal Republic of Germany paid 460 million marks to the same purpose, Sweden the equivalent of $54 million, Britain some £10 million. In Norway and Sweden an estimated 40,000 to 70,000 reindeer had to be slaughtered when they became contaminated by grazing on moss and plants registering a becquerel count from 10,000 to 20,000. In north-eastern Sweden alone the flesh of an estimated 25,000 head of livestock was unfit for eating for the same reason. In Turkey, the entire tea crop for 1986 had to be destroyed because of contamination. The list could be extended considerably.

As it was, the question of claiming damages from the Soviet Union was raised by the West Germans as soon as radioactive fallout was detected in Bavaria six days after the explosion in Chernobyl. It quickly developed, however, that there was no way to obligate the Soviet Union to pay such damages. According to the Paris Agreement dated 29 June 1960 concerning liability *vis-à-vis* third parties in respect of nuclear energy, a nation is liable for damage inflicted on the territory of any contractual partner arising from a nuclear incident taking place on its own sovereign territory. However, the Soviet Union was not a party to this agreement. Neither was the Soviet Union a party to the Vienna Treaty of the IAEA dated 21 May 1963, to the same effect concerning nuclear damage. It also developed that there is – as yet – no such thing as an internationally recognized conception of damage, a fact that imparts a clear impression of the state of international law in the first place. Thus, notwithstanding the great progress made in codifying human rights in terms of international law, the bulk of the problem of creating an effective international community still lies ahead.

The chief beneficiary of the Chernobyl disaster was the concept, policy and programme of *glasnost*. Another beneficiary was the International Atomic Energy Agency in Vienna. The meeting at which the Soviets presented the agency with their report on Chernobyl resulted in thirteen substantive suggestions for improvement on reactor safety the agency should pursue. By November 1986 the Supreme Soviet had approved two new conventions of the IAEA formulated in the light of the Chernobyl tragedy. And yet the Soviet Union ratified the treaties only in part. A special reservation was added to the effect that the USSR does not consider itself bound by the provisions of Article 11.2 of the Convention on Prompt Notification of a Nuclear Accident, nor by Article 13 of the Convention on Assistance in the Event of a Nuclear Accident or Radiation Emergency. Both these provisions refer to the submitting of any eventual dispute to arbitration or to an international court at the request of any side. The Soviet Union insisted on the same veto rights it enjoys as a founding member of the United Nations, stating that the consent of all sides must be obtained before any such submission can be made. By such rearguard action the Soviet Union managed to preserve a fig-leaf of its nuclear sovereignty.

The most fruitful bed for the deadly seed drifting in the winds from Chernobyl was the European ecological movement, using this term in its broadest sense. Over a period of several years and especially during the second half of 1985 in Western Europe, most particularly in West Germany, Switzerland and Austria, the public outcry had increased in stridency over the pollution of the atmosphere, the dying of forests, the poisoning of crops and then, well before the close of the year, the discovery in Switzerland and Austria that the very soil had been fouled by toxic wastes over extensive tracts. All this against the background of the pollution of European rivers by tributary cloacae from chemical plant and septic outlets, the disposal of toxic waste in the ground and in the sea, the fall of acid rain, etc. Perhaps the most striking picture of devastation over a twenty-year period had just been spotlighted underwater off the Côte d'Azure for a television programme by Jacques Cousteau. In Europe, in the five years before Chernobyl, never a day passed that some form of protest against pollution was not registered, particularly on television. Indeed, the emergence of the 'Greens' as political parties in West Germany, Switzerland and Austria (in both West Germany and Switzerland the Greens had entered parliament) remains the most conspicuous and substantial manifestation of ecological concern. The controversy in the European Economic Community over the introduction of the German catalysator, German production of environment-friendly auto-mobiles and the discount sale of non-leaded petrol for the purpose of reducing the toxicity of exhaust fumes was another case in point. In Sweden the government established a ministry of ecology, a move that was an example for other Western countries (West Germany followed suit a year later). It would be difficult to over-emphasize the importance of the pollution issue in Western Europe, the attention it publicly demanded and received, particularly in the industrial nations.

In the immediate aftermath of Chernobyl the Greens in West Germany and Austria increased their electoral standing by from six to eleven percentage points. Programmatically the Greens in Germany demanded the total rejection of nuclear power and the immediate shutting down and dismantling of all nuclear reactors. The German Social Democratic Party included the demand for the rejection of nuclear power in the party programme, but only over a period of ten years, regarding immediate shutdown and dismantle-ment as impractical and harmful to the economy (well over 60 per cent of West German energy is produced by atomic reactor). This was a panic reaction. Throughout German-speaking Europe there ensued an acutely heightened sensitivity to any accident or even irregularity in nuclear plant anywhere. (Here there is a bizarre discrepancy between Germans and French: the French are as good as utterly unconcerned over atomic energy – whether in the form of electricity or explosive – even though the French are far more dependent on nuclear power than are the Germans, 90 per cent of their industrial energy being nuclear-derivative. As a result of this sensitivity – and insensitivity on the French side – Europeans have been treated to the spectacle of Germans demonstrating on French soil over some announced, fairly minor defect in a French atomic installation, while the mildly curious French looked on. But the French are the exception.) Throughout Western Europe, thanks to Chernobyl, atomic power has become the symbol of pollution at large. The atom has become a symbol enveloping the whole of the ecological argument, blotting out every other consideration such as the energy quotient of the atom *vis-à-vis* the same amount of anthracite or bituminous coal (about 10,000,000 to 1) or the fact that pollution as it has come to be known in the industrial West is exclusively the product of non-nuclear sources of energy.

In the East, on the other hand, an almost totally different picture presented itself. In the Soviet Union the studied neglect of the very concept not to mention the practice of plant maintenance is immanent in the Soviet system. The Soviets have run roughshod over all such considerations as amenable working conditions and displayed a remarkable unconcern for the consequences of unending crash-programme production methods – such as the slighting of physical security precautions. It can be argued that, taken in its entirety, the anti-ecological nature of the Soviet system is the underlying cause of the general Soviet economic disaster. In any case it is that aspect particularly of the Soviet system that has given rise by reaction to the whole spectrum of conservationist, political, civic, cultural and artistic developments. The *vorozhdentsy* (adherents of the 'Russian national and religious renaissance'), the *derevenshchiki* (ruralist school of writers), the All-Russian Society for the Preservation of Nature and the widespread and numerous groups organized for the preservation of historical monuments are overlapping parts of the same general, conservative national movement.

The ecological situation of the Eastern European satellites of the Soviet Union is not markedly better. Indeed, a small, highly industrialized country like Czechoslovakia is certainly far worse off. Among German foresters Czechoslovakia has become known as 'the morgue of European forests': the ridges and upper reaches of the Erzgebirge and the Riesengebirge have been as bald as the mountains of the moon for some ten years now. What is worse, even Czechoslovak attempts at reforestation failed almost out of hand because of increasing pollution. There are enough natural reserves of coal in Czechoslovakia to last another fifty years at foreseeable rates of consumption. Unfortunately Czechoslovak coal contains a high percentage (10 per cent) of sulphur and the government contends that no funds can be budgeted for the construction of desulphurization works. Meanwhile the all-out drive to increase industrial production continued to enjoy top priority in Czechoslovak central planning.

The ecological plight of Poland was (and remains) likewise desperate. Early in September 1985 the correspondent of the French daily newspaper *Figaro*, Bernard Margueritte, wrote an article in which he described 'the catastrophic condition of the environment in Poland'. In the ensuing controversy with the Polish government Margueritte quoted excerpts from a discussion by experts published in the Polish weekly newspaper *Polytika*. In part, to the following effect:

> What is the psychological mechanism involved in the anti-ecological decisions taken by those responsible in these various areas? They are members of the same population, they take sick and die of the same civilizational and ecological maladies albeit, certainly, less often because they live in better conditions ... These ecological barbarians are everywhere but they are found most frequently in the echelons of technocracy. (*Wierbicki*)

Further in the discussion Professor Kozlowski revealed that the Institute of Marxism–Leninism had recently occupied itself with 'the problem of the menace looming over the working class as a result of environmental conditions'. Indeed:

> The principal threat to the Polish population concerns precisely the working class because it is above all the working class that lives in the twenty-seven ecological danger zones ... There are countries which, between 1993 and 1995, will reduce their emissions of CO_2 by 50 per cent. These are the Federal Republic of Germany and France ... but the situation is completely different in the Eastern bloc. In the German Democratic Republic as well as in Czechoslovakia and Poland we have programmes for the augmentation of CO_2. In these conditions, in the not distant future, Europe will be divided into two blocs fundamentally different from one another, a fact that will have very important consequences with regard to a host of economic problems. The dirty part of Europe will be confronted by a number of export barriers. The West will not wish to buy our dirty food products, our dirty automobiles, our dirty petrol, etc.

Professor Wierbicki then summed up:

> The lack of faith in the juridico-ecological domain and the failure to take punitive measures against those who infringe the laws protecting nature have assumed the dimensions of a national defeat for us.

The discussion ended on a sad note uttered by the vice-minister of environment, Zarek:

> It is evident beyond doubt that if we have destroyed Poland's environment during the last thirty years and most intensively during the last ten years, the process of reconstruction will not take less time.

384

This was the atmosphere, the sentiment and the outlook in the bloc countries in the winter before the black spring that brought Chernobyl.

It was not until the third day, Tuesday 29 April, that the Soviet government informed the West what had happened – at least twenty-four hours after ducks began dying for no apparent reason on Swedish ponds and Swedish technicians began to register radiation ratings indicative of the fallout resultant from a nuclear explosion. On the fifth day after the explosion, 1 May, the usual May Day parade was held in Kiev, which was well within the exposed and endangered area. After the passage of a full week the world was informed that two men had died, twenty were on the critical list and another twenty in 'serious' condition. Two hundred people were reported hospitalized.

The most important result of the Chernobyl disaster was the impression it made on the Soviet people as a whole and on the people resident in Chernobyl and the surrounding area, including Kiev, in particular. The impression was one of betrayal. For the people concerned were a classic example of 'an unevacuated and unsuspecting population'. Chernobyl brought with it the people's discovery that they had been kept in ignorance of the danger involved over the years and over the hours when they were left unevacuated and unwarned while receiving doses of irradiation that would prove to be fatal or disabling in later years. 'Why didn't they tell us?' was the question most frequently asked. The second most important result was that the catastrophe presented proof of the incompetence and unfeelingness of the authorities. It was a demonstration of the most convincing kind that the people on top did *not* know what they were doing. This realization effectively broke the ages-old hold of authority on the Russian soul. Chernobyl broke the spell under which the Russians had lived for a full millennium. 'Why, they treat us like children,' was the general reaction. The eternal *status infantis* of the Russian towards the state was recognized by all and sundry and rejected. The people could not trust its leaders, a fact that was illustrated every day that passed by the frantic attempts on the part of the authorities to regain control of the situation: they couldn't put the fire out in the fourth reactor for almost a full week while throughout there was danger of a meltdown in an adjacent reactor; irradiated

385

topsoil for miles around the installation had to be removed – at fearful risk for all concerned, some of whom were said to have been dragooned into the work, others reportedly deceived into believing there was no risk involved.

Above all, however, Chernobyl was the all-convincing argument for *glasnost* – freedom of thought, freedom of speech, freedom of communication, open-ended publicity in public affairs. It was this both domestically and in foreign affairs where the Soviet Union's notorious tradition of obsessive secrecy compounded the inevitable confusion surrounding such an occurrence and sowed suspicion unfoundedly. Indeed, the Western press had a field-day of vaulting speculations on the dimensions and true nature of the tragedy, a fact that infuriated the Soviets and added still further to the confusion. The Swedish press, stung by the failure of the Soviets to give timely notice of the catastrophe to a next-door neighbour, pronounced that the Russians were simply too uncivilized and uncultured a people to cope with so sophisticated a procedure as nuclear-energy production. As stated, the German government officially demanded compensation for ruined crops in Bavaria and Lower Saxony and suspended imports, especially of food and drink, from the Soviet Union and its satellites (just as Professor Kozlowski, cited above, predicted). But, again, the greatest alarm voiced by the Western democracies concerned the lack of information – especially the absence of an on-the-ground estimate of the damage real and potential stemming from the accident – the lack of international *glasnost*, so to speak. In connection with the absolute necessity for timely information in such matters came the ecological consideration. This is simply overwhelming in both the national as well as international sense. Ecology appeals directly to the strongest of human instincts, that of self-preservation. The nation, as the largest practicable ethnic–economic governmental unit, must be allowed to order its house in keeping with its immediate and lasting, life-and-death environmental interests. But in order to do so it must make allowance for the interests of its nation-neighbours far and near. Nowhere is Sakharov's dictum that 'there is no really important problem in the world today that can be solved at the national level' so cogent as in the general area of ecology. Here the tragedy of Chernobyl forced the issue of international cooperation. The days of Soviet secrecy on an international plane were over. Forever. The comity of nations, out of the instinct of self-preservation, were constrained to insist – by way of an ultimatum – that the Soviet Union provide all the necessary information as quickly as possible. The president of the International Atomic Energy Commission arrived in the Soviet Union just one week after the accident for consultations with Soviet authorities.

For their part the Soviets had no choice but to comply. There was the realization, which came with the first shockwave, that they, the Soviets, were now more dependent than ever on cooperation with the Western democracies. This recognition effectively closed the circle of defeats the Soviet Union had suffered in its attempts to secure and dominate relations with international agencies: there was the long struggle of Lysenkoism with the World Health Organization, the bitter controversy over the practice of confining political prisoners in psychiatric hospitals ending with the forced withdrawal of the Soviets from the International Psychiatric Association, the struggle to uphold the system of internal passports in direct violation of one of the cardinal conventions of the International Labour Organization, which ended provisionally with the Soviets being censured by that organization, the controversy over socialist realism with the international network of PEN clubs which brought that organization's retaliation of granting honorary membership to most if not all Soviet writers in exile. All this had to be viewed against the background of the covenants on human rights adopted by the General Assembly of the United Nations Organization on 16 December 1966. This was the historical point of departure of the human-rights movement in the Soviet Union and the Eastern European satellites. And it received an all-important confirmatory boost when the Soviet Union was constrained by general circumstances to ratify the covenants on human rights in 1973. The Helsinki Agreements were part and parcel of the same process, as were the follow-up conferences and the various Helsinki Watch Committees *et al.* And now the Soviet Union was being called to account before the International Atomic Energy Commission for the worst and deadliest mishap ever recorded in the nuclear-energy field. This was a language Everyman could understand – even those for whom talk of human rights was so much philosophical maundering: Chernobyl put the Polish Professor Kozlowski's message into clear-text – 'Would you rather be red *and* dead?'

For a while the Soviets tried to fight back on the public-relations front, charging the Western press with wilfully gross exaggerations of the damage caused by the explosion at Chernobyl, pointing out that 140,000 people were evacuated from Three Mile Island (needlessly, as it developed, since only a modicum of radioactive gases escaped from the installation), while the report on the American mishap was three months in coming, etc. But all this was of no avail. It merely made the Americans look good by comparison.

On the other hand, a very considerable amount of sympathy was generated in the West by the calamity. Dr Robert Gale, a specialist in bone-marrow transplantation, was sent from California under the auspices of the inevitable Armand Hammer to treat Soviet patients suffering from the effects of radiation. This was the obverse side of the fear of radioactive contamination, namely the desire to help the stricken Soviet Union and the identical twin of that desire, the realization that cooperation with the Soviet Union in all matters concerning the production and use of nuclear energy was imperative. This same concern and consideration categorically included nuclear weapons, but it also did more than that. It made it clear that in an industrial area laced with atomic plants such as the whole of Europe and the Soviet Union and North America had become, there could be no such thing as a merely conventional war. In any extensive artillery barrage or aerial bombardment an atomic installation of some sort was bound to be struck, damaged or demolished, whereupon that hideous strength would be loosed upon mankind – regardless of precautionary measures and contractual forbearances. The Soviets were among the first, naturally enough, to draw this conclusion, having just demonstrated that an atomic peace might be just as devastating as an atomic war, or that the difference between the two might well turn out to be – in terms of the humanity of it all – negligible. As a result the traditional truculence of the Soviets *vis-à-vis* the outside world changed over the next few months to the monitory reminder that 'We are all in the same boat.'

The tragedy at Chernobyl forced a whole series of foregone conclusions. In the first place it made a foregone conclusion of the disarmament negotiations between the Soviet Union and the United States resulting in meaningful agreements to curtail and reduce both production and stockpiles – if not indeed to eliminate them entirely in some categories. And this in both nuclear and conventional arms categories over what, historically regarded, would prove to be a comparatively short period. In the second place it guaranteed the persistence of the liberal reform movement under Mikhail Sergeievich Gorbachev. In the third place the accidental release of strontium at Chernobyl prefigured the deliberate release of the man who was largely responsible for the strontium, Andrei Sakharov, from Gorky. The accident at Chernobyl symbolized all the issues that Sakharov had harped on for twenty years and more. Chernobyl was the synecdoche (in which a part speaks for the whole) of the breakdown and bankruptcy of the Soviet system, the Soviet myth overtaken, exposed and destroyed by a cloud of strontium.

XVII

GLASNOST AND *PERESTROIKA*
WRIT LARGE

When Mikhail Sergeievich Gorbachev became General Secretary of the Communist Party of the Soviet Union in March 1985, he inherited a problem that almost defies description. It was, in fact, a vast complex of problems that had been steadily building for at least sixty-eight years. For one thing, he found himself in charge of a nation with 40 million officially acknowledged alcoholics, and the number was growing. In 1983, 11.7 million – one-eighth of the Soviet labour force – were arrested at one time or another on charges of drunkenness. In his first hundred days Gorbachev introduced laws increasing the penalties for alcohol abuse, but his most draconian measure was raising the price of a bottle of vodka 200 per cent, to 9 roubles, and cutting back the production of hard drink by 60 per cent. Alcoholism, however, was a problem the Soviets had inherited, untroubled, from tsarist officialdom. One quarter of government revenue in the year 1903 was provided by the state spirits monopoly established in 1894. This gave the treasury a vested interest in the production of spirits for popular consumption and thereby in the perpetuation of drunkenness, particularly in the countryside. But what had been the acknowledged bane of the peasantry became the acknowledged bane of all Slavs in the Soviet Union. In 1982 the per capita consumption of alcohol in the Soviet Union had more than doubled, to about 16 quarts per year, from 7.5 quarts in 1955. In 1983 the US Census Bureau reported that the death rate for alcohol poisoning in the USSR was eighty-eight times higher than in America.

In 1982, for another thing, after the fourth poor harvest in a row, a special commission reported a tenfold increase in Soviet food imports over the past ten years, 'staggering levels of mishandling of agricultural equipment, catastrophic losses in harvesting and in procurement of all crops – amounting to 20 per cent in the case of grain and 33 per cent for potatoes – and a diet that was significantly below medically recommended standards'. The report offered no prospect of improvement.

The official statistic for the annual per capita consumption of meat and meat products in the Soviet Union was 57 kilograms in 1977 whereas, according to the Academy of Medical Sciences, the level of sustenance necessary for the normal physical and mental functioning of the individual adult requires an annual per capita consumption of 81 kilograms of meat and meat-derivative products or their protein equivalents. This made for a shortfall of some 30 per cent. It is hardly a question of not having meat on the table once a day, writes Lev Timofeev in his book, *The Peasant Art of Starving*, nor is it a question of having meat as often as once a week among the rural population. The rural rule is to have meat on holidays only. This works out in the best of cases at about half of the national statistical average annual per capita meat consumption.

This deficiency takes its toll in various ways. On an average, children and adolescents in rural areas are from 10 to 20 centimetres shorter than their compeers in the cities. There is also the downright tragic consequence mirrored in the statistic that among village youths between fifteen and nineteen years of age the incidence of fatal cases of 'psychic aberration' is three times higher than in the cities and towns.

In the Soviet countryside, continues Timofeev, only 17 per cent of the populated areas have water sources that are rated by the authorities as of good quality. Seventy per cent are rated as 'satisfactory', while 13 per cent are found to be 'saline or polluted'. The average family in the city uses the equivalent of 150 litres of water a day. But every second rural family is obliged to carry its water home from a source more than 100 metres distant and every tenth rural family must fetch its water from a distance of more than two kilometres. The result, as Timofeev sums it up, is that the average citizen of rural Russia 'does not know the taste of pure water'. And then he cites Kosygin who, at the time he was prime minister, wondered about the habitual mass exodus of youth from the villages.

But the chief, the overwhelming concern of Timofeev in his remarkable book is theft. In the first place, he says, theft in the Soviet Union cannot be couched in statistics. In the second place it is not at all a matter for punitive justice. Theft, especially in village life, has become a profession by main force of circumstance. Without the practice of this profession it is impossible to survive. Theft makes up the commerce of the black market. Now the private plots of the kolkhozniki are well known to be an indispensable part of the Soviet collective farming system, supplying anywhere from 30 to 50 per cent of the entire agricultural produce, excepting only grain and beef. The private plots, in fact, are small farms under intensive cultivation. In order to run a small farm, as Timofeev points out, an entire inventory of hardware is prerequisite. But where to get such basic necessities as nails, rope, wire and the like? In the stores there is nothing for sale except buckets and shovels. The only possibility, then, is to steal the various necessities from the kolkhoz, which has everything. This is because the kolkhoz has its own supply system – it is part of a supply network from which it receives items and articles that are not – anywhere – for sale. Hence, if the kolkhoznik and his family are to survive, these things needs must be stolen. The children, says Timofeev, do not know what it is to steal. They hide the milk in the kolkhoz so that it can be picked up on the sly later and taken home (much of the theft is practised through the agency of children, a sort of collective Fagin syndrome); for them it is like a game of 'hot and cold'. But the grown-ups do not know what it is not to steal. In the Soviet Union there is no legal market of goods and services necessary to the running of a farm. Instead there is a flourishing market of stolen goods.

Timofeev returns at the end of his discussion of theft in the Soviet Union to the sombre statistic concerning village youths between fifteen and nineteen years of age whose mortality rate from 'psychic aberration' is three times higher than that of the comparable age group in the cities and towns. Could it not be, he asks, that the sensitivity of this age group is heightened still further by the gaping discrepancy between the ideal inculcated upon them daily and hourly by every means at the disposal of the state and the reality that stares them in the face at every turn? Could it not be that this acute sensitivity of the late teenager registers all too painfully the lie which the child cannot yet perceive and to which the adult has already become inured? 'If,' writes Timofeev, 'a person is forced day in, day out to violate the generally accepted moral norms, if the sermon he hears daily in no way conforms and cannot conform with the only possible conduct, then either words lose their imperative meaning or they tear apart the psyche of the individual concerned, they destroy his personality.'

As already indicated Gorbachev also found a critical public health problem. This manifested itself principally in a rising rate of infant mortality. Unquestionably, the steeply rising consumption of alcohol and tobacco had much to do with this, but another salient cause is the annual total of 10 million abortions in the Soviet Union. The average Russian woman has six abortions performed in her lifetime. This is twelve times the average in the United States. One of the chief causes of this sad record is the fact that in the Soviet Union abortion is virtually the only available means of contraception.

But the worst news was that the Soviet Union had passed the turning-point in its development as an industrial state – the transition between extensive mass production in heavy industry and the new intensive high-technology, quality production necessitated by the computer age. In terms of intensive high-technology production, the Soviet Union was working against itself, being fundamentally, structurally, sociologically and psychologically wrong for this kind of work.

In the spring of 1983 there appeared a thirty-eight-page paper written by A. T. Zaslavskaya, a member of the Academy of Sciences for the Study of the Economy at Novosibirsk. Beginning with the fact that for the last twelve to fifteen years the 'economic development of the USSR has exhibited a tendency toward a perceptible decline in the growth rates for national income' (from 7.5 per cent to 2.5 per cent), the paper examined the causes of this decline and quickly concluded that the 'state management of the economy' (exhibiting a 'high degree of centralization of . . . decision-making') is fundamentally, qualitatively and generally unable 'to ensure completely an efficient enough utilization of the working and intellectual potential of society'. The original (and still prevailing) system was intended for a 'comparatively low level of development of working people' and 'proves to be incapable of regulating the behaviour of workers who are more advanced in individual attitude and economically free' (Soviet workers change jobs frequently and had, at that time, more than 200 billion roubles in savings banks – a considerable problem in itself; they had nothing to spend their money on). Obviously, wrote Zaslavskaya, 'the existing system of production relations has fallen considerably behind the level of development of production forces'. And this at a time when the imperative need to change the economy over 'from an extensive to an intensive path of development can be done only by making use of all existing social reserves, of all the creative potential of the workers'. Then the blow fell. 'The posing of these problems,' continued Zaslavskaya, 'presupposes a profound restructuring of state economic management, that is, specifically the abandonment of administrative methods with a high degree of centralized decision-making and the consistent comprehensive transition to economic methods of production regulation.'

This was clearly a call for a market economy. It was a question, therefore, of the very existence of the Communist system. It was then more than twenty years since Nikita Khrushchev promised and threatened to 'bury' the Americans, confidently predicting that the Soviet gross national product would be greater than that of the United States by 1980. Instead, the Soviet public was presented with a catalogue of the multifarious ills that afflicted the Soviet body economic, sociological and politic – and affected them chronically, as it turned out. The catalogue had been public property for almost twenty years, having been the cause for the 'major' economic reform under Leonid Brezhnev in 1965. The Brezhnev reform accomplished nothing except the setting of a style for economic reform, including Andropov's 'reform' calling for increased worker and managerial discipline and greater general effort. The situation had steadily worsened over the intervening twenty years. Corrective measures that might have proved adequate then were by no means adequate 'now'. The huge investments in agriculture from the mid-seventies on were, according to experts, exactly half enough and hence 'not half enough' to produce reasonable returns.

Worse still, there was a historical factor hard at work: the Soviet Union was undergoing a 'demographic squeeze' of colossal proportions. In the sixties there was a growth birth rate of 17.8 per thousand; in the eighties it had already fallen to 8 per thousand, thus representing a reduction of more than 55 per cent over a period of twenty years. In the seventies 24 million workers entered the production process; in the eighties it was to be – on projection – hardly more than 6 million, a reduction of 75 per cent over a period of ten years. At the same time – and this was a crowning irony – the Soviet Union supported a very large army of 'hidden unemployed'. Communist doctrine demands that full employment be secured at all times and at all costs. This exaction is one of the chief factors in the confusion of concepts omnipresent in the Soviet Union. Many – far too many – Soviet enterprises were working at a loss. In a capitalist society they could have declared bankruptcy or been written off as a loss. In the Soviet Union this could not be done because the enterprise provided employment. (Something rather like this consideration has crept into the counsels of nationalized firms in the West: a firm is maintained at a loss because it is still cheaper than paying unemployment insurance.) In the Soviet Union the percentage of the labour force in 'non-productive branches' of industry continued to grow. In the seventies it was 11.7 per cent; in 1981 it was 26.7 per cent.

There was another debt that had increased by inexorable accumulation and had to be dealt with urgently: the general obsolescence of plant in all branches of industry – metallurgy, mining, refining, the electro industry and transport. While the obsolescence of plant has no direct ecological bearing, it does complicate and enlarge the problem of maintenance which, as indicated earlier in this account, is an ingrained Soviet weakness. This, in turn, was chiefly responsible for the looming ecological calamity symbolized by Chernobyl.

Worst of all, the leitmotiv of the Soviet economy as a whole was the concentration of all means on armaments and the armed forces, beginning with research and development and proceeding through priority procurement for the mass production of arms and accoutrement of all kinds. (Forty per cent of all machine construction and 20 per cent of all energy production plus 5 per cent – and the best 5 per cent – of the labour force. Also three-quarters of all top-flight scientists go to the military.) In a very direct sense the *nomenklatura* was an integral part of the armed forces; both the armed forces and the *nomenklatura* through conspicuous privilege were the embodiment of security measures. Soviet society was the most militarized society in world history. This systematic concentration on a few priorities was the underlying cause of the Soviet economic dilemma. It has skewed the entire system of priorities from the beginning. It was responsible for the studied neglect of agriculture and everything that went with it, including the development of an essential infrastructure – road-net, road-bed, rolling stock – in short, a well-developed and smoothly functioning transportation system. The pivotal industry between armaments and agriculture was, as always, the chemical industry. No country in the world is rich enough to force the development *à la longue* of armament industries and agriculture at the same time. But even under its lopsided dispensation in favour of the military the Soviet Union found it impossible to sustain the level of military expenditure. It was this fact, above all others, that forced the second serious attempt at reform in the history of the Soviet Union (the first was the NEP). And this was only because it had already forced the recognition by the Soviet military of the necessity for the reform.

Forcing the production of armaments resulted early on in the creation of highly specialized heavy and precision industries, a development that left the Soviet economy with a technological base effectively too narrow to compete on the world market at rational cost. The overall result was a paradox: an industrial base large enough to attract a wide variety of demands, but so distorted that it could not possibly meet them. The inability to meet an increasing number of demands of increasing volume over several decades had long ago forced the creation of what came to be called the second economy. The older name for it was black market. The black market, even when euphemized as the second economy, was both a drain on and supplement to the economy proper. With it the state commercial system could not function as it should have; without it the state commercial system could not have functioned at all. It came to account for as much as 25 per cent of the Soviet Union's turnover.

The classic Communist feature of a planned economy was the central planning system. The basic unit was the five-year plan, which rigidly shortcut consumer interests and needs in favour of heavy industry. In addition to the most formidable mass of military hardware in the world, it produced a vast backlog of unsaleable products – poor quality across the board and an extraordinarily high incidence of rejects. Various factors, moreover, combined to exacerbate the dilemma. In addition to the unfavourable demographic trend that brings less and less new blood every year to the labour force, there was the exhaustion of abundant and cheap raw materials, the erratic and cumbersome development of energy resources, the lack of suitable infrastructure, particularly in transport, the lack of sufficient investment in modernization against the background of poorly maintained, long-outmoded plant.

Between 1965 and 1970 the gross national product of the Soviet Union rose from 45.5 per cent of that of the United States to 53.7 per cent. In 1975 there was a rise of almost 5 per cent (to 58.2), which proved to be a flash in the pan. The percentage then fell back to around 54 per cent and has pretty much remained there. The same was true of the figures for the USSR's per capita GNP compared in percentages with that of the United States. There was a jump of slightly more than 10 per cent (35.3 to 45.5) between 1965 and 1970, and since then a levelling off between 46 and 47 per cent. So there had been a gain of roughly 10 per cent since Khrushchev made his threat to bury the United States in open economic competition in twenty years. But ominously for the Soviet Union there had been no gain and even a loss in the last ten years (a loss of almost 5 per cent in gross national product and a loss of more than 2 per cent in GNP per capita since 1975). It was, indeed, in the last ten years – 1975 to 1985 – that the great rude awakening for the Soviet utopians had come.

To be sure, the five-year plans had not been met for the past twenty-five years, but only since 1975 had the percentage increase of Soviet economic capacity fallen from 7 to between 2 and 3 per cent. And the longer the Soviet leaders delayed a meaningful reform of the economy, the greater the role the second economy would play. Thus the Soviet leaders had the choice of giving up some of their control to regional managers or having that control pass from them by default in the inexorable usurpation of the economy by the black market. The fact that the black market managed to assert itself in the face of the Soviet Union's imposition of the death penalty for economic crimes is a tribute to the indomitable ingenuity or the 'commercial depravity' (as the Soviets view it) of mankind. The phenomenon begins with the most famous of all unofficial Soviet slogans: 'They [the government] pretend to pay us, and we pretend to work.' The point is that when the Soviets began tinkering with the traditional value systems of the human race, they did not know what they were doing. They had only the foggiest notions about how the concept of state property as a universal system would affect the population at large.

397

If 'property is theft', as Proudhon insisted, then what is the theft of property? As Marx commented when he first read Proudhon's famous battle-cry, the word 'theft' itself implies property; theft has to be a stealing from some entity – corporeal or corporate. The concept of property cannot be abolished; it has to go somewhere. If private property is abolished it becomes perforce state property: it has nowhere else to go. If all – or practically all – property belongs to the state, then ownership becomes anonymous. Neither appeal to nor theft from an anonymity (the state) has anything like the force or meaning as when these actions concern a private person – however remote that person may be from the actual management of the entity concerned.

The idea that property equates with theft violates the concept of theft. If property is theft, then the theft of property is not a crime – in the conventional democracies rewards are given for stolen goods returned to the owner and no questions asked. If all men are thieves then no man is a thief, and if no man is a thief then all men are thieves. And indeed, theft of state property for private consumption or for resale on the black market is the most widespread form of corruption in the Soviet system. This kind of theft is practised without compunction (among adults – not forgetting Timofeev's teenagers) and no social stigma attaches to it. Indeed, employees often regard such theft as their good right, a sort of perquisite that goes with the job – especially if they happen to be employed in a butcher shop or supermarket or other form of highly prized consumer outlet.

It is little known and less remarked that the death penalty for economic crimes was introduced in the Soviet Union only in 1959 and by none other than Nikita Khrushchev ('We have to stop these speculators!') – as a desperate measure against the wildfire spread of the black market. But the necessity of maintaining the concept of state property (in order to prevent its becoming private property) rules out the disappearance of the state. The abolition of private property meant state property; state property meant the state – forever. Moreover it meant a particularly exacting, stringent, officious, meddling, suspicious ('vigilant!') type of state. In short, it meant the totalitarian state *par excellence*, a state forced by its very nature to intervene in the personal affairs of its citizens at every turn and without surcease. In the final analysis it meant a state doomed to pursue the phantom of the fulfilment of missions impossible – posed by the dilemma inherent in its nature. Such a 'mission impossible' is the discriminatory *payok* or package system of the sale of food products.

Tourists who marvel at how badly Soviet food shops are stocked even in Moscow are not aware that most Muscovites, like the majority of Soviets anywhere, are dependent for the bulk of their food on weekly or monthly food-parcels made available for sale at the 'company store'. Every large firm, enterprise or institution in the Soviet Union – from the Central Committee of the Party down to the local rubber-tyre factory – draws and distributes its own stocks to its employees. The quality, but not the quantity, of the food-parcels varies somewhat if not considerably depending on the organization involved: the food-parcels of the Central Committee, for example, are excellent – those of the Academy of Sciences are good, those of the ministry for foreign affairs are adequate. By and large the quality is what one would expect to find in an ordinary supermarket in Western Europe or North America. The standard *payok* contains a two-pound cut of beef or pork, a chicken (sometimes with four legs, as at the Academy), some canned fish and fruit of good quality. The food-parcel system was introduced in 1919 at a time of great scarcity. Except for a very few years in the early seventies, the Soviet system never really surmounted the scarcity of food. But the chief reason for keeping the food-parcel system is for control purposes – to see who gets what and why. (When preparing for the Moscow Olympic Games in 1980, one of the paramount problems confronting the Politburo was the decision on how much cauliflower to order for the occasion – especially if the Americans participated.) The *payok* system excludes those who work for firms too small to organize their own food procurement, part-time workers in services and, of course, the *tuneyadsye*, the do-nothings or so-called parasites (like the Nobel laureate poet, Joseph Brodsky). Such people are forced to live 'on the economy'. Thus the food-parcel system is the central planning of food procurement and distribution, both exclusive and highly prioritized, a rather finely tuned discriminatory sales procedure designed to work both as incentive and penalty.

One of the most aggravating aspects of the Soviet and satellite economic crisis is the hard-currency debt to Western nations, the total of which at this writing is well over $130 billion (of this, the debt of the USSR is over $40 billion). In 1986 the total annual

399

hard-currency income of the Soviet Union was hardly more than $30 billion, or a little over one-quarter of the sales total of General Motors for the same year. Soviet hard-currency expenditures in 1986, including Western imports, the servicing of debt and the cost of empire, exceeded this level of income by approximately 100 per cent. (A Rand Corporation study found that in 1983 Soviet military aid to Libya, Cuba and Vietnam exceeded $15 billion: total cost of empire for the year can be estimated at twice that amount.)

In 1986 nearly all hard-currency requirements to support Soviet global commitments and activities were funded on Western financial markets, the total of which funding amounted to some $38 billion when short-term credits are included. (The Soviet Union has already entered the international securities markets as a new source for untied funds, that is, the issuing of bonds, notes, etc.) Hence the empire is being kept alive by foreign-currency loans of ever-increasing amounts. Between 85 per cent and 90 per cent of these Western loans to the Soviet bloc are from private commercial banks (this compares with a 30 per cent to 40 per cent share in the 1970s). Approximately 80 per cent of medium-term Western credits take the form of untied, general-purpose loans. In mid 1988 Secretary Carlucci in testimony before Congress acknowledged that the American government was very much against these kinds of loans because they 'put an added defence burden on the NATO allies'. When Lenin wrote what amounted to the statement so often attributed to him, that 'the capitalists will sell us the rope with which we will later hang them', he might well have added that the capitalists would also lend the Soviets the money with which to buy the rope.

But easily the greatest in the voluminous catalogue of Soviet failures was that of the anti-religious or atheistic agitatorial work of the Party: the concerted and unceasing attempt to put down religion – especially Christianity – by demolition of places of worship, by dispossession and disenfranchisement of all religious institutions and communities, by dissuasion of members of congregations through argument, propaganda, discrimination, administrative and physical coercion. By way of positive measures the Soviets emphasized the Marxist tenet of the 'new man' who, shriven of all selfishness, devotes himself wholeheartedly to the building of socialism. This was, after all, the cardinal article of the

Communist faith – the denial of God and the affirmation of man, following Feuerbach's exposé of God as a figment of man's imagination.

Typically, the Soviets thought this fundamental reorientation of the human animal would be a relatively easy business, that it would follow naturally once the basis of human misery had been removed and the exploitation of man by man done away with. Instead, they were baffled from the start. On serious and prolonged inquiry the task the Soviets had set themselves proved to be surpassingly difficult and intricate. Recent reports inspired by *glasnost* reveal that the traditional practice of mass atheist propaganda – in the form of atheist clubs, compulsory courses in scientific atheism in high schools and institutes of propaganda in the media – has boomeranged. The teachers of such courses could not even grasp the complicated psychological reasons leading to religious faith – neither, for that matter, could the chief ideologues of the Party. Here the anti-intellectual atmosphere in the Soviet Union, so often mentioned by Sakharov, took its toll. Soviet ideologues were unable to comprehend the fact that religion is culture and that both are the result of tradition. To do what they wanted to do the Soviets would have had to rewrite the New Testament. This could not have been done without a lively appreciation of the antecedence of the Old Testament.

In the end the Soviets were reduced to mimicry of Church pomp and procession: the carrying aloft of huge portraits of Soviet leaders at parades, for example. But the iconization of Party bosses redounded to the nostalgic advantage of the Church and the defamation of the Party. Meanwhile (even before Chernobyl), popular concern over conservation – cultural as well as natural – forced a policy change from the demolition to the restoration of churches as historical monuments. More recently the Soviet authorities have even gone so far as to build new churches – in keeping with the gradual realization that religion is an essential element of the complex of forces that make for a productive relationship of the citizen to the state. Most recently the Soviets have turned – after long postponement and with extreme reluctance – to religious communities for help in offsetting the acute lack of nursing staff in the general misery of Soviet hospitals.

XVIII

FREEDOM AND THE MOSCOW SPRING

In the evening of Monday 15 December 1986, two electricians accompanied by a KGB officer appeared in the Sakharovs' apartment in Gorky and installed a telephone. By way of explanation they offered the following: 'Tomorrow you will receive a very important telephone call.' The next day when the phone rang Sakharov found himself in conversation with Mikhail Sergeievich Gorbachev. Said Gorbachev: 'The government has decided to end your exile and to pardon Elena Bonner so that the two of you can return to Moscow.' At this point Sakharov interrupted the general secretary, saying that he must speak with him on a different and far more important subject. He then reminded Gorbachev that a few days earlier 'his close friend' Anatoly Marchenko 'was killed in prison' and that there were still many prisoners of conscience in Soviet prisons who would have to be freed. To this, Gorbachev's rejoinder: 'Well, you know, among them there are very different people.' 'Yes,' replied Sakharov, 'very different. And all of them must be set free.' Gorbachev tried to change the subject by saying that it was necessary above all for Sakharov to return to Moscow and start working again in the scientific field, to occupy himself in his favourite activity for the good of his native country (a turn of phrase that has given rise to much speculation in émigré circles). Sakharov answered that the freeing of all prisoners of conscience in the Soviet Union, first and foremost, would be a move for the good of their native country. On that note the conversation ended.

Sakharov returned to Moscow on 23 December after an exile that had lasted seven years lacking one month. Besieged by foreign correspondents at the Moscow station, Sakharov repeated his plea for the release of all prisoners of conscience and added that it was also important to end the war in Afghanistan by withdrawing Soviet troops, since this was 'the greatest and most savage injustice being committed by the Soviet Union'. He would in future, he said, continue to insist on the release of all prisoners of conscience but would not follow and publicize individual cases with the same intensity as before. He was sixty-six years old; he was ailing; he had been under tremendous pressure for twenty years. And he had made his point, been borne out by history in spectacular if terrible fashion. He had won at least a very important battle. Perhaps he had won the war, but that remained to be seen, that lay in the future – but not far in the future. Before the end of the year, 1987, some 200 prisoners of conscience had been released from Soviet prisons. Equally important, throughout the next two years and more, no one was arrested on the basis of Article 70 of the Criminal Code (anti-Soviet agitation and propaganda). Before the end of 1986, Mikhail Gorbachev had made a virtue of necessity and proclaimed the advent of *glasnost* as official Soviet policy. (Actually, Gorbachev had first used the word *glasnost* publicly in a speech to the Central Committee in December 1984 when he was still secretary for ideology and second man in the Party behind the moribund Konstantin Chernenko. At that time Gorbachev declared *glasnost* to be the 'norm of the whole of social life'. In his inaugural address as secretary general three months later Gorbachev repeated this declaration. However, *glasnost*, along with *perestroika*, did not become campaign slogans until the immediate aftermath of the Chernobyl disaster.)

Remembering that reality in the Soviet Union is an artificial reality, perhaps the best way to put Gorbachev's decision to adopt *glasnost* and *perestroika* into its proper Soviet perspective is to cite the statement made by a Soviet observer, Mikhail Borodin, hardly three years earlier:

Sakharov is a wonderful person. He wants only goodness. But what he wants today, now, is just impossible. 'A man wants to talk, let him talk; he wants to organize, let him organize.' But let's assume that such wishes were suddenly realized, and that all who want to talk could speak as they liked, and go there, come here. You understand, at the level of consciousness that exists today, it would be a national catastrophe, a slaughter-house.

Today, in our conditions, all classes, all groups are located in a kind of rigid good will. They are held in a balanced positiveness by the authorities. And imagine that today there was no authority. But give us a million copies of *Gulag*, understand? [Solzhenitsyn has said that he will return to the Soviet Union when *The Gulag Archipelago* is freely published there.] Let's not give any positive thing except the slogan 'Freedom', etc., etc., without a moral basis, without any special systematic view of the world. And what would happen? People would begin to settle scores. It would simply be anarchy. People would begin to settle scores.

It's fine, freedom of speech, it's fine. Freedom of assembly – excellent. But in our conditions, in which popular consciousness is, all told, lower than before the revolution of 1917, how can this freedom be realized? Who will come to power? Sakharov? No ... the first who would perish under the guillotine's blade would be Sakharov.

It has not worked out that way. In the two years since Sakharov's return from exile, Soviet society, as hermetically closed as it had been for well-nigh seventy years, has burst wide open. Apart from the international military pacts such as the Intermediate-range Nuclear Forces (INF) Treaty with the United States (here for the first time the Soviets struck and carried out a nuclear-arms reduction agreement proportionately weighted against them), and the agreement within the UNO framework to withdraw all Soviet troops from Afghanistan by the spring of 1989, apart from the reciprocal summit visits between the Soviets and the Western Allies (during which Western heads of state invariably made a point of meeting with Sakharov), with a host of ancillary cultural and commercial agreements resultant, Mikhail Gorbachev took a seven-league step toward free enterprise with the introduction of a system of fifty-year leases for private farm plots to families and the establishment of so-called cooperatives, semi-private firms in which the state controls a 50 per cent interest. Gorbachev went on, announcing the introduction of legislation to effect the separation of powers, particularly that of Party from state (the while insisting that this could be done within a one-party system). By the end of 1988 the Supreme Soviet had dissolved itself by a vote of 1,468 against five, with twenty-seven abstentions, setting up a bicameral legislature with clearly stipulated powers, unlimited debate, elections from a plurality of candidates and an independent judiciary.

At the same time Gorbachev cleared his decks in Party and government in-fighting by suddenly restructuring the Politburo to the exclusion of Andrei Gromyko (whose place as president of the Soviet Union Gorbachev himself assumed with a legislated increase in the executive power of the office) and the demotion of his arch-rival Ligachev from chief ideologist to scapegoat for agriculture. This spectacular action – accomplished during an abruptly called extraordinary session of the Central Committee at the end of September 1988 – was widely regarded as a *coup d'état*. Thus less than two years after he had released Sakharov, Mikhail Gorbachev – in the name of *glasnost* and *perestroika* and rampant democratization – had gathered the reins of political power into his own hands.

But the greatest and most startling change was that which took place in the Soviet media. To an extent that would scarcely have been credited as possible by even the most sanguine optimist, the Soviet press, radio and television threw off the yoke of conformism and broke loose in all directions save only those of pornography and sexual scandal. Suddenly government ministers were almost daily involved in panel discussions defending Party policy and their own performances – for the most part clumsily and even plaintively, for lack of practice. Literally hundreds of articles appeared in the press condemning Stalin and all his works – most especially the awesome atrocities committed in his name: tens of millions murdered in the process. There were dozens of articles roundly condemning the Soviet perversion of psychiatry to political purpose, thousands execrating the insolence of the Party in all its dealings with the citizenry – especially in the article of filling the pockets of its functionaries. Here the field was led by Gorbachev himself. In a speech to the Writers Union in the summer of 1987 he put it baldly: 'In the Soviet Union, nothing is exploited so much as an official position.'

Today in private homes the Soviet television set is left on most of the time. When guests are present the sound is turned off. Whenever a talking head appears on the screen the sound is turned up to catch the forthcoming announcement or discussion. Criticism of Soviet officialdom is more voluble and unbridled on television than it is in the streets. Lengthy film footage is shown comparing Japanese and Soviet supermarkets, working a shock by opulent contrast with the gaping scarcity of Soviet consumer goods on display. The question thrown up every which way – publicly, privately, officially, artistically – is why, why, why? Against the background of economic collapse, amid the most resounding failure of a doctrine known to the history of man, the Communist Party of the Soviet Union is running for its life.

From 14 to 16 February 1987 the Kremlin held what it called an International Forum for a Non-Nuclear World and the Survival of Humanity. According to the official Soviet statistics, 1,559 invitations were sent out, of which 853 were accepted (nothing like this result could have been achieved if the release of Sakharov had not preceded the occasion in good time – a fact often enough expressed by those who attended). The forum was divided into six working committees and some reasonably serious overtures were made. One of the chief reasons, it was rumoured, for inviting so many film stars was to counteract the attraction of Sakharov who remained the cynosure of the international media on the occasion (he was all but ignored by the Soviet media), even managing to eclipse Claudia Cardinale. At the forum Sakharov made three appearances to read as many papers, the first two concerning nuclear disarmament negotiations (here he made a case for not linking other forms of nuclear disarmament to the Strategic Defence Initiative – SDI – of the Americans), the third and final concerning the peaceful use of atomic energy, in which he recommended the installation of atomic reactors underground as the best protection against a repetition of the Chernobyl tragedy.

As for Sakharov and his Lusia since then – it would be misleading to say that they have been rehabilitated. One cannot be 'rehabilitated' into a largely new situation. But they have led a kind of charmed life since their return from Gorky. Sakharov was soon back at his old place of work and with an office in the Academy of Sciences. He and Lusia were free to come and go as they pleased – at first within the boundaries of the Soviet Union, but in time this, too, changed. By the end of 1987 Sakharov appeared thrice in the Soviet press, twice with articles in the weekly *Moskovskye novosti* (*Moscow News*) and once with an article in *Sovietskaya Rossiya*. Thereafter his appearances in the press became more frequent. In early summer 1988 he and Lusia were provided with the site and facilities of the ministry of foreign affairs for an international press conference. In the autumn of the same year Sakharov was elected to the presidium of the Academy of Sciences by a vote of 178 to fifty-three. Within a month thereafter it was announced that Sakharov would travel to the United States to participate in a conference of the International Forum for a Non-Nuclear World and the Survival of Humanity to be held in Washington, DC at the beginning of November. In the event his visit in the United States, which lasted some six weeks, had all the earmarks of a triumph. He was received by the president (whom he had already met during the latter's summit visit in Moscow some eight months before). He was made an honorary member of the American Academy of Science and fêted as widely and variously as his time and patience would allow. During his sojourn it became known that he had insisted as the *sine qua non* of his trip that six Soviet dissidents be allowed to visit America at the same time. The six made the most of the opportunity by giving interviews to the press on conditions past and present in the Soviet Union.

Beginning in February 1989 Sakharov, accompanied by Elena Bonner, travelled to Italy where he spent more than an hour in private audience with the Pope and received an honorary doctorate in astronomy from the world's oldest institution of learning, the University of Bologna. Here he was hailed as 'the roving ambassador for *perestroika* in the Soviet Union'. The couple then went on to Canada and the United States whence Sakharov returned to Moscow alone in mid-March in order to contest the first free elections in Soviet history. Sakharov's candidacy for the new parliament was rejected by the Presidium of the Academy of Sciences in a secret vote, but he was reinstated as a candidate by popular acclaim within the physics department of the Academy. He won the primary, as it might be called, in early April and resoundingly: in late April he won the election itself and became a member of the Congress of People's Deputies, from which in turn would be elected the new Supreme Soviet.

But there was a huge question as to whether these elections had any real meaning. In the new parliament, as decreed, 85 per cent of the seats would go to Communist Party members, leaving the rump 15 per cent dependent on elections. And then there was the unique case of Boris Yeltsin, the former 'lord-mayor' of Moscow and Politburo member who had widely been regarded as Gorbachev's most able lieutenant, but was then thrown out of both positions and shunted into the office of deputy minister for housing construction. Yeltsin, as if out of spite, chose to contest the election to parliament for the city of Moscow, running against another Central Committeeman and Party favourite. In the event, Yeltsin won 85 per cent of the vote, a sensation that prompted the Muscovite dissident Vladimir Korsunski to comment that 'the overwhelming majority votes for the members of the overwhelming minority', that is, the Communists who make up 10 per cent of the population but will take 85 per cent of the seats in the new Supreme Soviet. By this reckoning, only those who abstained from voting showed the good sense or the courage of their convictions – and indeed, in the city of Moscow 949,515 citizens did just that: abstained. Moreover, of those Muscovites who voted, 578,611 crossed out the names of all uncontested Party candidates. Those who voted for Yeltsin, therefore, were simple dupes – taken in by the confidence-trick of the Party's quarrel with Yeltsin. Korsunski concluded that in reality nobody was elected. Perhaps next time, he said. But this time was merely a swindle.

It is not that simple. The Communist Party of the Soviet Union is split. It cannot stay that way and it cannot – for all the pessimistic speculation abroad – go back to the way it was. The electorate was wise to support the liberal members of the Party where it could. If the elections were largely a sham they were not entirely so. There was the publicity of open contests, the unprecedented demonstrations and campaigning for and against candidates, many of whom were non-Party. In the great majority of cases where Party and non-Party candidates contested the same seat, the non-Party candidates triumphed by margins averaging 80 per cent of the vote. And where Party candidates in such stand-offs fared well, they did so only because they enjoyed the support of the non-Party People's Front organizations. Moreover, scores of prominent Party candidates – generals, ministers or those of equivalent rank – were discountenanced publicly: 'running' uncontested, they were simply crossed off the ballot by overwhelming majorities – pointed demonstrations of a near-total absence of popular support which, according to Party spokesmen in the aftermath, would necessarily have its consequences for the 'candidates' concerned. By and large, then, whenever the Party exposed itself to electoral contest, its performance was so poor as to give wings to the saying that in a referendum on whether it should remain 'the guiding force' in Soviet life, the Party would be wiped out. Hence this was merely the beginning of a new experience, the electoral process. It was a confused beginning: 'We have a great deal of chaos in the Soviet Union,' ran one comment, 'but not enough to make a world.' Still, it was not an inauspicious beginning. It remains perhaps the most important of Gorbachev's initiatives because it opens the prospect of the people's making its own changes in legislation that is truly representative.

Sakharov himself became, as did most if not all of the released prisoners of conscience, a fervent advocate (but also an outspoken critic) of Mikhail Gorbachev and his policies. Sakharov has openly expressed his misgivings about the way Gorbachev, in combating Stalinism, has concentrated power in his person and position as did Stalin. Good, says Sakharov, Gorbachev needs the power to achieve the changes he himself has set, but is he not continuing a bad precedent? How do we know the man who follows Gorbachev will have the qualities of Gorbachev?

There was nothing unusual about the Sakharovs' advocacy of Gorbachev: in war there are only two sides, and in the nature of things dissidents were generally on the side of Gorbachev and the reformers. The Sakharovs had never been for revolution or any-thing like it. Gradualism was the catchword: the process had begun; it was already, for the most part, moving fast enough – there was no need to push. For the fact was that with the introduction of *glasnost* and *perestroika* as official Soviet policy, the Communist Party of the Soviet Union, for the first time in its history, was split – leaving the issue itself in the balance. The policy was announced and propagandized as official, but remained to be implemented. There was plenty of resistance to *perestroika* through-out the Party machine. Indeed, Gorbachev himself admitted that the full realization of the programme would take generations.

To mark one of the sorest points at issue, here is an example of Sakharov's steadfastness in the cause from his contribution to a book published under the title *The Inevitability of Perestroika* by the Moscow Progress Publishing House in June 1988. He asks the question whether there were 'connections of the KGB with the "terrorist Internationale" which emerged in the sixties and sev-enties or with other destructive actions'. Under the new conditions of *glasnost*, continued Sakharov, all such cases would have to be brought under scrutiny. This demand was part and parcel of Sakharov's attitude that higher interests of state could only be served by bringing to light the full truth 'about past and present'. One need not imagine the unprecedented confusion entailed by this on-going process toward full exposure. It is amply documented. As a Muscovite joke put it, it is becoming more and more difficult to predict the past. And indeed, in early 1988 it was announced that the key history examination held at the end of the tenth school year throughout the Soviet Union to test the ideological maturity of the students had been discontinued. The examiners were no longer in possession of the answers to their own questions.

The result of all this was a strange set of circumstances, a sort of *drôle de guerre* in the official media between the two factions of the Party, in which the reformists bombarded their opponents unceasingly while these were reduced to sniping and an occasional broadside. Then in the second half of 1987 there was an explosion in the unofficial media: several dozens of 'independent publications' sprang up in and around Moscow and Leningrad. By far the largest of these was a magazine that took *glasnost* as its title. It was edited – as it, at this writing, still is – by Sergei Grigoryants, an Armenian-Russian, a literary critic by profession and a doctor of philosophy in Soviet penology, as it were, having spent eight years in the gulag during two terms. Pardoned in February in the wake of Sakharov's release from exile, Grigoryants founded his magazine in July, as he put it, 'in order to fill in the white spots' or gaps in the government's new information policy. He began, understandably, by concentrating on the KGB, its activities, its history and its archives, which were said to be undergoing systematic destruction. He also gave considerable space to the plight of the Crimean Tartars on the occasion of their unprecedented demonstration in Moscow in the summer of 1988.

When Grigoryants tried to register *Glasnost* with the appropriate authority, he was told that this was impossible because his publication did not represent anything – which was to say, it did not represent any official Soviet entity. In the Soviet Union the public domain is – or was – the preserve of the Party-state. Thus the status of *Glasnost* – like that of *glasnost* – remained unclear. But in general terms the state ownership of the means of production proved to be not nearly so important as the state ownership of the means of reproduction – such as mimeograph and photocopy machines. If someone uses a state-owned photocopy machine – as someone recently did – to make sixty copies of *Glasnost*, that person can be – and was being – prosecuted for the theft of (the use of) state property. By the same token, *Glasnost* must be sent to all corners of the Soviet Union by courier. It was soon learned that the Soviet mails could not be used: copies posted were confiscated. By contrast, well before the end of the year there was an English edition of *Glasnost* out of New York, a French edition published in Paris under the auspices of the French minister of culture and a Scandinavian edition out of Norway. There was also a German edition published in Switzerland. In sum it is clear enough that the Soviet government would like to keep *glasnost* – as wide-open and free-wheeling as it has come to be – strictly official. Officials are reluctant to clamp down on the 'independent publications'. They are content, so far, to starve them out by denying access to the necessary facilities and materials.

Grigoryants has his own view of how *glasnost* and *perestroika* came about. 'The Soviet system,' he said, 'made inhumans out of people and the people retaliated by refusing to work. And now? Now the situation has not changed but the atmosphere has changed. Now there is some hope. I know that Mikhail Gorbachev is a highly intelligent man. I am perfectly prepared to believe that he is a sincere man, that he wants the best for everybody. What I cannot believe is that the Party is introducing democracy as an end and not merely as a means ... The Party is calling for democratization because it knows that it has to have democracy in order to improve and increase production by any appreciable amount. In the computer age secrecy only hurts those who try to impose it. No, I never expected anything like this to happen. I thought the future would look like George Orwell's *1984*. Instead we have a situation in which freedom is the *sine qua non* of a functioning economy. That is the big surprise.'

In this sort of no man's land of media legality (the Soviet Union has never had a press law, but now there is one in the making) the old saw about the elaborate controls over information in the Soviet Union forcing anyone trying to communicate to take recourse to the mediation of the corps of foreign correspondents in Moscow still applies. The information has to get out in order to get in – by foreign radio broadcast. As Grigoryants, who receives a flow of foreign visitors and dignitaries that would do credit to the consulate of a small country, explained to this writer: 'What really counts is that foreign radio stations broadcast our material in Russian-language programmes beamed to the Soviet Union. Radio Liberty, for example, broadcasts our material.' This was and is true: radio is the only means of breaking the Soviet monopoly of information on a mass scale. When Grigoryants made this statement in November 1987 the Soviet Union had already ceased to jam the Voice of America and the BBC. By the end of November 1988 the Soviets had ceased to jam Radio Liberty and the Deutsche Welle. This was unprecedented.

But just one month later, on 29 November 1988, a proscriptive ordinance, 'On the Activity of the Cooperatives', was published, outlawing, among other things, the storage or production of tapes, records or other means of audio-reproduction, video-tapes, films, television cassettes, clips and the like, or any form of printed matter on the part of the cooperatives. This ordinance quashed the hopes of those who, like the singer–composer Bulat Akhudzhava, saw the institution of the cooperatives as a way to establish private or semi-private publishing or broadcasting facilities and firms, these same being for good measure also specifically proscribed.

Until the release of Sakharov at the end of 1986, the war of words in the media was being fought out in the West by the West, with the Soviet Union adding a nudge here and there, or withholding information as it saw fit in order to guide the controversy along lines favourable to itself – in the same fashion, incidentally, as the Soviets release and withhold from their stock of hostage peoples, the Soviet Jews in the first instance and the Soviet Germans, formerly Volga Germans, in the second. Horse trading with people for lack of horses had long been a speciality of *la prison des peuples* as tsarist Russia was styled in the nineteenth century.

There is, of course, a deeper significance in this constellation of circumstances. How is it that a people numbering less than 1 per cent of the population of the Soviet Union plays such a disproportionately large role in the opposition (between 30 and 40 per cent of the material broadcast by Radio Liberty is of Jewish origin or orientation – and justifiably so)? The answer seems to be that the Jews are the key to 'the prison of peoples' – whether that prison of peoples happens to be the Austro-Hungarian Empire, the German Empire, the Russian Empire or the Soviet Empire. The turning-point came in 1892 when an idea germinated in the mind of Theodor Herzl. It was based on the realization that the assimilation of the Jews in Europe was not going to work. Herzl, who was the Viennese *Neue Presse* correspondent in Paris, wrote his book, *Judenstaat* (*The Jewish State*) under the immediate influence of the Dreyfus scandal. But the fate of Captain Dreyfus was merely the precipitating factor: Herzl's knowledge of the situation in his homeland was massive confirmation of the Dreyfus message.

In other words, the defection of Herzl signalled the disaffection of the minority nations that made up the empire in addition to the Austrians and the Hungarians. 'Austria,' wrote the young Benito Mussolini at the beginning of World War I, 'the age-old enemy of national existence.' It was the Austro-Hungarian Empire with its fermenting nationalities that contained the seeds of World War I. What an irony of history that Ludendorff's master-plan of providing safe passage for the revolutionary leader Lenin and his entourage to Petrograd crippled Russia for a time surely enough but could not save the German Empire. Instead it unleashed the one force that was capable of preserving the Russian Empire, albeit in a different form. For in truth the Russian Empire was saved by the October Revolution. Communism was probably the only ideology that could have solved the nationalities issue by eclipsing it in the class concept. The young Mussolini had a vision when the revolution appeared on the eastern front in 1917.

> The red flags planted on the Galician trenches have the highest symbolic value. It is the revolution which does not fear war, it is the war which rescues the revolution. The flags with the imperial eagles: they will not withstand the red flags of the revolution. THE RED FLAG WILL RISE on the palace at Potsdam too when the armies of the revolution and of the Western democracies have shattered the Germany of the Hohenzollerns . . .

It is instructive to compare this quote with that of Winston Churchill in a minute in Parliament on 8 April 1945, when World War II in Europe was all but over: 'This war would never have come unless, under American and modernizing pressure, we had driven the Habsburgs out of Austria and Hungary and the Hohenzollerns out of Germany. By making these vacuums we gave the opening for the Hitlerite monster to crawl out of its sewer on to the vacant thrones.' Within a month the red flags of the revolution were flying over both the palace at Potsdam and the Reichstag in Berlin. Within a month the Western democracies had met the armies of the revolution in the middle of Germany. And yet the revolution had betrayed all its peoples including the majority people. The revolution had produced a dictatorship not of the proletariat but of a Georgian bandit whose real name was

Djugashvili and who was on a perfect par with the Hitlerite monster. The Soviet Union remained the last great colonial empire on earth, the last 'prison of peoples'. And once again the Jews were the key to the prison. In retrospect it is clear how much depended on the fate of the Jews in the Communist Party of the Soviet Union. If they had fared as they had hoped to fare in and after the October Revolution – representatively, standing in the stead of all the minority peoples of the Soviet Union – it might have been a different story. As it was, the same retrospect makes it clear that the Soviet leadership never managed to pay anything like the attention to the nationalities question that the vast complex of problems that goes under that name not only deserves but demands. And this was because Stalin's 'classic' work on the subject was slavishly considered to be the last word, blocking all discussion and stifling all initiative. It is small wonder that today, seventy years after the October Revolution, Mikhail Sergeievich Gorbachev announces that the entire nationalities problem in the Soviet Union must be restudied.

The occasion for the first such announcement was Independence Day of the Lithuanian nation when thirty-six would-be demonstrators were arrested – as reported – by Soviet authorities. This was followed within two months by the uproar among the Armenians both in the Soviet republic of Armenia and in the Armenian enclave of Nagorno Karabakh in the neighbouring republic of Azerbaidzhan. The issue was the Armenian demand that the enclave be united with the Armenian republic. By the end of March 1988, thirty-four Armenian demonstrators had been killed in what was reported to be a pogrom carried out by the Azerbaidzhani. The Soviet government sent army units and police detachments into the area to keep the peace but refused to meet the demand for annexation. Hereupon Sakharov wrote a letter to Gorbachev, urging him to reconsider the Armenian demand. Sakharov's letter was indicated because the Soviet decision to let matters stand satisfied no one including the Azerbaidzhani who were left with the situation smouldering as before.

Meanwhile the unrest in the Baltic states spread and intensified. In the spring of 1988 the secret clause of the Molotov–Ribbentrop Pact, which gave the Baltic states to Stalin as his part of the deal partitioning Poland with Hitler, was published by the Estonian party press. Scarcely eight months later the Supreme Soviet of the northernmost Baltic state declared Estonian independence and, while not seceding (as each Soviet republic has the right to do under the constitution) and thus acknowledging Soviet sovereignty in matters of foreign policy, decreed its right to veto Soviet federal legislation. The Supreme Soviet of the USSR promptly declared the Estonian decree illegal. But the demand throughout the Baltic states for a far-reaching autonomy stood. In all three republics the red flag of the Union disappeared, to be replaced by the national flags and the national hymns. To this the Union did not react. Something on the order of a settling of accounts was clearly under way. And although Soviet official coverage was markedly better than it conceivably could have been before the advent of *glasnost*, the government's performance fell far short of expectations. Indeed, the Armenians accused the Soviet authorities of having precipitated the situation with the declaration of *glasnost* and then provoking bloodshed by refusing to honour their own declared policy. This was hardly more than an accurate description of what actually happened. According to official reports eighteen people were dead as the result of violence done to Armenians in Azerbaidzhan in the autumn and early winter of 1988, while as many as 250,000 were said to be on the move out of the Muslim republic in search of safety. Despite the massive commitment of troops, the situation was all but out of hand. Gorbachev, it was said, now had his 'ethnic Chernobyl'.

One answer to the 'ethnic Chernobyl' came in the spring of 1989, when Soviet soldiery killed a number of young Georgian nationalists by beating them to death with their entrenching spades. Estimates on the number of victims ranged from nineteen (official) to 150 (samizdat). Genadi Gerasimov, Foreign Office spokesman, pointed out by way of extenuation: 'At least we didn't shoot anybody.' Here the military and special anti-riot units were working under new decrees, numbered 504 and 505, published by the Presidium of the Supreme Soviet on 28 July 1988, 'concerning the duties and rights of the internal forces of the Ministry of the Interior for the maintenance of public order – during assemblies, gatherings, demonstrations and street processions'. When Mikhail Gorbachev promised a lawful society he apparently meant – at least in the first instance – legislation to cover with the mantle of legality whatever measures should prove necessary in putting down unrest of any and every description. This was not what Sakharov and other dissidents had had in mind.

As for Radio Liberty – its existence presents certain problems. Chief among these is the fact that the radio represents and practises a form of moral irredenta. It is a constant reminder that the United States does not accept the Soviet Union – either for what it is or what it claims to be. Now, however, it is a question of whether the United States will accept the Soviet Union for what it is trying to become. In any case the controversy over and within Radio Liberty was and is given – regardless of programme content.

Either conservatives or liberals would be upset; there is no way to satisfy both sides at the same time. One side strives to neutralize the rhetoric of the station in order to make the sedition that is the radio's mandate as bland and inoffensive as possible. The other side is intent on increasing the effectiveness of the broadcasting in order to break the communications quarantine of the Soviet Union. And despite *glasnost* that quarantine, although greatly lightened, has not been lifted. As a German saying has it, there is no such thing as a general basis of understanding among humankind. The same basic difference in approach has polarized the interpretation of Aristotle's ethical guidelines down through the ages.

In other words it is the same old dichotomy: for the one side the Soviet Union, despite all that has happened, remains a 'progressive' force trying to find itself and its place in the world; for the other side the Soviet Union remains – until that day when it institutionalizes the basic democratic principles and practices – the 'Evil Empire'. In the former case, should that side prevail, the Soviet Union will find itself showered – at least for a time – with long-term credits and grants in aid *à la* pump-priming funds for *perestroika* provided by emotionally moved, Gorbachev-charmed majorities among the industrial nations of the West. In the latter case the American–Soviet relationship will remain – at least for a time – reduced to disarmament treaties plus the all-important function of implementing the Universal Declaration of Human Rights, which gives Soviet citizens the right to know and others the right to provide them with what they have a right to know. Indeed, on the face of it, with the advent of the official Soviet policy of *glasnost* and *perestroika* the interests of the Soviet government and Radio

416

Liberty are now identical – or rather, the interests of part of the Soviet government, the comparatively liberal part that supports the declared policy of *glasnost*, and the interests of Radio Liberty are now identical. With this qualification, the twain have met.

In establishing human rights in the Soviet Union by example and by ordeal, Andrei Sakharov – by no means alone but by all means first and foremost among the dissidents – put an end to the prospect and rationale of Soviet totalitarianism, and with it in that end, to Soviet imperialism. Perhaps Sakharov's greatest service to his cause and his country has been that he has accustomed the Soviet government, by a persistent course of ethical instruction, to the idea of a legitimate opposition.

Is Sakharov a religious man? This question is often asked, because Sakharov conducts himself in word and deed like the paradigm of a Christian. Should the question be asked? Among scientists, physicists have the reputation for being passionately attached to their particular discipline. But apart from such detachment scientists do not believe because their business is not to believe but to find out – to know. With him, the scientist – as Thomas Mann said of Gotthold Ephraim Lessing – scepticism is his passion.

Instead of the religious question this writer asked Sakharov if he had ever dreamed of being anything other than a physicist. 'Physics,' said Sakharov, 'is the study of everything in the world that is not living matter. I decided to concentrate on the subject because it is the basis of everything, it is what preceded life. Now, I think that microbiology is very interesting; knowing what I know today I might well have chosen to study microbiology as the most fruitful field of inquiry.'

Sakharov used to go to church, not regularly but frequently. As a close friend put it, 'not because he was a believer but because he liked the music and the choral singing and took aesthetic pleasure in the elaborate Russian Orthodox service; he may very well also be convinced that the church service, taken as a whole in itself and as an integral part of the weekly routine, has a salubrious effect on mind and body.' But in the mid-seventies, when the pressure brought against Sakharov by the government was at its highest, the priest in charge of the local congregation took Sakharov aside and asked him to refrain from attending services for the

417

good of the church. Sakharov complied – with what feelings may be imagined.

In November 1987 in Moscow, when this writer ventured to characterize Sakharov's struggle as a confrontation between centralism and pluralism and referred to Andrei Dmitrievich as 'the voice of pluralism', Sakharov replied succinctly: 'I can tell you that "the voice of pluralism" was very much alone out there for quite some time.' He was certainly thinking not only of the Orthodox priest who asked him to desist from attending church services. This writer then mentioned the declaration of Soviet scientists which appeared in the 26 October 1983 issue of *Izvestia* accusing Sakharov of 'undermining the cause of peace and acting like an enemy of the Soviet Union'. It was followed by seventy-two signatures, or only slightly more than 10 per cent of the total membership of the Academy of Sciences. Was it this obvious failure to achieve a majority of the Academy membership in support of the campaign against Sakharov that stayed the government's hand? 'Not at all,' said Sakharov; 'what saved me was the fact that the Politburo was split on the issue: that is all.' Similarly, when the very sore subject of the continuing misuse of psychiatry in dealing with political prisoners – despite *glasnost* and *perestroika* – was broached, Sakharov replied matter of factly that one of Gorbachev's main pillars of support within the Party was the KGB; hence he (Gorbachev) was obliged to do something to keep that support. Sakharov did not elaborate, but it was not difficult to discern the figure of Yuri Andropov, patron and mentor of Gorbachev, as the champion over the years in the Politburo of a more tolerant line in dealing with the phenomenon of Sakharov. For it is perhaps the signal irony in the human-rights struggle in the Soviet Union that the KGB, as the best informed element of the Party, has from the very beginning been most open to the arguments for *glasnost* and *perestroika*.

There was no mistaking Sakharov's admiration of Gorbachev. When this writer broached the matter of Sakharov's relations with other dissidents he replied that many of them took exception to the fact that he had expressed his gratitude to Gorbachev. Said Sakharov: 'I will express my gratitude to Gorbachev a hundred times over if necessary.' And then he added, 'Gorbachev called me at a time when Ligachev was in Vietnam. That took a lot of courage!' (There is a particular aspect to the dissidents' attitude to Gorbachev: whether for or against they have a very lively appreciation of the magnitude of the task before him; as Ruth Grigorievna put it in a burst of enthusiasm, 'What grandiose audacity!')

This writer explained that he had concluded from reading Sakharov's political writings that he, Sakharov, had made a basic calculation on a perceptive analysis of the Soviet situation, a calculation of how things would inevitably have to work themselves out, so that from the very first Sakharov must have been sure of his ground. 'That is correct,' said Sakharov, 'but only for the philosophical calculation. In practice, in life, matters can turn out very differently.' (A footnote in Kant's *Critique of Pure Reason* warns against 'inferring at once from the possibility of concepts – logical – the possibility of things – real.') Was he then surprised at how quickly the change had come? 'Yes,' he said. 'I thought it would take much longer.' Sooner or later, then, his calculation would be borne out fully by events; *perestroika* and pluralism in the end would have to succeed – was that it? 'Yes,' he rejoined, 'but don't forget that you can have *perestroika* without pluralism.' The trouble was, he went on, that if *perestroika* failed the danger of war would be greatly increased because the fanatics in the Party would do anything rather than give up their power. When this book was mentioned, with its comparisons, Sakharov said that he could stand the comparison with Oppenheimer but not that with Galileo.*

It is noteworthy but hardly surprising that Sakharov should contemplate (retroactively, as it were) transferring his efforts from physics to microbiology. Having been significantly involved in one of the two most portentous scientific discoveries of all time, the splitting of the atom and its uses, it is small wonder that Sakharov should turn his attention to the other, namely the splitting of another core, the human cell, as in the discovery of the chemical process of heredity or the unscrambling of the genetic code revealed by the British–American team of Watson, Crick and Franklin in 1956 in the now famous model of the double helix.

It was, the reader will recall, the discovery in the mid-fifties that radiation exposure could alter the genetic code of cells and cause mutations that set Sakharov on the path of non-conformism, dissidence and confrontation with the Soviet state. At this very juncture

* It developed that he had read the transcript, *In the Matter of J. Robert Oppenheimer* – all one thousand pages of it. But the book that had made a greater impression on him was one he had read long before. This was *Lawrence and Oppenheimer* by Nuel Pharr Davis.

419

another scientific field, biology, opened the prospect of genetic manipulation. This prospect contained vistas of radically effective cures for hereditary diseases, the plague of humankind from time immemorial. But it also offered, for the first time in history, scientifically certified approaches to the premeditated genetic concoction of a super race – once again the old, old dream of the 'new man'. But this time the dream had a basis in scientific research. It boots little that medical authorities of high standing assure the public of the sheer impossibility of such a line of experimentation. The point is, rather, that Baron von Frankenstein and his like (namely, humanity at large) now have food for dreams and temptation to experiment far greater than anything seen or imagined heretofore – and this against the background of the 'hip-hooray and bally-hoo' commercialization of science that has increased the volume and accelerated the pace of experimentation a hundredfold in the past fifty years. To paraphrase the disgruntled eminent chemist Erwin Chargaff, 'a new, epoch-making scientific breakthrough every Thursday' has become a perennial motif of the media. Sakharov was right to include the dangers of gene manipulation in his catalogue of caveats for modern humanity.

In the 11 October 1988 issue of the Russian-language newspaper *Youth of Estonia*, Andrei Sakharov gave what is to date the most revealing interview of his life. It was his first published interview in the Soviet press. 'Don't you ever regret,' he was asked with regard to the hydrogen bomb, 'the fact that you took part in the creation of that horrible weapon?' Sakharov answered, as he had often enough before, that he and his collective considered their work absolutely imperative as a means of restoring the balance of power in the world. The absence of such a balance, he went on, was extremely dangerous, because the country with the advantage of power would be tempted to use it while the advantage still obtained, whereas the weaker side would be moved to act in desperate apprehension of falling still further behind. Then as now this was the only excuse for working on the construction of the Super. In the final analysis their work was justified just as the work of the scientists on the other, American, side was justified. (According to this reckoning Oppenheimer was right to endorse the atom bomb and wrong to oppose the Super, while Teller was wrong to oppose the atom bomb and right to endorse and develop the Super.) After all, continued Sakharov, the world restrained itself from descending to perdition, to the horror of Hiroshima and Nagasaki, and continues to restrain itself lo these forty years. Nevertheless it is always wrong to hold to one and the same position and assessment despite the movement and change of the times. He quoted Thomas Mann to the effect that to do so was 'historical stupidity', and added that he had tried to avoid such stupidity. (German is the only foreign language Sakharov knows; when this writer visited him in Moscow he was reading *Faust* in the original.) Nevertheless his, Sakharov's, fate had been in a certain sense 'exclusive':

> Not out of false modesty but out of a desire to be accurate I note that my fate revealed itself to be more powerful than my personality. I only tried to attain the level fate had set for me while avoiding the temptation of just such an 'historical stupidity'.
>
> YOE: Do you believe in fate then?
>
> SAKHAROV: I scarcely believe in anything – apart from some sort of general feeling for the inner sense of the course of events. And the course of events not only in the life of humanity but generally in the universe at large. I do not believe in fate as destiny. I consider that the future is unpredictable and undetermined. It is created by all of us – step by step in our endlessly complex interaction.
>
> YOE: If I understand you correctly then you consider that all is not in God's hand but in human hands?
>
> SAKHAROV: Here there is an interaction between the one and the other but the freedom of choice rests with man. Hence the magnitude of the role of the personality whom fate places at certain key-points in history. Personal fate is in part also predetermined, in part – not. In my case, for example, I was several times offered the chance to participate in the work on nuclear weapons . . . but each time I refused. However, my fate overtook me . . . And when I finally was called to this work (and we, I repeat, considered it important and necessary) then I began to work not out of fear but in conscience and with a great deal of initiative. But then I cannot hide the other side of the matter: I found it very interesting. This was not because of what Fermi calls 'interesting physics'; here the interest was evoked by the grandiosity of the problem, the possibility to show what you could do. That's the way scientists are. I wish to add that all this was churning around against a background formed by the still very fresh memory of the terrible war that had only just come to an end. I did not take part in that war, and now here was

421

my war. It was like war ... And now I was in the very front line. Later I even joked that if they were going to decorate us with gold stars then it should be as Heroes of the Soviet Union [the highest military decoration] and not as Heroes of Socialist Labour because we were required to take upon ourselves great responsibility for technical and political decisions of tremendous significance. And that required gallantry ...

YOE: Which is to say that you already realized that the political significance of your research, your experiments, your tests, was not transitory? That your bomb would change the political and psychological climate of the world?

SAKHAROV: Not quite. The full understanding of this came later, some time in the mid-fifties, about the time of the second thermonuclear test. But I want still to talk about our psychological motivation ... I once confessed to Igor Yevgenyevich [Tamm] how difficult it was for me, how painful to realize what a dreadful business we were concerned with. He very attentively listened to what I had to say although my words came as a surprise to him. After all, we were overcome by the sheer magnitude, the grandiosity of the thing we had to do with. Here I remembered the words of Eichmann about the ecstasy of his realizing that to him and him alone, the simple son of a German villager, should fall the lot of carrying out so great a project ... This excitement and this pride in the magnitude of things are very human traits, although I hope, too, that the parallel with Eichmann is only very partial ...

Not content with the parallel with Eichmann, at this point Sakharov goes on to give a description of the top security area where he worked on the bomb:

In our city all construction work up until 1953 was done by prisoners. And all of us understood, of course, that many of them were subjected to terrible atrocities and injustices. We were not, to be sure, in charge of these people, but we had to do with those who were in charge of them. This fact also had a double significance, as strange as it may seem. On the one hand, since such sacrifices were involved, it behoved us to justify them with the results of our work. We could not allow ourselves to forget those who worked in the uranium mines or those who marched in columns under our windows at dawn under guard with police dogs ... On the other hand it was necessary to reflect – and what are you yourself doing? Are you not taking part in a dreadful crime? That is to say, it was necessary to mobilize yourself in such a way that your actions would not seem criminal.

Shades of Arthur Rudolf, the administrative director of Wernher von Braun's V–2 factory at Peenemünde during World War II! Rudolf was hounded out of the United States, on charges of keeping slave labour at Peenemünde, forty years after being invited there along with the rest of von Braun's team of rocketeers by the American government (Operation Paperclip).

At this point Sakharov's interview logically turned to the problem of good and evil:

SAKHAROV: A phrase from Brecht's play about Galileo comes to mind. In the play a student remarks: 'Unhappy that country that has no heroes,' but Galileo replies, 'No! Unhappy that country that has need of heroes.'

YOE: And our country?

SAKHAROV: . . . has always needed heroes. But in addition to heroes it has also needed people who simply preserve their dignity, who are able to seek and find a dignified course of conduct – in their work and in concrete assistance to someone. Such a position is after all almost always possible. Of course, in our country often enough a situation has arisen in which one is forced to make a choice: hero or villain. Even so, we have always had people of dignity.

YOE: But where can one draw the strength necessary to preserve one's dignity?

SAKHAROV: From oneself.

One of the late Vladimir Visotski's most popular songs has the refrain: 'I don't believe in fate and I believe in myself still less.' But 'people,' says Sakharov, 'dispose over the broadest diapason of virtues – from unbounded rascality to unbounded self-sacrifice . . .' This is what the gaze turned inward finds. But 'the gaze turned inward with a moral purpose,' wrote C. S. Lewis,

does not discover *character*. No man is a 'character' to himself, and least of all while he thinks of good and evil. Character is what he has to produce; within he finds only the raw material, the passions and emotions which contend for mastery. That unitary 'soul' or 'personality' which interests the novelist is for him merely the arena in which the combatants meet: it is to the combatants – those 'accidents occurring in a substance' – that he must attend. Nor will he long attend them . . . without giving them their Hegelian 'hands and feet'.

Here, then, is Sakharov's guiding Hegelian hand:

This is ... the source of the conservatism of the moral type of society: it changes slowly. I would put it still more pointedly: it changes slowly for the better. For the worse it can be changed very quickly. And it is very difficult to correct the direction of a society once it has taken a turn for the worse. When our fellow citizens – even while they are still very young – are hung up, so to speak, on the idea of a career at any price, then this is an alarm signal. The sirens are screaming! Because the readiness to pay any price signifies, in its essence, a profound indiscriminateness and indifference toward other people – toward everyone except oneself. This tendency, unfortunately, is widespread in our country. It can be outlived only slowly. But the chief danger is that it may be impossible to outlive this tendency at all.

YOE: In such a case what is, from your point of view, the most powerful corruptive factor? After all, the moral disintegration in society (and of society) has now been under long and painful discussion in our country . . .

SAKHAROV: The most dangerous thing for the youth of the country is the lie, social hypocrisy. When everybody lies – social and youth leaders, parents . . . This factor has been at work here for a long time, and for this reason it can be said that this society is to some extent sick: it has been poisoned by the lie.

In short, the interview here quoted is a sermon, a lay sermon dealing with religion in its civic sense (as the Soviets have rediscovered, religion has a profound civic sense). This is low Church good citizenship. Sakharov is, in effect, a Christian apologist. He works (out of necessity, as C. S. Lewis did by choice) from a secular base. His thinking on ethical questions follows the causeway of Western idealist philosophy. His emphasis on the development of personality and insistence on the dignity of the individual are strongly reminiscent of Hegel, as quoted earlier in this book: '. . . the individual can therefore not know what he is until he has brought himself to reality through action . . . Talent is likewise nothing other than the original individuality regarded as inner means or the transition of purpose to reality.' Sakharov's assertion of the individual's disposition of 'the broadest diapason of virtues – from unbounded rascality to unbounded self-sacrifice' and the struggle involved in the active antithesis of these is straight out of Hegel. The striking juxtaposition of Sakharov with Eichmann is not casual. It took his complicity in the construction of the hydrogen bomb, that most terrible of all weapons, to force the choice between hero and villain and make Sakharov what he is. To become 'Sakharov' he had to go through an 'Eichmann' phase in which, by a masterstroke of rationalization, he mobilized himself in such a way that his actions would not seem criminal.

The word 'mobilized' in the above context is important. Sakharov's service to the state took place at the height of the cold war. It was not really wartime but it was his, Sakharov's, war. The best way to survive was to bring himself to believe in what he was doing. He accepted tremendous responsibility and this responsibility brought with it not only privileges but rights, rights that even the Soviet Party-state could not but recognize – he had done the state some service and they knew it. In his struggle against the Party-state he capitalized on his rights, as it were, to the full. In this sense Sakharov was a one-man opposition. But he was not alone: he was the natural focus and rallying point for opposition at large. And on the horizon of Sakharov's insistence on a comprehensive and exhaustive exposé of the Soviet 'past and present' – KGB archives *et al.* – looms the figure of Solzhenitsyn. For Sakharov's insistence entails, among many other things, a historiography of the Soviet Union, a task more complex and more painful (because of the mass of disenchantment and reluctance involved) than the scarcely begun historiography of the Third Reich and its aftermath in Germany.

How does one account historically and generally for the rupture that separated Soviet Communism from reality? It began, formally, with the proclamation of 'Socialism in one country'. For this was the beginning of the studied and fiercely enforced isolationism of the Soviet Union, the quarantine of the Soviet experiment. Now the rationale of the quarantine was to guarantee ideal conditions for the experiment, to free it from outside influence. Control was introduced not for its own sake but to protect the conduct of the experiment, to give it every possible chance of success. But there were other reasons. For one, the obsessive Marxist opposition to capitalism. In this opposition, Marx was forced to jettison whole disciplines as parts of the system of bourgeois oppression. Many of these disciplines were integral parts of the traditional instrumentalities of the arts and sciences, beginning with 'conventional' economics and ending with philosophy *in toto* (a dumbfounding exclusion). Timofeev makes the point again and again that Stalin

425

insistently emphasized he did not want just any kind of productivity ('We do not need every kind of productivity of the people's labour'). It had to be productivity achieved according to the rules of socialist collective labour. After all, the main purpose of the exercise was not production but the creation of 'the new Soviet man' from the alembic of the great experiment. And this required the destruction of the old, non-Soviet man – the bourgeois and all that he stood for. Hence the elaborate (and asphyxiating) catalogue of prohibitions and regulations as to how things in the Soviet Union and its satellites were *not* to be done.

In trying to provide a utopian alternative to bourgeois capitalism, the Soviet Union created a system in which man would no longer have to be good, simply because he would have no option for evil. To remove the option by way of removing temptation the Soviets removed the market and introduced a wilderness of controls to insure its continuing absence. As early as 1739 David Hume realized how essential to human activity the market was: the market made it possible 'to do a service to another without wishing him a real kindness', even though the beneficiary of the transaction remained unknown; to act 'to the advantage of the public, though it be not intended for that purpose by another', because the market by its very nature rendered it in the 'interest even of bad men to act for the public good'. Instead, the Communists made a fetish and fixation of central direction, an idea lineally descended from Descartes's fatal reservation of 'the single unifying mind as the source of absolute order'. So doing they created a production machinery-*cum*-bureaucracy so cumbersome as to be incapable of adapting to the spontaneous expression of change in popular taste which is fashion. As for quality, a quip made the rounds in the early sixties that the cardinal mistake of the founding fathers of Communism had been their failure to codify a penalty for sales resistance.

There was also the philosophical problem that Marx inherited from Hegel, of transcending the dichotomy between subject and object, between theory and practice (this came down to denying the neutrality of the observer whatever his intentions: 'You are either part of the solution or you are part of the problem!'). This, in turn, was the informing spirit of socialist realism which demanded from the artist 'a truthful, historico-concrete representation of reality *in its revolutionary development*' (author's italics). To

426

repeat Radek's injunction: 'We should select ... all phenomena which show how the system of capitalism is being smashed, how socialism is growing ...' The artist as cheerleader. But for all and sundry there was the doctrine of partisanship as the prerequisite of the very understanding of Communism. With all these factors operative in isolation, undisturbed (and unhelped) by reality, the mechanism of myth-making was installed and working full speed in less time than it takes to tell.

But surely the chief determinant of Soviet isolationism was the fact that the Communist Party is infallible only within the framework of its own terms. Similarly, utopia can be realized only on the basis of its own terms, and the only way to realize such terms is to fake them, having taken the precaution of isolating the whole so that none of its parts can be decried as bogus. Within the field of these categorical constraints the efforts of the Party at crash-programme construction aborted in a magniloquent exercise in self-deception. How else is one to account for the irresponsibility of the 'ruling class', as Timofeev calls it, in its economic policies? How else account for the crass stupidity of going on record with purely utopian claims in so important a document as the official Party programme? 'In the coming decade (1961–70)', runs the relevant passage from the programme,

> the Soviet Union, in creating the material–technical basis of Communism, will surpass the most powerful and richest country of capitalism – the USA – in terms of per capita production; the material well being and the cultural–technical niveau of the workers will improve significantly, everyone will be provided with a sufficiency of material goods; all kolkhozes and sovkhozes (state farms) will be transformed into highly productive and highly profitable undertakings; basically the needs of Soviet people for well-built and comfortable living quarters will be met; heavy physical labour will disappear; the USSR will become the country of the shortest working day.

Of course, nothing of the sort happened. To the contrary, the vaulting claims of the Party merely served to expose and emphasize the gaping (and increasing) discrepancy between goal and reality. In the end, the Party was reduced to proclaiming the advent and achievement of Communism – all evidence to the contrary notwithstanding. The profligate quixotism of this move was tantamount to an admission of failure.

Twenty-two years later, in 1983, Yuri Andropov took the Party sharply to task on the subject of its programmes. 'Some of the provisions' of the 1961 programme, he said, had 'not stood the test of time'. They 'contained elements of separation from reality, of running ahead of things, and of unjustified detail'. The current Party programme (it finally emerged in 1986) is a comparatively sober document, emphasizing the difficulties still facing the Party and the need for more discipline.

If progress has any direct meaning in this world it is the development of increasingly sophisticated ways and means to examine the accumulating evidence of life: we learn more about the past as we progress and the future unfolds.

But humankind is stuck with its past. The past cannot be changed, it can only be reinterpreted. A heritage is a particular, cumulative interpretation. It, too, cannot be changed; it can only be reinterpreted. A heritage is irreplaceable because only the actual historical process is creative of values. The New Testament is a quintessential reinterpretation of the Old Testament. As such it universalized Judaism. This is the significance of Luther's reading 'change' in the most profound psychic sense into the Greek word μετάνοια instead of the Latin Vulgate's fobbing in of the harmless partial equivalent 'repent'. John the Baptist did not say 'Repent!' to his brethren; he said 'Change your mind – forever! Become a different person!' He said all this in one word: μετανοεῖτε. And by way of emphasis he cited the prophet Isaiah who condemned the people of Israel for their utter corruption.

The significant aspect of Luther's discovery was the Isaian reflection on the venality of the Church in the form of the sale of indulgences, the sanctioned and highly organized practice of collecting money for the remission of sins: absolution for a price. This was the pinnacle of corruption. Isaiah's accusation of the people of Israel is repeated by Luther in his accusation of the Church. In this sense Lutheranism was a reinvigoration of Christianity as a whole.

Significant, too, is the way Luther and Galileo complemented each other. When Luther denied the monopoly of exegesis to the Church he universalized the implement, putting the means of reinterpretation into the hands of Everyman. Galileo reinforced this movement by inventing and applying increasingly sophisticated means of examining the evidence of life. He gave a stupendous impulse to the process of secularization, to be sure. But secularization may be regarded as the obverse evidence of religious envelopment. It was the Church's apprehension of reinterpretation, fully conscious as it was of this aspect of the birth of Christianity out of Judaism, that led to its prosecution of Galileo and the suppression of his works.

In the suite of Robert Oppenheimer's Alamogordo and its consequences, Andrei Sakharov discovered the secret of the 'solar phoenix', the spontaneous recreation of energy such as takes place in the sun's core, and with it the release mechanism of the greatest and most destructive force the world has ever known. The combined weight of nuclear discovery and invention has forced a new reinterpretation of the lot of humankind. It is one that squares, fairly and fully (but then this, too, is a matter of interpretation) with the reinterpretation made in Galilee two thousand years ago.

Marxism, on the other hand, is not a reinterpretation of Christianity but a negation of it. It is more (or less) than that. It is also a negation of the course of human history, of Socrates as well as of Christ. And in point of fact Marx was forced to jettison the whole of the Judaeo-Christian ethical–aesthetic heritage and the Graeco-Roman classical tradition with it. As noted, a heritage is irreplaceable – unless one proceeds like the mid-Western American college where it was announced that 'As of Monday morning it will be a tradition that students wear academic gowns in the quadrangle.' To say the replacement of humanity's cultural heritage at large undertaken by the Soviet Communists was a big order is to put the matter facetiously. But it does at least explain the unconscious frivolity of the Soviet attempt to reverse the whole of the 'bourgeois system'. Marxism was a break in the continuity of the development of man through the ages. As it turned out, the break was not a new departure but a breakdown. This year, 1988, most officially, the Soviet government celebrates the millennial anniversary of the Christianization of Russia. For the occasion it is allowing the import of one and a half million Russian-language Bibles. A full year before the anniversary, but with a belatedness that stretched over several decades, Yevgeny Yevtushenko protested that Gosizdat, the state publishing house, had never published the Bible – 'without the knowledge of which Russian classical literature cannot be understood'.

The world has watched the struggle between the last great colonial empire on earth, the Soviet Union, and the first great anti-colonial empire. If 'anti-colonial empire' is a contradiction in terms it is because America is a contradiction in terms. For anti-colonialism, like anti-clericalism or anti-anythingism, inevitably takes on many of the properties of the thing it seeks to destroy. However, the 'charitable inconsistency' with which America as an empire pursues its goals is its saving grace. Not for nothing did H. L. Mencken describe the greatest nation on earth as 'the only comic society in history'.

Thus the struggle between the two superpowers was also the global confrontation of two Internationals. The Soviet Union, by means of its vast resources and native manpower and aided immeasurably by the intoxicating doctrine of Marxism (Communism is the opiate of atheists and agnostics), tried to impose an international order of its own making – and unmaking. America in its diametrically different way, in its looser, less organized but more organic fashion, tried to bring the Soviet Union and its satellites into the general order of more or less democratic states within the secularized tradition of the Judaeo-Christian ethic backed by the rule of law. This is the empiricist philosophy with a pedigree stretching from Roger Bacon through Hobbes, Locke, Hume, Burke and the Austrian school of economics to F. A. Hayek. It is a philosophy that insists on evolution and deplores revolution as criminal, wasteful and blindly aberrant. In the last four hundred years this position has been what might be called the undersong of the overprivileged. It is an establishment philosophy, the closely reasoned justification of private property. But the opinion of an elite is by definition a minority opinion and therefore condemned in perpetuity: the communist–socialist ideal though inhuman is humane, and the capitalist ideal though human is inhumane. As Hayek puts it: 'Evolution cannot be just.' The left is not going to disappear simply because the right has been proved to be right and the left wrong. Indeed, because of the very hopelessness of the odds, the left appears to be more than merely humane. 'Man's inventiveness,' writes Hayek, 'contributed so much to the formation of super-individual structures within which individuals found great opportunities that people came to imagine that they could deliberately design the whole as well as some of its parts ... Although this is an error, it is a noble one, one that is, in [Ludwig von] Mises's words: "grandiose ... ambitious ... magnificent ... daring".' In short, this is the humanist fallacy in all its specious splendour.

The Soviet error has evidenced itself spectacularly. Its nature was largely due to Marx who, for all his genius, was basically a myth-maker, a mythopoeist. And 'no legend . . . is safe from the hermeneutics of a thorough-going mythologic theorist' (Tylor). He was therefore the opposite of a scientist and he had no grasp of economics. He was, in fact, an 'anti-economist'.

The 'fierce miscreed' of Communism was based on a fierce misreading of the evidence of history, a wilful misconceiving of the principles operative in society. In practice, the Marxist–Leninists got it exactly wrong, sending (to cite but one example) politicians to run corporations while the capitalists sent corporate executives to run governments. In effect, then, for almost seventy years the Soviets had been trying to run an anti-economy for purely ideological reasons. They succeeded, but at the consequent price of general bankruptcy. Mikhail Gorbachev is the Party-appointed conservator of that bankruptcy. The emphasis in this description falls on the word *conservator*. Gorbachev has made it amply clear that he means to conserve the Soviet Union within its present territorial limits. 'There is no joking with [Soviet] power,' he told Hans-Jochen Vogel, the chairman of the West German Social Democratic Party, in early April 1989 when commenting on the unrest in Georgia. And indeed: on 10 April 1989 a decree was published over the signature of Mikhail Gorbachev in which were entered Articles 7, 7–1 and 11–1, replacing the infamous Article 190–1 of the Soviet Criminal Code, which set forth the penalties for slandering the Soviet government and its works. The new decree, instead of the hoped-for alleviation, constitutes an aggravation (in place of 'slander', the broader term 'discredit' has been introduced). How this new draconian measure is to square with the policy of *glasnost* is a question. There is no question about the purpose of the decree. It is meant to repair the damage done by *glasnost* to the Soviet state in keeping with the axiom that sums up the Soviet dilemma: 'There is an essential connection between human rights and the nationalities problem. It was, in fact, merely the same old shift of redeclaring a national emergency and making that emergency serve as the statutory foundation of Soviet society. In this sense the flaring-up of the nationalities problem even proved to be a convenience. There was no longer any need to simulate acute revolutionary urgency; the urgency was genuine, provided by the nationalist unrest – thanks to *glasnost*. Sakharov still had his work

431

cut out. The American attempt, on the other hand, has succeeded, succeeded because it is fired by a commercial romanticism that necessitates freedom as its sole prerequisite, because it harnesses the force of habit just as instinctively as it caters to every conceivable form of economic impulse, and because it idolizes the machine. Over and against the Communist 'new centurion' (the low-level political officer) the Americans have posed the 'new centaur' – not a cross between man and horse, but a cross between men and horsepower, between man and machine. The new superman in the American mythopoeic projection is half man and half machine, a development that has nicely kept pace with the surgical interchangeability or reinforcement of human organs by artefacts and mechanical systems in an increasingly computerized medical science. This was the crux, the foreseeable compromise of the primordial urge to make machines like men and men like machines.

There is such a thing as a nobility of the downtrodden, 'the humiliated and insulted' as Dostoyevsky called them, in the Russian Empire – Soviet Union – those singled out for special spirit-breaking treatment by an oppressive regime; there is a nobility of suffering (as well as an arrogance) by virtue of a pedigree of persecution. Elena Bonner, Sakharov's 'Lusia', heiress of five generations of political exile, ranks high in that nobility.

As for her mother, when Ruth Grigorievna Bonner died in Moscow in 1987 a few days before the new year, she had spent almost twenty-five of her eighty-seven years in prison camps and in exile. To be sure, eight of those years were spent in the comfort and warmth of her American exile with grandchildren and great-grandchildren. And yet her anguish then, too, was great: her American exile coincided with the exile of Sakharov in Gorky while her daughter, Elena Bonner, shuttled between Moscow and Gorky until she was sentenced to share her husband's exile in 1985. After her daughter's return to Gorky from America in June 1986 following six months of medical treatment and convalescence, Ruth Grigorievna decided to spend her remaining time with her daughter and Andrei Dmitrievich in her home country. The release of the Sakharovs and their return to Moscow in December 1986 made this possible. Ruth Grigorievna returned to the Soviet Union in June 1987. She was a most valuable re-addition (back in her old apartment) to the community of dissidents in Moscow. For she had all the dignity, grace and warmth and none of the arrogance of suffering – a great, pure heart in love with life. She had six months of it at home.

Ruth Grigorievna often told the story of Andrei Sakharov's drawings, his sketching for the entertainment of the family and especially, of course, of the children. He always drew fantastic figures, either from the remote past – prehistoric animals – or for the distant future – animals with hoofs instead of horns on their heads because the conditions on various stars and planets would so condition thenm over the aeons. All this to the puzzlement of the grown-ups but to the great delight of the children. Apparently a Soviet astronomer discovered a new star and named it after Sakharov. The children were sure that they would all live on that star at some time in the future and see the fantastic animals Sakharov had drawn.

BIBLIOGRAPHY

Avtorkhanov, A.: *Tekhnologia Vlasti* (*The Technology of Power*), Frankfurt-on-Main, 1973

Bakunin, M.: *Staatlichkeit und Anarchie*, Frankfurt-on-Main, 1972

Berdyaev, Nikolai: *The Origin of Russian Communism*, London, 1937

Berg, Hermann von: *Die Analyse der europäischen Gemeinschaft, das Zukunfts-modell für Ost und West*, Cologne, 1985

——: *Marxismus–Leninismus – das Elend der halb deutschen, halb russischen Ideologie*, Cologne, 1986

Berlin, Isaiah: *Karl Marx. His Life and Environment*, London, 1939

Blumberg, Stanley and Owens: *The Life and Times of Edward Teller*, New York, 1976

Bonner, Elena: *Alone Together*, New York, 1986

Chargaff, Erwin: *Das Feuer des Heraklit. Skizzen aus einem Leben vor der Natur*, Stuttgart, 1981

Clebsch, William A.: *Christianity in European History*, New York, 1979

Cohen, Stephen F.: *Bukharin and the Bolshevik Revolution 1888–1938*, New York, 1973

Conquest, Robert: *Harvest Sorrow. Soviet Collectivization and the Terror Famine*, New York, 1986

Davis, Nuel Pharr: *Lawrence and Oppenheimer*, New York, 1968

Ehrenfeld, David: *The Arrogance of Humanism*, New York, 1975

Einstein, Albert: *La Relativité*, Paris, 1956

Faye, J. P.: *Langages Totalitaires*, Paris, 1972

Fireside, Harvey: *Soviet Psychoprisons*, New York, 1979

Fischer, Ernst: *Was Marx wirklich sagte*, Vienna, 1968

Fischer Ernst, Franz Marek: *Was Lenin wirklich sagte*, Vienna, 1969

Fölsing, Albrecht: *Galileo Galilei, Prozeß ohne Ende*, Munich, 1983

Friedell, Egon: *Aufklärung und Revolution*, Munich, 1928

Friedenthal, Richard: *Luther, sein Leben und seine Zeit*, Munich, 1967

Fritz, Kurt von: *Grundprobleme der Geschichte der antiken Wissenschaft*, Berlin, 1971

Fromm, Erich: *Haben oder Sein. Die seelischen Grundlagen einer neuen Gesellschaft*, Stuttgart, 1976

Grigorenko, Petro G.: *Memoirs*, New York, 1982

Groff. W. F. and D. E. Miller: *The Shaping of Modern Christian Thought*, Cleveland, 1968

Guthrie, W. K. C.: *The Greeks and the Gods*, Boston, 1950

Hamilton, Alexander, James Madison, John Jay: *The Federalist Papers*, New York, 1961

Hayek, F. A.: *The Fatal Conceit*, London, 1988

Hebleben, Johannes: *Galilei*, Hamburg, 1969

Hegel, Georg Wilhelm Friedrich: *Phänmenologie des Geistes*, Berlin, 1970

Hendel, Samuel (ed.): *The Soviet Crucible. The Soviet System in Theory and Practice*, Princeton NJ, 1959

Kermode, Frank: *Romantic Image*, London, 1957

Kochan, Lionel (ed.): *The Jews in Soviet Russia since 1917*, Oxford, 1978

Koestler, Arthur: *The Sleepwalkers*, London, 1959

Kolakowski, Leszek: *Main Currents of Maxism*, 1. *The Founder*, 2. *The Golden Age*, 3. *The Breakdown*, Oxford, 1978

Krasnov, Vladislav: *Soviet Defectors*, Stanford, 1986

Küng, Hans: *Existiert Gott?*, Munich, 1978

Lasky, Melvin J.: *Utopia and Revolution*, Chicago, 1976

Lenin, V. I.: *Sotschineniye*, Vols. 1–55, Moscow, 1950

Lewin, M.: *Russian Peasants and Soviet Power. A Study of Collectivization*, London, 1968

Lukacs, G.: *The Historical Novel*, Boston, 1963

Macpherson, O. B.: *The Political Theory of Possessive Individualism*, Oxford, 1962

Mandelstam, Nadezhda: *Hope against Hope*, New York, 1976

Marx, Karl: *Das Kapital*, Berlin, 1968

Medvedev, Roy: *A Question of Madness*, New York, 1971

Medvedev, Zhores: *The Rise and Fall of T. D. Lysenko*, New York, 1969

Moraze, Charles: *The Triumph of the Middle Classes*, New York, 1966

More, Thomas: *Utopia*, Amsterdam, 1969

Needleman, Jacob: *The New Religions. The Meaning of the Spiritual Revolution and the Teaching of the East*, New York, 1970

Nove, Alec: *An Economic History of the USSR*, Harmondsworth, Middlesex, 1969

Nyomarkay, Joseph: *Charisma and Factionalism in the Nazi Party*, Minneapolis, 1967

Payne, Robert: *Lenin*, New York, 1964

Plamenatz, John: *German Marxism and Russian Communism*, London, 1954

Pryce-Jones, Alan (ed.): *The New Outline of Modern Knowledge*, London, 1956

Riasanovsky, V. A.: *Historical Survey of Russian Culture*, New York, 1947

Ringer, Fritz K.: *The Decline of the German Mandarins. The German Academic Community 1890–1933*, Cambridge Mass., 1969

Sakharov, Andrei, and Edward Lazansky (eds.): *Andrei Sakharov and Peace, An Anthology*, New York, 1985

Santillana, Georgio de: *The Crime of Galileo*, Chicago, 1955

Schapiro, Leonard: *The Communist Party of the Soviet Union*, London, 1960

Schdanov, A., M. Gorky, N. Bukharin, K. Radek, A. Stetsky: *Problems of Soviet Literature*, Moscow, 1935

Sherrard, Philip: *Greek East and Latin West*, London, 1959

Spencer, Benjamin T.: *The Quest for Nationality*, Syracuse, 1957.

Spengler, Oswald: *Der Untergang des Abendlandes*, Munich, 1923

Stalin, I. V.: *Sotschineniye*, Vols. 1–13, Moscow, 1953

Stern, Philip M.: *The Oppenheimer Case*, New York, 1969

Szczesny, Gerhard: *The Future of Unbelief*, New York, 1961

Teller, Edward: *The Legacy of Hiroshima*, London, 1962

Theobald, Robert: *The Challenge of Abundance*, New York, 1961

Trotsky, Leon: *My Life*, London, 1975

——: *Über Lenin*, Frankfurt-on-Main, 1964

Voslensky, Mikhail: *Nomenklatura*, London, 1984

Waddams, Herbert: *The Struggle for Christian Unity*, New York, 1968

Webb, Wilfred D., Edward G. Lewis, William L. Strauss, Malcolm H. MacDonald, (eds.): *Readings in American Government*, New York, 1963

Weber, Max: *Methodologische Schriften*, Frankfurt-on-Main, 1968

——: *Soziologie, Universalgeschichtliche Analysen, Politik*, Stuttgart, 1973

Weizsäcker, Karl Friedrich von: *Die Tragweite der Wissenschaft*, Stuttgart, 1964

Wells, H. G.: *The Outline of History*, New York, 1949

Wyden, Peter: *Day One. Before Hiroshima and After*, New York, 1984

York, Herbert: *The Advisors Oppenheimer, Teller and the Superbomb*, San Francisco, 1976

Meschdunarodnoye Sluschanye Sakharova, The Sakharov Hearing Committee, Copenhagen, 1977; Second Session, Rome, 1979; Third Session, Washington, 1979; Fourth Session, Lisbon, 1983; Fifth Session, London, 1985

Survey, Vol. 29, August 1987, London, Social and Economic Rights in the Soviet Bloc

Independent Ukrainian Association for Research of National Problems in Soviet Theory and Practice: *Russian Bolshevism*, Munich, n.d.

Istoria Kommunistitscheskoy Partiy Sovietskovo Soyuza, Gospolitizdat, Moscow, 1959

Samisdat: Chronik eines neuen Lebens in der Sowjetunion, Herausgeber: pro fratribus, Koblenz–Mailand, 1975

Kontinent: Paris, 1974–88

U.S. Atomic Energy Commission, Personnel Security Board: *In the Matter of J. Robert Oppenheimer* (Hearings), Washington, 1954

INDEX

439

440

442

443

444

445

446

448